'Brian Toohey's book is a deeply troubling history of the Australian government's love affair with secrecy and state power. We present ourselves as one of the world's great liberal democracies, yet Toohey's research shows that our security agencies have so many of the powers that our governments rightly condemn authoritarian dictatorships for. This book should serve as a wakeup call for anybody who cares about the fundamental principles of human rights, transparency and accountability in Australia.'

Peter Greste

'Brian Toohey brings half a century of reporting on national security issues to the task of framing our modern discussion—powerfully documenting the layers upon layers of apparently small, incremental policy changes that have led us to where we are today: an often fearful nation that has given away many of its citizens' rights.'

Laura Tingle

'As the recent AFP raids on national newspapers demonstrate all too clearly, an obsessive over-reach by politicians and bureaucrats in their definitions of "national security" denies the Australian public its right to hold intelligence agencies accountable for lack of intelligence. Brian Toohey's rambunctious account of 70 years of cock up and cover up illustrates how unnecessary much secrecy is, how it conduces to foreign policy failures and feeds political paranoia—a problem today when our traditional allies are discombobulated—the US by the unpredictability of Trump and whilst the UK is constipated by Brexit. Some secrets must be kept whilst others should be exposed: the recent avalanche of anti-terrorism legislation fails to make the distinction.'

Geoffrey Robertson

'Toohey's insights into this new age of surveillance are scary (but it's a book that demands to be read).'

Kerry O'Brien

SECRET

THE MAKING
OF AUSTRALIA'S
SECURITY STATE

BRIAN TOOHEY

MELBOURNE
UNIVERSITY
PRESS

MELBOURNE UNIVERSITY PRESS
An imprint of Melbourne University Publishing Limited
Level 1, 715 Swanston Street, Carlton, Victoria 3053, Australia
mup-contact@unimelb.edu.au
www.mup.com.au

First published 2019
Text © Brian Toohey, 2019
Design and typography © Melbourne University Publishing Limited, 2019

Typeset in 11/13.5 pt Bembo by Cannon Typesetting
Cover design by Phil Campbell Design
Printed in Australia by McPherson's Printing Group

A catalogue record for this book is available from the National Library of Australia

9780522872804 (paperback)
9780522872828 (ebook)

To Sue

CONTENTS

ABBREVIATIONS

ABM Treaty	Anti-Ballistic Missile Treaty
ADF	Australian Defence Force
AFP	Australian Federal Police
AFR	*Australian Financial Review*
AIRAC	Australian Ionising Radiation Advisory Council
AJA	Australian Journalists' Association
ALIS	autonomic logistics information system
ANU	Australian National University
ARL	Australian Radiation Laboratory
ASD	Australian Signals Directorate
ASIO	Australian Security Intelligence Organisation
ASIS	Australian Secret Intelligence Service
ATO	Australian Taxation Office
AUSMIN	Australia–US Ministerial Consultations
AUSTRAC	Australian Transaction Reports and Analysis Centre
AWM	Australian War Memorial
AWRE	Atomic Weapons Research Establishment (UK)
BWC	Biological Weapons Convention
CBW	chemical and biological warfare
CGS	chief of the general staff
CNE	computer network exploitation
DFAT	Department of Foreign Affairs and Trade
DGSE	General Directorate for External Security (France)
DIO	Defence Intelligence Organisation
DPP	Director of Public Prosecutions
DSB	Defence Signals Bureau
DSD	Defence Signals Directorate/Division (name changed to Directorate in 1978)
DSL	Defence Standards Laboratories

DSP	Defense Support Program (USA)
EEZ	exclusive economic zone
FITS Bill	Foreign Influence Transparency Scheme Bill
FOI	freedom of information
FPDA	Five Power Defence Arrangement
GCHQ	Government Communications Headquarters (UK)
GCSB	Government Communications Security Bureau (NZ)
HF	high frequency
IAEA	International Atomic Energy Agency
ICAN	International Campaign to Abolish Nuclear Weapons
ICBM	intercontinental ballistic missile
IMF	International Monetary Fund
IS	Islamic State
ISDS	investor-state dispute settlement
ISI	Inter-Services Intelligence (Pakistan)
JIC	Joint Intelligence Committee
JIO	Joint Intelligence Organisation
MEAA	Media, Entertainment and Arts Alliance
MIRV	multiple independently targetable re-entry vehicle
NAA	National Archives of Australia
NATO	North Atlantic Treaty Organization
NBN	National Broadband Network
NCC	National Civic Council
NIC	National Intelligence Committee
NID	*National Intelligence Daily*
NPT	Nuclear Non-Proliferation Treaty
NSA	National Security Agency (US)
NT	*National Times*
NWC	North West Cape
NYT	*New York Times*
ONA	Office of National Assessments
OPCW	Organisation for the Prohibition of Chemical Weapons
OPEC	Organization of the Petroleum Exporting Countries
PAT	Political Action Team (CIA)
RCIS	Royal Commission on Intelligence and Security
SALT	Strategic Arms Limitation Talks
SANAAC	State, Army, Navy, Air Force Coordinating Committee (US)
SAS	Special Air Service
SDI	Strategic Defense Initiative (US)
SEATO	Southeast Asia Treaty Organization

SIGINT	signals intelligence
SIO	Special Intelligence Operation
SIOP	Single Integrated Operational Plan (US)
SIS	Secret Intelligence Service (UK)
SLBM	submarine-launched ballistic missile
SMH	*Sydney Morning Herald*
SOLAS	Safety of Life at Sea
SOTG	Special Operations Task Group
SPA	Special Political Action
TAG	technical assessment group
UCS	Union of Concerned Scientists
UNCLOS	United Nations Convention on the Law of the Sea
VLF	very low frequency
WMD	weapon of mass destruction

PREFACE

'*We the Government have vital information which we cannot disclose. It is upon this knowledge that we make decisions. You, who are merely private citizens, have no access to this information. Any criticism you make of our policy, any controversy about it in which you may indulge, will therefore be uninformed and valueless. If, in spite of your ignorance, you persist in questioning our policy, we can only conclude that you are disloyal.*'

Harold Thorby, Minister for Defence, Australia, 1938[1]

Step by step, a succession of new laws and policies have provided the building blocks for Australia to become a country in which secretive officials and ministers wield unprecedented levels of peacetime power. Secrecy, ignorance and fear are being used to deprive Australians of basic liberties and increase the risk of being dragged into a devastating war that could escalate into a full-scale nuclear catastrophe.

As a measure of just how far Australia has changed in recent decades, there are now seventy-five new laws to deal with terrorists who murder someone. Terrorists murdered people in earlier eras, but special laws were not considered necessary to cover those crimes. *Secret* shows how the tough provisions of these new laws have been extended to areas not remotely connected to terrorism. The national security juggernaut has reached the point where Australia is now chained to the chariot wheels of the Pentagon at a time when America has become an increasingly dangerous ally. The US-run bases in Australia secretly lock the nation into participating in the Pentagon's plans for 'full spectrum' warfare ranging from outer space to the ocean depths. Australia's leaders have let the US control so many critical components of the nation's weapons systems that it would not be possible for Australia to defend itself, for example, in a future conflict with Indonesia against America's wishes.

No major political party is offering to restore the values of an earlier era in which habeas corpus prevailed; the onus of proof was on the prosecution; the accused was allowed to see the evidence relied on by the Crown; and Australian Security Intelligence Organisation officials could not legally kidnap people or raid a lawyer's offices and seize documents in a commercial case directly involving the government on the other side. No major party seems bothered by the use of new surveillance technology that allows governments to detect contact between journalists and their sources, effectively denying whistleblowers the opportunity to reveal abuses of power and criminal behaviour.

The past was by no means a golden era. A dean of medicine at Melbourne University in the 1960s advised the Defence Department on how to kill people with chemical and biological weapons. Labor governments in the 1980s fell for the fairytale that the US-run Pine Gap base in Central Australia was all about arms control.

State-enforced secrecy in the name of national security increasingly covers up war crimes, phoney intelligence, abuses of power, incompetence, folly and hugely wasteful spending. Too often new laws make it legal for governments to take actions that would be illegal if done by corporations or individuals, including breaking and entering, assault, electronic eavesdropping, and stealing computer hard drives.

Few deny there can be a legitimate role for government secrecy. For example, there is usually little justification for revealing the names of informers working for the police and intelligence agencies, or for publicising plans for lawful wartime operations such as the Normandy landing. But just as secrecy enabled the churches to conceal child sex abuse and the corporate sector to suppress evidence about the harmful effects of tobacco, asbestos, pesticides, pharmaceuticals, pollution, tax evasion and fraud, so too has secrecy encouraged governments to demolish long-standing freedoms and deny the public's right to know what is being done in its name. Court suppression orders mock the notion that justice must be seen to be done.

I hope *Secret* provides a modest counter-narrative to the official accounts of Australia at war and the role of its intelligence services and the foreign-run bases. Although the book challenges some of the assumptions underpinning the mainstream interpretation of Australia's recent history, I am indebted to the outstanding work done by many historians, commentators and journalists.

Secret draws in part on my fifty years as a journalist and, briefly, a political staff member. A posting to Washington gave an appreciation of the best and worst aspects of the American political system and the importance of its constitutional protection of free speech. Like many other journalists, my goal is to let people know more about what governments do in their name, subject to the usual constraints of time and resources.

Over the years, massive efforts have been made to discover the sources of journalists' revelations about government actions, information about which ought to have been publicly available. Governments have made repeated attempts in the courts to discover the sources and suppress publication. Along with other journalists, I have been taken to court a number of times over such matters. In my case, and in most others', the courts didn't find that publication harmed national security, and no sources were unmasked.

Today's generation of journalists have a much tougher job. Governments have introduced new laws making it a criminal offence to receive a wide range of information. The June 2018 *Espionage Act* provides a glimpse of the future where it will be an offence to receive 'information of any kind, whether true or false and whether in a material form or not, and includes (a) an opinion; and (b) a report of a conversation'. George Orwell could never have dreamt that one up.

PART 1
THE CLANDESTINE AGENCIES

1

THE SECURITY SCANDAL THAT THE US HID FROM THE NEWBORN ASIO

'Perhaps the most significant intelligence loss in US history ...'
US National Security Agency[1]

The birth of the Australian Security Intelligence Organisation in 1949 is widely attributed to the discovery that two Australian diplomats, Ian Milner and Jim Hill, had spied for the Soviet Union in Canberra at the end of World War II. But there are three far more important, but rarely noticed, secrets behind the birth of ASIO.

One is that nothing Milner and Hill handed over mattered. Another is that the USA used highly classified nonsense to harm the Chifley Labor government. The third and most important is that the Americans harboured a much bigger traitor, William Weisband, but kept his genuinely damaging activities from ASIO on a 'no need to know' basis. Weisband was an American counterintelligence official who told the USSR in October 1948 how to stop the US deciphering its top-secret cables. ASIO was not informed about Weisband before the US National Security Agency (NSA) publicly revealed the secret in 2000. So much for the closeness of the US-Australia alliance.

The ultra-secretive US deciphering project called Venona decoded the content of cables sent between Moscow and its intelligence officers in several countries in the 1940s. In 1995, the NSA released the translations of every message the codebreakers deciphered fully or partly, and the suspected identities of those whose real identities were hidden behind unbreakable pseudonyms in the original messages.[2] The following analysis is based on the material released about the messages communicated between Moscow and the Soviet embassy in Canberra from 1943 to 1948.[3]

In contrast to Weisband's efforts, it is clear that the highly classified material handed over by the Australian spies was of no consequence. Supposedly, the most valuable were two top-secret British papers written in May 1945 that Milner and Hill indirectly passed on to Moscow in March 1946—assuming double agents in London hadn't already done so. The original documents in the British archives show banal, often erroneous predictions by UK officials about the strategic circumstances between 1955 and 1960.[4] It is hard to believe anyone in Moscow took any notice, especially Soviet leader Joseph Stalin. For example, he ignored numerous intelligence warnings of the German invasion of Russia on 22 June 1941, codenamed Barbarossa.[5]

The two British papers that were sent to Moscow from Canberra, written for the UK Cabinet by the Post-Hostilities Planning Staff, were called 'Security of India and the Indian Ocean' and 'Security in the Western Mediterranean and the Eastern Atlantic'.[6]

The first said the continuing 'integrity of India' was of major strategic significance but didn't foresee that the British government would grant India independence in 1947. Nor did it realise the government would destroy India's integrity by partitioning the country into Pakistan and what was left of India in 1947. It did raise concerns about possible civil unrest after 1955, but partition immediately created tremendous civil upheaval and loss of life. The paper also stressed India's strategic importance as a base and the contribution its fighting forces could make to Britain in future. India contributed two million troops to Britain in World War II compared to Australia's 993,000 to the overall war effort; 89,000 Indian soldiers (4.5 per cent of those who served) were killed compared with Australia's toll of just over 27,000 (2.7 per cent).[7] Since independence, successive Indian and Pakistani governments have shown no interest in making further troop contributions to Britain. However, partition did result in several wars between Pakistan and India, the first in 1947–48. The paper described the Soviet Union as the only major power capable of seriously threatening British interests in India. After independence the Soviets and India freely formed an enduring friendship. China now has more influence in Pakistan, as does Islamic extremism.

The other paper stated the obvious: that by 1955–60 Britain would want to control sea communications in the East Atlantic, retain its bases on Gibraltar and avoid the rise of hostile or neutral countries around the Western Mediterranean.

The biggest strategic factor missing from the papers is the development of nuclear weapons, something other British officials already knew was underway in 1945. By 1955–60, the nuclear stand-off effectively meant the Soviets could not invade countries in the Western Mediterranean, nor control the East Atlantic sea lanes.

Clearly, the fatuous predictions made in both of these papers would have been of little use to the Soviets. But David Horner, author of the first volume of the official ASIO history, states that several documents handed over 'would have been of great value to the Soviet Union, especially when it was negotiating with the allies over postwar arrangements in Europe'.[8] He doesn't support his claim by discussing the content of the documents. ANU researcher Adam Hughes Henry says the British had already alerted the Soviets to their desire to 'hold on' in the Mediterranean when Churchill negotiated his October 1944 'Percentages Agreement' with Stalin on allocating spheres of influence.[9]

The rest of the British papers sent from Canberra were trite. A typical example was a Foreign Office telegram in October 1945 stating, 'Argentine export of meat is a vital factor for Great Britain'.

Apart from Milner and Hill, non-diplomats in Australia also supplied documents sent to KGB headquarters in Moscow.[10] Contrary to widespread assumptions, this so-called Australian 'spy ring' was not the result of skilled recruitment by the KGB. Instead, an exceptionally energetic member of the Communist Party in Australia, Walter Clayton (codenamed Klod), organised a small band of people to give him information that he passed indirectly to the KGB without it having to lift a finger. One striking feature of the Venona transcripts is how the KGB's Moscow headquarters urged its Canberra representative, Semyon Makarov, to stop sending so much material. But Makarov, who didn't meet Clayton until 1948, had no direct control over what Clayton supplied to a go-between. Despite his diligence and skill, Clayton got few thanks from KGB headquarters. Moscow told Makarov not to let him recruit new agents, not to send any document that was more than a year old, not to be overeager to achieve success, and to stop obtaining information of little importance. Moscow even complained that Clayton had obtained material (including the British telegrams sent from Australia) without first asking for approval.

Clayton's most productive period was 1945–46, when many Australians saw the Soviet Union as a wartime ally whose population had made horrendous sacrifices to ensure victory over Hitler. But on 24 October 1946 Moscow ordered Makarov to suspend all contact with Clayton. This was effectively the end of the 'spy ring'.

On the available evidence, some of Clayton's agents knew they were passing information to the local Communist Party but seemed genuinely unaware that it was then passed on to Moscow. Others who didn't hand anything over are still often described as part of a spy ring simply because they were mentioned in the messages, were suspected by ASIO, or were a target of KGB recruitment. None of this meant they were agents. Some commentators still bluntly state that another diplomat, Ric Throssell, was an agent. After interviewing him in 1953, ASIO concluded that he 'is a loyal subject and is not a security risk in the department in which he is employed'.[11] Frances Garratt (née Bernie) is often still viewed as being a Soviet agent while she was working mainly on political party issues as a young secretary/typist in the Sydney office of the External Affairs minister, Bert Evatt, between November 1944 and April 1946. She later told ASIO she handed over information to Clayton but stopped in 1945. She insisted that she thought she was simply giving the local Communist Party some political information. She acknowledged being a party member during 1941–44, saying, 'It was a period … of youthful idealism but has completely finished'.[12] She was never charged.

One message Garratt passed on revealed nothing more than the parochial approach of one of Evatt's private secretaries, who wrote to him in April 1945 suggesting he return immediately from a San Francisco conference to deal with domestic political matters. Evatt stayed in the USA and made a widely praised contribution to the landmark conference that culminated in the formation of the United Nations.

Although the existence of Clayton's 'spy ring' caused understandable concern in Washington and London, other pressures on Canberra to replace the existing security organisations in Australia with ASIO are more troubling. The US relied on crude prejudices to try to damage Prime Minister Ben Chifley and his Labor government. In 1980, the *National Times* unearthed voluminous files in the national archives in Washington about a US Navy–inspired ban on the supply of any classified information to Australia in mid-1948. The files show the State, Army, Navy, Air Force Coordinating Committee (SANACC) imposed the ban after a navy submission in May 1948 claimed Australia was a poor security risk because of a leftist government 'greatly influenced by Communist-infiltrated labour organisations'.[13] The US army and air force opposed the ban, as did the British government. The navy then produced its trump card: it claimed to have fresh evidence of 'breaches of Australian security in the handling of highly classified US military information' in 1947.[14] No evidence has emerged to support the navy's claim about a security breach involving highly classified US military information in Australia in 1947, or at any other time. The US army and air force and the UK continued to argue against a complete ban on the supply of classified information to Australia, but SANACC cut off everything, including information in the lowest classification.

In a highly damaging example of foreign interference, the navy relied on shoddy information from fervently anti-Labor US officials in the Canberra embassy, based on accusations fed by Australian security and military officials. ASIO historian Horner says these officials supplied what he describes as 'wildly extravagant reports'.[15] He says the Defence Department head, Sir Frederick Shedden, later acknowledged he shouldn't have discussed the ban with the US ambassador, Myron Cowen, and the naval attaché, Stephen Jurika, because their views 'were adverse to Australia'. Jurika told Washington there was 'not one chance in 10 million' of any effective action against communism being taken until the Labor government was removed, and also claimed communism was 'rife in the highest governing circles' and had spread throughout the armed services.[16] Jurika was peddling malicious rubbish. Chifley sent in the army to break a coalminers' strike in 1949—the first time the army had been used in peacetime for strikebreaking. Although the Communist Party was active in Australia, it was small compared to Labor and the Coalition parties.

Chifley replaced the existing security bodies with ASIO on 2 March 1949, but the ban remained and was only lifted in mid-1950. The US even threatened to cut off the flow of information to Britain in early 1949 unless it stopped supplying Australia with information on guided missiles being tested at the Woomera Rocket Range. The British put up fierce resistance but eventually succumbed to preserve their own access to US data. Australia had paid for the range's construction and for a large number of security staff who vetted all Australians working there, but this meant nothing to the US.

The most disturbing secret at the time of ASIO's birth is that the most important traitor was Weisband, who worked on the Venona project decoding messages between many countries, including Australia and the USSR. The online chronology posted by the NSA says that its forerunner, the Army Security Agency, made an initial break in decrypting Soviet messages in late 1947 as part of Venona's cryptology attack undertaken with its British counterpart, the Government Communications Head-quarters (GCHQ). The NSA chronology revealed that Venona was so sensitive that the CIA was not officially briefed until 1953.

Senior officials from the British counterintelligence body MI5 took the lead in trying to convince the Chifley Government to set up its own counterintelligence agency. But secrecy meant they couldn't explain how they knew that the Australian spies actually existed. Horner says they decided that Chifley would be the first person in Australia to be told that the evidence came from intercepts of communications between Moscow and its Canberra embassy. Horner quotes MI5 officials as saying that the head of the External Affairs department, John Burton, probably had more influence than they did in convincing Chifley to act.[17] Yet evidence-free claims still appeared decades later claiming that Burton was part of the KGB 'spy ring'.

The Soviets switched to unbreakable encryption systems in October 1948 after Weisband, an employee of the US Army Security Agency, told the Soviets what Venona did. He had started working for the KGB in America in 1934 but was never charged because the authorities, reflecting a perverse official addiction to secrecy, feared the publicity would reveal that the Soviets already knew of Venona's existence. The significance and sensitivity of Weisband's activities resulted in suppression of any public acknowledgement of his treachery until 28 June 2000, when the NSA released a report saying he had been responsible for 'perhaps the most significant intelligence loss in U.S. history'.[18] Undeterred by hypocrisy, the US imposed a complete ban on supplying any classified information to Australia in May 1948, although Weisband had done vastly more damage than any Soviet agent in Australia would ever do.

Despite the fact that Venona was no longer a secret from the Soviets when it switched encryption systems in October 1948, Horner notes that 'For the next 20 years, American, British and Australian security agencies, including ASIO, would work with almost fanatical diligence to preserve the Venona secret, while the Russians knew about it the whole time.'[19] He doesn't reveal how long it took US officials to tell their Australian counterparts about Weisband. I asked ASIO when the US informed it (or its predecessor) that Weisband had told the Soviets that Venona was able to read its messages; ASIO replied in an email on 30 June 2017: 'The information you refer to is not drawn from ASIO records.' ASIO also told the National Archives of Australia (NAA) that it does not hold any open period records (i.e. up to 1993) about the US notifying it that Weisband told the Soviets about Venona.[20] The US should also have told the Defence Signals Directorate (now the Australian Signals Directorate, or ASD). When I asked ASD, via Defence, it declined to answer.

If the supposedly close intelligence relationship were to mean anything, the US should have told Australian counterintelligence about its own massive counter-espionage failure immediately it found out about it, and apologised. It should also have told the Defence Signals Directorate. Yet the US decision to withhold this crucial information is never mentioned by the many gullible political commentators and journalists who worship the wonderful intelligence the US supplies to Australia. Weisband's case brutally demonstrates that the US will withhold what it wants, when it wants, even when Australia has every right to know.

2
ASIO STRUGGLES WITH CHANGE

'I passed the ball to Hawke, who kicked it out of the ground.'
Harvey Barnett, ex–ASIO head[1]

The Chifley Labor government's appointment of the South Australian Supreme Court judge Geoffrey Reed as the first head of ASIO in 1949 reflected a short-lived concern that secrecy gave the new body an ingrained potential to abuse its powers. Instead of replacing Reed with another judge, in July 1950 the Menzies Government appointed the director of military intelligence, Brigadier Charles Spry, as ASIO's director-general. Spry brought a habitual commitment to secrecy to the job. His activities soon spread well beyond communists to targeting people who were simply exercising their rights of free speech and association. In 1960 Spry believed there were as many as 60,000 potential subversives in Australia.[2]

The ASIO official history argues that Spry went beyond the organisation's charter by giving political support to the Menzies Government during the 1951 referendum on the dissolution of the Communist Party.[3] Menzies held the referendum after Labor's opposition leader, Bert Evatt, decisively won a High Court challenge to the ban's constitutional validity. The Communist Party continued to exist for decades without posing a threat to the elected government, and in 1991 it dissolved itself. A tiny version has since reappeared.

There is little reason to believe Spry conspired with Menzies to engineer the 1954 defection of the KGB chief in the Canberra embassy, Vladimir Petrov, and his wife, Evdokia. But ASIO arranged the defections, which helped the Coalition parties, particularly after Menzies established a royal commission into espionage. Petrov couldn't give the commission any information about a current Soviet spy ring because there wasn't one. Nor did he have any knowledge of any Soviet 'illegals' (intelligence officials embedded in the community). Despite intensive ASIO efforts for many years, none were ever found.

Petrov was a heavy drinker with no appetite for the tedious work of agent handling, preferring to visit Kings Cross to drink and find prostitutes who would accept his money. By the time he arrived in February 1951, none of the agents from the mid-1940s were still active. The only important secret he brought with him after defecting was that he hadn't recruited any agents to replace the earlier ones.

Although the defections were widely acclaimed as a triumph for ASIO, which babysat the Petrovs for decades, their sole value was to help overseas counterintelligence agencies identify a few KGB officers. Other defectors have given more valuable information without a high-profile royal commission. The commission contributed nothing other than a political advantage for the Menzies Government following Evatt's fierce and sometimes intemperate attack on the commission.[4] The attack helped trigger a split in the Labor Party. A minor new party emerged, largely organised by the secretive National Civic Council (NCC) led by a zealous Catholic, Bob Santamaria. Called the Democratic Labor Party, it wrecked Labor's election chances until 1972.

Commissioned by the Whitlam Government, the Hope Royal Commission into Intelligence and Security (RCIS) produced a report in 1976 that was released by the NAA in May 2008. It gives a damning portrayal of ASIO as a dysfunctional agency that was much too close to particular political organisations (although unnamed, Santamaria's NCC was the key body). In a speech at the official release of the report, the commission's secretary, George Brownbill, said it had found 'a security service that was badly politicised ... The ASIO files disclosed numerous cases where gossip and tittle-tattle about people and their so-called communist sympathies was recounted to certain figures in the Menzies governments and then revealed in some cases under parliamentary privilege. As we found with a more detailed enquiry, much of this was no more than slander under privilege.'[5]

Although David Horner's first volume of the official ASIO history is called *The Spy Catchers*, the organisation never caught any Australians working as agents for a foreign intelligence service. Governments over the years expelled a couple of KGB officials whom ASIO had assessed as trying to recruit Australian agents, but for ASIO, catching spies took a back seat to snooping on innocent Australians. Although not a trenchant critic of Spry, Horner concluded, 'ASIO officers came to believe that any political movement or society or societal group that challenged the conservative view of society was potentially subversive.'[6] He also noted: 'It is now clear that ASIO's surveillance of academics, intellectuals, writers and artists and the gathering of information into voluminous files was a massive waste of time and resources.'[7]

After Peter Barbour took over from Spry in 1970, he tried to introduce reforms but was often frustrated by senior officers from the Spry era, some of whom were strongly influenced by Santamaria. John Blaxland's chapter called 'Shaping and Influencing' in the second volume of the ASIO history gives details of operations conducted by a new Special Projects Section established in 1965 to influence the debate over the Vietnam War. Its head, Bob Swan, said these 'spoiling' operations were initially 'designed primarily to debunk, discredit, disillusion or destroy' the Communist Party and later extended to the anti–Vietnam War protest movement, which merely exercised the democratic right to oppose government policy.'[8] ASIO's attempts to damage the government's critics went far beyond its charter. It made extensive use of journalistic stooges in major media outlets who would put their name on material prepared by ASIO.[9] One journalist, Robert Mayne, later revealed details of this activity in the *National Times*.[10] For many years during this period the ABC and the Melbourne *Age* let ASIO vet journalists to weed out people who might be regarded as subversive.[11]

ASIO's faction-riddled behaviour after Labor won the December 1972 election is covered in the chapters on the Whitlam years in this book. After 1975 the new Coalition prime minister, Malcolm Fraser, did not revert to politicising ASIO. However, when the *Australian Financial Review (AFR)* repeatedly published leaked Cabinet and other documents, Fraser wanted ASIO to tap my phone in the *AFR*'s Parliament House office where I covered national security, among other topics. Fraser faced opposition from senior public servants, who persuaded him that the phones in Parliament House, including those of journalists, should remain immune to official interception.[12] ASIO then tapped my family's home phone without discovering anything of value.

After I switched to the *National Times* following a posting to Washington, I published on 15 March 1981 a long article based on a leaked copy of the top-secret Hope report on the Australian Secret Intelligence Service (ASIS). Fraser told the new ASIO head, Harvey Barnett, that he wanted the leak investigated with the aim of prosecuting. Barnett, who had been deputy director of ASIS, told Fraser that those responsible would have ensured they couldn't be detected.[13] He was right.

Blaxland and Crawley's third volume of the official ASIO history chastises Barnett for taking a softer stand than the Labor prime minister Bob Hawke after ASIO discovered in 1983 that a KGB officer, Valeri Ivanov, was allegedly cultivating David Combe, Labor's former national secretary. Combe, who had become a lobbyist, was looking for work, including consulting on trade with Russia. Blaxland and Crawley criticise Barnett for focusing on expelling Ivanov while being 'oblivious' to Combe, who he didn't see as a target and to whom he gave 'the benefit of every doubt'.[14]

Barnett's approach made sense. Once the government had expelled Ivanov and banned Combe from having contact with ministers, Barnett correctly concluded that any national security risk had abated. Nevertheless, Hawke insisted on continuing an investigation into Combe that yielded nothing adverse. After listening to surveillance tapes, Attorney-General Gareth Evans and Foreign Minister Bill Hayden were not as convinced as Hawke that Combe had overstepped the line. Evans told the Cabinet Security Committee meeting that there was little in the bugged conversations 'that might constitute a viable charge of impropriety, or even worse, against Combe'.[15] Much of the ASIO case was based on the transcript of a conversation between Combe and Ivanov in the latter's home, which was bugged. The error-riddled transcript was incomprehensible in places, containing phrases such as 'even old stacks talk'. If Ivanov had been trying to recruit Combe as an agent, why would he have asked him to his home where the conversation might be bugged?

After retiring, Barnett told me in Melbourne, 'I passed the ball to Hawke, who kicked it out of the ground.' Barnett drove a red MG, the same colour and brand he used to tool around Jakarta while ASIS station chief. When I suggested he might be slightly conspicuous, he insisted that his 'tradecraft' let him foil Indonesian counterintelligence efforts. He clearly enjoyed his time in ASIS a lot more than his time in ASIO.

Following the Combe affair, the Hawke Government took the unprecedented step of making it a criminal offence to reveal the identity of ASIO officers. This raised ongoing difficulties for the justice system. In December 2007 an ASIO member named 'Officer 1' appeared by video link as a News Limited witness in a defamation action brought by a Sydney man, Mamdouh Habib, after one of its papers allegedly accused him of lying about being tortured. Officer 1 gave evidence about interrogating Habib after he was arrested in Pakistan and subsequently flown by the CIA to Egypt where he plausibly claimed to have been tortured. The former chief economist for HSBC in Australia, Jeff Schubert, who followed the case from Moscow, said, 'For all we know Officer 1 is an actor. If not, how did News Limited find him? Presumably, it asked ASIO to provide him as a witness, believing that he would readily tell the story it wanted the court to hear. Sitting here in my Moscow apartment, I wonder what News Limited would have to say about this practice in a Russian court.'[16]

Hawke also watered down Fraser's 1979 *Australian Security Intelligence Organisation Act*, which imposed severe limits on what ASIO could consider subversive activities. Fraser essentially confined domestic surveillance to groups likely to be involved in politically motivated violence. When Hawke's changes were introduced in parliament on 3 June 1988, the mainstream media did not bother to report them. But the amendments allowed ASIO to inquire into matters or persons 'reasonably believed' to be relevant to security, and said acts of violence or threats of violence were not a prerequisite.[17]

The weakening of Fraser's legal protections did nothing to discourage the kind of ill-disciplined thinking that flourishes in a culture of secrecy. In November 1995 ASIO's deputy director, Gerard Walsh, made sensational claims that people had been murdered in Australia as a result of irresponsible disclosure of intelligence secrets.[18] Following his speech, Walsh gave an off-the-record media briefing in which he referred to three murders since 1990. The ABC's national news that night reported that three people had been killed as a result of intelligence disclosures. The next day *The Australian* led with the headline 'Suspected Spies Killed Here: ASIO'.

But after checking, the attorney-general, Michael Lavarch, publicly rejected the claims, saying that nobody had been killed as result of media or other disclosures. The correction prompted the obvious question of how many other glaring errors senior ASIO officials have made—and continue to make—that never see the light of day.

Walsh subsequently told Lavarch's staff he never meant to imply that the murders had resulted from intelligence disclosures. But it was more than implied: in his speech he attacked the media and disaffected intelligence officers for showing an 'arrogant' disregard for the national interest by disclosing intelligence secrets, and said, 'In the most dramatic cases it has cost lives.'[19] The episode does not bolster confidence in the ability of high-ranking officers to give even a vaguely accurate account of what has happened.

ASIO has been widely criticised for not catching more hostile foreign intelligence officers. After the 11 September 2001 terrorist atrocities in the US, ASIO's director-general, Dennis Richardson, got this task into perspective: he shifted all counterintelligence staff to counterterrorism duties until more resources became available. Although many commentators are convinced that one or more of ASIO's officers spied for the Soviets for decades, it is hard to justify devoting resources to trying to discover the identity of a 'mole' who might have existed sixty years ago. Today, he or she would probably be dead, demented or disinclined to confess. The official history puts great emphasis on ASIO's suspicions and investigations about the existence of a mole, but they never actually found any, let alone showed they did serious damage to ASIO or the nation.

A former head of ASIS, Ralph Harry, said the success of former West German chancellor Willy Brandt's policy of détente 'was greatly assisted by the presence of a senior Soviet bloc agent in Brandt's office'.[20] The chapters in this book on nuclear risks reveal that moles even helped avert an accidental nuclear war by telling the Soviets that Western preparations for a nuclear attack were only an exercise. Catching the spies who engage in this type of espionage could end in a catastrophe and would benefit neither side.

Yet in an interview with the *Canberra Times* in November 2016, an excitable Blaxland spoke about the intense battles he alleges took place in the national capital between Russian spies and Australian spycatchers in the 1970s and 80s. He said 'It was on for young and old' in shops, restaurants, cafes and bars in Manuka, Kingston, Deakin, Yarralumla, Red Hill and parks near the Soviet and Chinese embassies. Blaxland claimed Russian spies were waiting for 'a pre-arranged contact to turn up to drop something off or have a "brush-past"' (jargon for a quick handover of information).

This is exhilarating stuff, but did it happen? The question is worth asking when one realises that ASIO gave the Australian National University $1.7 million to fund the research and writing of the official history volumes. When asked to confirm that Russian spies met their Australian contacts in shops, cafes, etc. in each of the locations, Blaxland referred me to the official history, which finished in 1989. It gave no instances of ASIO detecting a KGB officer actually meeting an agent at any of the locations mentioned in Canberra or anywhere else. On the contrary, it says ASIO admitted it never detected a decorated KGB officer called Pavlovich Lazovik actually meeting an agent during the seven years he spent in Canberra in the 1970s.[21] To some, this is proof he must have been protected by a mole within ASIO. To others, that way lies madness, and a life trapped in a 'wilderness of mirrors'.[22]

Although ASIO keeps tabs on Chinese and Russian activities, there is no suggestion that its counterintelligence role covers the activities of other foreign governments. Fairfax media reported on 9 December 2010 that WikiLeaks had revealed that several US cables from its Canberra embassy referred to Mark Arbib, a minister in the Rudd Labor government, as a 'protected source'—someone whose name should not be disclosed as a source of information. When I asked ASIO if it had investigated whether Arbib had disclosed sensitive information, it declined to answer. Without any examples, there is no reason to believe he did.

3

AN INFORMATION GATHERER MUTATES INTO A SECRET POLICE AGENCY

'*[Two ASIO officers] committed criminal offences of false imprisonment and kidnapping … ASIO's conduct constituted an unlawful interference with personal liberty … by agents of the state.*'

Justice Michael Adams[1]

When the Hawke Government made it illegal to name ASIO members, the blow to accountability was limited by the agency's inability to detain or interrogate anyone. This changed in 2002 when Coalition attorney-general Daryl Williams introduced a bill to allow ASIO officers acting as anonymous agents of the state to detain and question people for seven days, even when they were not suspected of committing a crime. An innocent person who refused to answer questions or revealed that they had been detained, let alone what they were asked, could be jailed for five years. So could others who revealed what happened, even if they exposed a serious miscarriage of justice.

Although subsequent amendments have taken some of the sharper edges from the bill, the key features remain to this day. The politicians who enacted the new law not only trashed legal protections built up over centuries—they ignored the potential of these powers to facilitate extrajudicial executions. This is not a fanciful concern when Australia's overseas intelligence partners assassinate people. If the CIA or its French counterpart wanted to kill someone in Spain, they could ask ASIO to use its coercive questioning powers to force an innocent relative in Australia to reveal the target's location.

Intelligence information is often wrong. Identities can be confused, intercepts misconstrued, and informants give false information about rivals. For this reason police are not allowed to assassinate people suspected of committing a crime—at least not in liberal democracies.

How readily ASIO uses its special questioning and detention powers depends on who happens to be director-general. It is not even required to reveal how many warrants it has received each year to use these powers. In 2017, it argued for an extension of its special questioning powers to include espionage, communal violence and foreign interference. These extra powers had not been granted at the time of writing.

The secretary of the Hope RCIS, George Brownbill, said at the public release of the commission's papers, 'One of people's great fears, and rightly, is of secret police.'[2] He noted that ASIO was never intended to be more than an intelligence-gathering and assessment agency that left breaches of the law to the police, and said Hope believed these functions must remain separate. Brownbill correctly identified the dangers of ASIO turning into a secret police agency, but failed to foresee that most people wouldn't care.

The case of ASIO kidnapping a University of New South Wales medical student, Izhar ul-Haque, is instructive. Ul-Haque attended a training camp in Pakistan in 2003 where he said he had hoped to find a role as a medic in the continued fighting over India's disputed control of Kashmir. The camp was not run by a declared terrorist organisation. Ul-Haque didn't like it and left after only three weeks. On returning to Australia, he told officials at Sydney Airport what he'd done. Neither ASIO nor the Australian Federal Police (AFP) showed any further interest until almost twelve months later, when they asked him to become an informer against other Muslims in Sydney. He declined, saying he wanted to concentrate on completing his degree, and was subsequently charged with terrorism offences.

The case collapsed after NSW Supreme Court judge Michael Adams found that prior to the charges being laid, two ASIO officers had 'committed criminal offences of false imprisonment and kidnapping … ASIO's conduct constituted an unlawful interference with personal liberty … by agents of the state'.[3] Although kidnapping is a serious criminal offence, no one in ASIO was subsequently charged. However, the head of the Attorney-General's Department, Robert Cornall, asked the NSW Judicial Commission to discipline the judge for being unfair to ASIO. The commission found no grounds to do so.

The overall lack of checks and balances on ASIO's powers extended to John Howard's Cabinet. One member told me on a non-attributable basis that three ministers questioned ASIO's role in the protracted imprisonment on Nauru and elsewhere of two Iraqi refugees, Mohammed Sagar and Muhammad Faisal, after they had fled Saddam Hussein's brutal regime. In line with this, the ministers wanted to know what the men had done to be incarcerated without trial from 2002, contrary to the basic principles of our justice system. The attorney-general, Philip Ruddock, refused to answer on 'national security' grounds. In effect, he denied Cabinet members the information they needed to decide whether there was any justification for depriving people of their liberty in such a fashion. The two were eventually released in early 2007. Often they had been the only refugees on Nauru, meaning their detention was extremely expensive.

To its credit, ASIO opposed the AFP's unjustified pursuit of Gold Coast doctor Mohamed Haneef. In July 2007, the AFP commissioner, Mick Keelty, approved charging Haneef with the 'reckless' provision of material support for a terrorist group: Haneef had given a second cousin a phone SIM card with unused credit that he no longer needed since he was leaving the UK for the job in Australia. The cousin was not a terrorist, as the British police established several days before the AFP charged Haneef. Shortly after the case began, the Director of Public Prosecutions (DPP) recommended that the charges be dropped because of a lack of evidence. More than twelve months and $8.2 million later, the AFP admitted Haneef was no longer a suspect.[4]

Well before the AFP charged Haneef, ASIO head Paul O'Sullivan had given written advice to the Howard Government that there were no grounds for believing Haneef was involved in terrorism. Instead of combating terrorism, the AFP's behaviour risked radicalising young Islamic people. Yet the Rudd Government expressed its full confidence in Keelty. In contrast to its relentless pursuit of Haneef, the AFP responded with remarkable nonchalance to an online post in Melbourne's *Sun Herald* on 10 July 2011 which said, 'Someone needs to assassinate Julia Gillard NOW before she totally destroys our way of life'. After I queried the AFP about its inaction, it said, 'Such comments can and do occur regularly in a range of online forums', later adding, 'A distinction should be made between inappropriate or offensive comments and comments that constitute someone making a specific threat to a person's life.'[5] In this case, the post, which was below an Andrew Bolt column with a large audience, specifically threatened Gillard's life.

Despite the AFP's attitude, inciting acts of politically motivated violence, whether in print or online, is a serious criminal offence. Ignoring menacing online posts by an Australian white supremacist culminated in the mass murder of 50 people at two Christchurch mosques in March 2019.

In 2014 the Coalition and Labor parties backed new laws imposing five- to ten-year jail sentences on anyone who revealed anything about what ASIO designates a Special Intelligence Operation (SIO). Numerous official inquiries and media reports in Australia and overseas have shown that highly secretive bodies will abuse their powers in the absence of strong checks and balances. Yet these changes have empowered intelligence operatives to commit criminal acts other than murder or serious violent offences—but the prohibition on revealing almost anything about these operations still covers murder and other crimes, as well as endemic incompetence or dangerous bungling. The loosely worded law shields ASIO officials and its agents and 'affiliates'—the latter could include other Australian and overseas intelligence agencies, police forces and commandos. It removed the long-standing defence that publication in the public interest can be legally justified. Countries such as the US and Israel do not have an equivalent law.

Bank robbers at least know they are breaking the law. Under the 2014 law, journalists, documentary makers and others who report on crimes, stuff-ups and abuses of power don't know whether a violent assault, for example, is part of an SIO. If asked by a journalist, ASIO will not even say if what the person wants to report might have been part of an SIO. Australian media reporting has never resulted in the death of an intelligence operative or undercover police officer—far more people have been wrongly killed as a result of intelligence operations being kept secret. Based on erroneous intelligence, drones and special forces repeatedly kill people, including children, around the globe.

Limited changes to the SIO laws were made after the head of the National Security Legislation Monitor, Roger Gyles, recommended in February 2016 that there should be differentiation between breaches by 'outsiders', such as journalists, and 'insiders', such as ASIO members, and that 'express harm' would need to have occurred to obtain a conviction. He said the existing law meant journalists could be jailed for an article 'regardless of whether it has any, or any continuing, operational significance and even if it discloses reprehensible conduct by ASIO insiders'. But he said 'outsiders' should still be considered to have breached the law if their reporting was reckless and endangered an operation or people's lives. Whistleblowers, such as ASIO officers, would still face the brunt of the law by revealing morally repugnant behaviour during one of these operations. Later in 2016, the inspector-general of intelligence and security, Margaret Stone, reported that ASIO had failed to meet a requirement to report to her within ten days of being authorised to conduct an SIO.[6]

4

ASIS: THE GOVERNMENT AGENCY YOU PAY TO BREAK THE LAW

'ASIS exists to conduct espionage against foreign countries … In all cases, espionage is illegal and the clandestine service's job is to break those laws without being caught.'

Justice Robert Hope[1]

It is not clear what the Menzies Cabinet thought it had agreed to when it decided in May 1950 to set up the Australian Secret Intelligence Service and appoint a Melbourne establishment figure, Alfred Brooks, to head it.[2] Brooks' patron, External Affairs Minister Dick Casey, wrote in his diary that he'd told the Cabinet meeting about 'the "dirt" boys' stuff, bribery, deception, whispering, underground methods generally'. ASIS did not begin operating until 1952. Even then, the External Affairs Department didn't want to breach international law by providing 'cover' for its operatives.

In 1954, the new head of external affairs, Arthur Tange, objected to Casey helping Brooks gain high-level access to senior figures in Washington, such as Secretary of State Foster Dulles, without letting him know what was said. On one occasion, Brooks told Dulles that the US could, in effect, base nuclear weapons in Australia.

ASIS was modelled on its British counterpart, the Secret Intelligence Service (SIS), where secrecy was institutionally ingrained along with a reflex willingness to withhold crucial information from governments. In an audacious rejection of accountability, the SIS in 1956 refused to tell UK Prime Minister Anthony Eden for over a fortnight that a former World War II frogman, Lionel 'Buster' Crabb, had died while diving on its instructions around a Soviet warship in Portsmouth Harbour. Eden had invited the new Soviet leaders, Nikita Krushchev and Nikolai Bulganin, to visit Britain on this ship and explicitly ordered that the dive not occur. By 1956, the diminutive 46-year-old Crabb was a chain-smoker, heavy drinker and poor swimmer. While on a drinking spree the night before the dive, he attracted attention for his monocle and personally embossed swordstick and his reported boast that he was going to 'take a dekko at the Russians' bottom'.[3]

Crabb disappeared during the dive on 19 April, most probably from drowning. The SIS and the Admiralty not only withheld the information from the PM but also from the public. Eden still hadn't been told on 29 April, when the Admiralty released a readily discredited story that Crabb was somewhere else. Amid frenzied media speculation, Eden was finally told on 4 May. Even then, the Foreign Office asked him to lie by saying Crabb was on an unauthorised 'adventure' of his own.[4] An outraged Eden refused, and on 9 May he told parliament the dive had been undertaken without the government's knowledge; he later sacked the SIS head.

Like Casey, Brooks had a 'Boys' Own' view of his role. In a note to Casey on 14 March 1955, he said diplomacy was 'as dead as a dodo' and a clandestine service could let you 'find the soft spot on the other chap's jugular'. A former adviser to the Defence Committee later told me on a non-attributable basis that 'Under Brooks, we regularly knocked back proposals to assassinate someone.' But Brooks soon had to defend his own job. Apart from Tange, the CIA wanted him sacked, as did the Australian-born Dick Ellis, an influential member of the British Secret Intelligence Service. On 16 May 1957, ministers and the heads of key departments agreed to disband ASIS. It eventually survived, unlike Brooks: he was the first of three heads to be sacked.

Brooks was replaced by a senior diplomat, Ralph Harry. When he left in 1960, ASIS had only three overseas stations—Jakarta, Tokyo and Dili—and a couple of staff embedded in the UK's SIS Hong Kong station. Harry established ASIS's clandestine warfare training centre on Swan Island at Port Phillip Heads as part of its Special Operations role. Officially Special Operations covered 'raising, directing and supporting indigenous guerrilla movements, and sabotage and small party operations'—tasks better left to the military.

Harry's replacement, Walter Cawthorne, rejected a CIA request for ASIS to have a military role in Vietnam. As a former major general, he realised ASIS wasn't up to the job. Instead, he let small teams of Australian military officers train at Swan Island before they were sent to Vietnam from 1962. Some were loosely attached to ASIS; actual ASIS members were later posted to Vietnam solely in an intelligence-gathering role. All their Vietnamese agents (informants) had been killed by the end of the war.

ASIS also conducted operations known as Special Political Actions (SPAs) against Indonesia's President Sukarno in the early 1960s. Six separate SPAs were undertaken, including covert funding for Sukarno opponents, distributing propaganda, and issuing a fake booklet at a major Communist Party conference. Delegates were so overburdened with literature that none noticed the booklet, which was supposed to split the party.

A joint Foreign Affairs/Joint Intelligence Organisation (JIO) report for the newly elected Labor PM, Gough Whitlam, and another from two senior military officers concluded that ASIS should not have a covert action role. Uncharacteristically, Whitlam took no action on these reports. In early 1973, however, he ordered ASIS to withdraw its operatives from Chile after its director, Bill Robertson, told him they were there against his wishes—because the McMahon Coalition government had agreed to an American request. Robertson argued that no Australian interests were served by ASIS taking over three experienced CIA informants when the US government was trying to destabilise President Salvador Allende's elected government. The intelligence that had been collected by the Australians fed into the overall pool used by the CIA for its program intended to culminate in the overthrow of the Allende Government. Allende died during the 11 September 1973 coup by General Augusto Pinochet, who went on to run a particularly vicious dictatorship.

Only the terminally naive would pretend ASIS wasn't involved in Chile around that time. Yet a Labor attorney-general, Gareth Evans, told parliament on 29 November 1983: 'There is no foundation whatsoever for any suggestion that any Australian intelligence agency was engaged in any activity whatsoever in Chile at or around the time of the coup against President Allende.' Pinochet later told Reuters that the origin of the September 1973 coup dated back to 13 April 1972.[5] This was while the ASIS operatives were helping the CIA, which they did until May 1973.

From the start, ASIS faced the problem that its activities were illegal. Bob Hope, the well-regarded NSW Supreme Court judge whom Whitlam appointed to head the RCIS, said, 'In all cases, espionage is illegal and the clandestine service's job is to break those laws without being caught.'[6] He did not explain what was so special about information dubbed 'intelligence' that makes it acceptable to break the law to get it.

Apart from this inherent problem, Ian Kennison headed ASIS without mishap from 1975 to 1981. He was replaced by a former diplomat

John Ryan, established a new Directorate of Covert Action that attracted some thrill-seeking, part-time members. One young part-time recruit, Alexandria Smith, who worked in the *Canberra Times* advertising department, later wrote about how much she enjoyed the chance to practise offensive driving, board a submarine from a Zodiac, learn unarmed combat, and strap her personal weapon, a Browning .22 pistol, to her leg.[7] She said the project's head told her to buy imported underwear to ensure that during an overseas operation any 'ill-intentioned searcher would have a tough time working out my origins from French bras, Italian panties and British socks'.

The 30 November 1983 raid on Melbourne's Sheraton Hotel was designed to enable officers to practise rescuing someone being held overseas or, in this case, in a room at the Sheraton. In some ways, the raid reflected the risk-taking ethos that Hope had urged ASIS to adopt in his top-secret RCIS report.[8] After Hope was appointed to examine the raid on the Sheraton, however, he was highly critical of what had happened.[9] ASIS didn't give the hotel or the Victorian police advance warning of the operation. After the trainees ran around the hotel dressed in garish party masks and armed with hypodermic syringes, automatic pistols and silenced submachine guns, the management called the police. The trainees were lucky the police didn't shoot them.[10] The Victorian government wanted to charge them, but Foreign Minister Bill Hayden refused to divulge their identities. There was no need for such protection, as none of them had been posted overseas. Once again, the mystique surrounding intelligence excused criminal behaviour that should have been prosecuted.

In his RCIS report, Hope said he wanted ASIS to adopt an 'attack' role to penetrate overseas intelligence services. He listed the Russian, Chinese, Vietnamese and North Korean intelligence services as suitable for penetration, plus others in South-East Asia. For this purpose, he recommended posting ASIS operatives to Pyongyang—a dangerous fantasy that, if implemented, would likely have resulted in the operatives and their agents being detected and jailed. When ASIS tried to infiltrate the KGB in Bangkok in 1984, the operation backfired badly. On 6 April, the Soviet embassy held a press conference revealing the name of the ASIS officer and what he had done. One experienced ASIS official later commented on a non-attributable basis: 'Why divert resources into a game the Soviets know backwards, when your real job is to find out what is happening in Thailand? That's hard enough on its own without trying to twist the tail of the KGB.' Hope also seemed unaware that leaving foreign spies alone can be highly beneficial when they supply reassuring information that alleviates governments' unfounded fears.

In 1990, my co-author of *Oyster*, Bill Pinwill, gained access, on a non-attributable basis, to a senior diplomat's diaries from the 1950s and 60s. They revealed that ASIO was training Indonesians as spycatchers while ASIS spies were trying not to be caught in Jakarta. The diplomat also said that ASIS had attempted to 'buy elections' in Asia and recruit Colombo Plan students to spy on their own governments when they returned home.[11] Like many diplomats, this man was highly critical of the quality of ASIS reporting. The historian Alan Fewster unearthed a study by former head of Foreign Affairs Keith Waller of the intelligence reporting from Indonesia during two months in the 1970s. Waller concluded, 'Much of the ASIS reporting was over-classified and given to trivia, or simply retailed gossip that was "endemic" in any capital like Jakarta.'[12]

In addition to diplomatic cover, ASIS had corporate assistance. AWB (previously the Australian Wheat Board) provided it with cover for a small number of its officers by employing them in difficult locations, including Iraq.[13] ASIS's role there included the period when the Howard Government wanted to maintain wheat exports before and after the overthrow of Saddam Hussein. Although the government denied any knowledge of wrongdoing, it appointed Terence Cole QC to head a commission of inquiry into AWB, which had paid almost $300 million in kickbacks to Saddam.[14] The kickbacks were in violation of UN sanctions.

Successive governments deployed far more ASIS officers to the war in Afghanistan than to any other part of the globe. Their precise role is not publicly known, but they provided intelligence to Australian special forces there. Apparently, this intelligence was passed on by the USA. Accurate intelligence is notoriously difficult to obtain in Afghanistan because enterprising locals are sometimes rewarded for falsely claiming that a traditional enemy is a Taliban insurgent. The contribution of false intelligence to the killing of innocent people by Australian and other Western special forces has helped strengthen support for the Taliban.[15]

The annual average growth in funding for ASIS in the ten years up to 2017–18 was 10.5 per cent.[16] The annual average for all government spending, including on schools, hospitals and age pensions, was under 3.5 per cent.

In July 2017, two ABC journalists, Dan Oakes and Sam Clark, published a detailed seven-part series about behavioural problems in Australian special forces in Afghanistan. In one case, they reported that a Special Air

Service (SAS) soldier had pulled a loaded Glock pistol on a female ASIS officer after a large amount of alcohol was consumed on 7 December 2013. The incident occurred at covert premises in Kabul where twelve SAS troopers were guarding several ASIS officers.[17]

ASIS's biggest recent blunder involves the decision by the then foreign minister, Alexander Downer, to authorise it to bug government offices in Dili in 2004 so the government could eavesdrop on Timorese Cabinet discussions about negotiations with Australia over petroleum leases and royalties in the Timor Sea. Australia then won a resources boundary well beyond the normal median line between it and its impoverished neighbour. The bugging operation followed the Howard Government's decision to withdraw from the binding application of the Law of the Sea's territorial dispute settlement procedures two months before Timor-Leste gained independence in 2002. (This cynical move didn't stop the Turnbull Government from warning China to obey the Law of the Sea in its territorial disputes in the South China Sea.) All went smoothly until Timor-Leste found out about the bugging and took action in the International Court of Justice in The Hague in 2013, arguing that Australia had gained an improper negotiating advantage in the dispute over the petroleum leases.

I asked Mark Dreyfus, Labor's attorney-general before the change of government in 2013, if he had authorised warrants to intercept the phones of the ASIS whistleblower who was in charge of the bugging and his lawyer, Bernard Collaery, who had acted for Timor-Leste. Dreyfus replied that he 'never comments on intelligence matters'.[18] He would be an exception—many ministers in the national security arena barely manage to talk about anything else.

The new Coalition attorney-general, George Brandis, authorised ASIO to raid Collaery's Canberra office on 3 December 2013. The raid was ordered by ASIO head David Irvine—the same man who had headed ASIS during the 2004 bugging in Dili. During the raid, officials seized documents, including an affidavit from the ASIS whistleblower (later called Witness K). ASIO also took Witness K's passport, thus preventing him from giving oral evidence in The Hague that Collaery had foreshadowed in the normal exchange of information in commercial litigation. There is no precedent for ASIO's seizure of the plaintiff's documents in a commercial case with the government as the defendant. The operation had nothing to do with national security and everything to do with helping Woodside Petroleum gain access to more natural gas.

Collaery said Witness K came forward after learning that Downer had become an adviser to Woodside. Woodside's board already included

Ashton Calvert, a former head of the Foreign Affairs Department. Witness K's affidavit reportedly said he considered the bugging was immoral because it was in the interests of a petroleum company, not the nation.[19] After setbacks in The Hague, Australia agreed in March 2018 to give Timor-Leste a more equitable revenue share from the gas fields.

A former intelligence analyst, Andrew Wilkie, then revealed in parliament on 28 June 2018 that the government had approved the prosecution of Witness K and Collaery for allegedly breaching the *Intelligence Services Act* by revealing the information they had obtained from ASIS. Collaery told a press conference later that day that Witness K had received approval from the inspector-general of intelligence to approach him over the bugging. He also told the media that the government had used the anti-terrorism laws as the basis for the original raids on his office and Witness K's home. Wilkie told parliament that rather than engaging in terrorism, the two defendants were exposing a crime the Howard Government had committed in Dili. The trial will be secret. ASIS must be relieved that Timor-Leste dropped the idea of charging the dozen or more Australians involved in the Dili bugging, who had no indemnity from criminal prosecution for breaching that country's laws.

This episode exposed governmental hypocrisy on two fronts. First, Woodside, with the benefit of ASIS's bugging, was technically 'innocent' of any wrongdoing—any other company using industrial espionage would have been viewed as having committed a serious criminal offence. Second, the government has enacted laws savagely penalising anyone involved in foreign interference in Australia, yet defends its own grubby act of foreign interference in Timor-Leste.

5

ASD/NSA: THE FIVE EYES CLUB SHOWS THE STASI HOW IT'S DONE

'The National Security Agency is authorised to spy upon the citizens of America's closest allies including Britain [and Australia] … The NSA can go it alone if permission is not forthcoming—or if the US chooses not to ask.'
James Glanz, *New York Times*, 20 November 2013[1]

Intercepting someone else's private communications or breaking into their computer hard drive is a criminal offence, except when governments to do it. The Australian Signals Directorate (ASD) makes no attempt to hide its enthusiasm for doing so as a member of the 'Five Eyes' group, with the most intrusive global surveillance network in history. ASD's mission statement reads: 'Reveal their secrets, protect our own'. Its website says it intercepts and decrypts other countries' communications—called signals intelligence (SIGINT)—while protecting Australia's own communications. This statement ignores how ASD, in conjunction with the NSA, also intercepts SIGINT emitted by radar and weapons systems that feed into the US war-fighting machine.

ASD's ability to protect Australian communications is limited. It can't ensure that the NSA or other governments don't spy on Australians. The internet's use of packet-switched global networks means that domestic messages can be routed overseas before reaching their Australian-based recipient. This makes it almost impossible for ASD to protect these messages from interception elsewhere.

Although ASD has improved recently, it has normally refused to answer innocuous media questions despite being a far more powerful intelligence agency than either ASIO or ASIS.[2] Nor, according to the NAA, have its predecessors ever lodged any significant documents with it as required by law.

ASD's roots trace back at least as far as the Allied Central Bureau during World War II, which was staffed by Americans and Australians. After the war, the Chifley Government established the Defence Signals Bureau (DSB), which began operating in 1947. Its name changed to the Defence Signals Division, then Directorate, before becoming ASD in 2013.

There was no doubt about who was calling the shots when Australia and New Zealand were formally accepted in 1956 as members of a British-American SIGINT agreement called UKUSA. An annex to the updated 1956 agreement said DSD had to perform tasks determined by the NSA—in effect it became an NSA subsidiary.[3] Initially, US and UK signals intelligence officials decided not to tell elected Australian political leaders about the agreement, which was signed on an agency-to-agency level rather than between governments. Interviews in 1982 with former prime ministers and other ministers confirmed that they were never shown the agreement. Almost none were even told it existed.[4] This is only one example of the NSA-orchestrated intercept network considering itself independent of national governments. It continued to supply signals intelligence to New Zealand despite the US government ordering all intelligence links to be severed in 1985 following a row over nuclear ships' visits.

Although Canada, Norway, Denmark and West Germany were all invited to join UKUSA before Australia and New Zealand, the agreement designates the US as the first party and the four other Anglo-Saxon countries (Australia, Canada, New Zealand, UK) as second parties in what is called the Five Eyes club. The club is not as exclusive as many assume—dozens of other countries are third-party members. The US chooses recipients that give it a political advantage or reciprocal intelligence. Insiders say some of these countries are often given the same intelligence as the Five Eyes members. One group, dubbed Fourteen Eyes, is more formally known as SIGINT Seniors Europe and comprises the Five Eyes countries plus Belgium, France, Germany, Italy, the Netherlands, Norway, Spain, Sweden and Denmark; SIGINT Seniors Pacific comprises Five Eyes plus France, Singapore, India, South Korea and Thailand.[5] Another group includes all twenty-four NATO countries. The NSA also has bilateral

agreements with Japan, Israel, Finland, Algeria, Tunisia, Saudi Arabia and
the United Arab Emirates.[6]

Hardly anyone in Australia had heard of DSD until the Whitlam
Government's defence minister, Lance Barnard, revealed in parliament on
1 March 1973 that no previous army minister had been told it existed.
Yet important DSD facilities (such as its Singapore intercept station) were
in the army portfolio. The NSA also installed SIGINT antennas at the
US-run North West Cape communications base in Western Australia in
1967 without telling the government.[7] Documents leaked to the *National
Times* in 2003 threw new light on what DSD did.[8] Few even considered
the legality of its behaviour before the Hope RCIS in the mid-1970s.
Hope looked at the Overseas Telecommunications Commission's earlier
practice of illegally handing over customers' messages to DSD. He also
examined DSD's practice of intercepting phone calls in Australia, sometimes when ASIO couldn't obtain a warrant. In one example, DSD
intercepted phone calls made from within Australia by Denis Freney, a
leading campaigner for East Timorese independence.[9] In response, the
Fraser Government confined the warrant system to ASIO while letting it
subcontract the job to DSD.[10] Today, ASD needs ministerial authorisation
to deliberately intercept Australians.

Australia initially relied heavily on military units to collect SIGINT,
mainly from wireless transmissions. Over time, DSD employed more
civilians, broadened its intercept targets, and exploited the huge volume
of communications sent over optical-fibre cables and satellites. As well as
high-frequency and direction-finding radio masts, ASD/NSA now has
ground stations at Kojarena near Geraldton, Shoal Bay outside Darwin and
Pine Gap near Alice Springs that intercept signals sent over commercial
communications satellites. Pine Gap is also linked to satellites tasked by the
NSA to intercept a huge range of signals.

Shoal Bay provides an example of US business practices. In the mid-
1970s the Hughes Space Group built satellites and ground stations for a
new Indonesian telecommunications system. It also built a near-identical
ground station at Shoal Bay to let DSD/NSA intercept everything sent
via the Indonesian satellites. Hughes did not tell its Indonesian customer
about this side deal, which compromised the system that country had
just bought.

The NSA does not always share relevant intelligence with Australia. For
example, it cut off the flow of sensitive SIGINT to the Fraser Government
in early February 1979 when the Chinese were preparing a military
incursion into Vietnam.[11]

Another supposed strength of the global network operated by the NSA and ASD and their partners is that it can provide policy-makers with the truth about big issues, such as whether Saddam Hussein's Iraq possessed weapons of mass destruction (WMDs) in 2003. It failed miserably, and the world is still paying the price.

DSD, in conjunction with the NSA, installed interception equipment in Australian diplomatic premises in Papua New Guinea, Indonesia, Thailand and other countries for a program called Reprieve to intercept local phone calls in those countries.[12] After I revealed this in 1983, these target countries objected to hosting diplomatic premises that spied on them. Australia later joined the NSA in a new program called Stateroom to expand these operations to Beijing, New Delhi and other capitals.

China and Russia also collect SIGINT, but they lack access to the many fibre-optic cables and satellite links in the NSA's global network. ASD has formidable defences, as well as powerful encryption, to stop Russia and China intercepting Australia's top-secret communications. These communications are inherently safe because they use a separate secure network and data storage facilities that are inaccessible to the rest of Australia's telecommunications links, including the National Broadband Network (NBN). Nevertheless, in 2012 Prime Minister Julia Gillard announced that she had protected the national security communications system by banning a staff-owned Chinese company, Huawei, from tendering for any part of the NBN.[13] Huawei was offering to supply switches and routers for sections of the NBN at a highly competitive price. The ban ignored the fact that hackers will attempt to break into computers regardless of who supplies the routers—the US has no Chinese equipment on its telecommunication system, but overseas hackers often penetrate American computers. In 2018, the government banned Huawei from supplying its 5G mobile system to Australia although it was the most advanced in the world and much cheaper than those of its rivals.[14]

In 2013 a former NSA contractor, Edward Snowden, transformed the world's knowledge of the immense scale of US-led interception activities and raised questions about the legal and moral difficulties involved. His documents, shared with selected media outlets, showed how the NSA and its partners have reduced traditional secret police, such as the former East German Stasi, to bit players.[15] Online news site *The Intercept* revealed that one NSA system, called XKEYSCORE, utilises over 150 sites around the world to access, sort and analyse staggering amounts of information sent over optical-fibre cables and satellites; this information includes not only emails, chats and web-browsing traffic, but also pictures, documents,

voice calls, webcam photos, web searches, advertising analytics traffic, social media traffic, logged keystrokes, username and password pairs,
file uploads to online services, and Skype sessions.[16] The US population
wasn't exempt: a top-secret court order required one of America's largest
telecoms providers, Verizon, to give all its customers' telephone records
to the NSA on a daily basis, regardless of whether the customers were
suspected of wrongdoing.[17]

Snowden's documents revealed that ASD had intercepted the mobile
phones of Indonesia's president, Susilo Bambang Yudhoyono, his wife
and senior colleagues in 2009.[18] The Indonesians strongly objected to
this deceitful behaviour by a neighbour who professed to be a friend.
Apparently, the spying operation produced nothing of value. Other
Snowden documents showed that in 2013 ASD offered to supply the NSA
with SIGINT involving an American law firm representing Indonesia in
trade disputes with the US, including 'information covered by attorney–
client privilege'.[19] There is no public policy rationale for ASD to help the
US oppose Indonesia in a commercial law case.

The UK's Investigatory Powers Tribunal exposed large-scale illegal
behaviour in February 2015 when it found that UK–US sharing of
bulk intercepts of electronic communications had been unlawful for the
previous seven years and that GCHQ had breached human-rights law by
accessing emails and phone records intercepted by the NSA. The European
Court of Human Rights ruled in 2018 that the UK mass interception program violated the rights of privacy and freedom of expression. The court
found that the program 'is incapable of keeping the interference to what is
necessary in a democratic society'.[20]

Another Snowden memo revealed that UK officials had approved a
secret deal in 2007 to allow the NSA to analyse and store phone, internet
and email records and IP addresses of British citizens who were not
suspected of any wrongdoing. One analysis suggests that 'three hops'
(friend to friend to friend) from a typical Facebook user could pull the
data of more than five million people into the dragnet.[21] It's not publicly
known if ASD has a similar arrangement.

Snowden released documents showing that in 2005, 'The NSA is
authorised to spy upon the citizens of America's closest allies including
Britain [and Australia] … The NSA can go it alone if permission is not
forthcoming—or if the US chooses not to ask.'[22] Given the nature of US
money politics, it would be surprising if American firms didn't receive
intelligence about their competitors in Australia and elsewhere.

ASD is so intertwined with its intercept partners in collecting intelligence that it often has no way of knowing whether this information is used for good or evil. Snowden provided documents showing that the US gave Turkey SIGINT identifying the location of Kurdish rebels; this information allowed the rebels to be captured or killed.[23] Killing Kurds—who are known to be the most effective fighters against Islamic State terrorists—would not be in Australia's interests.[24] ASD could serve Australian interests with no moral qualms by helping police identify those who make anonymous threats on social media to rape and murder people. It could also improve the ability of the Australian Tax Office (ATO) and the Australian Transaction Reports and Analysis Centre (AUSTRAC) to investigate tax evasion and money laundering.

Taking recklessness to a new extreme, the NSA has developed a huge array of offensive cyber-tools to introduce malware onto computers; this malware can be employed to steal documents, hack into emails, and subtly change data or destroy it. A group called Shadow Brokers is reportedly responsible for stealing some of these malware tools and putting them online, where others have used them for criminal purposes.[25] More than embarrassment is at stake: a government agency has lost control of weapons it developed, and these weapons are now causing serious damage to corporations and individuals. Imagine the equivalent of US fighter planes being used to damage property across America and its allies. The danger is real. Media around the world reported in 2017 that ransomware allegedly stolen from the NSA infected tens of thousands of computers in 100 countries around the globe, disrupting the UK health system, Russian banks, Spain's Telefónica, and police departments in the US.[26]

WikiLeaks made a valuable contribution when it revealed on 7 March 2017 that the CIA had lost control of its global covert hacking program, including its arsenal of 'weaponised' malware.[27] The documents showed the extraordinary scale of the CIA's attacks against a wide range of products and operating systems, including Apple's iPhone, Google's Android and Microsoft's Windows. In its series called Vault 7, WikiLeaks said the CIA had undermined the Obama administration's undertaking that the intelligence agencies would tell manufacturers promptly about any serious vulnerabilities discovered in their products. It said vulnerabilities not disclosed to the manufacturers placed huge swathes of the population and critical infrastructure at risk to foreign intelligence or cyber criminals who could utilise the vulnerabilities. Similar outcomes are now possible in Australia due to the encryption laws introduced in December 2018, which allow intelligence and police agencies to build weaknesses into tech companies' systems.

Far from denying the authenticity of the USA's weaponised malware documents, the Trump administration said it was investigating CIA contractors as the probable source of the leaks.[28] It said nothing about addressing the problem of telling the technology companies how to overcome the vulnerabilities, let alone stopping the CIA or the NSA from creating malware that can sabotage many of the advantages cyber-technology delivers to humanity.

6

THE USES AND ABUSES OF INTELLIGENCE

'Through the seven and a half years in which I was prime minister, I can't recall a single decision of government that was significantly influenced or altered as a result of defence signals intelligence.'

Malcolm Fraser[1]

Daniel Ellsberg, who exposed the US government's lies about the Vietnam War by leaking the *Pentagon Papers*, had access to numerous classified documents while he was a high-ranking Defense official. He later told an interviewer that he warned Henry Kissinger about the traps awaiting him when Kissinger became Nixon's main security and foreign policy adviser in 1969, saying, 'Henry, you are about to receive a whole slew of clearances, maybe 15 or 20 higher than top secret. After you read all this intelligence ... you will think that others who don't [have it] are fools.'[2] He said he told Kissinger the information was often inaccurate and omitted much of relevance: 'In the meantime, you'll become incapable of learning from most people in the world, no matter how much experience or knowledge they may have of their particular area.' Ellsberg then likened secrecy to 'the potion Circe used to turn men into swine'. Kissinger thanked him and promptly embraced secrecy.

Ellsberg's warning has lost none of its force. Today, many politicians, think-tank analysts and journalists seem to believe in the infallibility of the secretive bodies who turn raw information into a processed commodity called intelligence. Too often, the more accurate description for what they produce is propaganda, designed to shape government policies and public opinion. At its most useful, accurate intelligence and other information can help reduce tensions by showing two rivals that neither is a threat to the other. At its worst, governments can falsely claim they have intelligence that justifies aggression and wasteful national security spending, and helps demonise foreign political leaders.

Intelligence, even if accurate, is not automatically valuable. After retiring, former Australian PM Malcolm Fraser wrote, as quoted above, that during the seven-and-a-half years in which he was prime minister, he couldn't 'recall a single decision of government that was significantly influenced or altered as a result of defence signals intelligence'.[3] Alan Wrigley, a former deputy Defence Department head in charge of strategic policy, told a conference in 1993 that none of the massive volume of intelligence material that had crossed his desk over a ten-year period 'was of any significant value to policy-makers'.[4] Gareth Evans said that in his thirteen years in Cabinet 'very little of any of the stuff that was … gleaned [by ASIO or ASIS] added much value to our understanding of what was going on let alone vital to our security interests'.[5]

On other occasions, secret agencies don't supply crucial intelligence. For example, the Five Eyes signals intelligence club failed to give New Zealand prior warning about the French secret service operatives who blew up the Greenpeace ship *Rainbow Warrior* in Auckland Harbour in February 1985.[6] It also failed to respond to the threat posed by an Australian white supremacist who murdered 50 people in Christchurch in March 2019 after posting increasingly menacing messages online. As explained previously, Australia and New Zealand are part of NSA's global surveillance network that intercepts, analyses and stores almost all communications by phone, radio or the internet. There were ample opportunities to put the killer on watchlists and later alert Christchurch police closer to the attack. Shortly after the massacre, the head of ASD, Mike Burgess, gave a speech boasting about how his agency had countered the online activities of Islamic extremists in the Middle East.[7] Simpler action could have prevented the March 2019 massacre.

Burgess also announced in his speech that he would be recruiting 'many hundreds' of hackers for offensive cyber operations, sometimes involving the destruction of computer systems. This is an act of aggression, little different to a missile attack, and a long way from the DSD's earlier role of simply intercepting communications. Careful outside examination should be given to every proposed hacking operation before it is approved.

It might have been different if Dwight Eisenhower's farewell speech as US president on 7 January 1961 hadn't fallen on deaf ears. In the widely quoted speech, Eisenhower voiced his deep concern about the military-industrial complex's unwarranted influence and the danger to 'our liberties or democratic processes'. His warning followed the 1960 presidential election campaign in which John Kennedy used false intelligence to claim there was a missile gap with the Soviet Union that required huge sums to be spent on the military. There was no gap: the US Air Force claimed the Soviets had hundreds of intercontinental ballistic missiles (ICBMs), but in fact the Soviets had two and the US slightly more. After becoming president, Kennedy acknowledged there was no gap, but then committed troops to the war in Vietnam based on intelligence assessments that fatally ignored the importance of Vietnamese nationalism. Frank Snepp, for five years the CIA's chief strategy analyst in Vietnam, later recounted how the agency's station chief in Saigon, Ted Shackley, pushed his staff to recruit more and more paid informers, enabling him to send a record 500 intelligence reports a month to Washington. Snepp said it only became clear in 1974 what 'havoc Shackley's zeal had visited upon us: over 100 of his Viet Cong agents were discovered to be fabricators; clever Vietnamese entrepreneurs who knew nothing of Communist plans but supplied what looked like valid intelligence'.[8]

After the US lost that war, another threat soon emerged. US Secretary of State Alexander Haig announced on 11 September 1981 that the Soviets were supplying toxic chemical agents to the Laotian and Vietnamese governments to use against resistance groups. Rod Barton, an Australian scientist at the JIO, wasn't convinced.[9] He concluded that the supposedly toxic 'yellow rain' was merely bees defecating in swarms after eating pollen that caused yellow droppings. Although Barton and others clearly demonstrated that the bizarre claims were false, a new secretary of state, George Shultz, presented what purported to be new evidence to Congress in 1982. He had no evidence. Nevertheless, US intelligence officials angrily denounced Barton to his bosses, and the US ambassador even complained to Prime Minister Fraser about Barton. Although the US had over 100 specialists working on the 'threat' compared to Australia's two, Fraser backed his intelligence officers, whose work proved accurate.

On other occasions, senior Australian officials ignored accurate intelligence that did not fit their own policy positions. A leaked transcript of talks in Washington on 22 February 1999 revealed that the Foreign Affairs head, Ashton Calvert, had strongly rejected the concerns of a senior State Department official, Stanley Roth, that there would be a bloodbath in

Timor-Leste during the independence ballot in August that year. Roth wanted to send a peacekeeping force but Calvert saw no need, despite Australian intelligence warnings and media reports that the Indonesian military's plans could result in carnage. Subsequent events proved Roth had been right, and the Australian public's horrified reaction forced the Howard Government to organise an Australian-led international force to stop the killing, rape, torture and destruction.[10]

The March 2003 invasion of Iraq stands out as the greatest intelligence failure in decades and provides a powerful reminder that intelligence, like other forms of information, can be used to deceive policy analysts and the public. In this context, a former Defence Department head, Bill Pritchett, said, 'The great bulk of what we receive will already be processed, analysed, collated and presented: our ability to check it out is very limited. It means that our policy ... can be, or is, already largely shaped.'[11]

It shouldn't be surprising that intelligence agencies have trouble predicting what will happen in the radically uncertain future often confronting human societies, but there was much less excuse for blunders when sensitive sensors could make detailed observations about Iraq's supposed possession of WMDs in 2003. Following the Iraq debacle John Howard described the supply of US intelligence as 'priceless'.[12] Far from being priceless, the massive supply of phoney intelligence on WMDs caused enormous damage.

Following a visit to Washington, the head of the British SIS, Sir Richard Dearlove, gave an honest account of the role of intelligence when he reported to a meeting held by British prime minister Tony Blair on 23 July 2002. Dearlove said, 'Military action was now seen as inevitable ... justified by the conjunction of terrorism and [WMDs]. But the intelligence and facts were being fixed around the policy.'[13] It's now clear that George W. Bush, Blair and Howard, wittingly or not, relied on a propaganda campaign that used distortion, fabrication and lies to make the case for war. Secretary of State Colin Powell fell for the fraudulent intelligence in delivering a speech at the UN on 5 February 2003. He got off to a bad start by saying, 'Every statement I make today is backed up by facts, solid facts. These are not assertions. These are facts corroborated by many sources.' One 'fact' relied on satellite photos of trucks outside buildings in Iraq and later photos showing the trucks no longer there. This supposedly proved that they had taken away WMDs, but in fact all it proved was that trucks can move. It's why they have wheels.

The official post-invasion inquiries clearly established that the CIA had relied heavily on a transparent con man codenamed Curveball to 'prove' the existence of Iraqi WMDs. His 'intelligence' appeared in Powell's UN speech even though the CIA had never spoken to Curveball. As has been widely reported, Curveball, whose actual name was Rafid Ahmed Alwan, had been jailed for embezzlement in Iraq before going to Germany, where he claimed to have first-hand knowledge of Iraq's alleged mobile biological-weapons laboratories. The CIA took his word over that of UN weapons inspectors in Iraq who had investigated his claims and found them false.[14] Before Powell spoke, the German Federal Intelligence Service (BND) had repeatedly interviewed Curveball and concluded he was lying.

Others still behave as though the intelligence agencies' devastating self-deception never occurred. An ANU professor of national security studies, Michael Wesley, even asserted: 'There is only one genuine source of trust in our world and that is intelligence.'[15] Wesley, who was deputy director-general of the Office of National Assessments (ONA) during 2003–04, didn't explain how trusting the phoney intelligence on Iraqi WMDs made the world safer.

Undeterred by the Iraq lesson, governments relied on intelligence to justify attacks on Syria. In July 2018 the Organisation for the Prohibition of Chemical Weapons (OPCW) reported on its investigation into an alleged Syrian government chemical weapons attack in Douma in April— the incident that had led the US, France and the UK to launch air strikes on Syria. Contrary to US claims that the nerve agent sarin had been used in the Douma attack, the OPCW fact-finding mission found that 'no organophosphorous nerve agents or their degradation products were detected in the environmental samples or in the plasma samples taken from alleged casualties'.[16] Freelance journalist Paul Malone also investigated the US targets in Barzah and Jamrayah, which were said to be chemical weapons facilities. When he asked if the OPCW had investigated these sites, the organisation referred him to publicly available documents on its inspections of the facilities in 2017 and 2018. The inspectors had reported that they 'did not observe any activities inconsistent with the obligations under the [Prohibition of Chemical Weapons] Convention'.[17] Malone says, 'On the evidence we have, there was no Syrian government sarin attack on Douma in March 2013 and no justification for the airstrikes.' Nor, he says, was there evidence that the facilities the US attacked in Damascus were producing chemical weapons.

The mainstream media's failure to scrutinise Western government claims about Syrian sarin attacks and Iraqi WMDs is a major shift from the 1970s, when many journalists became sceptical of secret intelligence, especially after US congressional committees found that the CIA had severely abused its powers. Today, many politicians and commentators in the US and Australia behave as if unproven allegations leaked by intelligence agencies about Russia or China must be true. Writing in *Salon*, political commentator Danielle Ryan saw another possibility. After WikiLeaks released the Vault 7 documents, she noted that they revealed that the CIA 'can cover its tracks by leaving electronic trails suggesting the hacking is being done in different places—notably, in Russia'. She said that according to WikiLeaks, there was an entire department '[whose] job was to "misdirect attribution" by leaving false fingerprints'.[18] In these circumstances, Ryan said evidence of wrongdoing 'becomes flimsier'.

Nevertheless, many senior journalists seemed to be in league with the intelligence agencies in trying to portray President Donald Trump as a Russian dupe. Much of the reporting presumed that anyone who has spoken to a Russian should be suspect.[19] Had such beliefs been held in the past, Robert Kennedy would not have played a key role in 1962 in resolving the Cuban missile crisis by speaking to the Soviet ambassador, and President Richard Nixon and President Leonid Brezhnev would not have achieved the landmark treaties in the 1970s to slow the nuclear arms race.

An experienced American journalist, Glenn Greenwald, commented in 2017 that the Trump presidency was extremely dangerous, but so was the CIA. Unlike the CIA, he said, 'Trump was democratically elected ... To urge that the CIA and the intelligence community undermine the elected branches of government is insanity.'[20] Greenwald cited many serious mistakes that had been caused by relying on intelligence sources: for example, the *Washington Post* had to retract a report that the Russians had hacked into the US electricity grid; and three leading CNN journalists resigned after the news agency retracted a report falsely linking a Trump ally to a Russian investment fund.[21] The US Homeland Security Department received widespread media coverage for claiming Russia had hacked into the voting systems of twenty-one states, but that claim quickly fell apart.[22]

Greenwald says the vast majority of reporting about Russia has come from anonymous intelligence officials, many of whom had concealed agendas: 'The importance of this journalistic malfeasance when it comes to Russia, a nuclear-armed power, cannot be overstated. Ratcheting up tensions between these two historically hostile powers is incredibly inflammatory and dangerous.'[23] Many journalists and Democratic politicians pushed the line that Trump had colluded with the Russians. After an exhaustive investigation, Robert Mueller found that the evidence 'did

not establish that members of the Trump campaign conspired or coordinated with the Russian government in its election interference activities'.
Mueller found that Trump may have attempted to obstruct justice during
the investigation, but said a decision to charge a serving president was a
matter for Congress.[24]

Concern about the uses of intelligence and other information is not
confined to the international stage. In Australia, security 'expert' Peter
Jennings claimed that Russia or China was likely to be responsible for
hacking and crashing the 2016 Australian census computer, but there was
no hack—only a failure of the IBM-developed system.[25]

Meanwhile, there has been a rapid growth in governments' creation and
use of vast databases on Australians, including their telecommunications
'fingerprints' and facial recognition characteristics. Amid a bewildering
array of examples, new powers initially confined to preventing terrorism
have been extended to unrelated offences. Simultaneously, the ability
of whistleblowers and the media to expose abuses of these new powers
has been severely curtailed by the threat of ten-year jail sentences for
performing what used to be considered their proper role in a democracy.

Not everyone faces such harsh penalties. After former CIA director General David Petraeus gave highly classified information to Paula
Broadwell, the uncleared biographer with whom he was romantically
entangled, he initially faced potential felony charges of lying to the FBI
and leaking classified information under the US Espionage Act. Instead,
he faced a lesser charge in 2015 and was sentenced to two years' probation
and fined US$100,000.[26]

On 23 June 2017, Petraeus addressed a Liberal Party gala dinner in
Sydney. How did Australian politicians, who want to crack down hard on
leaks, react? One attendee, Foreign Minister Julie Bishop, described Petraeus
as a 'friend and valued sounding board'.[27] The Coalition's fiercest national
security hawk, Peter Dutton, also attended, apparently unperturbed by the
party's choice of a notorious leaker as its honoured speaker.

PART 2

AN IDEAL PLACE FOR DANGEROUS
TESTS AND DANGEROUS BASES

7

MEDICAL SUPPORT FOR TRIALS TO KEEP THE ASIAN HORDES AT BAY

'The most effective counter-offensive … [would be] the destruction by biological or chemical means of tropical food crops and the dissemination of infectious disease'
Sir Macfarlane Burnet[1]

Winston Churchill was an ardent supporter of chemical and biological weapons, as were many US generals and, more covertly, some Australian medical scientists.[2] In a famous memo to his military chief of staff, General Hastings Ismay, on 6 July 1944, Churchill said he would ignore 'the psalm-singing uniformed defeatists' when he asked his generals to 'drench Germany with poison gas'.[3] The generals successfully argued that the attacks would not be as effective as the existing bombing campaigns and would invite German retaliation. Unknown to Churchill, the Germans had developed a new category of chemical weapons involving lethal nerve agents, such as one now called sarin, that could have delayed the Allied cross-channel invasion.

US historian Barton Bernstein wrote in 1985 that the US Army wanted to conduct gas warfare against Japan in 1945—the *Washington Times-Herald* agreed, with the headline: 'You Can Cook 'Em Better with Gas'.[4] Mark Weber reported that American military plans included a massive pre-invasion attack against Japanese cities with phosgene gas, which a declassified June 1945 report said 'might easily kill 5 million people and injure many more'.[5] If German military leaders had approved a similar plan to gas London, Weber said, 'Doubtless it would have been cited endlessly as a striking example of Nazi evil, and those responsible for drafting it would have been vilified.'[6] Presidents Roosevelt and Truman rejected this plan. But the US Air Force mounted massive incendiary attacks on sixty-six Japanese cities in the last months of the war, and 300 B-29 heavy bombers burnt most of Tokyo to the ground on 9 March 1945, killing over 100,000 civilians and destroying 250,000 buildings.[7]

The Japanese made little, if any, use of poison gas against the US in the Pacific War, but used chemical and biological weapons during their 1937 invasion and occupation of eastern China. In the Sino-Japanese conflict, between 10 million and 25 million civilians, along with four million troops, are estimated to have died by 1945—more than the total casualties elsewhere in the Pacific War.[8]

There are now several well-regarded accounts of the harrowing Japanese program to develop biological weapons at a complex of extensive laboratories and production facilities outside Harbin in Japanese-controlled Manchuria in 1932.[9] Among other atrocities, the Japanese scientists and medical specialists conducted biological-toxin experiments on live prisoners, including women and children. Prisoners at the laboratories known as Unit 731 were injected with bubonic plague, anthrax, cholera, gangrene, typhoid, tuberculosis, syphilis, gonorrhoea, dysentery, small-pox and botulism. Some were subjected to live vivisection and women were raped as part of a program to conduct tests on those who became pregnant. Multiple limbs were amputated without anaesthetic. Prisoners were attacked with hand grenades, flamethrowers and bombs to obtain data on the resulting injuries.[10] Although there was little outside media reporting of what was happening, many Chinese knew. President Chiang Kai-shek's government released a report in 1942 on the use of fleas to spread bubonic plague.[11] Journalists in the Allied countries ignored this widely disseminated document until Franklin D. Roosevelt referred to it in mid-June 1943.

The lesson from Unit 731 is not that the Japanese were uniquely cruel—they also suffered the cruelty of the firebombing of Tokyo and the first nuclear attacks on cities. The lesson is that secrecy allows zealots to go beyond normal human boundaries, especially when the media fails to keep the world informed. Although Roosevelt warned the Japanese on 5 June 1943 to stop using both chemical and biological weapons against the Chinese in what he called 'this inhuman form of warfare', he approved large increases in US spending to develop similar weapons.[12]

In 1945, the Allied media failed to uncover the deliberate refusal by the US to put the Unit 731 perpetrators on trial for the most heinous crimes committed during the Pacific War. This failure made it much easier in 1945 for the US government to grant immunity to the unit's head, Dr Shiro Ishii, and many other members of his team. In return for this immunity, the US gained a huge amount of information for its own biological weapons programs.[13] Unsurprisingly, extreme secrecy surrounded the deal. Meanwhile, those responsible for the conventional military attack on the US base at Pearl Harbor were prosecuted and executed.

Unit 731's members returned to civilian life, with many taking high-level jobs in universities and industry. Ryoichi Naito, a military physician at Unit 731, became the founder of the Japan Blood Bank.[14] Subsequently, the US was accused of using germ warfare in the conflict with North Korea. This issue is unresolved.[15]

Australia also experimented with chemical agents, importing large quantities of mustard gas and other chemical weapons during World War II. Their only use was on Australian soldiers, who suffered severe burns after volunteering to participate in trials.[16] Secure disposal of onshore stocks was not completed until many decades after the Japanese surrender.

Following the war, the head of the Walter and Eliza Hall Institute of Medical Research, Macfarlane Burnet, advocated the use of chemical and biological weapons yet won the Nobel prize for medicine in 1960. His role was publicly disclosed only after the historian Philip Dorling found documentary evidence in the NAA. Brendan Nicholson reported in 2002 that Burnet wrote a top-secret report in 1947 for the Defence Department's Chemical and Biological Warfare (CBW) Subcommittee, in which he said. 'The most effective counter-offensive to threatened invasion by over-populated Asiatic countries would be directed towards the destruction by biological or chemical means of tropical food crops and the dissemination of infectious disease capable of spreading in tropical but not under Australian conditions.'[17]

Nicholson said that in June 1948, Burnet wrote that the strategic value of biological warfare was that 'it has the tremendous advantage of not destroying the enemy's industrial potential which can then be taken over intact'.[18] After Burnet visited Britain in 1950, he told the subcommittee that this type of biological warfare might succeed 'in a country of low sanitation [where] the introduction of an exotic intestinal pathogen, e.g. by water contamination, might initiate widespread dissemination'.[19]

Burnet wasn't reflecting the prevailing norms. After World War II, the public still supported the 1925 Geneva Protocol's ban on the aggressive use of chemical and biological weapons. Nor was Burnet arguing that it doesn't make a lot of difference if it is a nerve agent or a bullet that quickly kills a soldier on the battlefield. Instead, he advocated a policy of deliberately creating mass starvation in Asia by using biological agents to destroy crops and spread diseases that would kill civilians as well as crops. Either way, the Nobel-laureate-to-be was advocating that Australia commit repugnant war crimes. Nevertheless, the Defence subcommittee in 1951 recommended that a panel report on the 'offensive potential of biological agents likely to be effective against the local food supplies of South-East Asia and Indonesia'.[20]

However, Defence took little further interest in crop destruction until the 1960s Vietnam War, when Australia participated in the US chemical warfare program, spraying crop-destroying toxic herbicides, such as Agent Orange, in an effort to deny food to the Vietcong. Non-combatants also suffered because they lived in the sprayed areas. These herbicides were also used to destroy jungle foliage in an attempt to deny cover to the ultimately successful Vietcong.[21] The terrible multi-generational human harm continues.

The Defence Research and Development Policy Committee at its June 1959 meeting noted that big changes had occurred in CBW since 1952, especially the discovery of the 'V series' of agents, which were extremely toxic and entered the body through the skin or inhalation.[22] Melbourne University's dean of medicine, Professor Sydney Sunderland, was an enthusiastic member of the Defence R&D Policy Committee in the late 1950s. After Defence commissioned him to visit highly secret facilities in the US and UK in the 1960s, he produced top-secret reports on CBW in September 1960 and April 1961. The archives show that Defence Minister Athol Townley acknowledged using these reports as the basis for a 1963 Cabinet submission supporting US chemical weapons tests in Australia. In the reports, Sunderland welcomed new developments in CBW and strongly supported testing in Australia. He said there was a growing feeling abroad (i.e. in the US and the UK) that CBW was just as effective as nuclear weapons for killing people, but had the 'decided advantage' of producing short-lived contamination of the environment 'without destroying the capital assets and industrial resources of the defeated'.[23]

Sunderland noted that 'an active [American] program on crop diseases continues' and the Americans were also interested in studying Indigenous Australian toxins and poisons and would be prepared to support such projects financially.[24] He did not elaborate. However, the US Church Committee on Intelligence revealed in 1975 that the CIA wanted shellfish toxins and cobra venom for assassinations and suicide pills, and to use as ammunition for a gun (called a 'microbioinoculator') that could fire poison darts about 100 metres.[25] In 1960, the CIA had planned to poison the elected Congo prime minister, Patrice Lumumba, with a venom that would appear local to the area. Instead US-backed local forces tortured and killed Lumumba in January 1961. The CIA also proposed assassinating Cuba's Fidel Castro with shellfish toxin.[26] In the end, Castro lived to the age of ninety. Gary Powers, the American pilot of a U2 spy plane shot down over the Soviet Union in 1960, was supposed to commit suicide using shellfish toxin; sensibly, he refused and was later exchanged for a Russian prisoner. The Defence Standards Laboratories (DSL) at Maribyrnong held stocks of the shellfish toxin in Melbourne where the research, at least in one case, appeared to be for public health purposes.[27]

The first public disclosure that Australia was involved in CBW research was on 9 March 1967, when the *Sydney Morning Herald*'s science writer, Noel Limblom, reported that DSL was doing so in collaboration with the US, the UK and Canada.[28] Answering a question from Gough Whitlam in parliament on 15 March 1967, Prime Minister Harold Holt gave what was to become the standard comment: a small group of scientists was keeping up to date with the technology for 'defence against chemical warfare'. This distinction between offensive and defensive weapons is meaningless. Once produced, chemical and biological weapons can be used for either purpose. Shortly after the *SMH*'s revelation, two anti-war researchers, Humphrey McQueen and Ian Morgan, wrote that the principal research scientist at DSL, Dr Archie Gillis, had published five papers on nerve gases and two on stonefish since 1958.[29]

The head of the School of Biological Sciences at the University of Sydney, Professor Charles Birch, was one of the strongest opponents of using scientific knowledge for making chemical and biological weapons. He told the ABC radio program *The World Tomorrow* on 27 July 1968 that there was no excuse for scientists to keep their work secret.[30] An ABC journalist, Michael Daley, noted that DSL's annual report for 1967 referred to research it was doing into the movement of chemical and biological aerosols through foliage, the action of drugs on the nervous control of muscles, and the reaction impact of bacterial endotoxins in rabbits' blood—all were of particular relevance to CBW.[31]

It is almost certain that no Australian dean of medicine would advocate testing such agents today. Nor should doctors in the 1960s have done so—they were ethically required to do no harm, and the 1925 Geneva Protocol outlawed the offensive use of chemical and biological weapons. It's unclear if Melbourne University knew about Sunderland's work for Defence. The 150th-anniversary biographical sketches of Melbourne University's medical-school staff in 2012 mention a minor role undertaken with the Defence Department by wartime Faculty of Medicine dean Peter MacCallum, but make no reference to Sunderland's extensive work with Defence on CBW.[32] Nor is this important aspect of his work mentioned in a prominent biographical dictionary.[33]

8

THE BEST PLACE TO TEST THE DEADLIEST NERVE AGENTS

'The scale and type of trials now necessary are such that these cannot be conducted inside the US due to the dangers involved and the lack of suitably spacious sites.'
US General Lloyd Fellenz[1]

Defence Department scientists in 1961 were keen to test the most potent nerve agent known, VX, in Australia and produce highly toxic biological weapons locally. The NAA shows that the official report of the Defence R&D Policy Committee's July 1961 meeting said it regarded the VX nerve agents as of 'great potential importance to Australia and consideration should be given to conducting trials in tropical areas here'.[2] The committee also said there were important developments in biological warfare, including the ability to produce pathogens cheaply and in bulk. It concluded: 'The possibility of attacks with biological agents must be taken seriously.' However, the Joint Intelligence Committee (JIC) said in a top-secret report in March 1962: 'The possibility of mass attack with chemical and biological warfare agents against the civilian population of Australia is extremely remote ... The clandestine use of CBW agents for sabotage or against base facilities or key installations is technically feasible but, in our view, unlikely.' JIC also concluded that any other form of military attack by the Soviet Union or Communist China was unlikely because of Australia's 'relative insignificance in Communist strategy'.[3]

JIC's assessments were in sharp contrast to the Menzies Government's alarming references to the communist threat. Secrecy ensured that the public was not allowed to hear the contrary view from the civilian and military specialists in the government's peak intelligence committee. The main reason JIC's relaxed conclusions remained highly classified seemingly had little to do with national security and everything to do with preventing public exposure of the Menzies Government's politically motivated fearmongering.

The pressure for increased Australian involvement in US CBW programs gathered momentum after the US defence secretary, Robert McNamara, wrote to Defence Minister Townley in October 1962 saying that Australian Defence scientists had proposed US testing of chemical weapons in Australia. The archives show that Cabinet had not endorsed the actions of the Australian scientists, but McNamara used their suggestions to propose sending a US survey team to Australia to pursue the idea. He did not disclose that his main interest was in VX. Although Townley did not have Cabinet approval at the time, he agreed to tropical tests provided their existence was classified. As well as trials in north Queensland, obliging Australian officials suggested that the US should look at Maralinga and Emu Field in the South Australian desert for the tests, which would include spraying VX from planes or dropping it as bombs. They didn't mention how dust storms could distribute the toxin, as had happened when the wind scattered dangerous levels of plutonium from British nuclear tests in the 1950s (see Chapter 13).

The US already had a publicly known site for testing CBW, at Dugway in the Utah desert outside Salt Lake City. This program sometimes relied on sick humour to describe tests that spread deadly diseases and bacteria—for example, Operation Big Itch tested ways to spread diseases via fleas, and Operation Big Buzz tested spreading using mosquitoes.[4] Big Itch was a particularly sensitive operation. After it was revealed to widespread condemnation that the Japanese had used fleas to spread disease during their occupation of China, the US denied accusations that it had spread diseases using the same insects during the Korean War.

A new centre in Utah trialled the more toxic agents, including VX. General Lloyd Fellenz, who had overall responsibility for the US testing program, headed the survey team that arrived in Australia for a secret visit in January–February 1963. The record of a meeting Fellenz held with senior officials shortly after arriving says he warned them that the subject of CBW was 'political dynamite', so it might be best not to mention his name. Professor Sydney Sunderland, who was a secret CBW consultant to Defence, attended the meetings.

Fellenz candidly revealed to the Australians that the US program involved both offensive and defensive CBW trials—contrary to the

Australian government's subsequent spurious claims that everything was defensive. Fellenz also explained why the trials of VX had to be held in Australia: he said it was because the scale and type of trials necessary 'cannot be conducted inside the US due to the dangers involved and the lack of suitably spacious sites'. This was the main appeal of a new site at Iron Range, on the east coast of the Cape York Peninsula. British officials had earlier given a similar explanation for why their misnamed 'minor' Maralinga plutonium trials had to be held in Australia rather than the UK.

The survey team visited Iron Range, Innisfail, Emu Field and Maralinga. Iron Range was used for Operation Blowdown in July 1963, in which 50 tonnes of TNT was exploded on the top of a 40-metre steel tower. The blast allowed a US, British, Canadian and Australian technical group to collect extensive data about the explosion's impact on the forest. The real purpose of the explosion was not officially explained, but journalists reported that it was intended to see if nuclear weapons would be an effective way to clear jungle that was concealing insurgents in South Vietnam.

The purpose remained an official secret for almost forty years until Defence Minister Robert Hill answered a 25 June 2002 parliamentary question on notice by saying Operation Blowdown used conventional high explosives 'to simulate, on a very small scale, the blast effects of a nuclear explosion in a jungle environment'. He told parliament: 'The data collected allowed scientists to extrapolate what would be the effects on social mobility and patrol activity if a 10-kiloton tactical nuclear weapon had been used in the jungle.' The eventual assessment was that nuclear weapons were not suitable, so the US instead sprayed huge quantities of Agent Orange and other chemical defoliants in Vietnam between 1962 and 1971.

A key objective of the proposed US chemical weapons tests in north Queensland was to overcome the main difficulty with VX. Although it is often described as a gas, VX is a viscous liquid with a tendency to stay as small droplets when sprayed, thus reducing its chances of killing soldiers by inhalation. Small quantities in contact with the skin are fatal.[5] Without mentioning that Vietnam was the intended target, Townley said in a Cabinet submission on 9 October 1963 that Fellenz had explained that 'one important objective would be to prove the effectiveness of weapons systems using operational CW agents and means of distribution under conditions as near as possible to those of actual operations. The trials would include the dispersal of real CW agents from [low-flying] jet aircraft at night.'

On 16 August 1963, the US Army asked for a second survey team to have a look at the Iron Range proposal. Townley sought permission in

October 1963, but Cabinet did not make a decision and would continue to procrastinate, mainly because it didn't like the idea. Townley's Cabinet submission said safety would be a prime consideration and suggested that the involvement of an organisation along the lines of the Atomic Weapons Tests Safety Committee 'would appear to be appropriate'. It is hard to think of a less appropriate body—the 1984–85 McClelland Royal Commission into British Nuclear Tests in Australia found the safety committee was a disgrace. Townley said safety had 'not yet been determined for tropical forest conditions'. He also noted that safety considerations would need to include the possible contamination of streams and how long the toxic agents would persist after the trials—but he was willing to let the US undertake large-scale tests without credible information about safety.

In another echo of the Maralinga debacle, Townley's Cabinet submission said the possibility of 'disturbance' to the Aboriginal population would need to be examined, without mentioning that the Lockhart Aboriginal township was within the Iron Range precinct. The experience at Maralinga showed it wasn't easy to warn all Aboriginal people in the general vicinity and that some wandered into prohibited areas (see Chapter 10). Cape York Aboriginal people could do likewise. Townley said the initial trials were expected to take two to three years, during which jet planes would spray toxic agents over an area 20 × 3 miles (32 × 5 km) at night, within a public exclusion area of 30 × 40 miles (48 × 64 km). The Cabinet submission noted that Britain, Australia, the USSR and China—unlike the US and Japan—were parties to the 1925 Geneva Protocol prohibiting the use of chemical and biological weapons in war.

After Townley's submission said that the existence of trials was likely to become public knowledge, External Affairs advised that an official statement might say they were 'not being conducted with a view to producing offensive weapons'. This would have been an outright lie—the submission acknowledged that the US was developing 'both offensive and defensive' weapons. An External Affairs cable from Australia's UN mission in New York on 10 October 1963 wanted to delete a suggested reference to tests of 'bacteriological and chemical weapons' and say only that the tests would use 'conventional means'. This was an even more palpable lie. A more realistic External Affairs draft note later cautioned that when the US's use of non-lethal agents in Vietnam was revealed in 1965, 'there was a world-wide reaction of condemnation and hostility. In Asia, the reaction reflected, among other things, a feeling that a weapon of warfare that would not be used in Europe was being directed against Asians.' The US Defense Department sought to put a positive spin on the use of chemical agents in

1966 when it argued that their use in Vietnam 'is not only militarily useful, but more humane than bullets or explosives'.[6]

Rigid secrecy ensured that in the 1960s the public was given no inkling of the proposals for the US to test VX in tropical north Queensland. It was not revealed until May 1988, when I wrote an article describing how VX could cause a horrible death, with a victim's body 'twitching in a pool of vomit and diarrhoea'.[7] With the benefit of background details from a diplomat, my article said that after 'much hesitation and embarrassment' the Menzies Government informed the US in June 1965 that it had decided against a visit by the survey team. The US accepted Australia's reservations.[8]

The archives show that the defence attaché in Australia's Washington embassy sent a cable in 1967 giving some indication of the likely sensitivities if the US tested biological weapons in Australia. It summarised revelations in the *Washington Post* on 13 January 1967 that universities and private firms were helping the government to develop weapons, including dysentery, plague, Rocky Mountain spotted fever, yellow fever and botulism.

A resourceful television journalist, Ross Coulthart, cited recently declassified documents to report on the Nine Network's *Sunday* program on 8 July 2008 that in the 1960s the US had been 'strongly pushing the government for tests on Australian soil of two of the most deadly chemical weapons ever developed, VX and sarin nerve agents. The plans called for 200 mainly Australian combat troops to be aerially bombed and sprayed with chemical weapons—with all but a handful of the soldiers to be kept in the dark about the full details of the tests.'[9]

Exposing unwitting soldiers to the inherent dangers would have been an unconscionable repeat of what had happened at Maralinga (see Chapter 10). This time Menzies said no to the Americans—which is not something recent Australian governments have done when faced with a supposed national security requirement.

9

FIGHTING THE GOOD FIGHT AGAINST CHEMICAL AND BIOLOGICAL WARFARE

'It remains a matter of some mystery to me why [the US refusal to ratify the Biological Weapons Convention] ... has not registered a little more visibly on the international rage-meter.'

Gareth Evans[1]

Shirley Freeman was a leading medical scientist who made a significant contribution to Australia's support for a complete ban on chemical and biological weapons. Freeman's work was in contrast to some high-profile medical scientists who championed these weapons. In 1966 Freeman became acting head of the Pharmacology Department at Melbourne University while the dean of medicine, Professor Sydney Sunderland, supported CBW in his secret role as an influential consultant to the Defence Department. Freeman shifted to the Defence Science Laboratories, where her work included trying to develop treatments for victims of chemical and biological weapons and better detection technologies. She then joined the Defence Science and Technology Organisation, where she had a key role in advising departments on negotiations for a complete ban on chemical weapons.

After retiring in 1989, Freeman became a forceful public critic of CBW. Shortly after she retired she told me that, contrary to the hopes of the fervent advocates of CBW in the 1950s and 60s, the US eventually lost interest in deploying these weapons because it couldn't make them as effective on the battlefield as conventional weapons. She remained one of many scientists concerned that CBW could still be used destroy crops and create mass starvation—as Macfarlane Burnet had passionately recommended.

Because they are hard to disperse, most existing chemical and biological weapons are not suitable for causing mass casualties other than through crop destruction. Anthrax bacteria can be spread widely as a fine aerosol and might kill unvaccinated people. In 2001, 2 grams of finely milled anthrax spores were sent in a letter to US senator Tom Daschle. When the letter was opened no one in the room was killed, but five US postal workers who had handled the envelope died.[2] The anthrax had been produced and stored at the Fort Detrick chemical and biological weapons laboratory despite the Biological Weapons Convention (BWC). It took the US government over eight years to establish that the source was one of its own laboratories. The FBI announced in 2010 that the culprit was Bruce Ivins, a scientist at the laboratory, who suicided before he could be arrested.[3] The BWC is still crucial to stopping production of contagious bacteria that can spread quickly, such as smallpox and new genetically engineered toxins that are immune to existing antibiotics.

Because nerve agents deteriorate quickly unless stabilisers are added, they are usually of little battlefield value to developing countries. For example, unlike the US, the UK and the Russians, whose bombs and artillery shells can keep the components of the nerve agents separate until shortly before they reach their target, Iraq couldn't stabilise its VX and sarin. Difficulties in dispersing the liquid nerve agents remained. One drop of VX can kill an individual, but one million drops in a bomb won't kill one million people—unlike a high-yield nuclear weapon used on a large city.

Modern protective suits, masks and antidotes render chemical weapons almost useless for the opponents of major military powers on the battle-field. Poorly protected troops are more vulnerable to chemical weapons, but these weapons are still far less effective than conventional ones. During Iraq's 1980–88 war against Iran, it killed an estimated 10,000 people with traditional chemical weapons such as mustard gas, compared to a total of about one million killed on both sides by conventional bombs, artillery shells and bullets.[4] In 1995, the religious sect Aum Shinrikyo attacked five trains on the Tokyo subway with sarin and small quantities of anthrax and botulism, but dispersal problems meant they killed only twelve people rather than the thousands theoretically possible.

Australia can be proud of its role in the 1980s and 90s in trying to bring about effective bans on nuclear, chemical and biological weapons. After the Hawke Government's first foreign minister, Bill Hayden, instructed his department to do more about disarmament, John Gee, a diplomat with an Oxford PhD in chemistry, was instrumental in establishing what became known as the Australia Group. This informal group promoted strict export licensing and inspection regimes to prevent the proliferation of precursor materials and dual-use equipment for CBW programs. The group now has over forty members.

Gee's contribution helped ensure that the Chemical Weapons Convention was much more comprehensive than the 1925 Geneva Protocol. It banned the development, production, stockpiling and use of chemical weapons, and established rules for the destruction of existing stocks and for substantive verification processes. Most stocks have now been destroyed, particularly by the US and Russia, each of which had staggering amounts of VX, and nearly all countries have ratified the convention. Reports from the Organisation for the Prohibition of Chemical Weapons (OPCW) say that Syria has destroyed chemical weapons. Israel has signed, but not ratified, and Egypt has done neither.

Although the BWC was signed in 1972, fewer countries have ratified it, leaving the 1925 Geneva Protocol as an inadequate backup. The 1972 convention suffers from the US's continued refusal to support a verification regime with onsite inspections, even though one of its ostensible reasons for invading Iraq in 2003 was that it was not cooperating sufficiently with the UN weapons inspectors there.

In 2007, Hayden's successor as foreign minister, Gareth Evans, paid tribute to Gee's achievements in a memorial lecture at the Australian National University. Evans said that Gee, working closely with Freeman and another Defence scientist, Bob Mathews, crafted the critical path to accelerate long-stalled negotiations for a chemical weapons convention that ultimately bore fruit with the signing of the treaty in 1993.[5] He was much gloomier about progress on biological weapons, saying that part of the practical problem was that biological weapons don't need large industrial plants or huge sums of money to manufacture. He said, 'Very significantly, [the BWC] contains no requirements whatever for national declarations of existing biological weapons programs, and no verification or inspection regimes whatever governing research facilities and the destruction of biological weapons stockpiles.'[6] He said that negotiation of a detailed protocol for the BWC to cover these gaps began in 1995 but was broken off in 2001 when the US withdrew from the drafting group. The US was supposedly concerned that the inspection regime would compromise the commercial integrity of its pharmaceutical industries. Evans was particularly caustic about the obstacles the US had created by refusing to accept onsite inspections to verify compliance with the treaty. He said it remained a matter of some mystery to him why the behaviour of the US 'has not registered a little more visibly on the international rage-meter: maybe it's because the Bush administration was at the time walking away from so many multilateral treaty commitments and negotiating obligations that it was simply lost in the crowd.'[7]

Although arms-control agreements have been good at preventing most states from stockpiling huge quantities of chemical weapons, only tiny quantities are needed for assassination purposes, and they can be produced as needed. Since Evans spoke at ANU, nerve agents have been used to murder individual people, or to attempt to do so. The North Korean leader Kim Jong-un apparently used VX to kill his brother at Kuala Lumpur Airport in February 2017, and a nerve agent called Novichok was used in the attempted murder of former Soviet double agent Sergei Skripal and his daughter, Yulia, in Salisbury in the UK on 4 March 2018. A Soviet chemist, Vil Mirzayanov, said he had worked on Novichok before moving to the US in 1995, where he published a book containing the Novichok formula.[8] As a result, other countries could have produced it, including his American hosts. In January 2017, Iranian researchers synthesised Novichok nerve agents and added the spectral data to the OPCW's database.[9] Novichok produced by the Soviet Union could also have been destroyed or stolen in the chaos following the disintegration of the communist regime. Leonid Rink, a scientist who worked at a Soviet nerve agent facility, was convicted after he admitted to Russian investigators in 1995 that he had sold a capsule of Novichok to gangsters who killed a Russian banker.[10]

One puzzling aspect of the Salisbury incident is that the UK government initially said the agent used was much more powerful than VX. Ten milligrams of VX is enough to kill if the contact is with the skin; less than 1 milligram is needed if inhaled.[11] The Skripals survived, although another woman later died after coming in contact with a discarded container. The UK government identified two Russians as responsible, and an investigative news site gave supporting evidence that they worked for a Russian military intelligence organisation known as GRU.[12] While he may well have done so, it's hard to see why President Vladimir Putin would directly order the attempted murders in Salisbury: he is keen to reduce, not increase, sanctions that might harm Russian economic growth, which he sees as one of his successes. If he had wanted to murder Skripal, it would have been cheaper and safer to shoot him with an untraceable gun. Russian authorities also had ample time to kill Skripal after they arrested and jailed him in 2004 before swapping him five years later for a Russian spy caught by the West.

This incident and the earlier one, cited above, involving anthrax produced at the Fort Detrick chemical and biological weapons laboratory provide good reasons to try to enforce bans on the production of chemical and biological weapons—let alone nuclear weapons, which are vastly more destructive.

10

MENZIES' GIFT

'No conceivable injury to life, men or property could emerge from the tests.'
Prime Minister Robert Menzies[1]

In 1950, Bob Menzies indulged a fading power's demand for a level of extreme secrecy whose malign consequences remain today.[2] It was a generous gift from Menzies to a country that many Australians felt had abandoned them during World War II. Although he had only been elected as the Liberal/Country Party's coalition PM in 1949, Menzies had confidence in his own judgement. Without consulting any other Australians, he agreed to let Britain explode prototype nuclear bombs in Australia and conduct even more dangerous trials of highly toxic bomb components from 1952 until 1963. The British also wanted to examine the impact of the explosions on soldiers and equipment for future military use. Menzies was not told initially that another key British objective was to help it develop much more destructive thermonuclear (hydrogen) bombs. Given the growing public revulsion at the H-bomb's power, Britain was keen to keep this activity secret.

The biggest secret was that there was almost no justification for secrecy on national security grounds. Edward Teller, US physicist and passionate advocate of the H-bomb, opposed classifying any scientific research and only wanted weapons to be classified for a couple of years after their development.[3] Australian scientists and public servants couldn't give informed advice on the wisdom of agreeing to the tests because none were briefed by the British. This mix of secrecy and ignorance resulted in the unnecessary deaths of some Australians and left others to suffer from debilitating health effects for decades afterwards.

The only thing Menzies told the public about the atmospheric weapons tests was that they were occurring—he could hardly do otherwise when they produced telltale mushroom clouds. The 20,000 British and 15,000 Australian soldiers and other personnel involved in the tests were given scant information about the potential risks when they were ordered, for example, to fly through radioactive clouds immediately after an explosion, or handle contaminated vehicles or test equipment.

The wider Australian public was exposed to fallout from radioactive clouds blown thousands of kilometres across the mainland from the test sites. Because the bomb tests were at or near ground level, they sucked up much more radioactive dust than if they had been higher up or underground. Menzies did not reveal that other less obvious, but riskier, trials were also occurring. However, in answering a question in parliament on 21 October 1953, he said it had been 'stated most authoritatively that no conceivable injury to life, men or property could emerge from the tests'. He did not name these 'authorities'.

Some ministers were told just before the first explosion that the tests would occur, but the supply minister, Howard Beale, was basically kept in the dark even though his department was in charge of facilitating the tests. Beale later revealed that he had only found out that the British decided he shouldn't be told after his department head, Sir George Stevens, told him. Beale said, 'I boiled and fumed at what I regarded as an insult.'[4] It was an insult Menzies was prepared to ignore.

A subsequent royal commission in the mid-1980s chaired by former judge Jim McClelland, who had been one of the Whitlam Government's more effective ministers, broke through much of the secrecy to let Australians know more about what had happened. Dr Bill Yonas, a geographer, and Jill Fitch, a health physicist, were the other two members of the commission.

The British exploded twelve nuclear bombs in Australia between 1952 and 1957: three on the Monte Bello Islands off the Western Australian coast, and nine in the South Australian desert—two at Emu Field and seven at Maralinga. In addition, they conducted almost 600 trials that were misleadingly described as 'minor'. These trials were less obvious, but some were potentially much deadlier. Total secrecy about them prevailed until a few details were leaked in 1973.

One of the atomic bombs tested had an explosive power four to six times larger than those the US had dropped on Hiroshima and Nagasaki.[5]

The fact that many of the Japanese victims of those bombs suffered from radiation sickness was already known: senior UK scientists, military personnel and politicians, unlike the public, knew that a Medical Research Council study in 1947 had found that 'Even the smallest doses of radiation present a genetic affect, there being no threshold dose below which no genetic effect is induced.'[6] It is now known that genetic damage can be passed on to subsequent generations.

The head of the British nuclear weapons program, Sir William Penney, asked Sir Ernest Titterton to be the technical director of the first British test at Monte Bello. Titterton worked on the program and effectively kept doing so after taking a job as a nuclear physics professor at ANU in 1951. Mark Oliphant, an Australian who had worked on the US Manhattan nuclear weapons project, was a more distinguished physicist than Titterton, but he criticised unnecessary secrecy and the British warned Menzies that he was not acceptable to the Americans.[7] Following the Monte Bello tests, the Menzies Government appointed Titterton to the committee charged with the safety of the atomic tests. He went on to head this body despite remaining a British citizen for the rest of his life.

Titterton was not an objective observer. McClelland said Titterton 'regarded himself as a member of the British team rather than the custodian of the safety of Australian citizens'[8] and cited numerous examples of Titterton taking unilateral decisions to endorse high-risk options, mislead Australian governments and repeatedly act as the de facto representative of British nuclear interests. If ASIO had done its job, it would have discovered that Titterton was a British agent who deceived the Australian government he supposedly served.

One example of Titterton's disregard for safety is what happened when Australian health physicists discovered unexpectedly high levels of radiation while they were conducting a routine survey of the site shortly after one of the 1957 Maralinga tests. It turned out the source was cobalt-60, scattered in small pellets across the site after being part of the test. Cobalt-60 has a radioactive half-life of five-and-a-half years and is potentially deadly, but no one told the members of the health physics team that it was present before they were sent into the area. McClelland concluded that Titterton was the only member of the safety committee who knew the cobalt was there and his failure to inform others 'contributed to an unnecessary radiation hazard'.[9] Tittterton was removed from various official Defence advisory bodies only after the 1972 election of the Whitlam Government.

In 1957, three tests codenamed Antler were held at Maralinga to evaluate thermonuclear (H-bomb) components and their triggers to help

Britain develop these bombs, nine of which were subsequently tested in the Pacific on what is now Kiribati. Thermonuclear bombs generate far more power from their fusion reaction than the fission reaction in the kind of atomic bombs that were dropped on Japan. The fusion reaction itself creates little radiation, but weapons designers now use the fusion explosion to create a second fission reaction that then creates a much bigger explosion and a lot more radioactivity.[10]

In 1955 the British prime minister, Sir Anthony Eden, told Menzies two new tests codenamed Mosaic would be held at Monte Bello in 1956 and would be boosted by light elements, such as tritium, used in thermonuclear bombs. He reassured Menzies the bombs would remain atomic bombs, but well-regarded author Liz Tynan says many scholars now accept that the last Mosaic test at Monte Bello had a yield of 98 kilotons—over six times bigger than the Hiroshima bomb.[11]

The media failed to inform the Australian public about the dangers of the tests. Despite this failure, a gallup opinion poll in 1957 showed only 39 per cent of the public favoured the tests and 49 per cent opposed them.[12] The media muzzled itself by voluntarily accepting government 'D-notices' that even prevented it from reporting information that had been previously published in the UK. Journalists failed to reveal that the dangerous 'minor trials' were occurring.[13]

There was no need for confidential contacts when a scientific report revealed the alarming levels of radiation caused by the nuclear tests. In 1956 a CSIRO scientist, Hedley Marston, conducted a biological survey of the fallout from the tests and found that thyroid iodine levels in animals were 4000 times higher than expected in central Queensland—far from Maralinga and Monte Bello.[14] After a small test in 1956, Marsden measured radiation levels on the roof of his Adelaide laboratory and found thyroid results almost 5000 times higher than normal.[15] Journalist Frank Walker gave a disturbing account of attempts to cover up Marsden's findings. Several scientists denigrated the politically conservative Marsden as a communist, and Titterton stopped his findings being published in the *Australian Journal of Biological Sciences* until a censored version eventually appeared in 1958.[16] Apart from the small-circulation rural publication *Stock & Land*, a compliant media ignored the article.

Robert Milliken, a journalist who covered the McClelland hearings, says, 'For more than 30 years after the tests the British and Australian governments maintained the fiction that no Aborigine strayed into the vast zone, and that no Aborigine suffered from the tests.'[17] Defence Department documents uncovered by *Canberra Times* journalists Paul Malone and Howard Conkey show that Aboriginal people were kept out of the Maralinga prohibited areas. Before the first test at Maralinga in September 1956, the Supply Department chief scientist, W.A.S. Butement, wrote that if Aboriginal people should 'wander very far to the south outside the reserve, some harm might result'.[18] Native patrol officers W.B. MacDougall and R. Macaulay were given the impossible task of ensuring that Aboriginal people were kept out of danger. Butement took issue with MacDougall's efforts to protect the locals, but MacDougall's boss, the controller of the Weapons Research Establishment, H. J. Brown, wrote to Butement about his officer's concerns.[19] Butement replied on 16 March saying, 'Your memorandum discloses a lamentable lack of balance in Mr MacDougall's outlook in that he is apparently placing the affairs of a handful of natives above those of the British Commonwealth of Nations.'[20]

At Monte Bello, despite the clear public danger, security was non-existent following the tests. Scavengers removed steel and other material left at the bomb sites to sell on mainland Australia, while others salvaged equipment including contaminated copper wire, trailers and hydraulic jacks from the South Australian sites—a souvenired Land Rover was even driven to Melbourne.[21]

Apart from the inherent dangers for military and civilian personnel during the tests, the deliberate exposure of troops who were tasked with gathering data on the impact of radiation increased the risks for military and civilian personnel. After academic researcher Sue Rabbitt Roff discovered archives showing that twenty-four Australian personnel were ordered to walk across contaminated craters after atomic blasts to test protective clothing, she said, '[this] puts the lie to the British government's claim that they never used humans for guinea pig type experiments in weapons trials in Australia'.[22]

Following the main atmospheric tests in 1957, the British conducted research to extend their knowledge of the damage nuclear weapons can inflict in wartime, rather than advancing public understanding of the dangers. Walker says 22,000 bones, mostly of babies and young children, were removed from corpses in morgues as part of a classified program to examine the effects of the radiation that spread across large parts of Australia.[23] With few exceptions, the grieving parents were not asked if the remains of their children could be used for scientific studies relating to the development of nuclear weapons. The existence of the program, which ran from 1957 to 1978, was kept secret until 2001.[24]

Some sites of the mushroom-cloud explosions might have been relatively safe to enter after several years—unless all the plutonium used in the tests wasn't consumed in the fission reactions. Alan Parkinson, an experienced nuclear engineer who worked on later clean-up attempts, says that perhaps only 25–30 per cent of the plutonium was 'fissioned'.[25] In these cases, he says, some of the non-fissioned plutonium particles would have been left at ground zero and the remainder sucked up in the air and deposited as fallout further away.

It was not feasible to protect people against fallout that reached distant parts of the mainland, which helps explain why the Menzies Government was so insistent that the fallout was not a problem. Although estimates vary, it is now accepted that atmospheric testing in the 1950s and 60s caused a serious increase in deaths and illness. A 2008 study using the US Environmental Protection Agency cancer risk coefficients estimated that the number of deaths worldwide from fallout will total 200,000 to over 500,000 by the end of the twenty-first century.[26]

Proving that an individual cancer was caused decades earlier by UK tests in Australia is extraordinarily difficult. For this reason, McClelland recommended that governments reverse the onus of proof to make it easier for plaintiffs to succeed. However, the Australian and UK governments refused this recommendation and continued vigorously defending cases for compensation. Belatedly, they have paid compensation in cases involving two types of cancer.[27]

Australian governments have not produced figures for the number of deaths or the number of disabled children resulting from the tests that Menzies assured parliament posed 'no conceivable injury'. Although some British troops also suffered, the biggest toll will be in Australia, because that's where the radiation fell and where plutonium remains in the shifting winds and dust.

11

THE DECEPTIVELY NAMED MINOR TRIALS

'I doubt if the people owning the estates in Scotland would look on that with very great favour. They are interested in pheasants and deer in Scotland.'

Noah Pearce[1]

Almost 600 trials falsely described as 'minor' were held at Maralinga and five at Emu Field between 1953 and 1963, not counting the full-scale nuclear weapons tests that finished in 1957.

If the trials were minor, why not hold them in Britain in a remote part of Scotland? The barrister assisting the McClelland Royal Commission on the tests put this question to a British official, Noah Pearce, during the hearings. Pearce replied with the words quoted above.

The consequences of the trials were far from minor—most of the radioactive and other contamination remaining at Maralinga is due to them.[2] McClelland said secrecy was so tight that no Australian scientists or other officials were allowed to observe any of the trials. He said they were 'characterised by persistent deception and paranoid secrecy. In their desire to avoid international repercussions, the British authorities embarked on a course of determined concealment of information from the Australian Government aided and abetted by [Sir Ernest] Titterton'.[3] If the existence of the trials were to have been publicly announced, the international repercussions could have meant that they were covered by the proposed nuclear test ban that had already begun on a voluntary basis in 1958.

The main purpose of the most important of the trials was to improve Britain's nuclear weapons and help design nuclear triggers for H-bombs.

These trials resulted in the extensive dispersal of radioactive material and toxic chemicals, particularly beryllium, uranium and plutonium, and over 800 tonnes of debris from destroyed equipment. Beryllium was used as a reflector to enhance the nuclear reaction in some H-bomb designs. Plutonium 239, with a radioactive half-life of 24,000 years, was by far the most toxic material used: minute particles can enter the body via inhalation, ingestion, cuts or wounds and cause lung, blood, bone and liver cancers. One kilogram of plutonium contains over 16 billion times the international standard for the maximum permissible body burden in humans.[4] Officially, a total of 24.4 kg of plutonium was used in the trials, although we have to take the word of British nuclear officials that there wasn't more.[5]

Powerful explosions caused much of the 22.2 kg used in the last of the 'minor tests' to be dispersed as fine plumes. Most initially fell on nearby areas, but unknown quantities were blown further away in the dust storms common to the area. Some was later found to be attached to small fragments of metal debris distributed well beyond the presumed areas of contamination. This represented a particular danger to Aboriginal people who wandered around the test sites.[6]

The McClelland Royal Commission agreed with the analysis of John Symonds, who had written an official study of the British tests in which he said the PM's Department advised Menzies that Australia had 'very little information concerning these particular trials at a time when delicately balanced discussions were proceeding in Geneva towards a complete cessation of nuclear weapon testing. Although government officials viewed these tests as involving matters of deep political significance beyond safety and public health, they considered Australia should not agree to the tests without an informative statement from the UK authorities about their nature.'[7]

Given the diplomatic issues arising from the trials, including the test-ban negotiations and the proposed nuclear non-proliferation treaty, the Foreign Affairs Department would normally have been deeply involved in advising the government. But Menzies preferred Titterton's unswerving advice that there were no problems.

McClelland said the biggest question mark about the exact purpose of the trials and the degree of British frankness about them hung over the series held between 1959 and 1963 called Vixen A and B. Although plutonium had been used in all the trials since 1959, Symonds said it was not specifically mentioned in any safety reports until 1962, when concealing its presence on the range would have become impossible.[8] The fate of the massive steel structures called 'featherbeds' on which the twelve Vixen B trials occurred gives an idea of the power of the explosions that spread the plutonium. McClelland said the damage to each featherbed and concrete pad was so extensive that a new featherbed had to be used for each new trial. In destroying the featherbeds and other equipment and buildings, the explosions created three million plutonium-contaminated fragments in the area of the Vixen B trials.[9]

Asked by the British authorities to help gain political support in Australia for the Vixen B tests, Titterton argued that no new approval was needed as they were simply an extension of the recent Vixen A tests. In reality they were very different, as senior scientists with Britain's Atomic Weapons Research Establishment (AWRE) told the commission. One explained that the Vixen A tests were safety trials to find out what happened if plutonium caught fire, whereas the Vixen B trials involved detonating 'something which looks like the heart of a nuclear weapon and involved a much bigger dispersal of plutonium'.[10] Another AWRE witness admitted that a Vixen B test could fairly be described as a 'very small atomic explosion'.[11] Yet McClelland quoted Titterton as telling the AWRE, 'It would perhaps be wise to make it quite clear that the fission yield in all cases is zero.'[12]

Had the AWRE done so, it would have been lying to the Australian government. Nor was this what the AWRE told Titterton: what it actually said was that the quantities of materials 'are such as to ensure a low limit on any fissile reaction'.[13] That's not zero. But Titterton told the government that the AWRE had satisfactorily 'answered everything we asked',[14] and the government went ahead on that basis.

In his formal finding, McClelland said, 'In view of the known long half-life of plutonium (24,000 years), the Vixen series should never have been conducted at Maralinga.' Or Scotland!

12

BRITISH PERFIDY, AUSTRALIAN TIMIDITY

'Secrecy strikes at the very root of what science is, and what it is for ... It is not good to be a scientist ... unless you think that it is of the highest value to share your knowledge ... and believe that ... [it] is a thing which is of intrinsic value to humanity.'

Robert Oppenheimer[1]

The 1967 British attempt to clean up Maralinga, called Operation Brumby, was a demonstrable failure. Nonetheless, British nuclear weapons physicist Noah Pearce wrote an official report that concluded the operation was a success. The Pearce Report formed the basis of the Gorton Coalition government's decision to sign an agreement backdated to December 1967 stating that the UK government was 'released from all liabilities and responsibilities' relating to Maralinga.[2] Never mind that Operation Brumby involved using graders and ploughs that made it easier for the dust storms common to the area to distribute soil contaminated with plutonium.

The safety issues were revived when I revealed extensive details of the still-secret sections of the Pearce Report in May 1984.[3] My article noted that some of the tables in the report showed that the plutonium contamination was as much as 100 times higher than Pearce's own benchmark for what was permissible. It also said that the 'minor trials' were usually described as 'point safety' tests, when the reality was that some of them were extremely unsafe operations that left plutonium scattered across the countryside after the heavy loss of topsoil at some of the trial sites. On 25 May 1984, Deborah Smith and I reported in the *National Times* that

Labor's energy minister at the time, Peter Walsh, who was responsible for the site, doubted the reliability of Pearce's claim that 18 kg out of the 20 kg of plutonium used had been buried in pits at Maralinga. Walsh was told that Pearce had admitted to some Australian officials in late 1968 that as much as 18 kg was left on the surface and only 2 kg was buried.[4] The official figure given to Justice McClelland at the royal commission was that 24.4 kg had been used—excluding the plutonium that settled on the ground as part of the 'mushroom cloud' bomb tests.

On 8 June 1984, Smith and I explained in the *National Times* that the discovery of pieces of plutonium weighing up to 2 grams at Maralinga meant the public could have little faith in the assurances given by the Australian Ionising Radiation Advisory Council (AIRAC) about safety, although AIRAC included some of the nation's most prestigious scientists.[5] Our article said a 2-gram piece of plutonium was about 300,000 times bigger than what the council's reports said was there. Perhaps more disturbingly, we said that the latest AIRAC report on safety at Maralinga accepted that neither 'the detail nor purpose' of the British tests and trials using plutonium should be of concern. Australian scientists let secrecy ensure they remained ignorant of crucial facts about the nature of the trials, at great cost to the accuracy of their findings—and to public safety. To do their job properly they should have heeded the warning quoted above from the head of the US nuclear weapons project, Robert Oppenheimer: 'Secrecy strikes at the very root of what science is for.' Robert Milliken noted in his book *No Conceivable Injury* in 1986 that AIRAC stated in its 1983 report that none of the explosions in Australia had a bigger yield than 20 kilotons,[6] but the biggest had been officially stated publicly to be 60 kilotons[7] and was later estimated to be 98 kilotons.[8]

In contrast, the Australian Radiation Laboratory began a survey in 1984 to find what was still on the ground at Maralinga. The ARL's report, released in 1985, found that the contaminated areas and radioactivity measurements were much larger than Pearce had concluded and that Pearce had entirely missed huge numbers of test fragments contaminated with plutonium. The ARL scientists later estimated that there were as many as three million fragments, many of which were outside the supposedly safe areas. That posed a serious danger to visitors who might pick one up. Small amounts of highly toxic beryllium were also found.

Some of the scientists involved told Melbourne-based journalist Ian Anderson that the plutonium contamination was ten times as much as the British had claimed and sometimes extended 150 kilometres from the site instead of the 2.2 kilometres Pearce had reported. Anderson quoted one

scientist, Geoff Williams, as saying, 'For a nation to conduct such a technically sophisticated program and then get contamination levels wrong by a
factor of 10—it's just unbelievable.'[9] What is more believable is that the
UK cared far more about developing bombs than about the contamination
they caused. Anderson reported that the ARL study also found that Pearce
misunderstood how plutonium particles in the soil were suspended in the
air if disturbed, so the amount that could be inhaled by Aboriginal children
playing in the sand was six to twenty times higher than he had suggested.

The US Department of Energy gave the ARL scientists a large amount
of data from Operation Roller Coaster, the joint US-British trials carried
out in the early 1960s that were similar to the Vixen B trials at Maralinga.
In her chapter on the US-UK trials in her book *Atomic Thunder*, Liz Tynan
sets out how senior ARL scientist John Moroney's analysis of the Roller
Coaster data found the plutonium contamination at Maralinga would have
spread much further than the British claimed.[10] Although the British had
the Roller Coaster documents well before Pearce wrote his report, they
never told the Australians about them.

The 1985 ARL report led to the establishment of a joint American,
Australian and British technical assessment group (TAG) to develop a new
clean-up plan that eventually got underway in 1996. Nuclear engineer
Alan Parkinson was appointed as a government representative to oversee
the project but was removed in 1977. In a 2002 article, he said a huge
amount of plutonium-contaminated debris was found outside the concrete
burial pits—one loose concrete cap was several metres away from a pit and
another was one-fifth of the required size.[11]

Journalist and author Robert Milliken records that South Australian
scientists collected nineteen rabbits and a dingo near the radioactive burial
pits at Maralinga and elsewhere in the area and discovered that plutonium,
caesium and strontium had been taken up on the fur and in the gut and
the respiratory systems of all the animals. One of the industrious rabbits
had been picked up from a warren next to the burial pit, making it 'almost
certain' the animals would burrow their way into the pits that were
supposed to remain intact for 24,000 years.[12]

Parkinson explained in his 2014 book that heavy equipment was
initially used to try to shift contaminated soil, in much the same way as in
the failed 1967 effort that allowed plutonium to blow away in dust clouds.
He said on at least fifteen occasions the airborne dust was so thick that
the heavy machinery had to stop work, and on one occasion health physicists evacuated facilities.[13] Yet he records how a departmental official told
a Senate inquiry in May 2000 that no measurements were kept of how

much plutonium blew away during the operation. Better dust-control measures were later introduced and a more thorough attempt was made to remediate the site. How effective this will prove over the longer term remains contentious.

The many years of negligence towards the severe failure to safely contain Maralinga's highly toxic plutonium contrasts with the effort to safely contain low and medium radioactive waste from industrial and medical uses. Nothing contained the radioactive fallout across much of Australia during the British bomb tests—which is why they should never have been held.

After explaining that Maralinga means 'thunder' in an Indigenous language, Tynan gave the word a broader contemporary meaning in her book's final paragraph: 'If there is a word that speaks not only of thunder but also government secrecy, nuclear colonialism, reckless national pride, bigotry towards indigenous peoples, nuclear-era scientific arrogance, human folly and the resilience of victims, surely that word is Maralinga.'

13

THE STRUGGLE TO REVEAL MARALINGA'S MALIGN SECRETS

'A small determined band of men could mount an operation … to quickly remove this plutonium and use it for terrorist purposes.'
Jim Killen, Defence Minister 1975–82[1]

The secrecy and ignorance surrounding Britain's nuclear tests in Australia and their malign legacy remained largely intact until the mid-1970s, when nuclear veterans, politicians and journalists started to highlight the issue. Avon Hudson risked breaking the *Official Secrets Act* by going on ABC television in Adelaide on 2 December 1976 to explain that dangerous waste remained at Maralinga.[2] Hudson, who worked at Maralinga while in the RAAF, also spoke to an Adelaide newspaper, which reported that he had helped bury twenty-six boxes of waste, including plutonium.[3] On 4 December, Hudson took a Channel 10 crew to Maralinga, where he uncovered part of the waste-disposal site for the camera.[4]

Labor frontbencher Tom Uren asked Defence Minister Jim Killen in parliament on 9 December 1976: 'Is it true that, during the moratorium on nuclear weapons testing between 1958 and 1961, Australia cooperated with the British on conducting secret atomic "trigger" tests at Maralinga and that waste and debris were buried at Maralinga?' After Killen replied, 'Urgent inquiries have been set in train to establish precisely what has been buried at Maralinga', Robert Milliken suggested the issue deserved more media attention than it got.[5] The obvious follow-up question was why Defence didn't already know the answer to Uren's question. Killen certainly didn't, but ministerial ignorance was not confined to him: the

Coalition's supply minister, Vic Garland, had falsely told parliament on 14 September 1972 that the radioactive waste at Maralinga had only a half-life of fifteen to twenty years, when Maralinga's plutonium-239 actually had a half-life of 24,000 years.

Many journalists admired Killen as a wit and bon vivant, but as well as being pompous, he was an anti-fluoridation crank who passionately supported white rule in Rhodesia and South Africa while his prime minister, Malcolm Fraser, actively opposed it. He also had a habit of launching intemperate and error-riddled attacks on anyone who criticised him. Milliken quotes a letter Killen wrote to Uren in February 1977 in which he said the matter he raised had been 'confused and distorted by several unfounded allegations' and bluntly rejected Uren's claim that '800 tons of nuclear waste material, including plutonium, is buried at Maralinga'.[6] Killen was forced to retract his inaccurate denial after his department told him that Uren was correct.

It didn't help Killen's mood when I revealed on 16 December 1976 that the Fraser Government was going to ask the British government to upgrade the security of the plutonium and other nuclear waste material at Maralinga.[7] My article said no armed guards patrolled the area and a fence around the waste site had been removed. The government was eager to go ahead with large-scale exports of uranium under what it called 'the strictest safeguards' following a recommendation from Justice Russell Fox's inquiry into uranium mining. However, I explained that Fox had not been told about the plutonium at Maralinga despite his clear need to know. I also said government advisers recognised that waste disposal techniques at Maralinga would need to be of the highest standard to meet Fox's conditions on uranium exports.

When my article appeared, the chief Defence scientist, John Farrands, sent a minute to Defence head Arthur Tange dismissing as 'speculation' its reference to the trials having involved 'small nuclear explosions'.[8] It wasn't speculation. My source correctly said this was how some British nuclear weapon scientists had described the trials—a description later repeated to the McClelland Royal Commission.[9] Farrands' minute demonstrated how the public service's failure to challenge British secrecy undermined its ability to advise governments about what had happened during the most important and dangerous military tests ever conducted in Australia. Farrands admitted, 'Very few, and only one in Defence, [have] any particular insight into the trials which would help in answering Mr Uren's question.'[10] To his credit, Farrands subsequently pressured the British for more information.

The issue returned to the public spotlight after I revealed in October 1978 that a Cabinet submission from Killen warned that 'extremely toxic' plutonium at Maralinga included a 'discrete mass' of half a kilogram of plutonium buried near the airport, which created a terrorist problem.[11] Killen's submission said a 'small determined band of men' could quickly remove this plutonium and use it for terrorist purposes.[12] Although the amount was not enough to make a standard nuclear bomb, the submission warned that plutonium's extremely toxic properties meant terrorists could threaten to disperse it in a city.

My article reported that Killen also said that the plutonium, whose existence he had previously denied, 'probably represented a breach of Australia's obligations' under the International Atomic Energy Agency (IAEA) requirement for Australia to properly safeguard and account for the material. Another disturbing aspect of the Cabinet document was its admission that Australia would have trouble meeting a key IAEA requirement to 'characterise' the plutonium's exact weight and chemical composition—a task it described as being on the 'borderline of Australia's technological ability'. The submission did not explain why the well-funded Australian Atomic Energy Commission couldn't do this job.

Cabinet preferred the option of repatriation of the plutonium to Britain, but admitted this was likely to be rejected by the British. My article said this was because the then government had signed a memorandum in 1968 releasing the British from all obligations in regard to Maralinga. Given that Australian officials had almost no knowledge of what had been left at Maralinga, it was a reckless decision that greatly complicated the task of future governments.

Prime Minister Fraser told parliament on 10 October 1978 that he hadn't known about the presence of the plutonium until earlier that year. He should have been told while he was defence minister in 1970, when Australia signed the Nuclear Non-Proliferation Treaty requiring it to declare and safeguard any fissionable material, especially plutonium. Killen was soon back-pedalling. The Cabinet submission created extensive media and public interest. He suggested in parliament on 10 October 1978 that there might be no need to do more than repeat his earlier announcement about upgrading the police guard.[13] This was an abject repudiation of the clear statement in his own Cabinet submission that the plutonium needed to be removed for safety reasons and to meet our international obligations.

Killen then took the strange step in parliament of appearing to deny my report about what was in his Cabinet submission, even though his Cabinet colleagues knew my report was accurate. This did not stop him launching a florid parliamentary attack on me the following day, enlivened by the line that I wouldn't be capable of 'accurately reporting a minute's silence'.[14]

Fraser insisted the British must remove the half-kilo of plutonium buried near Maralinga Airport and they eventually agreed, provided Australia paid. Fraser agreed in January 1979 to absolve Britain from any further responsibility to repatriate waste once it had removed the half-kilo of plutonium. The operation took place in dusty conditions in February 1979, with temperatures of over 40°C and winds up to 130 kilometres an hour—hardly conducive to containing any loose plutonium at the site.[15]

Fraser replaced Killen as the minister responsible for Maralinga, but no one in the government seemed to understand that other highly dangerous plutonium remained on the ground to be blown around in the winds.

14

A WISE MANDARIN IGNORES LEAKS

'That is not a role that would fit well with this department.'

Mike Codd[1]

It is almost unthinkable today that any public servant wanting to hold onto their job would follow Mike Codd's approach to leaks while he was deputy head of the Prime Minister's Department in 1978.[2] Codd was unfazed by the leaking of Jim Killen's Cabinet submission on the terrorist and other dangers posed by plutonium at Maralinga. I published the details of the submission in the *Australian Financial Review* two days after it was circulated to a small number of ministers and officials on 5 October 1978. On the same day, the Cabinet Office told Codd that the submission had been circulated to 'a wider range of ministers than departments'.

On 9 October, Codd wrote a note to Prime Minister Malcolm Fraser that began by stating: 'Mr Toohey clearly had knowledge of the Cabinet submission (of which he may have had a copy) and in broad terms of Cabinet's decision.' Codd said he was satisfied the leak had not come from the department's officers, and seemed happy to leave it at that. He said statements had not been sought from the heads of other departments, and added pointedly, 'Nor have we made any check on handling in ministers' offices.' He ended by asking Fraser, 'Do you want to proceed with such an exercise?' and adding: 'The chances of it leading to the identification of source of the leak are not high.'

The Maralinga leak to the AFR was followed in quick succession by reports of the content of three Cabinet submissions on economic issues. The full Cabinet then requested that the PM's Department devise measures to prevent a repeat of these leaks and the Maralinga one. Codd could not muster enthusiasm for doing anything much beyond discussing four possible measures.

He objected to Option 1—to discourage photocopying—saying there was 'already a widely held belief that we can trace Cabinet documents so any public announcement could be counter-productive'. He conceded that the department could enlist the assistance of the security agencies in 'quietly exploring the possibilities'. Left unspoken was the prospect of ASIO interrogating ministers.

Codd agreed to Option 2's mundane proposal that department heads maintain a record of who saw submissions, but said Option 3's proposed introduction of regular checks on the handling of Cabinet papers raised two difficulties. First, unless the checks included ministers' offices, he said they would be perceived as selective. Codd spelled out another difficulty: 'Regular checking of ministers' offices could be taken to imply … that unauthorised disclosures could originate from your ministers.' He saw a further problem in regular questioning of public servants: 'That is not a role that would fit well with this department.' He said, 'An alternative would be the appointment of a special security auditor, but this may be seen as heavy-handed. Altogether, we would not favour this option.'

Option 4—to call in the police—presented further difficulties. Codd said, 'Again the checks would need to be comprehensive, including departments and ministers' offices as well as relevant media sources. Such action has not been taken for many years—our recollection suggests not since the Maxwell Newton case—and may be seen publicly to be an overreaction by the government.' (In 1969, Cabinet asked police to investigate a leak to journalist Newton that was widely suspected to come from future prime minister Billy McMahon.) Codd had a further objection: 'It would, in any event, perhaps have only a short-term disincentive effect and lead sources to adapt their mode of operation rather than cease.' He strongly rejected this option 'other than in the most exceptional circumstances'.

Codd's candour did not stop him later becoming the department's head. Today, departments and ministers routinely call in the federal police to try to nail sources, and legislation in 2018 made it a serious criminal offence to either leak or receive a wide range of often innocuous information that ultimately belongs to the public.

15

HOW AUSTRALIA JOINED THE NUCLEAR WAR CLUB

'Mr Prime Minister, I want to present you with one peppercorn payment in full for the first year's rent.'

US ambassador Ed Clark[1]

The Coalition prime minister, Bob Menzies, had one overriding objective in letting the US Navy build a communications base in Western Australia for sending underwater signals to its nuclear-armed submarines: he wanted to use the base to gain an electoral advantage over his Labor Party opponents—as archives unearthed by the *National Times* in the Kennedy Presidential Library in Boston make plain.[2] In announcing his decision in parliament on 17 May 1962 to approve the base, Menzies didn't even mention submarines, although they were by far the most important reason the US wanted to build the base at North West Cape (NWC) near Geraldton. He merely said that the purpose of the base was to provide radio communications for the US and allied ships. The archives show that the US ambassador at the time, William Battle, pushed Menzies' partisan political interests behind the scenes.

Labor was concerned that the base could involve Australia in a nuclear war without its consent and make it a nuclear target. Neither concern bothered Menzies, who preferred to stress how Labor leader Arthur Calwell and his deputy, Gough Whitlam, were harming the American alliance by allegedly taking their orders from 'faceless men' at a special conference of the party. Calwell and Whitlam had adopted the policy that a future Labor government would renegotiate the NWC agreement regardless of outside pressure.

Although Ambassador Battle was a personal friend of John F. Kennedy's from World War II, the archives also show that the White House was not so biased against Labor, much to Menzies' annoyance. Battle was an example of an ambassador who is 'captured' by a host government. The White House wanted the NWC base to go ahead, but didn't want to upset Labor unnecessarily in case it won the next election. Battle sent a secret cable to Washington on 25 March 1963 welcoming Labor's problems: 'The recent difficulties in the Labor Party over our Very Low Frequency [VLF] radio installation [at NWC] have placed the Menzies government in an excellent position to make much needed political ground … The government is anxious to overcome the Labor charge, to which it is somewhat vulnerable, that it has not kept the country adequately informed of its intentions and of its negotiations with the US. In order to take advantage of the atmosphere of the moment, the government is now extremely anxious to move ahead full tilt with the VLF and status of forces agreement negotiations.'

Battle said Menzies told him that he wanted to table both these agreements in parliament before the end of the current session. He said in the same cable, 'This is very much to the advantage of the US. With the present precarious balance in the Parliament the government could be replaced by Labor at any time.' (The 1961 election had left Menzies with a one-seat parliamentary majority.) The briefing papers for Kennedy's scheduled White House meeting with Calwell on 23 July 1963 summarised Menzies' tactics more astutely than Battle had. The papers said that 'in trying to exploit' the establishment of the VLF station, Menzies introduced a bill for ratifying the agreement 'even though there was no obligation to obtain parliamentary approval … Apparently, the government hoped the ALP would introduce an amendment to make the bill conform to ALP policy, with the thought that left-wing members might split the party.'[3]

Battle ended his 25 March cable with a plea that the State Department stop issuing statements that annoyed Menzies. The cable said Menzies had been upset by a report in the Sydney *Sun* on 25 March 1963 in which a State Department spokesman made the diplomatically impeccable statement, 'As for which party should be in power, it's none of our business.'

Battle followed up with another secret cable, on 17 April 1963, giving tactical advice about the 'privileged status' being sought for the NWC facility. He said the Australian public favoured defence cooperation with

America, but cautioned, 'Public attitudes to detailed arrangements on US government and US forces privileges in Australia are likely to be entirely different … Many things to which the Australian government has already agreed will inevitably give rise to extensive press and public comment, much of it probably unfavourable.' Battle explained that the Menzies Government 'had already conceded points which he had expected they would be totally unwilling to grant'. The ambassador also said Menzies had offered to remove any further sticking points that the government had only put there to increase public acceptance. But Battle counselled Washington to accept the window-dressing, saying, 'If the Australian people are unwilling to accept its terms, the agreement would result in defeat for the present government at the polls. This would be too high a price for us to pay.'

The negotiations were a doddle for the US. The original text of the agreement that the external affairs minister, Garfield Barwick, presented to the embassy on 26 March 1963 said almost nothing about Australian con-trol—merely that the two governments would consult from time to time. But the text continued: 'The station will be open for inspection at all times by the Australian government and, except with the express permission of the Australian government, will not be used for purposes other than naval communication.' The owner's right to inspect proved too much for the US, and Barwick promptly changed it to say merely that the government 'will at all times have access to the station'. The stipulation confining it to naval communications was changed to 'defence communications'.

To reassure the Americans that Australia was not really asking for any-thing of substance, Barwick presented a clarifying letter to the embassy on 7 May 1963 saying that the word 'consultation' was 'not intended to establish Australian control over the use of the station', nor to prevent the US communicating with Polaris nuclear submarines, nor give Australia 'control over, or access to, the contents of messages transmitted'.

Menzies even tried to dictate US policy in South America. Battle warned Washington in a secret cable on 5 November 1962 that Menzies did not want Kennedy to back a Brazilian proposal for a nuclear-free zone in South America along the lines Calwell was proposing for the entire Southern Hemisphere. Unhappily for Menzies, the White House briefing paper prepared for Kennedy's meeting with Calwell in July 1963 suggested that if the Labor leader raised the proposed Southern Hemisphere nuclear-free zone, the president could say the 'US is sympathetic with the principle of a brake on further proliferation, but it should not upset the existing military balance'.

Battle objected that backing the Brazilian proposal would 'certainly be grasped by the Opposition as indirect US support for its own proposal' and would be an ideal weapon with which to attack Menzies, who had branded Calwell's idea as 'suicidal' and 'one of the craziest proposals I've ever heard'. Menzies took the bold step of publicly claiming that the US government had told him of its strong opposition to the Brazilian proposal. Calwell called Menzies' bluff, threatening to ask Kennedy when he met him in July whether this was true. The US secretary of state, Dean Rusk, refused to bail Menzies out, saying in a 23 November 1962 cable, 'We have no record of any such discussion by Menzies.' But he couldn't rule out the possibility that something might have been said while Menzies was alone with Kennedy.

It would be surprising if Menzies had raised Brazil in conversation. He wrote to Kennedy on 20 July 1962 suggesting, perhaps a touch pompously, 'I even hope that on my next visit to Washington I might have the opportunity not to discuss concrete problems, but have the kind of generalised conversations with you which is one of the advantages of civilised life.' Kennedy had ready access to just about any intellectual or artistic luminary he cared to meet, amid other sources of companionship. Had he known about it, Menzies would have been upset by the CIA biographical note on Calwell, which said the agency was unconcerned about the possibility that the Labor leader might become PM.

North West Cape's importance to the US at the time can be seen by its status as the most powerful of the three major US VLF stations. NWC had a maximum output of 2.5 million watts. The other two, one at Cutler, Maine and the other at Jim Creek, Washington state, were not as well situated as NWC for the US to communicate with its fleet in large parts of the Pacific and Indian oceans. All three utilised the way VLF signals follow the curvature of the earth, allowing communications with submarines over much longer distances than straight-line radio transmissions. Because submarines can receive VLF well below the ocean's surface, this avoids the riskier alternative of putting an antenna up to the surface to receive higher-frequency signals.

The NWC base is situated on a long peninsula at Exmouth Gulf, about 1200 kilometres north of Perth. The first design contract was issued without any public announcement in January 1961.[4] The 388-metre-high central tower was the tallest in the Southern Hemisphere at the time. It and a surrounding circle of 300-metre-high towers hold up a web of transmission antennas, with the receiving antennas 60 kilometres away. (NWC also hosts high-frequency antennas that are less important.)

Although not acknowledged for the first three decades of the base's existence, the VLF's radiated power at the normal operating level of one million watts posed a health hazard to staff, let alone at the much higher levels sometimes used. A 1993 US Navy report said new procedures could reduce the hazard to safe working levels.[5]

New US ambassador Ed Clark, a Texas lawyer close to President Lyndon Johnson, formally opened what was still officially called the US Naval Communication Station North West Cape on 16 September 1967. Clark is mainly remembered in Australia for his folksy speech that day, which stressed the great deal the US had got for leasing 2666 hectares of prime coastal land for the base. In a ceremonial handing-over of the rent to Menzies' successor, Harold Holt, Clark famously presented the prime minister with one peppercorn payment for the first year's rent in full. It was certainly a good deal for the tenant. The landlord wasn't allowed to inspect the place or have any say over how the tenant behaved.

Although the base was renamed the US Naval Communication Station Harold E. Holt on 20 September 1968, nothing else changed. There was no improvement in Barwick's abject definition of what constituted 'consultation'. The US Naval Security Group, a subsidiary of the NSA, operated a secret eavesdropping unit at NWC between 1967 and 1992 and still operates one under a different name at Pine Gap near Alice Springs.[6]

Congress was not told about the NSA unit at NWC until 1972, and Australian governments were not told until even later. However, a former NSA officer wrote that NWC 'intercepts traffic in the Sunda Straits and in the Indian Ocean'.[7] Because the NSA's electronic snooping goes well beyond military communications, this activity would not comply with the NWC agreement, which stipulated that the base's activities must be confined to defence communications. In addition, NWC's high-frequency transmitters were heavily committed to relaying signals to assist the US in mining Haiphong harbour and inland waterways in Vietnam in May 1972 without first consulting the McMahon Coalition government.[8] The US commitment to consultation meant nothing.

16

DANGEROUS ADVICE FROM IGNORANT AUSTRALIAN OFFICIALS

'The Soviets could decide to go after our communications system to our submarines.'

US Defense Secretary James Schlesinger[1]

The new Labor government elected in December 1972 picked the hardest way to implement its policies on the three most important US bases in Australia—North West Cape, and the ground stations linked to US intelligence-gathering satellites at Pine Gap near Alice Springs and Nurrungar near Woomera. Although in later decades Labor strongly supported the presence of US military facilities, Prime Minister Gough Whitlam and his deputy, Defence Minister Lance Barnard, had solid party backing to renegotiate all three bases.

Immediately after winning the election, Whitlam and Barnard accepted without protest the advice of the Defence Department head, Sir Arthur Tange, that the need for extreme secrecy meant Labor must abandon its clear election promise to tell the public, in general terms, what Pine Gap and Nurrungar did. This was bad advice—more could have been revealed without harming security.[2] In contrast, they made a much harder, and ultimately futile, attempt to assert Australian sovereignty over the US naval communications station at NWC. Barnard said in a parliamentary statement on 28 February 1973 that the government would negotiate changes to NWC to 'obviate any possibility that Australia could be in a war—and nuclear war at that—without itself having any power of decision'. Given the horrific destructive power of nuclear weapons it was an admirable goal, but probably unachievable without closing NWC. Barnard's statement upset hawkish US officials such as the defence secretary, James Schlesinger, and President Nixon's national security adviser, Henry Kissinger.

In April 1973, I reported that a senior Pentagon official had told the *AFR* that Australia would never be allowed to see, let alone veto, the coded messages sent to US nuclear submarines through NWC, but that the US would be willing to release more information about Pine Gap and Nurrungar.[3] When Whitlam asked his officials to convince the US to compromise on NWC, their response was reluctant, even derisory. Despite their disdain for the PM's supposed naivety, the officials' own understanding of US nuclear strategy was woefully inaccurate, or in some cases non-existent.

They got off to a bad start after Whitlam asked Australia's Washington embassy to find out where NWC stood in the American system for communicating orders to submarines. Although NWC had been an issue in Australia since Menzies had tried to damage Labor over the base in 1963, the ambassador, Sir James Plimsoll, replied on 20 March 1973 that he was unable to throw much light on the subject. In a stunning mix of insult and ignorance, Plimsoll's answer recommended a standard reference book that gave examples of 'radar and tracking facilities' in Canada and Alaska and had nothing to do with communicating with submarines. He also referred to a scholarly paper titled 'Reconnaissance, surveillance and arms control' and a book, *Secret Sentries in Space,* neither of which had the remotest relevance to the question he'd been asked.[4]

Undeterred, Whitlam then asked Plimsoll to lead negotiations on NWC in Washington starting on 11 June 1973, and Defence and Foreign Affairs officials prepared a position paper for the talks. Whitlam told the negotiators to make clear to the US that the Australian government had the power 'physically to stop the station functioning'.[5] There is no record of whether they did so.

The paper, stamped 'Secret', began with basic information confirming that NWC relayed messages to submarines, ships and planes via its VLF and high-frequency (HF) transmitters. It explained that VLF was crucial because it was the only effective way to communicate with submerged submarines, and gave the extraordinary range of the transmitters at NWC: far beyond the Indian Ocean, east to Panama, north to the Aleutians and west to Africa.

Despite repeated claims that the ANZUS alliance provided highly classified material from America to Australia, the paper revealed that Australian officials were disturbingly ignorant of US nuclear war-fighting policy. In discussing how submarines would be ordered to launch nuclear missiles, it wrongly stated that it seemed 'likely that the US would use only stations situated on its own territory for so important an order'.[6] When Plimsoll summarised the 11 June 1973 negotiations in a secret cable to Canberra on 15 June, he said the Americans had bluntly rejected the discussion paper's assumption that the US would only be likely to send a firing order from its own territory. Instead, the Americans said messages were always passed via multiple routes and multiple modes to ensure they were reliably received.[7]

The position paper also asserted that the possibility NWC would come under nuclear attack was 'extremely remote'. Schlesinger was much less dismissive. When asked in Congress on 7 February 1974 if his 'counter-force' strategic doctrine would increase the chances of nuclear war, the US defence secretary said, 'I think that is a fair, logical inference.' On 11 September that year he told Congress, 'The Soviets could decide to go after our communications system to our submarines' and gave the VLF station at Cutler, Maine as an example. Because NWC was at least as important as Cutler, it seems that all VLF stations could be nuclear targets. The Office of National Assessments, Australia's peak intelligence body, warned Prime Minister Malcolm Fraser in 1980 that if USSR cities were attacked or threatened, the ONA 'would rank North West Cape as an important target'.[8]

Despite the US's point-blank refusal to agree not to relay firing orders to nuclear missile submarines through NWC, Plimsoll reported that the Americans had said during the 11 June 1973 negotiations that 'consultation with Australia about any impending crisis would be automatic'.[9] This commitment soon proved worthless. There was no consultation before the Yom Kippur War later that year, when the US put NWC and other bases in Australia on full alert on 11 October. Nor was the government informed, much to Whitlam's displeasure, when NWC was used on 25 October to communicate a general nuclear alert to US military forces in the Western Pacific and Indian oceans. The US had clearly had enough time to notify the Australian government, but never thought to do so.

Barnard was dispatched to Washington in January 1974 to salvage something from the wreckage of his February 1973 policy statement to parliament. The upshot was that an Australian would be titled deputy commander of what would now be called a 'joint' communications station—but another US officer would take charge if the US commander was absent or indisposed. Australian submarines would gradually make more use of the VLF transmitter but would pay around $1 million a year for access to the base for which the US paid a peppercorn. More Australians would work there, but none could access the US cypher traffic. Apart from that, the best Barnard could extract from Schlesinger was an agreement to hold more policy consultations.

The first of the new wide-ranging talks between officials occurred in September 1974. In August 1976, I published extensive quotes from the top-secret official report of the talks.[10] This time the Americans had explained why NWC was particularly significant: it was the only VLF station whose signals could be received in the south-west Indian Ocean—a factor that could 'become more critical later in the decade' if the US deployed submarines with the powerful Trident missiles in the Indian Ocean.[11]

NWC was also important for communicating with US nuclear attack submarines in the Indian Ocean and elsewhere. The Americans conceded that these submarines sometimes operated in the Indian and Pacific oceans without explaining their potentially destabilising impact on the nuclear balance. Sometimes called 'hunter killers', they have a critical role in US nuclear war-fighting strategy as they are able to trail Russian nuclear-missile-carrying subs with the aim of sinking them at the start of a nuclear war.[12] This would undermine the other side's retaliatory capability to deter a first strike—something the US refused to rule out. The Australian officials did not mention this problem, although it was of obvious relevance to NWC and became more so after China later deployed four nuclear-armed ballistic-missile submarines.

However, the officials did criticise Schlesinger's nuclear war-fighting doctrine during the September 1974 talks, saying that Australia could support NWC's role in the doctrine of mutually assured destruction where submarine-launched missiles were likely to be confined to deterrence. They said with uncommon bluntness that Schlesinger's proposed use of nuclear weapons for 'surgical strikes' could change the character of the nuclear relationship to one where 'Australia might see US policy as risking the use of nuclear weapons in circumstances that were unacceptable to us. In these circumstances, Australia could hardly be expected to facilitate a nuclear campaign in support of US policy.'[13] The US side responded by saying that 'relying on massive retaliation, with all its catastrophic risks, was essentially a bluff', so more limited options were needed. The difficulty with the doctrine was that a limited war could easily escalate into a full-scale nuclear exchange.

After raising good questions that didn't attract convincing answers, the Australian side ended the talks by saying they were satisfied that the existing arrangement for the US to use NWC 'was unimpaired'.[14] It was not clear why.

I reported in August 1974 that after the Australian officials returned to Canberra they complained that they had not seen Schlesinger's congressional evidence where he said the Soviets could decide to attack VLF stations. A senior JIO official, Bob Mathams, cabled the Washington embassy to follow up these concerns.[15] The answer was that both the diplomatic and military officials in the embassy had failed to understand the crucial importance of Schlesinger's congressional answers about VLF stations being targets and had never relayed them to Canberra. Mathams said in a subsequent top-secret minute that my article's reference to the officials' concerns about Schlesinger's statement to Congress 'may be used to support a contention that NWC is a nuclear target and that US officials were less than honest in the discussions of this matter with the Australians'.[16] They were indeed less than honest.

The same lack of candour applied to the Americans' claim during the joint discussions that tight controls would prevent an accidental or unauthorised launch of a submarine ballistic missile. A fuller account would have acknowledged the serious risks of a nuclear war starting by accident or misunderstanding, as evidenced by the numerous close calls during the Cold War. As the Canberra Commission on the Elimination of Nuclear Weapons concluded in 1996, 'The proposition that nuclear weapons can be retained in perpetuity and never used—accidentally or by decision—defies credibility.'[17]

Given the risks, Whitlam's desire to have greater control over NWC was not quixotic. Until all nuclear weapons were abolished, he accepted a role for deterrence between the superpowers. But the magnitude of the destruction if a war occurred by accident or otherwise helped explain his desire to stop Australia, a signatory to the Nuclear Non-Proliferation Treaty, relaying orders via NWC to fire nuclear-armed missiles from submarines. The practical sticking point was that the US—which hadn't ruled out the first use of nuclear weapons—would never agree not to use NWC in a nuclear war. Whitlam ended up accepting this, but he was entitled to feel that a more determined diplomatic effort could have achieved a concrete commitment from the US to consult Australia.

My observation as a journalist during the Whitlam years is that most government departments made a serious effort to serve the government. This was a key reason why much of Labor's policy was quickly implemented. Some senior diplomats and officials in Defence were the dishonourable exceptions.

A summary of the destructive power of submarine-launched warheads also helps explain Whitlam's approach. When Labor came to power, the Polaris submarines each carried sixteen missiles, whose lack of accuracy best suited them to attacking cities and industrial centres. China was the main target for the submarines based in the Pacific. Each missile could hit a city with an explosive power of 1 megaton (over sixty times bigger than the power of the bomb the US dropped on Hiroshima). The more devastating Poseidon missile began to replace the Polaris in the early 1970s, and was itself replaced by the more powerful and long-ranging Trident missile. The precision and manoeuvrability of the Trident's warhead lets it attack military targets as well as cities anywhere on the globe. Each of the US Navy's fourteen big Ohio-class submarines can carry up to twenty-four Trident missiles, each with up to fourteen manoeuvrable warheads with a yield of up to 475 kilotons. Each submarine could destroy 336 cities.

The US and Russia have since agreed to reduce the number of submarine-launchable warheads on each side to 700, but that's still enough to destroy 700 big cities and kill hundreds of millions of their inhabitants. Worse, these agreements seem unlikely to be renewed.

17
BLUSTER AND BELLIGERENCE

'We have been seriously embarrassed by US failure to convey relevant information on this matter in a timely way.'

Bob Hamilton, Australian Defence official[1]

Most sensible ministers are irritated when classified information leaks (other than when it leaks for their own political advantage). The Fraser Government's defence minister, Jim Killen, was different: leaks drove him into extraordinary rages.[2] In May 1978, he fiercely denied the accuracy of an article by me in the *AFR* while simultaneously asking his department to berate US officials for not telling him about the information in the article.[3] Killen's fury was triggered by my report saying that contracts had been let for the US to build a new satellite ground station at its politically sensitive base at North West Cape. This was the first either Killen or his senior departmental policy advisers had heard about it.

The article said the US Defense Department's evidence in the 1977 congressional budget hearings showed that it had contracted the American company Philco Ford to build the new ground station at NWC as part of a worldwide system of stations linked to a new series of satellites for US global military communications.[4] Construction at NWC was due to start in the second half of 1978 and finish in 1980.

My report from the congressional record caught Australian defence policy advisers off-guard. They reacted by accusing the US of breaching the January 1974 Schlesinger–Barnard agreement that required it to give

Australia 'full and timely information' about the installation of significant new equipment and any other notable changes at NWC.

Despite denying the article when it appeared, Killen asked a senior official in Defence's Strategic and International Policy Division, Bob Hamilton, to send a tough message to Australia's Washington embassy. On 10 May 1978 Hamilton instructed the head of the embassy's defence section to personally inform the relevant Pentagon officials that 'We have been seriously embarrassed by US failure to convey relevant information on this matter in a timely way'. In the same cable, Hamilton instructed the embassy to 'register our strong concern that this material is being made available publicly in US Congressional hearings, which is of direct interest to the Australian government, but no steps have been taken either to inform Australia or to seek prior formal clearance from here'.[5]

He then told the embassy to inform the Pentagon: 'No consideration can be given by the Australian government to the proposed replacement of the satellite terminal at NWC until a formal proposal is received from the US, and that it is necessary for the minister so to inform the Parliament.' The embassy would not have relished delivering these instructions, which were blunter than any complaints the Whitlam Government had made to the Pentagon.

Hamilton also told the embassy that Killen wanted the Pentagon to provide full information on whether the new terminal would extend the capability or function of NWC. The terminal was the key component of twenty-one new AN/MSC-61 ground stations being built around the globe to transmit a wide range of US military communications over the latest Defense Satellite Communications System (DSCS 111). Hamilton said he was concerned this enhanced system would plug NWC into the entire US global military communications networks in ways that could make significant changes to the station's existing satellite systems.

Killen became directly involved when he wrote stiff letters to the US ambassador, Philip Alston, on 25 May and 29 May asking him for answers from the US about other equipment installed earlier at NWC without the Australian government's approval. In his 29 May letter, Killen wrote that the equipment for receiving and transmitting signals to the US fleet provided a 'particular type of capability not hitherto installed at Harold E. Holt [NWC]'.[6] He said he could not be expected to publicly support changes at NWC in the absence of authoritative advice from the US government, and that the proper course would have been for the US to have provided 'the requisite information and sought formal concurrence. Failing such action already, I believe that it were best done now.'

The Americans were not accustomed to such a sharp rebuke from an Australian defence minister, especially from the Coalition. It is unclear why Killen muddied the waters by raising a less contentious piece of equipment than the new one he asked Hamilton to complain about. Alston replied on 31 May that this older equipment was a simple ground-station receiver that did not alter NWC's function. He also reminded Killen that he had written to him on 16 May explaining that the Australian deputy commander at NWC was always fully informed of what was happening there. At least Alston's answer gave Killen grounds for complaining about the failure to obtain Australian government approval before letting this contract, even if Defence's internal communications should have been better. Alston ended on an insouciant note: in order to ensure that there were 'no surprises at policy levels', he said he wished to inform Killen that staff at the station's newspaper would be moving into new quarters and new colour TV equipment would be installed.[7]

In a further setback for Killen, I reported in the *AFR* on 23 May 1978 that the US embassy had received a State Department cable the day before telling it that the US was now taking the hard line that the Australian Defence Department had been informed about the NWC proposals.[8] My article also reported that local Defence sources said the US had briefed a senior Australian officer, Air Vice Marshal John Jordan, in detail in 1977 about the proposed new ground station while he was working at Defence's headquarters at Russell Hill in Canberra, and that he had distributed a minute reporting what was said.

This article was partly based on answers the local head of the US Information Agency, Robert Nesbitt, had given to questions from me. Later that day Hamilton called Nesbitt and the US embassy's political counsellor, Dixon Boggs, into his office. An embassy official later told me that Hamilton criticised Nesbitt for talking to a journalist about Jordan and other matters. His tone infuriated the impeccably mannered Boggs, who told me when we met up in Washington in 1980 that he had 'never been dressed down so rudely' in his diplomatic career. He particularly resented Nesbitt being admonished for doing his job of answering journalists' questions. According to Defence's record of the conversation, Nesbitt explained that he couldn't have been the source of the information about Jordan as he had never heard of him until that morning.[9] Hamilton seemed to have missed my article's clear statement that the source was an Australian official.

Killen was still stewing about the issue in late June when I put new questions to his department about another change at NWC. He banned his department from answering any questions from the entire Fairfax media group before accepting advice from Defence's PR director, Harry Rayner, that he confine the ban to the *AFR*. Killen wrote to the *AFR*'s acting editor, Fred Brenchley, on 29 June stating that my initial 8 May article was 'utterly false. One question asked of my office by Mr Toohey could have prevented the false and mischievous assertion he made.'[10] But asking Killen's office would have been futile, as neither he nor his office staff nor his departmental policy advisers knew the answer—hence the complaints to the US about not being told. Had my article been 'utterly false', a normal Cabinet minister, unlike Killen, would not have instructed Hamilton to berate the Americans on the basis that it was true.

Rayner suggested to Killen on 5 July that he might lift his ban after the Australian Journalists' Association (AJA) proposed banning its members from handling any material from the minister or his department.[11] Rayner also noted that the Melbourne *Sun News-Pictorial*'s bureau chief, Laurie Oakes, had asked a series of questions 'basically the same as those which Mr Toohey posed before the ban'.

Killen directed his department to answer Oakes' questions but not mine. The executive assistant to department head Arthur Tange wrote a note to Killen on the same day saying his stand was jeopardising the D-notice system of voluntary censorship of specified information, because the AJA, which was due to meet the Press Council the next day, would be even less disposed to sympathetically consider the D-notice issue than hitherto.[12] Killen lifted the ban later that day, but Defence was not suddenly converted to open government.

I asked the department a question on 27 November 1978 about the installation of an improved version of a vital piece of equipment at NWC that was used to communicate with submarines. A senior official, G.R. Marshall, explained in a minute to Killen on 29 November that Defence was willing to say that this version (designated ISABPS) had been installed with Australia's approval, but it didn't want to acknowledge that it was linked to another piece that had been installed in October (designated IEMATS). Marshall said IEMATS allowed emergency action messages, which may 'include firing orders for US submarines', to be sent directly from the continental US to nuclear submarines (via NWC) rather than relayed more slowly from elsewhere.[13] Moreover, the messages no longer had to be 'manually processed before they can be relayed from NWC'. In other words, IEMATS eliminated the previous small chance that some Australian staff member at NWC could discover what was happening and inform the Australian government. Marshall said, 'Given the potential significance of this system, we consider this information should not be volunteered to Toohey.'

Marshall left unsaid the fact that denying me the information was much less important than keeping the Australian public in the dark about what was being done in its name. A follow-up minute in December said Defence needed to be prepared for the possibility that I knew about IEMATS and would claim that 'we were being deliberately deceptive'.[14] Marshall's minutes demonstrate they *were* being deliberately deceptive. More importantly, the fact that the US had developed this automated system to send firing orders to its nuclear subs was not kept secret from the American public. Once again, Defence decided it should conceal information about a base in Australia from the Australian public when the US didn't conceal the information from its own citizens.

18

NORTH WEST CAPE: MORE DANGEROUS THAN EVER

'Donald Trump sets goal to create US military space force by 2020'
ABC News, 10 August 2018

By the 1990s, the North West Cape communications base had become less important to the US than in previous decades for ballistic-missile-carrying submarines. It handed the management of the base to Australia in 1999, but retained the ability to automatically relay signals to its submarines through NWC without Australia knowing. However, it has recently become more important than ever, playing a potential role in space warfare as well as terrestrial nuclear war.

By the early 2000s, the US wanted a new long-term lease—something the Whitlam Government had vowed it would never grant after the initial one expired. For Whitlam, choosing not to renew the lease was the only realistic way to restore the sovereignty that had been lost by hosting a base that a foreign country could use for a nuclear war without Australia's permission.

In July 2008, the Rudd Labor government dutifully signed a new treaty, giving the US 'all necessary rights of access to, and use of, the station' for the next twenty-five years.[1] The US wanted the new lease for two reasons that had emerged by 2008. Firstly, NWC was well situated for contributing to the US military-industrial complex's latest frontier: space warfare. Secondly, the rise of China made NWC more important in letting the US communicate with its nuclear-powered 'hunter killer' submarines in the Asia-Pacific via VLF underwater signals.

American hunter-killer submarines and Australia's conventionally powered ones are now the main users of the base's VLF transmitters.[2] China's submarines are effectively trapped not far from their coastline by a US-Japanese network of undersea and overhead sensors that monitor the various choke points preventing easy access to the open ocean.[3] In the unlikely event of any of China's four new ballistic-missile submarines reaching the relative safety of the open ocean, the most important task of America's nuclear hunter killers is to trail these boats and sink them at the outbreak of hostilities.[4]

This strategy is extremely dangerous. China's land-based retaliatory missiles have always been vulnerable to highly accurate US missiles, including non-nuclear ones. Sinking the submarines would destroy the supposedly invulnerable component of China's small retaliatory capability. Faced with a choice of using or losing their sea-based missiles as well as those on land, Beijing would have an incentive to launch first if it considered an attack was imminent. It has always vowed never to do so, but this may change.

The contentious role of US hunter-killer submarines may explain why Australian officials have become more secretive about NWC. When I asked Defence Media on 22 June 2016 if US nuclear submarines would receive VLF signals relayed through NWC in future, it replied by email: 'Defence does not comment on submarine operations nor capability' (other than when it suits it). A Defence official said privately that I might have a better chance asking the Americans. Another source verified that US submarines would definitely use NWC.

In a separate development, the Gillard Government let the US establish new facilities in Western Australia to improve the Pentagon's space-fighting capabilities. During the annual Australia–US Ministerial Consultations (AUSMIN) in November 2010 and 2012, the Australians agreed to let the US install space surveillance radar and an advanced space surveillance telescope at NWC. The radar is operated remotely from the Australian Air Force base at Edinburgh in South Australia. The US military was more forthcoming on this equipment than Australia.[5]

Australian ministers announced that both the radar and the telescope could help locate space junk, but they failed to say that the principal task of these sensors is to track and locate Chinese and Russian surveillance and communications satellites so that they can be disabled or destroyed. During AUSMIN 2010, the Foreign Affairs Department released a fact sheet denying that the new facilities would contribute to the militarisation of space, claiming instead that 'Australia, the US and other countries recognise the right of all nations to access space for peaceful purposes'.[6]

Once again Australian ministers and officials appeared ignorant of readily available information about major strategic issues involving the nation. Contrary to the official claims, the new facilities are incompatible with Australia's ratification of the 1967 Outer Space Treaty preventing the militarisation of space. Melbourne University's Professor Richard Tanter explained that the radar and the telescope would contribute to the militarisation of space because much of the data from the sensors will go back to the US Combined Space Operations Center, which supports the component of the US Strategic Command whose mission includes destroying or disabling Chinese and Russian satellites.[7] Although some of the administrative arrangements have changed, the US subsequently expanded its preparations for space warfare.

President Donald Trump took a further step to militarising space when he announced on 18 June 2018, 'We must have American dominance in space … We are going to have the Air Force and we're going to have the "Space Force".'[8] The White House announced a starting date of 2020 for what it called the sixth branch of the US military.[9]

Australian governments are still to tell their citizens that a base on their soil contributes to this sixth branch of the US military in violation of the nation's treaty obligations. Perhaps Australians will find out when some the world's communication satellites suddenly stop working and global war begins.

19

THE MAN WHO THOUGHT HE OWNED THE SECRETS

'What other contractors to the CIA, who may or may not employ Russian spies, are privileged to receive, analyse and transmit data from facilities on Australia soil?'

Gough Whitlam to parliament, 4 May 1977

The security seemed impenetrable at the windowless vault in the TRW corporation's compound in Redondo, California. The vault was a core element of the deeply secret eavesdropping satellite system called Rhyolite that TRW had built for the CIA. One of the vault's main functions was to handle messages to and from the satellite ground station that TRW operated under CIA guidance at Pine Gap near Alice Springs.

Redondo's security did not prevent Christopher Boyce, a young dope-smoking high-school dropout, from taking highly classified information from the vault in 1975 and 1976 and selling it to the Soviets. After the 24-year-old Boyce was sentenced in 1977 to forty years' jail for espionage, he explained to congressional committees and journalists how security really worked at Redondo. He said he and his co-workers held daily drinking parties in the vault, mixing daiquiris in a special blender meant for destroying code cards. Staff regularly took secure communication satchels out of the vault to carry back liquor supplies.[1] Boyce also took out classified documents in the satchels and returned with liquor. As was widely reported, he sold the Soviets detailed information about Rhyolite's ability to intercept a wide range of electronic signals and US plans for the next generation of satellites.

Meanwhile, the head of Australia's Defence Department, Sir Arthur Tange, took extreme measures to prevent Australian ministers knowing about the Rhyolite secrets. He insisted on briefing new prime minister Gough Whitlam and his deputy, Defence Minister Lance Barnard, about Pine Gap immediately after the Australian election in December 1972. The briefing, which included information about the US base at Nurrungar near Woomera, was inexcusably skimpy, confused and misleading. Tange insisted that neither Whitlam nor Barnard could tell the public that Pine Gap and Nurrungar were ground stations for satellites, although the Coalition defence minister, Allen Fairhall, had told parliament on 29 April 1969 that 'Pine Gap and Woomera [Nurrungar] … are concerned with satellites'. Whitlam and Barnard should not have agreed to be briefed in the intensely busy period immediately after the election—they should have waited until their staff could help them challenge Tange's refusal to let them repeat publicly available information, such as the links to satellites. This would have been at least a tiny step towards honouring their clear election promise to tell the public more about the bases.

Although Pine Gap did no research, its name remained the Joint Defence Space Research Facility until 1988. Nor was it 'joint':[2] the CIA ran it, and the handful of professional Australian staff had no say. Likewise, the name of the Joint Defence Space Communications Station at Nurrungar gave no hint of its role of detecting Soviet missile launches, although this was widely reported in the US media. Nor did the Labor ministers challenge the continuing official description that the Pentagon's Advanced Research Projects Agency operated Pine Gap. In an inexcusable lapse, Tange failed to tell the prime minister and the defence minister that Pine Gap was operated by the CIA's science and technology division, plus private US contractors, as part of a vast US intercept program that captured a wide range of communications and other electronic emissions across a large part of the globe, including Australia. Nor did Tange show them the secret 1966 Pine Gap agreement that explicitly stated that the CIA and the Australian Defence Department were the parties to the agreement.

Meanwhile, eight young daiquiri-swilling code clerks in TRW's Redondo centre, along with many other Americans in the CIA, the Pentagon, the NSA and the White House, and various contractors, were briefed in much greater detail than Australia's two most senior leaders.

When Tange, with chief Defence scientist John Farrands in tow, briefed the Australian ministers he adopted the obfuscatory technique of calling Pine Gap the 'twin' of the Nurrungar base. The stations were not remotely twins. They did not have the same parents, used very different technologies and had dissimilar purposes. Nurrungar, run by the US Air Force, was linked to a satellite that used an infra-red telescope to detect heat from missile launches. Whitlam later complained to staff that the way Tange had conflated the two left him so confused that he was often unsure which one did what.

Pine Gap did acquire a twin when the NSA began operating similar signals-intercept satellites a few years later at Menwith Hill in England. These twins use big antennas (now well over 100 metres in diameter) to intercept a huge quantity of electronic signals. The satellites are positioned 36,000 kilometres above any chosen spot on the equator in a direct line of sight to their ground stations. Geo-synchronous orbits let Pine Gap's satellites receive all electronic signals on any chosen frequency within the antennas' capabilities, including those involving phones, radars, missiles, fighter planes and so on, within a vast area covered by the antennas. Today, the satellites do not have to be precisely geo-synchronous and are part of a US global surveillance system run by the NSA. Whistleblower Edward Snowden explained in 2013 that the system has an extraordinary capability to intrude on the privacy of almost every individual and corporation around the globe, as well as supporting most US war-fighting operations.[3]

Given Tange's contemptuous briefing of ministers who were fully entitled to know as much as he did, it was no surprise that a disillusioned Whitlam complained in a parliamentary speech on 4 May 1977 that he had not been told core information about the bases. After the initial briefing, he had left it to Barnard to handle Labor's 28 February 1973 parliamentary statement that was supposed to fulfil the party's commitment to greater disclosure about the bases. At that time, the commitment reflected wide-spread public disquiet about being kept in the dark, particularly when the bases made Australia a potential nuclear target. Barnard, in turn, left it to Tange to decide what was to be in the statement, despite efforts by his highly qualified staff to keep at least part of the election promise. Barnard's principal adviser, Darcy McGuarr, was a former Pentagon-trained analyst who had worked in the Department of Defence. Another adviser, Derek Woolner, was a defence specialist from the parliamentary library's research service. Woolner later told me that the day before Barnard was due to deliver his statement in parliament, Tange ordered the recall of all copies of a more informative statement and replaced it with a gutted version that restricted Barnard to saying that everything had to be kept secret.

Tange was not particularly anti-Labor at that stage, just obsessively secretive. He acknowledged in his memoirs that the only comment he allowed Barnard to make was that 'neither station is part of a weapons system and neither station can be used to attack any country'.[4] This was untrue. A wide range of authoritative accounts have demonstrated that from the start Pine Gap's satellites collected a vast array of military communications, radar signals and other data that could be used in an attack on another country by locating targets and intercepting battlefield military signals. In 1972, a Pine Gap Rhyolite satellite was explicitly tasked to collect signals from within Vietnam while the war was still underway.[5]

In 1973, US Ambassador Marshall Green had no doubt about the bases' importance. Referring to the US's priorities, he later told me, 'The biggest issue was [securing] our facilities [i.e. bases]', followed by access for US investment, then Australian support in international forums.[6] A departmental minute written in August 1973 said Washington had agreed that Barnard's statement on 28 February could include four points about improving Australian involvement in the operation of the Central Australian facilities.[7] Barnard included none of these points in his statement, even though they would have added a little substance to his threadbare attempt to honour Labor's election promise. The additional points sank without a trace.

Tange's insistence on giving oral briefings didn't always assist ministerial understanding. Barnard suffered hearing difficulties from having served at Tobruk in World War II. He once told staff, for example, that he had just been briefed on one intelligence agency when the briefing had been on an entirely separate agency.[8]

Claims by successive governments that Pine Gap doesn't intercept Australians' phone calls, emails, faxes and so on have all been false. The technology dictates that these messages automatically include information about Australians within the footprints of Pine Gap's own satellites. Australians' communications are also routinely intercepted by ground stations at Pine Gap and those near Geraldton and Darwin that collect a huge number of transmissions to and from communication satellites. Once the data is transmitted to US intelligence agencies and military forces, they can do whatever they like with it. When he was defence minister in the 1980s, Kim Beazley told me that this outcome is unavoidable, 'unless you believe knowledge is divisible'. He later said he'd discovered there was an extraordinary lack of departmental documentation about the bases, prompting him to insist on a monthly report about their activities.[9] Apparently, there was no record of what Tange had or had not told earlier ministers.

Tange, perhaps through a misunderstanding, was on firm ground over Pine Gap's supposed role in monitoring the SALT I agreement to control

ICBM numbers. Stephen Stockwell, a Griffith University professor, discovered documents in the US National Archives showing that President Richard Nixon's national security adviser, Henry Kissinger, sent a message to the US embassy in Canberra in January 1975 prior to an impending Labor conference where the bases would be an issue. Kissinger claimed Whitlam knew Pine Gap 'played a vital role in détente and strategic arms limitations agreements'.[10] Although Kissinger wanted Whitlam to tell the conference that the bases had a benign role in arms control, Tange hadn't told Whitlam this. Contrary to Kissinger's assertion, Pine Gap had almost no role in monitoring arms control agreements.[11] Tange's classified briefing for Whitlam before the 1975 Labor conference said, 'Care will need to be taken to neither confirm, nor deny, the supposition … that the facilities have a capacity to police arms control and disarmament agreements'.[12]

Tange acknowledged in his memoir that he didn't tell Whitlam about Pine Gap's supposed monitoring role,[13] but muddied the waters by wrongly claiming that these agreements 'were not in place' at that time.[14] In fact, Nixon and his Soviet counterpart, Leonid Brezhnev, had signed SALT I in Moscow on 26 May 1972. The treaty was the culmination of the strategic arms limitation talks between the two countries. The Anti-Ballistic Missile Treaty (ABM Treaty), which bolstered deterrence by greatly restricting each side's ability to destroy the other's ICBMs, was also in place. Both treaties came into force on 3 October 1972, but Whitlam was not elected until 2 December that year. Peter Edwards, who edited Tange's memoir, did not pick up this basic error.[15]

Secrecy surrounding Pine Gap survived until mid-1975. Before then the common assumption, peddled by some academics, was that it was involved in satellite photo-reconnaissance. In July 1975, I reported that the NSA ran bases in Turkey that gave a pointer to what Pine Gap did. My article said that the most important base, at Sinop in Turkey, intercepted signals on Soviet missile tests and strategic and tactical operations.[16] It also said Pine Gap was engaged in collecting signals intelligence from satellites. The Turkish government had closed the US intelligence bases following a congressional arms embargo on Turkey, and my article reported that the White House wanted Congress to reconsider the embargo because 24 per cent of the US intelligence on the Soviet Union came via the NSA bases in Turkey. Consequently, the US would not want Australia to lose Pine Gap's significant source of intelligence on the Soviet Union. Chapter 20 shows that only a few months later, however, Tange warned Whitlam that the US would cut off its intelligence relationship with Australia if the PM revealed any more information about Pine Gap.

Tange's pivotal role in managing and shaping the Australian end of the US alliance derived in large measure from his decision that briefings on Pine Gap would be confined to the 'very top'.[17] This meant that he and Farrands would have the primary responsibility for Pine Gap and Nurrungar. Tange bypassed his deputy secretary, Gordon Blakers, who had been briefed before Tange headed the department. Blakers was a gentle soul who after retiring joined protests in Tasmania against damming lakes. Because his responsibilities included strategic policy and defence intelligence, he, not the chief scientist, should have had the task of oversighting Australia's interests at Pine Gap. This anomaly was only corrected after Tange retired in 1979.

Being at the 'very top' didn't mean you necessarily understood what was going on, as Tange inadvertently made clear in his memoir when he referred to Nurrungar's techniques for using 'space phenomena to study terrestrial objects in detail'.[18] His secrecy-induced habits of obfuscation seemed to leave him just as befuddled as the prime ministers he briefed. Nurrungar's satellites used infra-red sensors—human-made objects, not space phenomena—to capture images of what was happening on or near the earth.

20

THE MAN WHO THOUGHT HE OWNED A PRIME MINISTER

'This is the gravest risk to the nation's security there has ever been.'
Sir Arthur Tange, 6 November 1975[1]

Prime Minister Gough Whitlam, the son of a former solicitor-general, was initially attracted to the notion that Arthur Tange was a dedicated public servant. He later discovered that this public servant presumed he was entitled to withhold crucial information from prime ministers.

Tange was an abrasive personality who headed the Foreign Affairs and Defence departments for twenty years, broken only by a demotion to high commissioner to India after he fell out of favour with Prime Minister Robert Menzies. After he returned to head Defence in 1970, he quickly demonstrated that he hadn't lost his love of wielding power. He embraced Labor's proposal to incorporate five separate departments into a vastly enlarged Defence Department—a process that increased his own power without generating the anticipated efficiency gains—but he never fitted the stereotype of a 'hawk' eager to use military force.

His preoccupation with rigid secrecy and the control it gave him came to a head in November 1975, a month after the Opposition leader, Malcolm Fraser, announced that the Coalition would, in effect, block the budget supply bills in the Senate to bring Whitlam down. Tange became deeply alarmed at what he saw as Whitlam's willingness, in the heat of a political battle, to challenge his control over what ministers could say about the US's prize asset in Australia, Pine Gap.

Tange's alarm stemmed from information I received in mid–1975 about the role of Richard Stallings, who was Pine Gap's first head when it was established in the mid-1960s. Because Tange had not told Whitlam that the CIA ran Pine Gap, he was desperate to hide the fact that Stallings had worked for the agency when he was running Pine Gap.[2] After Labor staff independently found out from Adelaide sources where Stallings had worked, Whitlam asked Foreign Affairs on 20 October 1975 for a list of all CIA officials in Australia for the past ten years—information he was fully entitled to have and that the US was supposed to give Foreign Affairs. Stallings' name was not on the list, and ASIO also said it had not heard of him. Whitlam then told his department head, John Menadue, to ask Tange about Stallings. Tange told the PM's staff that he had informed the CIA of Whitlam's request.[3] Whitlam told parliament on 4 May 1977 that 'after some pressure' Tange had confirmed that the CIA had employed Stallings at Pine Gap during 1966–69 and that he had spent part of his time from 1971 to 1974 in South Australia, where he performed 'CIA service at Willunga', outside Adelaide.

A former highly placed CIA official, Victor Marchetti, was a friend of Stallings who had helped him draft the secret version of the Pine Gap agreement, which stated that it would be run by the CIA and the Australian Defence Department. On retiring, Marchetti co-authored *The CIA and the Cult of Intelligence*, a powerful analysis of the damaging mystique surrounding clandestine intelligence. He told me and other journalists in November 1975 that Stallings' service at Willunga had been for the CIA's covert action division, despite Stallings' earlier qualms about its activities. Marchetti also said Stallings told him that he was concerned in the 1960s that the then CIA station chief Ray Villemarette's interference against Labor in Australian politics could jeopardise the continued presence of Pine Gap.

Based on US sources, I reported on 3 November 1975 that Stallings had worked for the CIA as head of Pine Gap, and gave more details the next day.[4] The National Country Party leader, Doug Anthony, then told journalists that Stallings was a friend who had rented his Canberra house, and that his family and Stallings' family had subsequently holidayed together. On 4 November, Anthony denied in parliament that he knew that Stallings worked for the CIA. Later that day, at Tange's urging, Labor's defence minister, Bill Morrison, tried to get Anthony to stop talking about Stallings. Refusing to be silenced, Anthony put a question on the parliament notice paper on 6 November challenging Whitlam to provide evidence when parliament resumed on 11 November that Stallings worked for the CIA. Anthony referred to *The Australian*'s report earlier that day that the State Department said Stallings 'had never worked for any US intelligence agency'.

Given that Whitlam knew this was a lie—because Tange had belatedly told him the truth—he refused to mislead parliament by saying Stallings had not been a CIA employee. Shortly after Anthony put his question on the notice paper, Whitlam prepared a reply making it clear that Defence (i.e. Tange) had recently told him that Stallings had worked for the CIA. Later the same day, he read it over the phone to a horrified Tange, who then told Whitlam's staff: 'This is the gravest risk to the nation's security there has ever been.'[5] Others might nominate the early days of the Pacific War as a more serious threat than confirmation of the public knowledge that someone worked for the CIA.

Under the agreement between Australia and the US, notice to terminate Pine Gap's activities could have been given from 10 December 1975. Ted Shackley, the head of the CIA's East Asia division, gave ASIO's Washington representative a tough message on 8 November to send to ASIO headquarters. His telex to ASIO raised the possibility of cutting off the intelligence relationship unless ASIO gave him a satisfactory explanation of Whitlam's comments on CIA activities in Australia, which could 'blow the lid off' Pine Gap. ASIO passed the message on to Tange on 9 November and to Whitlam on 10 November.

On the morning of 10 November, Tange and Farrands sent Whitlam a note claiming that later that day the Pentagon would 'announce Stallings was employed by the US Department of Defense … This direct confrontation [with what Whitlam planned to say] must be avoided at all costs. Proposed formula for the answer to Anthony's question is overtaken by the intention of the US.' Tange should never have presumed he had the right to give the elected PM such a blunt order. The Pentagon made no announcement.

There was no reason for Whitlam to abandon his accurate answer based on what Tange had told Menadue earlier in the month. Shackley's telex removed any residual doubt about where Stallings worked by bluntly stating: 'Stallings is a retired CIA employee.' This demonstrated that the State Department's 6 November public denial was a straight-out lie, while the proposed Pentagon statement, if it ever existed, was little better. Even if Stallings had worked for the US Defense Department earlier in his career, Whitlam was correct to say that he was working for the CIA at Pine Gap.

In the event, Kerr sacked Whitlam at 1 p.m. on 11 November 1975 and installed Fraser as caretaker prime minister, although Labor still had a majority in the House of Representatives. There was no urgency—supply would not have run out for another nineteen days. Although information about the CIA's role in Pine Gap may have played no part in Kerr's decision, it meant that Whitlam could not give his proposed answer to Anthony's question. Much to Tange's and Shackley's annoyance, I reported the gist of the telex message eight days before the election on 13 December 1975.[6]

Tange's behaviour was reprehensible. A responsible public servant would not have behaved towards a prime minister in such an arrogant, unprofessional and bullying manner as he did about who ran Pine Gap. He should have replied immediately to the Pentagon urging it not to make any statement that clashed with Whitlam's intention to give an accurate parliamentary answer stating the already publicly known fact that the CIA ran Pine Gap.

Whitlam's refusal to take Tange's advice threatened to undermine much of the power and control Tange had built as the undisputed keeper of the CIA's secrets in Canberra. Other Defence heads and senior officials have not let an addiction to secrecy distract them from the many other important aspects of their jobs.

After the dismissal, former Labor defence minister Bill Morrison told me that Tange had claimed to him that the CIA's role at Pine Gap had to be kept secret because it was part of an intense political battle in Washington over whether the CIA or the NSA should run the facility in future. Morrison, who never told me anything about Pine Gap while he was minister, said he couldn't understand what Tange was on about. The key players in Washington knew who ran it, and Tange had no business taking the CIA's side.

The NSA claimed a compromise victory in 1977 when the US government gave it 'review and approval authority' over the CIA's signals intelligence programs.[7] The NSA is now clearly in charge of this program, as the ABC reported in 2017.[8] Moreover, US spy Christopher Boyce had already told the Soviets the answer to the minor puzzle of who ran the station.[9] Nothing Whitlam proposed to say could have compared with what Boyce did as an employee of a CIA contractor deeply involved with Pine Gap. The US deputy secretary of defence at the time, William Clements, said, 'Our intelligence community is in disarray. A major satellite intelligence system developed and deployed over the past decade without Soviet knowledge has been compromised by intelligence procedures as porous as Swiss cheese.'[10]

Tange later refused to answer my written questions about what communications he had with the US about Whitlam's behaviour during this period, including the purported Pentagon announcement on 10 November that Stallings worked for it. Tange's biographer, Peter Edwards, who had access to the Defence Department's classified archival records, told me he did not recall seeing any of this material.[11]

There was a further twist to Tange's attempts to downplay his over-bearing behaviour in the lead-up to 11 November 1975. In his memoir, he dismissed Shackley's telex as unimportant. Others called it 'one of the most dramatic cables in Australia's political history'.[12] Tange described Shackley as a 'ham-fisted' American intelligence official who 'fired off' a telex to ASIO 'extravagantly predicting serious consequences for Australia's relations which could follow the Prime Minister's disclosures',[13] but Shackley's language was not as extravagant as Tange's claim that Whitlam had committed the 'gravest breach of security ever'. Shackley was relaxed about Tange. When we later met in Washington, the first thing he asked was 'How's the old crocodile?'

What can the NAA tell us about these historic events in November 1975? None of the communications between Defence and the Pentagon and the CIA leading up to 11 November are available in the archives. This is not the NAA's fault—Defence often ignores its legal obligation to provide records to the archives. The Attorney-General's Department is little better. The NAA replied on 16 February 2016 to a request from me that it had identified a relevant document in records held in the Attorney-General's Department, which the department had destroyed. The only message of interest from the US in the archives is the Shackley telex to ASIO, but its content was still totally redacted in 2016. I published the full text in the *AFR* on 29 April 1977—almost forty years earlier—and Whitlam read it into Hansard on 4 May 1977.

21

THE MEN WHO SPREAD THE FAIRYTALE ABOUT ARMS CONTROL

'The US does not need telemetry from Russian missile flights to verify Russian compliance with the New START treaty.'

US Defense Secretary Robert Gates[1]

The biggest secret about Pine Gap is that it is essentially irrelevant to verifying compliance with arms control agreements. This has not stopped politicians from asserting that it is vital to arms control—a cover story concocted when Australian opposition to Pine Gap and the Nurrungar base was much stronger than it is today.

No one disputes that Pine Gap's satellites can intercept the 'telemetry' data sent to and from missiles during tests, but this is only a minute proportion of what is collected and has nothing to do with verifying whether the Russians have cheated on strategic arms control agreements. Pine Gap's satellites only provide information about a particular missile tested—the total number deployed is the central figure for arms control. The primary goal of the initial SALT I treaty, which applied from 1972 to 1979, was to limit the number of US and Soviet ICBM silos and the number of launch tubes on submarines carrying nuclear weapons on ballistic missiles. Later agreements included the number of nuclear-capable bombers, shorter-range missiles, warheads, production facilities, and so on.

The main reason the US wanted to intercept Soviet telemetry was to find out how Soviet missiles were performing. This is why the CIA began intercepting Soviet ICBM telemetry in the 1950s using planes and ground stations in Iran, Norway and Turkey. Iran's permission to establish bases overlooking the Soviet launch sites was one of the benefits of the US-British coup in 1953 to replace the democratically elected secular prime minister, Mohammad Mosaddegh, with a brutal, corrupt dictator, Mohammad Reza Shah Pahlavi. When the despised Shah fled to America in the February 1979 Iranian Revolution, fundamentalist Islamist ayatollahs were left in charge.

A few months later a former deputy director of the CIA, Herbert Scoville, gave an authoritative explanation about why the subsequent loss of the telemetry from the Iranian listening posts (called Tacksman I and II) didn't matter for arms control. Scoville, who was in charge of analysing the telemetry data from Iran, said intelligence gathering was not synonymous with treaty verification. He said photographic images from low-orbiting satellites were the crucial verification tool: 'They have little difficulty recognising all the weapons covered by the arms control agreements, such as land and sea-based launchers and heavy bombers. Satellites can now locate, count, and measure modern weapons from 100 miles [160 km] away.'[2] His article also explained that the US had extensive facilities to observe tests of all multiple independently targetable re-entry vehicles (MIRVs) carrying warheads as they moved towards their target zone in the Soviet Far East or the Pacific Ocean: 'Radar receivers and infra-red sensors on ships [and] planes and on land can determine the characteristics and the number of warheads they carry.' Advances in long-range optical sensors and other devices have since reinforced this capability. Later arms-control agreements required the destruction of some weapons and counted the actual number of MIRVs as well the number of missiles produced. Onsite sensors and official inspections of production facilities, launch and test sites and other measures reinforced earlier methods of verification. US officials claimed that even in the case of Russia's mobile missiles, they had 'cradle to grave' monitoring.[3]

Against this backdrop, US defence secretary Robert Gates told a press conference in 2010 that the US didn't need telemetry from Russian missile flights to verify compliance with New START (Strategic Arms Reduction Treaty). It seems the Soviets/Russia never had any geo-synchronous satellites capable of intercepting telemetry.[4] If Australian ministers were concerned about arms control, they should have pushed to internationalise the verification processes so all parties were subject to the same independent compliance procedures, as occurs with most other arms control agreements.

As well as SALT I, the US and the Soviets ratified the 1972 ABM Treaty, which put strict limits on the number of specialised radars and missiles needed to destroy incoming ballistic missiles. The treaty helped maintain deterrence by ensuring each side retained enough missiles to be able to retaliate after a first strike. Because it only allowed one missile field and one capital city on each side to be defended, satellite photography could easily verify the numbers. Space-based signals intelligence could contribute marginally to other means of verifying the treaty's condition that phased array radars could not be used.

This didn't matter much. Once the ABM Treaty was in place, the Soviets deployed their missile shield near Moscow. However, it was basically useless as it could only destroy a maximum of eight incoming US ICBMs. An authority on nuclear war, Eric Schlosser, has pointed out that US war planning envisaged hitting Moscow with 400 nuclear warheads during the Cold War—far more than needed to reduce the city to radioactive rubble.[5] The US didn't bother to defend Washington in the way the ABM Treaty allowed: it preferred to try to develop 'Star Wars' weaponry under its Strategic Defense Initiative (SDI) to destroy Soviet missiles with laser or particle beams fired from space.

Labor governments' statements on arms control have often been ill-informed. Prime Minister Bob Hawke's statement to parliament on 6 June 1984 said that the Central Australian bases provided information about nuclear explosions 'which assists in nuclear test ban monitoring and supports nuclear non-proliferation measures'. This was an implicit reference to Nurrungar. But its satellites' infra-red sensors had no role in monitoring nuclear test ban treaties or non-proliferation.[6] By the time Hawke spoke in 1984, all countries had already ceased atmospheric tests. Some underground tests continued, but they could and can be detected by the Comprehensive Test-Ban Treaty's international monitoring system, which has a large network of sites to detect the seismological, radionuclide, hydro-acoustic and infra-sound indicators of a test, backed by onsite inspections.[7] Russia, the UK and France are the only nuclear weapons states to have ratified the treaty; the US, China and Israel signed but didn't ratify, while India, Pakistan and North Korea refuse to sign.

Labor's defence minister, Kim Beazley, even asserted in 1986 that the Pine Gap and Nurrungar bases 'provide the only presently workable method of verifying arms control agreements. If it were not for the exist-ence of Pine Gap and Nurrungar it is highly unlikely that the SALT and START agreements could have been reached.'[8] This is rubbish, as Scoville explained above.

In 1986, Beazley offered me a lengthy briefing on Pine Gap from two knowledgeable officials (who didn't share my conclusions). Although unclassified, the briefing helped convince me to write that Pine Gap produced a vast array of intelligence that 'backed the global military and political ambitions of the US, however noble, bellicose or repugnant. Hosting Pine Gap meant we played a crucial part in collecting this intelligence, no matter what purposes it finally serves.'[9]

On 22 November 1988, Hawke made a further parliamentary statement in which he described Nurrungar as playing a 'fundamental role in preventing nuclear war' because its US Defense Support Program's satellites provide early warning of ballistic-missile launches. Because the DSP gave longer warning of an attack than other systems, Hawke said, it 'reduces the chances that US forces could be destroyed in a surprise attack, and that makes it extremely unlikely that anyone would ever try such an attack'. However, a serious effort to prevent war also required the Soviets to have sufficient warning to avoid being destroyed in a surprise attack, accidental or intentional. Moscow was right to be apprehensive: declassified documents show that US planning included nuclear first strikes;[10] the US still refuses to renounce a first-strike option. The Soviets did not have any infra-red early-warning satellites until several years after the US. As Schlosser pointed out in his article, this capability began to decline in 1996 and Russia now has none, leaving it with only a few minutes' warning from radars to decide whether to retaliate—a dangerous situation that exacerbates the chances of a launch by mistake.

Despite their righteous pronouncements about disarmament, Hawke's inner Cabinet secretly approved a US request to use Australian facilities to help test a heavy new ICBM called the MX that would have greatly strengthened its nuclear weapons capabilities and probably spurred a renewed arms race. After the *National Times* revealed this decision in February 1985, a party revolt forced Hawke to back off.[11] Hawke also approved a US request to shift one of Pine Gap's satellites to a better position to eavesdrop on Andreas Papandreou's government in Greece. This had nothing to do with verifying arms control treaties and everything to do with gathering intelligence on a government that favoured a more neutral foreign policy and reduced support for hosting US nuclear bases.[12] The *NT* then reported in May 1985 that the US had asked Australia to assist its Star Wars (SDI) research even after Hawke had told the White House earlier in the year that it wouldn't do so. The article revealed that Australia was cooperating with a key SDI program called Teal Ruby, but Beazley claimed the Australian component did not involve the SDI. However, a US official said on the record that the data collected from the Australian component would be 'of interest and value' to the SDI program.[13]

The US satellite ground stations were also ideally situated for communicating with the SDI's proposed space-based beam weapons.[14] Although the SDI was put on hold, the US has deployed land- and ship-based anti-ballistic missiles.

The US took advantage of the planned closure of Nurrungar in 1999 to introduce much more advanced satellites linked to Pine Gap. These detect heat using other parts of the light spectrum as well as infra-red. Both low- and high-orbiting satellites can now detect heat from engines in fighter jets, bombers and small missiles. This information is integrated into US war-fighting machinery that defies claims about Pine Gap's contributions to peace.

A Howard Government Cabinet submission on 3 September 1997 explained that a new relay ground station would be installed between Pine Gap and the US to transfer data from a new Space-Based Infrared System. The submission acknowledged that the changes were open to the criticism and would lead 'to the withdrawal from the Anti-Ballistic Missile Treaty and to the deployment of weapons in space'.[15] No one in Cabinet seemed bothered, although Australia had signed a treaty prohibiting space warfare and the ABM Treaty was essential to guaranteeing nuclear deterrence. Instead, Pine Gap became part of the US Space Tracking and Surveillance System designed to help destroy ICBMs, in contravention of the ABM Treaty.

In 2001 George W. Bush unilaterally announced that the US would abandon the ABM Treaty. Nevertheless, Australian journalist Peter Hartcher said in 2015 that Vladimir Putin's Russia 'has become a rogue state [that] is now threatening to no longer observe the Anti-Ballistic Missile Treaty'.[16] Given that the US withdrew from the treaty fourteen years earlier, presumably Hartcher also considers it a rogue state.

In a parliamentary statement on Pine Gap on 20 September 2007, the Coalition's defence minister, Brendan Nelson, dropped the pretense that Pine Gap isn't part of a weapons system, saying it provided 'priority intelligence on targets such as terrorism'. Labor's defence minister, Stephen Smith, then used a parliamentary statement on 26 June 2013 to trot out the tired line that Pine Gap helps monitor compliance with arms control and disarmament agreements. The US defence secretary, Bob Gates, had already clearly stated in 2010 that intercepted telemetry—supposedly Pine Gap's speciality—had no role in verification. However, Smith broke new ground by revealing that Pine Gap hadn't operated with the 'full knowledge and concurrence' of governments before Hawke's, and added the crucial caveat: 'Concurrence does not mean that Australia approves every activity or tasking undertaken … [It only means] Australia approves the presence of a capability or function in support of its mutually agreed goals.'

This revelation followed adverse publicity about Pine Gap's role in extrajudicial killings. The base cooperates with its UK counterpart at Menwith Hill to produce targeting data for drones or special forces to kill suspected terrorists, but they often kill innocent bystanders. In November 2014, *The Guardian* reported that attempts to kill forty-one men using US drones had resulted in the deaths of an estimated 1147 people.[17]

22

THE MEN SEDUCED BY THE SECRETS

'I do not like the idea of nuclear bombs falling on Australia, but the vision that some people have of what it would involve seems to be quite exaggerated.'

Des Ball[1]

More than any other minister, Kim Beazley was fascinated by the Pine Gap and Nurrungar bases. Despite the strong pressure in Labor circles in the 1980s to kick them out, Beazley as defence minister was determined to keep them. He later enthused about how an ANU strategic specialist, Des Ball, had been crucial to converting Labor to this cause, calling Ball a 'man of the left, not only intellectually but in lifestyle and demeanour' whom he had arranged for the ANU to appoint as a 'special professor'.[2]

After Ball's death in October 2016, Beazley and former Labor foreign minister Gareth Evans told a remembrance service that he had been enormously influential in gaining support for the bases. Each failed to mention that Ball later switched to vehement opposition.[3] Beazley said that Ball's 1980 book, *A Suitable Piece of Real Estate*, changed Labor's attitudes by showing that Pine Gap had a role in supporting arms control. The book contained a single sentence asserting that the ability of the base's satellites to intercept telemetry data was one of the principal means the US used to monitor 'Soviet compliance with the SALT agreements'. Ball opposed the base's continued presence on other grounds.[4] In 1979, Herbert Scoville had explained that the focus of international arms-control agreements was on reversing the nuclear arms race by cutting missile numbers and warheads. Because telemetry couldn't count total missile numbers, Pine Gap contributed next to nothing.[5]

A quick glance at a map rebuts Ball's claim that Pine Gap's isolation in the middle of Australia was essential to preventing adversaries getting close enough to eavesdrop on its satellite downlinks:[6] the US–UK signals intelligence base at Menwith Hill has links to geo-synchronous satellites similar to Pine Gap's, yet it is in North Yorkshire in a particularly narrow part of British Isles that is readily accessible to hostile eavesdroppers onshore and offshore. The CIA deceived the Defence head, Arthur Tange, who repeated its claim that ground stations had to be isolated geographically,[7] and in 1975, US government sources told *National Times* journalist Andrew Clark that it had considered shifting the ground station to its Pacific Island territory of Guam.[8]

Ball was much more enthusiastic about Pine Gap in his evidence to a parliamentary committee in 1981 than in his 1980 book. He said he had no doubt whatsoever that the Soviet Union would target Pine Gap, Nurrungar and North West Cape, and told the committee he didn't like the idea of nuclear bombs falling on Australia, but that 'I cannot imagine any scenarios involving nuclear bombs falling on Australian cities'.[9] Ball didn't mention that the Soviet warheads were far more powerful than the bombs the British had tested in Australia. Yet the radioactive fallout from the British tests spread across large areas of Australia. Unlike Ball, senior intelligence analyst Bob Mathams told the same committee that the JIO considered the Soviets able to target Sydney with a nuclear missile.[10] A million people could lose their lives.

Ball was more dogmatic in 1987 when he said, 'It is simply not possible to seriously support arms control and disarmament and at the same time argue for the closure of the Pine Gap station.'[11] On the contrary, it is entirely consistent to support the former and call for the latter. The reality was that Pine Gap had almost no role in arms control or disarmament, but a growing role in US mass surveillance programs and war fighting. Ball went even further in evidence to another parliamentary committee in 1999, when he scoffed at claims that Pine Gap would be used to pick up individual phone calls.[12] This is an odd statement from someone who stressed the importance of understanding technology. In this case, the receiving antenna automatically intercepts everything in its frequency range that is transmitted within its very large coverage, including phone calls, texts and so on, as part of a vast US eavesdropping network. The network can and does identify and access huge numbers of phone calls. Echelon was an early program with this capability; British journalist Duncan Campbell had publicly revealed its existence before Ball gave evidence in 1999.[13]

It is unclear why Ball became such a zealous supporter of Pine Gap that he thought hosting it was worth risking a nuclear attack—something he had dedicated a large part of his academic life to preventing. One possibility is he was misled by secret briefings in Australia and the US. Secrets can be seductive—and deceptive.

Pine Gap did not suddenly switch to a new role of contributing to US mass surveillance programs and war-fighting capabilities—that was its core capability from the start. Ball himself said that soon after Pine Gap became operational in 1970, one of its satellites was tasked to 'monitor signals coming from Vietnam ... The war was still going during this period.'[14] Continuing improvements in satellite sensors and data-processing power mean it can make a stronger contribution to these roles.

Starting in 2013, Edward Snowden provided vast amounts of information on the NSA's global activities for gradual release via sites such as *The Intercept*. In collaboration with *The Intercept*, ABC journalist Peter Cronau used unpublished Snowden documents in 2017 to make a Background Briefing radio program giving an authoritative account of Pine Gap's role in war fighting and mass surveillance. One of the key revelations in the program and the associated documents is that Pine Gap and Menwith Hill jointly collect and often analyse SIGINT before it ends up with the NSA in the US. The program showed the bases' core tasks, called Mission 7600 and Mission 8300, explicitly include 'support to US military combat operations'.[15] The combined coverage includes the former Soviet Union, China, South-East Asia, East Asia, the Middle East, Eastern Europe and the Atlantic landmass.

The program showed that the two stations collected SIGINT on radars and weapons systems such as surface-to-air missiles, anti-aircraft artillery, fighter planes, drones and space vehicle activities, along with other military and civilian communications. When combined with photographic imagery from sources such as the Australian Geospatial-Intelligence Organisation, the SIGINT can have a decisive role in detecting military and terrorist targets. Background Briefing interviewed two ex-members of the US military who worked on the drone program, Cian Westmoreland and Lisa Ling. Westmorland explained that drones are 'like the tip of the spear but the rest of the spear is actually the global communications surveillance system'.[16] Ling said it was not like she went to work in the morning and pressed the 'enter' key on a keyboard and suddenly a child died in Yemen. She said such a death would be the result of a much more complex targeting system and the contributing nation-states are 'complicit in what happens'.[17]

Although the US National Reconnaissance Office has a general supervisory role at Pine Gap and Menwith Hill, the documents used by the ABC program showed that an NSA official is firmly in charge of SIGINT collection under the direction of its Washington headquarters. An official from the the Australian Signals Directorate is called the deputy chief of facility and 'advises and assists on [the base's] overall management and administration'.[18]

In September 2016, Ryan Gallagher, using Snowden's documents, reported in *The Intercept* on the magnitude of Menwith Hill's ability to locate individual targets around the globe for 'capture kill' operations in collaboration with Pine Gap.[19] Gallagher reported that as well as links to geostationary satellites, Menwith Hill, the NSA's biggest overseas base, has ground antennas that in 2009 could eavesdrop on communications sent via 163 foreign satellites. The numbers have since grown. He said the NSA documents show that during a twelve-hour period in May 2011 its surveillance systems logged more than 300 million phone calls and emails. Since then, he said, a new collection posture had been introduced at the base, the aim being to 'collect it all, process it all, exploit it all'.[20] While figures for Pine Gap are not available, it should be able to generate similar volumes of material.

One of Snowden's documents showed that a more powerful version of the target-locating program called Ghosthunter would be installed at twenty-seven NSA-CIA Special Collection Service sites around the globe by 2010 to achieve more wide-ranging capture-kill operations. The global coverage requires the use of Pine Gap's geo-synchronous satellites as well as Menwith Hill's. Gallagher reported that Jemima Stratford QC, a leading British human rights lawyer, warned that if British officials facilitated covert US drone strikes outside of declared war zones, they could be implicated in murder. British MP Fabian Hamilton told *The Intercept*: 'I don't buy this idea that you say the word "security" and nobody can know anything. We need to know what is being done in our name.'

To his credit, Ball joined colleagues in publishing well-researched reports on Pine Gap that countered his earlier claims. A 2015 report set out how thoroughly militarised the base had become through its close involvement in operations of the US military worldwide, including in Iraq and Afghanistan.[21] A 2016 report said Pine Gap hosted a distinctively shaped torus antenna system that could intercept transmissions from thirty-five or more commercial satellites simultaneously, adding to the US's ability to collect, analyse and store enormous volumes of communications that have nothing to do with verifying arms control agreements.[22]

Faced with the evidence that Pine Gap had become fully integrated with the US military's kill chain, Ball told the ABC's *7.30* program on 13 August 2014: 'I've reached the point now where I can no longer stand up and provide the verbal, conceptual justification for the facility … We're now linked in to this global network where intelligence and operations have become essentially fused and Pine Gap is a key node in that whole network, that war machine … which is doing things which are very, very difficult, I think, as an Australian, to justify … It's now using data directly from … satellites up above, down to Pine Gap, directly to the shooters.' Ball said, 'I don't know how many terrorists have been killed by drones, but I would not be surprised if the total number of children exceeds the total number of terrorists.'

He was even blunter in an interview just before his death with a journalist friend, Hamish MacDonald, in the *Saturday Paper* on 1 October 2016, saying, 'The base now has nothing much to do with our requirements … it's about finding individuals and targeting them for killing by drone and air strikes … in places that are not designated war zones.' In Ball's obituary in Fairfax Media on 19 October 2016, MacDonald said that in his last email to him Ball had said, 'It's not my PG [Pine Gap] anymore. That means that if it is the strategic essence of the alliance, I now have to question my overall support for that too!'

It was never Ball's Pine Gap. It always belonged to those who controlled the US military-industrial-intelligence complex, to do with as they wished.

Beazley was confronted with the same evidence as Ball, but has become even more enamoured with the base following his posting as Australian ambassador to Washington in 2010 and his subsequent appointment to the Australian board of Lockheed Martin, the giant US weapons manufacturer whose space division makes the satellites used at Pine Gap, the rockets to launch them into orbit, and systems for the new era of space warfare. (He resigned from the board after becoming governor of Western Australia in May 2018.)

In 2016, Beazley said our 'interest is best served by expanding the joint facilities', i.e. Pine Gap and five other US intercept assets in Australia.[23] The man who once extolled these bases for their supposed contribution to arms control and peace has now embraced their use for war fighting in distant parts of the globe that pose no threat to Australia.

PART 3

ANZUS: THE TREATY WITHOUT A SECURITY GUARANTEE

23

THE DIFFICULT BIRTH AND EARLY YEARS OF A TREATY

'A superstructure on a foundation of jelly'

Robert Menzies[1]

Following victory over Japan in 1945, many Australians didn't know that General Douglas MacArthur had told Prime Minister John Curtin in June 1942 that America had been fighting to protect its own interests, not Australia's.[2] Most took it for granted that the US would always protect Australia, regardless of the circumstances. It took several frustrating years to convince the US to sign a treaty, and even then it lacked the desired security guarantee, unlike the NATO treaty.

Initially, the US didn't want a local treaty. This worried many Australians, who feared what would happen as the momentum for decolonisation gathered pace in Indonesia, India, Pakistan, Ceylon and Vietnam. Two influential Melbourne *Herald* journalists, Robert Gilmore and Denis Warner, reflected this fear when they wrote in 1948, 'A new chaos has spread through the Jap-pillaged lands of East Asia; the lust for independence has quickened.'[3] In China, the communists led by Mao Zedong defeated Chiang Kai-shek's government in 1949. Foreign Minister Bert Evatt and his department head, John Burton, wanted Australia to do more to make its own way in Asia, but Labor lost power in 1949. Most Australians expected the US to take over from Britain as the nation's protector.

Roger Holdich, Vivianne Johnson and Pamela Andre's official study of the ANZUS Treaty reveals a distinct US lack of interest in stepping up to the plate. It begins with a top-secret cable from the Australian embassy in Washington to Canberra in March 1949 reporting to the Labor PM, Ben Chifley, that a journalist had just told the ambassador, Norman Makin, that his State Department contacts were 'most frigid' towards the idea of any formal US commitment in the Pacific and were preoccupied with NATO.[4] According to the study, in January 1950 the US narrowly defined its security perimeter in the Pacific as encompassing the Aleutians, Japan, the Ryukyu Islands and the Philippines, but not Australia, New Zealand or Korea.[5]

After becoming Coalition prime minister in 1949, Bob Menzies didn't see an urgent need for a treaty. He sent a cable to the external affairs minister, Percy Spender, in February 1951 saying, 'I would earnestly advise you that we should not push the US too hard for a formal obligation. We have their goodwill and may tend to lessen it by insisting too much upon formula.'[6] Journalist Graeme Dobell noted that Spender quoted Menzies as privately stating that the formal alliance would be 'a superstructure on a foundation of jelly'.[7]

The US softened its stand on a treaty, but suggested it include Japan and the Philippines. This was definitely not what Australia wanted. In February 1951 the head of the External Affairs Department, Alan Watt, wrote a minute to Minister Spender endorsing the view of senior diplomat Arthur Tange that Australia 'wants a guarantee against attack from Japan itself'— not an obligation to defend it.[8] Tange also opposed backing a Filipino government that was against reform movements. In the same minute, Watt strongly favoured the proposed treaty's intention to include only offshore areas, arguing that if mainland areas were included and attacked, the US would have to enter into land warfare, which would 'probably be disastrous'. This observation may be more pertinent today, but it doesn't stop senior politicians and commentators wanting Australia to back the US in a war with China.

In a Cabinet submission later that month, Spender identified another problem: the US and the UK opposed a peace treaty restricting Japanese rearmament. Spender said this conflicted with the Australian government's consistent view that there 'is no evidence the Japanese [have] under-gone any fundamental change of heart and the danger from a revived and militant Japan, even in collaboration with Russia and Communist China, must not be ignored'.[9] This is a strange assessment. Rather than embracing rearmament, the Japanese people strongly endorsed the pacifist clause in their 1947 constitution. Partly in response to US wishes, the September 1951 San Francisco Peace Treaty allowed Japan to develop 'self-defence forces'. Nevertheless, Japan stayed within a relatively modest military budget of about 1 per cent of GDP for many decades. Even after a more militaristic prime minister, Shinzo Abe, relaxed the constitution's pacifist clause in 2015, public opinion remained in favour of the original version.[10]

The US signed separate security treaties with Japan and the Philippines, smoothing the way for Australian, New Zealand and US representatives to sign the ANZUS Treaty in September 1951 in San Francisco.

Today, many Australian politicians and commentators choose to ignore how the treaty imposes severe constraints on the use of military force. Article 1 states: 'The parties undertake, as set out in the UN Charter, to settle any international disputes in which they may be involved by peaceful means … and to refrain in their international relations from the threat or use of force in any manner inconsistent with the purposes of the UN.' This is the core of the treaty. If any of the parties are threatened in the Pacific, ANZUS states only that they should consult each other. If one is actually attacked, each would act 'in accordance with its constitutional processes'—which leaves them free to do nothing other than consult.

During the first few years of the treaty's existence, the US repeatedly showed just how little ANZUS meant to it. Australia's clout was not helped by what Menzies called the 'dead hand of Fred Shedden'.[11] Sir Frederick Shedden had risen from a pay clerk's job in World War I to become head of the Defence Department in 1937. A zealous advocate of secrecy, he had almost no interest in strategic issues but an obsession with protracted administrative processes.[12] The *National Times* published US archival documents in 1980 showing that Shedden sent a stream of pointless letters marked 'Personal' to the perplexed chairman of the US joint chiefs of staff, Admiral Arthur Radford.[13] In March 1956, Radford's handwritten annotation on Shedden's latest missive said, 'I am a little puzzled as to why Sir F keeps sending me this sort of info.' Shedden's relentless correspondence developed into a pass-the-parcel game in the American hierarchy. 'Dear Raddy', 'Dear Livie' and 'Dear Walter' letters flowed backwards and forwards as Radford and two senior State Department officials, Livingston Merchant and Walter Robinson, wrestled with new ways to write thank-you notes to him. Merchant told Radford, 'Apparently he does not realise that our representatives in Australia keep us fully and promptly informed on matters such as these.' Still the letters came. A weary Radford wrote to Merchant that he had returned from an extensive trip and 'there was another one lying on my desk … now here is another one'. Menzies and his ministers preferred to rely on External Affairs or themselves for advice on substantive issues.

Although Radford treated Shedden courteously, the *NT*'s report on the US archives shows he didn't hold back when dismissing proposals from Australian ministers or other officials that didn't fit the US agenda. Tight secrecy ensured that the Australian public had no inkling that the Menzies Government had almost no influence with the US. Radford brusquely explained what he thought of an Australian and New Zealand proposal to invite Britain to attend ANZUS council meetings after they had agreed it shouldn't be a member. He said in an August 1956 top-secret memo to other American officials, 'There is absolutely no reason for the British to be in [the meeting] except to exert pressure on the Australians and New Zealand.'

Although Menzies' visit to Washington in March 1955 was publicly acclaimed as a great success, the archival records show he failed to get American support for his proposal that US forces participate in naval exercises off Malaya's coast with Australia and New Zealand. A top-secret message from the US commander-in-chief in the Pacific, Admiral Felix Stump, on 20 December 1955 demanded the recall of significant parts of a report by staff planners to the ANZUS council because they disclosed information 'which is not permitted by current US policy and bilateral agreement'.[14]

The *NT*'s report shows that the external affairs minister, Dick Casey, got an unambiguous knockback after he asked Stump in Honolulu in September 1955 to base a high-ranking American military officer in Melbourne. Casey said he wanted a four-star general or admiral 'to look over our shoulder and take part in our military planning'. Today, such a request would be welcomed as enhancing interoperability between the forces. Back then, the US correctly assessed that Casey wanted the arrangement for domestic political reasons. Casey soon had another go: this time Stump reported to Radford that Casey wanted to be told the size and type of military forces the US desired Australia to have, and explained that the Labor Party strongly opposed the Coalition's military appropriation. Radford refused to accept this level of politicisation and replied to Stump that he 'held out no hope that military planning could go as far as the Australians desire'.[15]

Two other episodes illustrate the low level of Australia's standing in Washington. In one instance, Casey wrote a secret cable to US military headquarters in Hawaii saying that a Geiger counter had gone 'wild' near Australia's Antarctic base and he feared a uranium deposit there might attract the interest of the Russians. Casey didn't know that the US joint chiefs of staff wanted to annex part of Australia's territorial claim covering

42 per cent of the Antarctic. A document dated 3 April 1957 shows the joint chiefs had instructed their strategic planning group to draw up rec-ommendations for the 'establishment now of US claims to those portions of the Antarctic, including those claimed by our allies, to which we would have a basis for valid claims'.[16] However, Eisenhower and Khrushchev demonstrated the advantages of international leaders talking to each other when they were instrumental in creating the 1961 Antarctic Treaty, which declared that no one owned any part of Antarctica and put all existing claims on hold indefinitely.

In case there was any further doubt about where ANZUS stood in US priorities in its early days, the archival documents clarified the issue in the conclusion of a 1957 US security report: 'The US has adhered to a policy of not allowing ... ANZUS to become a NATO-type organization with significant standing military forces. This has enabled the US to avoid the formulation of approved combined requirement plans and resulting force commitments. This policy is still highly desirable.'[17]

The US's and Australia's subsequent use of force in Vietnam and Iraq shows they are willing to violate their obligations under ANZUS's Article 1 and the UN Charter regardless of the devastating human con-sequences. The current growing integration of Australian and US forces could generate a powerful expectation that Australia will be automatically involved in future US wars. This momentum is not unstoppable. The Menzies Government rejected numerous US demands in 1954–55 that it be prepared to back the US militarily after skirmishes broke out in the Taiwan Strait over the Quemoy and Matsu islands, situated just off the Chinese mainland.[18] Menzies was not persuaded by the fact that the islands were controlled from Taiwan (Formosa) by US ally Chiang Kai-shek, who had fled to the island after losing the Chinese civil war in 1949.

24
FOREIGN BASES AND FOREIGN POLITICAL INTERFERENCE

'Australia and the territories under its control have become increasingly important to the US defense and space establishments in recent years as a site for satellite tracking stations, nuclear test detection facilities, space research and related activities. With ample space, relatively advanced technology, political stability and conservative government, Australia has become a uniquely desirable base for both military and civilian programs involving operations in the Southern Hemisphere.'
White House position paper, 1962[1]

Following the US refusal to include a security guarantee in ANZUS, Prime Minister Menzies was keen to win Washington's favour by hosting American military and intelligence installations. As shown below, knowledge of what was happening on Australian soil was often kept secret from the Australian public and sometimes the government. From the American perspective, the use of Australian territory was usually more important than the contribution of a relatively small number of troops to add an extra flag to US military expeditions.

This focus remained in a high-level 1971 national security study that Queensland academic Stephen Stockwell discovered in the Nixon presidential archives. It stated: 'Our most direct stakes in Australia and New Zealand are: maintenance of continuing access to the territory for purposes of locating defense and scientific installations of significance to our strategic capability and space program … [and] a support base area in case of general hostilities with a major power.'[2] Again, there was no mention of contributing troops to US wars.

Some Australian commentators have trouble accepting that the US puts such a strong emphasis on Australia's importance as a base for American military and intelligence facilities, preferring to see the relationship as based on a warm friendship between the two countries. Marshall Green stated the unsentimental reality when he told me that his first objective as US ambassador to Australia in the 1970s was to maintain the US naval communications facilities at North West Cape and the secretive satellite ground stations in Central Australia at Pine Gap and Nurrungar.[3] His second objective was keeping Australia open to US investment, and his third was backing the US in international forums. He didn't mention contributing troops to US wars.

Other facilities were also important to the US in the 1950s and early 1960s. The Menzies Government didn't have the remotest clue about the purpose of some of the facilities established during its term; nor did it care. Its goal was to appear much closer to the US than Labor. In 1961, Menzies agreed to let the US establish TRANET Station 112 at Smithfield in South Australia as part of a network of ground stations for TRANET navigational satellites. The satellites' main task was to provide highly accurate navigational data for US submarines equipped with nuclear-armed ballistic missiles.[4] Defence academic Des Ball said, 'The government itself remained in blissful ignorance of the station's operations and its strategic implications.'[5] This was confirmed when the *AFR* published details of a cable Defence head Arthur Tange sent to Washington in May 1973 in an effort to find out what the TRANET station did—twelve years after it had been established.

In 1955, the Menzies Government signed a secret agreement to allow the US to establish what it publicly described as a meteorological station at Alice Springs, called the Oak Tree Project. The fact that it was really a seismic station for detecting nuclear explosions was not revealed until Labor's defence minister, Lance Barnard, said so in parliament on 28 February 1973. In 1960, Menzies agreed to let the US secretly operate U-2 spy planes from Australian airfields under projects called Clear Sky and Crow Flight. The historian Philip Dorling later discovered that the project was probably about trying to estimate the size of the Soviets' nuclear arsenal.[6]

Menzies was fully aware that ANZUS did not contain a security guarantee, but he pretended it did. He told the New South Wales Liberal Party's annual convention on 2 November 1962 that ANZUS meant that 'If someone attacks us we know America will come to our aid. Under Labor, the US could come to the aid of Australia in the event of a Chinese

Communist attack, but only with conventional weapons. What nonsense is this?' His purpose did not escape a US diplomat in Canberra who reported to Washington on 9 November, 'Menzies undoubtedly thought the moment was politically right, in the midst of public interest concern over the Cuban crisis, to attack Labor.'[7]

Menzies' speech did not reflect the key conclusion of the Joint Intelligence Committee about the likelihood of a Chinese or Russian attack on Australia. JIC's assessment in September 1961 was that 'In the event of global war or overt aggression in Southeast Asia involving Australian forces, no military attack on Australia or the island territories would be likely ... The only foreseeable circumstance that might alter this assessment would be the establishment in Australia of a base or staging area for the West's nuclear forces, in which case there would be a threat of direct attacks against Australia.'[8] In other words, Australia was fairly safe from attack so long as it didn't host bases such as the US naval station at NWC.

As Labor slowly gained more traction for its initially unpopular stand against Menzies' 1965 decision to send a battalion of troops to Vietnam, the US financed sympathetic Australians to counter opposition to the Vietnam War. Lincoln White, the US consul-general in Melbourne in the mid-1960s, told the National Times in 1980 that the CIA station chief, Bill Caldwell, had funded Australian supporters of the war. White said, 'The main thing we funded was counter stuff through our friends out there ... We also had people in the newspaper business who put our side.'[9] He said Caldwell had someone at the Melbourne Age that the US didn't have to fund, but White couldn't remember his name. A report in the Lyndon Baines Johnson Library in Austin, Texas shows that in July 1965 White recommended to Washington that 'an increase in effort and resources should be devoted by the US in preserving and further promoting Australian policy and effort on this key issue ... Unless strongly countered, trends might well develop which could defeat or at least modify federal policy for containing the spread of communism in South East Asia.'[10]

Declassified American documents also show that the US argued in the Supreme Court that allowing publication of the Pentagon Papers (Daniel Ellsberg's leaked report on how badly the Vietnam War was going) would damage the US goal of keeping Billy McMahon's Coalition government in power. The NT reported that in 1971 a State Department deputy secretary, William Macomber, gave a top-secret court deposition in which he claimed that publication would weaken the McMahon Government's tenure. He said, 'Anything that weakens the government in Australia ...

must be regarded as a serious setback for the security interests of the US.'[11] Macomber said McMahon had been appalled by the publication in June 1971 of a highly classified cable from General Maxwell Taylor in Saigon, the text of which 'can lead to the inference that the dispatch of Australian combat troops to Vietnam was not done at the genuine request of the South Vietnamese government but rather was facilitated through the South Vietnamese government by the US'.[12] The inference was true. The Supreme Court refused to stop publication of the *Pentagon Papers*—a victory for transparency that would be impossible under recent new laws in Australia that rule out the 'public interest' defence used in the *Pentagon Papers* case. Nor does Australia have anything similar to the protection of free speech contained in the first amendment to the US Constitution.

25

ENDURING FAITH IN A GUARANTEE THAT DOESN'T EXIST

'In practice, each of the parties to the ANZUS Treaty is going to decide whether or not to take action under the treaty according to its own judgement of the situation … The government is of the opinion that discussion of [the treaty's] meaning is almost certain to narrow its meaning.'
Foreign Minister Garfield Barwick, in a top-secret department memo[1]

In the late 1950s and early 1960s the Menzies Government kept pushing for US military backing in any conflict with President Sukarno's government in Indonesia, and the US kept refusing. Although Sukarno never showed any inclination to invade Australia, he certainly frightened our leaders as he tried to maintain a balancing act between the US-backed Indonesian military and a strong Communist Party (the PKI). The US National Archives show that at the ANZUS military representatives' meeting in Melbourne on 23 January 1956, Australia wanted treaty members to prepare for an invasion of Indonesia. But at a meeting on 26 May that year, the US military's joint chiefs of staff made it clear that they opposed 'overt military intervention in Indonesia'.[2] The joint chiefs said they would not 'authorize any US military representative to develop combined plans, allocate US forces to specific contingencies, commit the US to specific courses of action or place undue emphasis on ANZUS military planning'.[3]

However, the US fostered a rebellion in Sumatra and Sulawesi by giving covert military support to Islamist parties.[4] Former CIA official Fletcher Prouty, who was directly involved in what happened, told an interviewer that the agency managed to arm a rebel force of 42,000 and Australia was expected to supply administrative and medical help if the rebels succeeded.[5] He said the program collapsed after the Indonesians captured Allen Pope, the CIA pilot of a B-26 that crashed after bombing a hospital on Ambon. The US attorney-general, Robert Kennedy, negotiated Pope's release.

The Australian external affairs minister, Dick Casey, recorded in his diaries that he suggested to the Americans that covert action be used to undermine the Indonesian economy by sabotaging oil production. He sent a cable to his department conceding that 'The danger of such action could be nationalisation by the Jakarta government.'[6] The Americans saw no merit in risking the nationalisation of their oil interests. Casey's judgement of regional politicians was no better: he wrote in his diary that Singapore's prospective leader, the politically moderate, administratively competent Lee Kuan Yew, was 'a clever, impractical, left-wing theoretician'.[7]

After the rebellion failed, the US switched to trying to win Sukarno's favour with soft aid and political support in international forums. As a result, Australia was caught wrong-footed when Sukarno stepped up his attempts to incorporate the Dutch colony of West Irian into Indonesia. The US and the UK both supported him, with a US National Security Council paper in 1959 noting, 'The Australians are, if anything, more determined than the Dutch that West New Guinea [West Irian] should not come under Indonesian control.'[8] Cabinet noted that if Indonesia attacked West Irian the US would see its best interest 'as not antagonising the Asian nations, rather than supporting its allies'.[9]

Although a proposal to put West Irian under UN trusteeship gained wide approval, the UN agreed to transfer it to Indonesian control on 1 May 1963, to be followed by an act of self-determination in 1969. Historian James Curran, who researched the National Archives in Washington and Canberra, says the Australian government was only told of the deals, which effectively guaranteed the Indonesian takeover of the territory, after they had been done. Curran said one of Kennedy's advisers, Bob 'Blowtorch' Komer, explained, 'It was worth sacrificing a few thousand square miles of cannibal land to keep Indonesia out of the communist camp.'[10]

The act of self-determination was a travesty. Indonesia selected 1022 West Irians to vote from a population of about 800,000, and the entire 1022 voted unanimously to become part of Indonesia. Because of the secrecy surrounding the policy shifts, the Australian public were surprised and angered by an outcome they believed Menzies would successfully oppose. Despite some recent improvements, Indonesia has treated the locals badly. Likewise, the US corporation Freeport-McMoRan, which operates a vast copper and gold mine in the province, could have done much better.

The next shock occurred in 1963, when Indonesia introduced its policy of 'Confrontation' to oppose what it branded a British imperialist policy of encirclement through the creation of a new neighbouring state, Malaysia. Under the 1963 proposal, Malaya was to form a federation with Singapore and the two non-Indonesian parts of Borneo, Sarawak and Sabah. 'Confrontation' mostly amounted to strident Indonesian propaganda and small-scale military harassment and incursions, rather than a full-scale war against Malaysia, but Menzies and his foreign minister, Garfield Barwick, wanted to back the UK's call for a military response by sending troops to Borneo. This eventually occurred in January 1965. The problem disappeared when General Suharto ousted Sukarno amid horrific military and communal violence that is generally estimated to have killed between 500,000 and one million people in 1965–66.

Meanwhile, the Americans gave Barwick and Menzies, both lawyers, a painful rebuttal of any notion that the ANZUS Treaty was an enforceable contract. The same applied to the belief that Australia had paid the necessary 'insurance premiums' by sending 17,000 troops to the Korean War at the cost of 340 Australian lives and by making an initial contribution to the escalating war in Vietnam.

When Menzies met Kennedy in the White House in July 1963, the president explained that the American people 'have forgotten ANZUS and are not at the moment prepared for a situation which would involve the US'.[11] After another rejection, Barwick wrote the top-secret memo to his department quoted at the start of this chapter, which acknowledged that ANZUS left the US free to decide whether to take action when requested, and came to the abject conclusion that discussing the treaty's meaning 'is almost certain to narrow its meaning'. While in Washington, Barwick was given a secret record of understanding on 17 October that stated that the treaty 'related only to overt attacks and not to subversion, guerilla warfare or indirect aggression'.[12] It also said that any American assistance, if sent, would not include ground troops.

Kennedy could not have spoken more plainly, but Barwick lied when he subsequently told parliament in April 1964 that there was 'no question of doubt' about the US obligation to intervene if Australian forces in Borneo were attacked.[13] Lying to parliament is supposedly a sackable offence, but secrecy shielded parliamentarians and the public from knowing that Barwick had done so. His successor as external affairs minister, Paul Hasluck, acknowledged the truth in early 1965 when he publicly conceded, 'We have been put on notice by a former president that the American understanding of its obligations was such as to exclude help from them to Australia in certain circumstances.'[14]

Curran said that Kennedy's comment about the Americans forgetting about ANZUS 'punctured not only much of the rhetoric about an alliance forged in the crucible of the Pacific but questioned the foundational principle of Australia's Cold War policy. Kennedy had shown that the idea of common cause with an old wartime ally cut no ice in US domestic politics. The US, as all great powers do, had quite properly followed its own interests. Australia simply had to make do.'[15] He concluded, 'The lesson is clear. The warming rhetoric of the "Anglosphere" ought to recall that in the past Australian and US interests in Asia have collided as much as they have coincided.'[16]

Most Australian politicians, commentators and journalists still prefer to believe that the alliance provides a security guarantee like an insurance policy, in which Australia pays premiums by sending troops to support the US in overseas wars. The payout, they believe, is that the US will always honour the policy by coming to Australia's rescue, no matter where or how far in the future. However, most experienced politicians understand that a US president will act in his or her political interest, bolstered by a plausible interpretation of America's national interest. If a deeply unpopular intervention on behalf of Australia serves no core strategic interest, a future president won't send troops to support Australia, regardless of the cost in blood, treasure and votes.

John Howard demonstrated during the 1999 crisis in Timor-Leste that he did not understand the elementary lesson Kennedy had given Menzies in 1963—that US leaders will make their own self-interested decisions on whether to send troops to support Australian soldiers. Howard presumed President Bill Clinton would agree to his demand for American boots-on-the-ground in Timor-Leste in 1999. Clinton refused. The rebuff shook Howard, who had written to Indonesia's President B.J. Habibie in late 1998 suggesting that Timor-Leste become independent within the decade. Habibie promptly held a ballot, on 30 August 1999, that resulted in an overwhelming vote for independence. However, Habibie didn't control Indonesia's special forces and their militia units, who responded with devastating violence in Timor-Leste. An outraged Australian public demanded action, and Howard then organised an Australian-led intervention force with UN approval. But he desperately wanted US support on the ground.

The veteran ABC defence and foreign affairs correspondent Graeme Dobell observed, 'Australian policy makers should always be reminded of two images from the epicentre of the crisis in the days when failure was still likely.'[17] He said one snapshot was of Clinton's national security adviser, Sandy Berger, telling journalists that America had no more responsibility for solving Timor-Leste than he did for cleaning up a mess his daughter might create in her apartment. The other is of Howard sitting in a radio studio 'almost pleading over the airwaves for American "boots on the ground"'.

New Zealand's contribution of 1200 well-trained troops helped reduce the need for any US boots, although the US did make a significant contribution by persuading key Indonesian figures to prevent their military confronting the intervention forces. In contrast, Australia's defence minister, John Moore, could not even get his Indonesian counterpart to take his phone calls, despite a security treaty between the two countries. In September 1999 the Indonesians cancelled this security treaty, which former Labor prime minister Paul Keating had signed in December 1995 with the Indonesian dictator Suharto. The treaty had been rendered worthless in less than four years.

26

HOW NEW ZEALAND HAS SURVIVED WITHOUT ANZUS

'In February 1985, the New Zealand government's Communications Security Bureau was receiving reports about minute details of the Iran–Iraq War, a weekly list of all the Libyan students in Britain and a lot of other marginally interesting top-secret reports. But there was nothing, among the screeds of reports on international terrorism, about the French DGSE agents who were right then on their way to New Zealand to become the first foreign terrorists in New Zealand's history: blowing up the Greenpeace ship Rainbow Warrior.'

Nicky Hager[1]

In 1985 the US, backed by the Hawke Labor government, booted New Zealand out of ANZUS. Its sin was to elect David Lange's Labour government in July 1984, which had a policy of banning visits by ships that confirmed they were carrying nuclear weapons or were powered by nuclear reactors. The issue came to a head the following February with a proposed visit by an old, conventionally powered US vessel that Lange correctly assumed was not carrying nuclear weapons. The Americans refused to confirm or deny if this were the case. Implementing its policy, the NZ government exercised its sovereign right to ban entry to a foreign ship—a right possessed and exercised by the US, Australia and most other countries.

Australian Labor and Coalition governments in earlier years had banned the entry of similar US ships without being thrown out of ANZUS—back then, the US chose to cancel proposed visits rather than say whether the ships were nuclear armed. It's unclear why the US didn't follow this precedent in 1984 and quietly drop the proposed visit. Instead, in June 1985 President Ronald Reagan officially suspended New Zealand from ANZUS in what amounted to expulsion. He then banned NZ from receiving any US intelligence or armed-forces training.

The punishment did not have the desired effect: New Zealand not only lived to tell the tale—it thrived. Lange won the next election, and the antinuclear stance remains so popular with New Zealand voters that conservative governments keep it. Nevertheless, some scholars have trouble understanding what happened. American politics scholar Amy Catalinac, who has lived in Wellington, said the US formally suspended its 'security guarantee' to New Zealand under ANZUS.[2] Never mind that New Zealand could not be deprived of something that never existed.

The Hawke Government decided in March 1985 that it would no longer give New Zealand any document containing references to classified US information. Defence Minister Kim Beazley later told me that a laborious effort went into checking a wide range of Australian documents to ensure they didn't include material from US sources when passed on to Wellington. He didn't know at that stage that the NSA had secretly kept supplying New Zealand with the highly sensitive intelligence that the Australians painstakingly deleted. The NSA was defying government policy. A deputy assistant secretary of state, William Brown, officially stated that 'All intelligence flows to New Zealand would be stopped.'[3] The reason for the NSA's perfidy was simple: it considered the continued supply of signals intelligence from the intercept facilities it effectively ran in New Zealand as more important than punishing the country for refusing to let a ship into a port.

Nicky Hager, an authority on intelligence subjects, wrote that 'While governments, journalists and the public around the world were led to believe that United States–New Zealand intelligence ties had been cut, inside the five-agency network [US, UK, Canada, Australia and NZ] it was mostly business as usual. The US military was unsentimental about its decades of alliance links with the New Zealand armed forces. Military exercises, exchanges and other visible links were completely cut. However, New Zealand's involvement in the UKUSA [Five Eyes] intelligence alliance was too useful to the overseas allies to be interrupted by a quarrel over nuclear ships.'[4]

Hager obtained a copy of the 1985–86 annual report of the NSA's tiny partner the New Zealand Government Communications Security Bureau (GCSB), which confirmed that it continued to receive SIGINT from its partners. The GCSB even managed to increase its output of SIGINT reporting by 33 per cent over the year. The report said relations with the NSA evolved into a mixed state of 'official cautiousness and private cordiality', while 'close relations continued' with Australia's Defence Signals Directorate.

After becoming PM, Lange was never told that the GCSB's director of policy and planning was an American employee of the NSA.[5] It is less clear how much Lange knew in 1987 when he approved a new station that would deliver a large increase in New Zealand's SIGINT collection capabilities and would perform most of its intercept work on behalf of the NSA and its other Five Eyes partners. Like the DSD base built at the same time near Geraldton in Western Australia, the new station at Waihopai near Blenheim allowed the NSA and its local partner to intercept all signals transmitted via particular communications satellites in geo-synchronous orbit above the equator.

In 2013, Edward Snowden released details of the extraordinarily sophisticated new equipment at Waihopai and how it was being used for the bulk collection of communications in the Asia-Pacific region as part of an integrated Five Eyes system.[6] The NSA's closeness to the GCSB was also illustrated in a report by Hager and Ryan Gallagher about a joint hacking project to eavesdrop on Chinese diplomats in Auckland.[7] They said the project apparently required the agencies to violate international treaties, signed by New Zealand, that prohibit the interception of diplomatic communications. Diplomatic eavesdropping is widely practised, including by Australia, although it is against the rules. This does not stop Australia hypocritically insisting that China obey a 'rules-based international order'.

Snowden released a 2013 NSA report saying that China was first on a list of targets the GCSB monitored on the NSA's behalf. Hager and Gallagher said the documents highlighted discrepancies between secret and official foreign policy adopted by New Zealand in running spying operations against twenty or more countries, including friendly nations and trading partners. The GCSB targets these countries by using the Waihopai satellite intercept base and from covert listening posts hidden in New Zealand's diplomatic buildings.[8] The wider consequence of allowing the GCSB to follow the NSA's targeting directions is that it partly undermines the increased foreign policy independence New Zealand gained from being kicked out of ANZUS.

The value of participating in the Five Eyes arrangement was put to a crucial test when France undertook an act of state terrorism by attacking antinuclear activists in 1985. On 10 July that year, an arm of the French foreign intelligence service (DGSE) exploded two bombs on the Greenpeace ship *Rainbow Warrior* in Auckland Harbour. The attack killed a photographer on the ship, which was due to lead a protest at the site of forthcoming French nuclear tests at Mururoa Atoll in the Pacific. France denied responsibility well after New Zealand police caught two members of one of the three terrorist teams involved. Australian and NZ police arrested three of the other French terrorists on Norfolk Island after their boat stopped there following the sinking of the *Rainbow Warrior*. The police wanted to hold them on murder charges but Australian authorities, with the approval of their New Zealand counterparts, ordered their release on the grounds of insufficient evidence. Evidence materialised soon afterwards.[9] After the court case, the French government negotiated an extraordinary concession that allowed the terrorists to serve their ten- and seven-year jail sentences on the idyllic French island of Hao in the Pacific. Compounding the insult, the French government released them after less than two years and promoted both of them.

So what warning did the vast eavesdropping capability of the Five Eyes network offer New Zealand about what was planned? Given that these agencies stress how detecting early-warning signals is one of their most valuable attributes, it's reasonable to expect they alerted the government. But as quoted above, there was nothing among numerous reports on terrorism about the French state terrorists who were on their way to blow up the *Rainbow Warrior*.

Much of the original rationale for the US punishment of New Zealand disappeared after the September 1991 agreement between President George Bush and his Soviet counterpart, Mikhail Gorbachev, to remove all tactical nuclear weapons from surface ships and attack submarines. But the US didn't reinstate New Zealand as a functioning member of ANZUS.

Nor has New Zealand been eager to rejoin. A common explanation is that many voters fear this would increase US pressure on the country to boost its military spending and support tough American policies against NZ's major trading partner, China. Although President Bill Clinton tried to sell or lease twenty-eight F-16 jet fighters to New Zealand, Helen Clark's Labour government decided in 2001 not to go ahead with the deal because it didn't need—and couldn't afford—them. Conservative governments subsequently supported the decision.

Many Australian ministers and officials initially welcomed their enhanced status when New Zealand no longer attended ANZUS meetings, but the two countries have common defence interests regardless of ANZUS. In 1991, they agreed to a formal 'closer defence relations'

arrangement, and in 1999, New Zealand made a welcome military contribution to the Australian-led intervention to restore order in Timor-Leste.

In a paper published by the Australian Defence College in 2011, Mark
Keenan and Colin Richardson said New Zealand was a Pacific Island
country with an identifiable Polynesian element to its culture, and has
always felt it has a destiny separate from Australia. They said its remote
location meant there was no credible external threat to its territory or
immediate interests.[10] In these circumstances, most New Zealanders seem
comfortable with the added independence gained from being ejected
from ANZUS.

27

THE LONELY DEATH
OF A GOOD POLICY

'It is the Government's policy that our armed forces must be able to defend
Australia without relying on the combat forces of other countries. We must be
the sole guarantor of our own security. It is not healthy for a country to become
dependent on another for its basic defence. Further, if Australia was ever to
be directly threatened, our allies may well be engaged elsewhere and unable
to assist. This may sound unlikely, but it was a hard-learned lesson from the
Second World War.'

Australia's National Security: A Defence Update 2007[1]

The message above makes refreshing good sense, and was reinforced by
the reminder during the 1999 conflict in Timor-Leste that the US is not
obliged to provide troops at Australia's behest. Nor is Australia required to
do so at America's behest.

The lesson has been slow to sink in across the political spectrum, as
Foreign Minister Alexander Downer discovered during a doorstop inter-
view in Beijing in August 2004. Reflecting the wording of the ANZUS
Treaty, Downer said Australia was not bound to help the US defend
Taiwan in any future military action. Labor's shadow foreign minister,
Kevin Rudd, then promptly claimed that Downer had 'blundered into a
diplomatic minefield'.[2]

Downer's remarks were not a blunder, unless ANZUS can never be
discussed in other than reverential terms. His critics overlooked the fact
that Australia formally recognised China in 1972 as the 'sole legal government' of China, including both the mainland and Taiwan (as a province).

Most governments, including that of the US, have given a similar form of recognition, although the US's position is complicated by its security treaty with Taiwan. The upshot for Australia is that a conflict between China and Taiwan can be regarded as an internal Chinese issue. Either way, ANZUS does not oblige Australia to do anything. Prime Minister John Howard told ABC Radio National's *PM* program on 20 August 2004 that Downer hadn't 'stumbled' and that 'We must support the One China policy [and] make no apology' for our close relationship with China.

This did not stop the American ambassador, Tom Schieffer, claiming on the same program that Australia was obliged to come to the aid of the US if there were a conflict over Taiwan. Although the ANZUS Treaty is a brief document, Schieffer admitted he hadn't read it. Had he done so, he would have discovered that Australia has no such obligation, any more than the US did to support Australia in Borneo in the 1960s or in Timor-Leste in 1999. Another US ambassador, Robert McCallum, confessed at the National Press Club on 14 February 2007 to not having read the treaty.

Against this backdrop, the Howard Government publicly outlined the dangers of military dependency in its 2007 *Defence Update*, cited above. Despite the update's strong evidentiary basis, it surprised and annoyed some who had never expected a Coalition government to declare that it was unhealthy for one country to become dependent on another for its defence. Defence Minister Brendan Nelson, who wrote the introduction, clearly felt there was nothing controversial about this.

The Rudd Labor government had no intention of differing with the US. Thanks to WikiLeaks, we now know it secretly sucked up to the Americans by telling them to take no notice of what it said in its 2009 Defence White Paper, with the paper's principal author, Michael Pezzullo, telling the US embassy that the government would 'continue its missile defence research and development cooperation with the US system'.[3] But the White Paper unequivocally stated that the government was 'opposed to the development of a unilateral national system by any nation because [this] would be at odds with the maintenance of global nuclear deterrence'. Pezzullo, who now heads the Home Affairs Department, explained that the wording of this key policy document was only to mollify the Labor government's left faction. However, the White Paper deceived a lot more than a party faction—it deceived the Australian public, who were told that the wording represented government policy.

Some Labor politicians continued to sound more unthinkingly loyal to the US than some Coalition ministers. After Defence Minister David Johnston correctly stated on the ABC's *Lateline* on 12 June 2014 that

ANZUS didn't always require Australia to back the US militarily, Labor's Michael Danby claimed that Johnston's words 'will be causing shock waves in Washington, Tokyo, Hanoi, Manila and even in Beijing'.[4] No shock waves were detected.

A policy of not depending on an external guarantor doesn't mean that Australia must design and build all its own military equipment. It makes sense to import items such as highly sophisticated fighter planes, submarines, frigates and some electronic systems. The caveat is that the supplying nation doesn't have a de facto veto over their use.[5] The US doesn't need any incentive to sell expensive weapons systems to Australia and other countries—it pushed hard to sell F-16 fighter jets to New Zealand after kicking it out of ANZUS in 1985 and banning weapons sales to that country. In the unlikely event that the US refuses to sell weapons to Australia in future, high-quality alternatives are available from Europe and elsewhere.

The US's refusal to sell has been confined to technology considered too sensitive to supply to other countries. It banned the export of its F-14 fighter because it wanted to keep its Phoenix missile technology secret. The only exception was Iran: the US encouraged the big-spending Reza Shah Pahlavi to buy the fighters. The Shah had been restored to the Peacock Throne in 1953 by a covert US–UK operation that overthrew the democratically elected secular prime minister, Mohammad Mosaddegh. After the Shah fled the country in 1979, he was replaced by the distinctly non-secular Islamic Revolutionary Government, which was then able to use some of the world's most advanced jet fighters against the US-backed Iraq in the 1980–88 war between the two countries.

Australian forces don't need the same weapons as the US for the two nations' forces to operate together. They have done so in the past despite having different ships, fighter planes, tanks, artillery and rifles. The benefit from exchange of 'intelligence' is also open to question, as much of what the US supplies to Australia is irrelevant. Political leaders such as Malcolm Fraser and Gareth Evans have stated that they did not find intelligence information particularly useful when they were in office.[6] Intelligence, like any other form of information, can be distorted to influence or deceive governments—as happened before the 2003 invasion of Iraq, when the US eagerly supplied bogus intelligence about the continued existence of Saddam Hussein's alleged weapons of mass destruction. It quickly became obvious that Iraq didn't have these weapons—despite Howard's unqualified statement to parliament in 2003 that he 'knew' it did.

A refusal to join the invasion wouldn't have wrecked the alliance. Almost all members of NATO, except Britain, refused to join the initial invasion. The alliance wasn't destroyed. Nor did the US scrap its alliances with Japan and South Korea after they too refused.

In a carefully argued essay, former Australian diplomat Garry Woodard says the outcome of the war in Iraq 'strongly reinforces the most serious lesson of Vietnam, that the royal prerogative, or executive privilege, to decide on going to war which the Prime Minister exercises is an anomaly and should be made subject to rules and conventions'.[7] Former DFAT historian Bill Hudson noted the irony that 'if a Commonwealth government wished to declare war simultaneously on the United States and the Soviet Union it would be free to do so: if it wished to add a cent in tax to the cost of a packet of cigarettes it would have to arrange the preparation of appropriate legislation, survive debates in its own party room, pilot a Bill through each of the two houses of Federal Parliament, accommodate publicity and calculate the electoral impact of the ire of nicotine addicts'.[8] Woodard is one of many who say the obvious course is to require that authority for war should lie in a vote in parliament by the two houses sitting together after a nationally televised debate.

Woodard also said the Howard Government's decision immediately after the 11 September 2001 terrorist attacks to extend the geographical ambit of the ANZUS Treaty worldwide could come with a great many military and political costs. It could create perceptions that Australia will be involved if the US launches an attack elsewhere in the Middle East or worldwide. He added, 'It may narrow or eliminate Australia's options in regard to its biggest trading partner, China.'[9]

In these circumstances, the 2007 *Defence Update* was an important corrective to the impulse to join almost every US expeditionary war. Yet the wisdom embodied in the update has been cast aside in a bipartisan scramble to integrate Australian forces much more closely into the US military as the fear of again losing a big protector grows along with the rise of China's economic and military strength.

28
WHAT TO DO ABOUT A BELLICOSE ALLY

'It is hard to remember all the times we have invaded countries—or just bombarded or attacked them incessantly with drones—covertly or overtly, without any international benediction. The US is allowed to violate its own rules, as long as it serves our security and interests as every administration defines them.'

Former US ambassador Morton Abramowitz[1]

Most Australians appreciate the tremendous global contribution the US makes to areas such as the arts, science, technology, entrepreneurship and the media. For some, its music alone amounts to an unrivalled contribution. Its foreign policy is more problematic. The tendency of some Australians to brand any criticism of the US's use of force as 'anti-American' is a lazy attempt to win a debate. Does a dislike of Chicago politics but a love of Chicago blues make you 'anti' or 'pro' America? Many patriotic Americans also object to US foreign policies and are highly critical of what they see as their country's increasingly toxic political culture. In this context, some Australians worry that the US is an increasingly erratic ally that could become more repressive domestically and more aggressive internationally. Nevertheless, there is a high level of support among political leaders for Australia's military to become much more closely enmeshed with US forces, regardless of whether Donald Trump or someone worse is president.

Australia's mainstream political leaders are undeterred by the fact that the US has been involved in an astonishing number of wars and has repeatedly overthrown governments in defiance of international norms laid down at the founding of the United Nations. A Congressional Research Service study found that the US used its armed forces overseas on 215 occasions from its foundation in 1798 to 2016. The tempo stepped up greatly after the Cold War ended in 1991—since then, force has been used 160 times.[2] The US is commonly estimated to have around 800 overseas bases, compared with fewer than ten for Russia and China. Most countries have none. Research by a Carnegie Mellon scholar, Dov Levin, found that the US intervened in eighty-one foreign elections between 1946 and 2000, while the Soviet Union/Russia did so thirty-six times; Levin cautions that the latter figure could be an underestimate.[3]

US intervention in Russia's 1996 election was blatant. With President Boris Yeltsin's approval ratings in single digits, a reinvigorated Communist Party looked like winning. But the US moved to keep Yeltsin in power, as the 15 July 1996 edition of *Time* magazine detailed in its cover story, 'Yanks to the rescue: The secret story of how American advisers helped Yeltsin win'. *Time* said that after US advisers introduced typical American campaigning techniques, Yeltsin's daughter Tatiana complained that some of the lies being told were 'unfair' to their opponents. Yeltsin won but soon handed over to Vladimir Putin—not exactly the outcome the US wanted.

An assistant secretary of state, Victoria Nuland, later told a congressional committee that the US provided US$100 million 'to counter Russian propaganda in 2014 by measures such as supporting "independent" media within Russia, training journalists, and Voice of America broadcasts'.[4] Apparently this was part of an ongoing program. The US spent much more than this in Ukraine after that country gained independence in 1991. Nuland told a conference that the US had spent US$5 billion in Ukraine to support goals such as 'building democratic skills and institutions'.[5] On one occasion, she was directly involved in helping to form a pro-US government. A BBC analysis of a leaked phone call between Nuland and the US ambassador to Ukraine in 2014 clearly shows she intervened heavily in decisions about who should hold key positions in the new Ukraine government following the overthrow of the elected pro-Russian president.[6]

Russia allegedly intervened in the 2016 US presidential campaign at a much lower cost by hacking into computers in the Democratic campaign headquarters and posting items on Facebook in an attempt to divide an already-divided nation. That Russia interfered would not be surprising, but it is hard to assess what, if any, impact this might have had amid all the other influences swirling around in the election campaign, including huge spending by the political parties.

Some of the best-known examples of US covert action to overthrow governments or leaders include the removal of Iran's democratically elected prime minister in 1953, and the 1973 coup that replaced Chile's elected president, Salvador Allende, with the brutal dictator General Augusto Pinochet. Similarly, the overthrow of the elected Congolese prime minister, Patrice Lumumba, took a terrible human toll.[7] The CIA had initially planned to poison Lumumba before his US-favoured rivals killed him in 1961.[8] Joseph Mobuto took full control in 1965, and ruled until 1997 as one of the worst monsters of the twentieth century.

The Voice of America lists significant covert US interference in France and Italy (1948), the Philippines (1948–54), Albania (1949), Guatemala (1954), Cuba (1959 to the 1960s), Laos (1964), Vietnam (1949–73), Angola (1975), Nicaragua (1981) and Afghanistan (1979 to the present).[9] The US also supported coups in Brazil (1964), Argentina (1966), Grenada (1983), Haiti (1991 and 2004) and Honduras (2009).[10]

The US has been much more successful at instigating coups than the Soviets. An anti-communist historian, Walter Laqueur, said, 'The greatest shortcoming of Soviet [foreign] policy has been its overall inability to initiate coups. With the exception of South Yemen and Afghanistan in 1979, the USSR has not played a central role in any of the coups that brought pro-Soviet regimes to power [but] was probably involved in several failed coup attempts.'[11] The USSR did use tanks to crush the 1956 Hungarian revolution and prevent reforms in Czechoslovakia in 1968.

Morton Abramowitz, a former American ambassador and a co-founder of the International Crisis Group, is quoted at the beginning of this chapter. He wrote in 2012 that the core difficulties in US foreign policy stem from the belief that 'the use of its power can be unbounded since it is profoundly moral'.[12] He said the US constantly reminds other countries, particularly China, that they must play by the rules, but 'China has not invaded any country since [Vietnam in] 1979 and then it was only for three weeks'.[13] The US often refuses to obey international law while insisting that its own laws must have extraterritorial application to every other country.

Nevertheless, recent Australian prime ministers have effectively integrated Australian forces so tightly into their US counterparts in planning, training, doctrine, logistics and communications that Australia could find itself participating in a devastating war between the US and China.[14] Before the 2003 invasion of Iraq, Australian personnel were involved in planning at the US military's central command headquarters. Garry Woodard says in his study of what happened in that invasion that having all the preparations in place can create a momentum that's hard to stop.

He argues, 'Being embedded in military planning generates a moral commitment … It provides a charge like that of getting on the inside of policy-making.'[15]

Similar considerations apply to buying military equipment to plug straight into the American forces, which increasingly means Australia's procurement choices are less likely to be cost effective for meeting its own requirements. For example, Australia is paying $7 billion for six big unarmed Triton drones to be integrated into the US Navy system that uses the same drones for surveilling Asia, particularly the South China Sea. It would cost about $3 billion to buy thirty US Reaper drones instead[16]—which, unlike the Tritons, can carry powerful weapons when needed. They would be far more cost effective than the Tritons for Australian tasks ranging from spotting bushfires, asylum-seeker boats and illegal fishing activities to detecting and attacking hostile ships and land targets. They could also surveil the South China Sea and parts of the Pacific and Indian oceans.

The former Labor defence minister and ambassador to the US, Kim Beazley, is a keen supporter of close integration with the US military. He was in an expansive mood when he gave the Lockheed Martin Vernon Parker Oration in Canberra in 2016. (Lockheed Martin, America's biggest arms corporation, had put Beazley on its Australian board.) He happily admitted that he was a member of a 'deep state', but said it was not an evil one where 'the real power lies in a military/intelligence phalanx'—he called it a 'benign deep state'.[17] 'Benign' is not the word the victims would choose to describe what Beazley's deep state did to Korea, Vietnam, Iraq or Afghanistan, or to Mosaddegh, Lumumba or Allende.

Beazley said he used to wonder why the Americans let the Hawke Government 'get away with such crap in the 1980s [initiated by foreign ministers Bill Hayden and Gareth Evans]'. He then corrected himself to say, 'It wasn't crap … but they didn't like what we were doing on Cambodia [trying to help the country recover from the Khmer Rouge nightmare], they didn't like what we were doing on South Pacific nuclear-free zones, they were sceptical of what we were doing with weapons of mass destruction in so far as gas was concerned [trying to ban nerve gas].'[18] He explained that the US didn't really care what the Hawke Government did provided it gave them full access to the joint intelligence and communications facilities. He said Australia had been 'strategically irrelevant' during the Cold War and welcomed that it was now much more important to the US.

Beazley's myopic view does not include what is happening in Asian countries, which are unlikely to see Australia as important when it continues to slide down the indexes of economic size and power. Although precise predictions can be wrong, forecasts in the government's 2017 Foreign Policy White Paper show that the Chinese economy—the ultimate source of strategic power—will be about 75 per cent bigger than the US's by 2030.[19] Projections by the big accounting firm PricewaterhouseCoopers for GDP in 2050 show that China will be the biggest economy, followed by India and the US; Australia will drop from nineteenth in the world in 2018 to twenty-eighth in 2050; Indonesia will rise to fourth; and Vietnam, the Philippines, Bangladesh, Malaysia, Thailand and South Africa will all be ahead of Australia.[20]

Malcolm Fraser argued that Australia would be safer if it withdrew from ANZUS because it would make it easier to stay out of a disastrous war between China and the US. He said, 'Strategic independence will allow Australia to agree and disagree with both Washington and Beijing.'[21] Bill Pritchett, one of the finest strategic thinkers to have headed Defence, said after he retired that it would have been better if Australia had never joined ANZUS following World War II and if it had had to 'make its own way in Asia'.[22] Commentator Geoff Barker supports leaving ANZUS and dismisses the protection the US nuclear umbrella supposedly offers: 'No American president would risk sacrificing an American city to protect an Australian city from nuclear attack.'[23]

An alternative would be to stay in ANZUS but refuse to participate in wars of aggression. Supporters of this approach, including this author, say it would reflect the wording and intention of the treaty, especially Article 1's core focus on refraining from aggressive use of force in line with the UN Charter and, preferably, a reformed Security Council. By doing so, Australia would simply be adhering to the rules-based international order it is so quick to accuse others of breaching.[24]

PART 4
THE WHITLAM ERA

29

THE IRRATIONAL US HATRED OF WHITLAM

'Marshall, I can't stand that cunt.'
Richard Nixon's considered opinion of Gough Whitlam[1]

When a Labor government was elected in Australia on 2 December 1972—the first in twenty-three years—there was nothing surprising about its foreign policy. The core themes reflected the party's long-standing advocacy of a more independent and wide-ranging foreign policy within the American alliance.

The new prime minister, Gough Whitlam, was an internationalist whose eloquence, arrogance and patrician manner might have seemed better suited to the foreign stage than implementing the sweeping domestic reform agenda that dominated his time in office. His foreign policy changes were hardly radical, but this cut no ice with intransigent US leaders unable to accept that they were no longer living with one of the biddable Coalition governments that had been in power since 1949.

Many of Whitlam's policies, foreign and domestic, survived his political demise. He unambiguously rejected apartheid—unlike the US, whose policy of actively supporting minority white rule in South Africa, Rhodesia and Angola, dubbed the Tar Baby Option, was set out in its National Security Study Memorandum 39. Whitlam granted independence to Papua New Guinea, helped scrap the moribund Southeast Asia Treaty Organization (SEATO), enthusiastically abolished what remained of the White Australia policy, upgraded relations with Japan, recognised China, ended military conscription, withdrew the remaining Australian troops from Vietnam, abandoned the doctrine of forward defence, and cut trade barriers.[2] Although predictable, Labor's election win caught the notoriously prickly US president Richard Nixon off-guard. Nixon was poorly served by his political appointee as ambassador to Canberra, Walter Rice, who had advised that the Coalition would win.

Even astute US diplomats could be confused by the attitudes of some senior Labor ministers. At one extreme were those who said whatever they assumed the US wanted to hear; others disagreed with whatever the US said or did. In an extreme example of the former, Whitlam's deputy, Lance Barnard, had a short meeting near the end of the election campaign with a visiting staff member from a congressional foreign relations committee, in an air-force building at Canberra Airport. The first question asked of Barnard was 'How would a Labor government respond if it discovered ICBMs were based at Pine Gap in Central Australia?' Barnard, who was about to become defence minister, instantly replied it would not be a problem, although 'some party hotheads' might object. The two US embassy officials attending the meeting were aghast: they knew Whitlam would never host nuclear weapons but might accept Pine Gap's intelligence-gathering role. They indicated that they wanted me—attending as a staff member—to clarify Labor's position. I said it was widely understood that Pine Gap was linked to intelligence-gathering satellites, but Whitlam would reject the presence of nuclear weapons. I wouldn't normally have spoken, but I knew Barnard's unthinking acquiescence could create a furore on the eve of the election if the notoriously anti-Labor Ambassador Rice leaked it.

Other senior ministers were less accommodating than Barnard. Clyde Cameron found it amusing to ask Rice if the US would 'send in the marines' if Labor nationalised the economy—something the government had no intention of doing. The CIA station chief, John Walker, told me later in New York that he sometimes had a drink with Cameron, whom he'd first met in Paris in the 1950s while working on the agency's programs to infiltrate trade unions. Walker said he was surprised that Cameron became a such a bitter critic of Whitlam after the PM sacked him from Cabinet. Cameron told me he had drinks with Walker in Canberra but couldn't remember him from Paris. Other Labor figures sought to ingratiate themselves with US diplomats by warning them that a leading Labor frontbencher, Jim Cairns, was terribly radical. US concerns grew when Cairns replaced the hapless Barnard as deputy leader in the ballot following Labor's May 1974 election victory. The US fears were misplaced: Cairns focused more on a personal affair with a staff member than on fidelity to his previously held positions. Whitlam correctly predicted that Cairns wouldn't ask for a briefing on Pine Gap—to which he was entitled as deputy PM.

Soon after the election, Whitlam, who hated breaking election promises, tried to please the Americans by abandoning his commitment to tell the public what the US bases in Central Australia did. He made no substantive comment at a press conference after US president Richard Nixon embarked on a massive air attack on Hanoi, Haiphong and other parts of North Vietnam in late December 1972. The 'Christmas bombing' campaign involved the largest-ever deployment of B-52 bombers, each capable of carrying up to 40 tonnes of bombs, supported by a wide range of other combat aircraft. The US subsequently agreed to peace terms on essentially the same basis as the North Vietnamese had proposed.

Many leaders and commentators around the globe condemned the bombing, with some highly regarded US journalists denouncing the onslaught as 'war by tantrum' and the act of a 'maddened tyrant'.[3] Whitlam merely sent a polite private letter to Nixon, written by Keith 'Spats' Waller, the experienced head of the Foreign Affairs Department, arguing that the bombing was counterproductive and negotiations needed to resume. When Nixon got the letter he flew into an uncontrolled rage. The outrage of his national security adviser, Henry Kissinger, was equally irrational: he objected to the letter's call for both sides to resume negotiations, and angrily complained to an Australian embassy official that Whitlam had put an 'ally on the same level as our enemy'.[4] Would Kissinger have preferred that Whitlam call for only the US to resume negotiations but not its enemy? Marshall Green, then an assistant undersecretary of state for East Asia and the Pacific, who happened to be in Nixon's office when Whitlam's letter arrived, later said it 'was perfectly understandable and reasonable, but the president took great offence'.[5]

The record of conversation of a meeting of the PM with Ambassador Rice on 8 January 1973 shows that Whitlam said he would keep the US bases, which didn't appear to harm Australia and could help the US, but added, 'If there were any attempt to "screw us or bounce us" inevitably these arrangements would become a matter of contention.'[6]

The US opposed Whitlam's plans to withdraw the 1700 Australian troops in Singapore as part of his government's policy to drop the forward-defence doctrine and improve relations with Indonesia. The US said the withdrawal could undermine the Five Power Defence Arrangement (FPDA) signed in 1971 between Singapore, Malaysia, Australia, New Zealand and Britain. This arrangement did not require the permanent stationing of Australian, British or New Zealand troops in either country. There were no external threats to either Malaysia or Singapore at that time; nor have there been at any time since. A secret briefing paper from the Defence Department considered the FPDA mainly as a restraining influence on Singapore and Malaysia, whose relations were uneasy. In contrast to stereotypical views of Defence thinking, the brief said the English-educated leadership in Singapore could sometimes present the more plausible case to the European observer, but the Malays had a case to put: 'There are 130 million of them, Indonesians included. Singapore has only 2 million rich aliens living off their ability to skim cream from the regional economy.'[7] The paper also said, 'Singaporean military thinking countenances the possible need to make a lodgement in the Malayan Peninsula, e.g. to protect Singapore's water supplies.'[8]

Australia's withdrawal was complicated by the fact that the new government didn't know that some troops in Singapore intercepted communications for Australia's signals intelligence agency, the Defence Signals Division. After he was briefed, Whitlam reluctantly agreed to a slower withdrawal. Following an article in the US magazine Ramparts referring to the DSD's role in Singapore, the National Times reported on 12 February 1973 that the delay in the troop withdrawal was due to the DSD presence, which was unknown to Singapore. The US then falsely accused Whitlam of leaking the DSD information and ordering ASIO to stop targeting the Australian Communist Party. The interim head of the CIA James Schlesinger, asked the Australian ambassador, James Plimsoll, to see him with the rabidly anti-Labor head of counterintelligence, James Angleton, on 20 March. Plimsoll pointed out that ASIO still targeted the Communist Party and that Ramparts had named an ex-US intelligence official as the source of the DSD leak.[9]

Another Whitlam policy goal was achieved when the SEATO partners agreed in September 1975 to wind up the organisation. Despite its name, SEATO only ever had two South Asian members—Thailand and the Philippines—and six outsiders. It was a front for US power in South-East Asia, and vanished without trace.

Historian James Curran says Nixon didn't have time to talk to Marshall Green before Green took over as ambassador to Canberra in February 1973, but they had a brief discussion at a White House lunch, in which Nixon said of Whitlam, 'Marshall, I can't stand that cunt.' Green later said it was 'a strange kind of parting instruction to get from your President'.[10] After settling in as ambassador, Green accepted that Whitlam's centre-left Labor government was broadly similar to governments the US had managed to live with in Europe. From a broader perspective, it is difficult to think of a senior US diplomat at that time who was more in tune with aspects of Whitlam's larger global perspective than Green. He told me, 'It is now the American century, but East Asia—not the Pacific Rim—will be the next century.'[11]

Whitlam was deeply annoyed by the failure of the US to tell Australia that the North West Cape base was being used to communicate a general nuclear alert to US forces in the Western Pacific and the Indian Ocean during the Yom Kippur War in October 1973. This legitimate complaint enraged Kissinger and Schlesinger, the latter having become defence secretary in July 1973.

The secret report of the talks between Barnard and Schlesinger in Washington on 10 January 1974 (see Chapter 16) exposed Schlesinger's woeful ignorance of the pacifist influence in postwar Japan. He warned that the partial embargo on exports imposed in October 1973 by the newly established Organization of the Petroleum Exporting Countries (OPEC) could trigger the re-emergence of Japan's extreme prewar nationalism, and raised the prospect of a rearmed Japan establishing a 'quasi co-prosperity sphere' in the Middle East—a reference to Japan's prewar attempt to impose a co-prosperity sphere in the Pacific following a US embargo on supplying raw materials.[12] In language sounding like a parody of Cold War hyperbole, Schlesinger said that if the Soviets dominated Persian Gulf oil it would lead to 'the decline of the Western civilised world as we know it'.[13] He was also concerned that Japan had been attempting to buy Siberian oil: Japan was sensibly diversifying its supplies, but Schlesinger could only view this through a Cold War lens.

After Green left the Canberra posting in 1975, he was belatedly replaced by a Texas businessman, James Hargrove, whose priorities became clear at a lunch he invited me to in September 1976 (I covered energy for the *AFR*). I was the only guest and had barely sat down before Hargrove spread out large geological maps of the Great Barrier Reef and asked which areas were most likely to have oil. I said the recent royal commission on the reef had suggested there wasn't much oil there, but, more pertinently, drilling would never be allowed. Hargrove disagreed, saying his potential partner and good friend, Queensland premier Joh Bjelke-Petersen, was confident drilling would occur. Hargrove departed Australia without leaving any mark on the political or diplomatic landscape or extracting oil from the reef.

Some of the petty US techniques intended to belittle Whitlam only diminished Kissinger's reputation as a statesman. For example, he once rolled out a metre less of red carpet for Whitlam than for the visiting New Zealand Labour PM, Norman Kirk, whose protest letter about the Christmas bombing of Hanoi had been as strong as Whitlam's.[14] Curran notes that other leaders were on the receiving end of Kissinger's threats, bluffs and petulance. The UK's Conservative leader, Edward Heath, ignored Kissinger's fury after Heath adopted a more Europe-oriented foreign policy and refused to reverse Britain's military withdrawal from South-East Asia.[15] After Labour's Harold Wilson cut UK defence spending, Kissinger's threats to cancel intelligence sharing and nuclear cooperation proved nothing more than bluster.

Whitlam's worst foreign-policy mistake was to condone Indonesia's preparations to invade Portuguese Timor in December 1975, but the damage to his reputation was nothing compared to the dreadful suffering of the East Timorese people for twenty-five years after the invasion. Thanks to a JIO leak, Peter Hastings reported in detail on the Indonesian military's invasion plans in the *Sydney Morning Herald* on 21 February 1975; the Indonesians then delayed action. One of Hastings' long-term friends, JIO head Gordon Jockel, was concerned that the invasion, which some moderate generals opposed, would strengthen the political influence of the hawkish generals to Australia's long-term detriment. The head of Defence's strategic and international policy division, Bill Pritchett, wrote a briefing note to Whitlam on October 1975 warning him of the potential pitfalls and correctly predicting that an Indonesian invasion would cause many Timorese to resort to guerilla warfare. Pritchett said, 'The Australian domestic reaction would probably make it very difficult for the government to sustain cooperative policies towards Indonesia.'[16] He explained that 'Indonesia is the country most favourably placed to attack Australia … An attack would not necessarily involve such major changes in the global strategic order as would critically affect US interests compared to an attack by, for example, Japan. US involvement in support for Australia would therefore be more uncertain.' He said the Timor issue might develop in such a way as to identify Australia in Indonesian eyes 'as an adversary, or at least an unsympathetic and unhelpful neighbour', and that Defence had advocated very early on a policy with reasonable prospects of meeting the basic requirements of all the parties—namely, the acceptance of an independent state of East Timor. He said this would satisfy the demand for self-determination and move the Indonesians away from confrontation, as they would gain because the new territory would be heavily dependent on Indonesia's support and on Australia.

Pritchett's advice fell on deaf ears.[17] The enduring relevance of Pritchett's warning was demonstrated by the United States' refusal to meet John Howard's request for American 'boots on the ground' during the tense military stand-off with Indonesia in East Timor in 1999.

The petulant US treatment of Whitlam contrasts with the way the US usually accommodated the behaviour of Bob Hawke's Labor government—behaviour that would have enraged Nixon and Kissinger. The Hawke Government criticised the US mining of Nicaraguan harbours, supported a South Pacific nuclear-free zone, backed sanctions on South Africa for its apartheid policy, and objected to Ronald Reagan's Star Wars weapons because they destabilised the nuclear balance. The US did not publicly object when Foreign Minister Bill Hayden described those who objected to any criticism of ANZUS as 'craven and servile'.[18]

Politically, Whitlam's worst decision was to let his irascible energy minister, Rex 'The Strangler' Connor, pursue his obsession with using a con man, Tirath Khemlani, after November 1974 to seek a $4 billion petrodollar loan from the Middle East. The headstrong minister kept searching after Cabinet withdrew his authority on 20 May 1975. Although Whitlam did not find out until later, Marshall Green cabled back to Washington in July, 'There is every indication [Connor] is still exploring the possibility of a large overseas loan.'[19] The political impact of the 'loans affair' was disastrous. Without it, there is a good argument that Malcolm Fraser would not have been able to convince his colleagues to block the budget, thus removing the governor-general's justification for sacking Whitlam.

The Treasury head, Fred Wheeler, was so concerned about the petrodollar loans that he broke the law by taping his phone calls as part of a wider investigation. The transcripts, which were later leaked to the *National Times*, gave a disturbing account of the frenzied hunt for the elusive loan.[20] The US was deeply worried about any threat to Wall Street's dominant role in recycling petro-dollars, and Australia's search for a big loan in the Middle East became another black mark against the Whitlam Government. There would have been nothing wrong with bypassing Wall Street and seeking a Middle East loan using official channels, but Connor ignored warnings not to use intermediaries. By the time the Saudi Arabian Monetary Authority offered to lend in 1975, it had become political poison to touch a petro-dollar loan from any source.

The immense cost to Labor of this incident provides a salutary lesson about the damage secrecy can cause. Had Khemlani's role been made public at the start, the reckless decision would have been reversed in a day or two rather than remaining at the centre of a political scandal drawn out over nine months before Whitlam sacked Connor. I later discovered that the FBI arrested Khemlani in 1981. A New York court convicted him on charges relating to $2 million in stolen bonds previously held by the Mafia, but came to an agreement that saw him serve no jail time.[21]

The loans affair overshadowed the Whitlam Government's numerous enduring achievements. It introduced important structural reforms to open Australia's inward-looking industries to the global market, including the politically painful removal of rural subsidies, and importing frigates from the US rather than surrendering to intense pressure to build an Australian-designed light destroyer locally. Subsequent governments have supported the exceedingly costly policy of building submarines in Adelaide to uniquely Australian designs.

Few countries coped well with OPEC's unprecedented quadrupling of oil prices in 1973 and 1974, but thanks to a strong fiscal stimulus under Whitlam, Australia did not go into recession—unlike the US and the UK, which suffered long slumps. Australia was roughly in the middle of the international pack on inflation and better on unemployment, which rose to only 4 per cent. (It rose to almost 11 per cent in the early 1990s.)

When Whitlam died in 2014 at age ninety-eight, there was widespread recognition of the gains his government made for women, education, health, the environment, Aboriginal people, the arts and myriad other areas—gains that mostly survived the political turmoil of the time.

30

PUNISHING AN INNOCENT ALLY

'The [Nixon] administration was contemplating what course of action would have the most devastating domestic political effect.'

James Curran[1]

US and Australian intelligence officials made an early attempt to remove Whitlam as prime minister in 1973. Their failure didn't mean the idea was never resurrected. James Curran has revealed that 'some kind of covert CIA activity in Australian domestic politics' was at the very least considered by US policy-makers in 1974.[2] What had the Whitlam Government done on either occasion to warrant the possible resort to clandestine action? Whitlam hadn't burgled his political opponent's headquarters and covered it up; nor had he killed large numbers of people in Vietnam, Laos and Cambodia. Yes, there were the disputes with the US over issues such as the Christmas bombing of Hanoi, and more minor issues that caused disproportionate anger. Labor's approval of the opening of a Cuban consulate in Sydney in January 1974 enraged Kissinger, but this was innocuous compared with the US's attempts to assassinate Fidel Castro and the use of CIA mercenaries to invade the island.

Well before the 1974 discussions in Washington about how to damage the Labor government, senior US intelligence officers and renegade members of ASIO attempted to remove Whitlam. The PM was oblivious to the career history of a fervently anti-Labor US official, James Angleton, who tried to topple him. Angleton had headed the CIA's counterintelligence (spy-catching) division since 1954 until the CIA head, William Colby, sacked him in December 1974 because his briefings were incomprehensible and his wild accusations of treachery were driving good people out of the agency.[3] David Martin's book *Wilderness of Mirrors: Intrigue, Deception and Secrets* provides solid grounds for Colby to sack Angleton much earlier. David Wise does the same in *Molehunt: The Secret Search for Traitors that Shattered the CIA*. These authors and many others showed that from 1954 Angleton tore apart the CIA's Soviet section so thoroughly that it was impossible to imagine how a KGB mole could have caused more damage. Likewise, he undermined US foreign policy with unfounded allegations that foreign leaders were KGB agents.

Angleton supervised an extensive covert surveillance project called Operation Chaos against members of the American civil rights and anti-war movements. He also controlled a CIA network run by an ex-communist union leader, Jay Lovestone, that funded anti-communist unions in a large number of overseas countries, including Australia, and developed informers in others. One of the great lessons of Angleton's career is that obsessive secrecy and a lack of scrutiny can severely damage an organisation. It also demonstrates that elements within secret organisations can go rogue and undertake actions that aren't always approved by their political masters. Angleton would have been lucky to last a few weeks in a job where secrecy did not protect his tenure. By 1970 he was especially close to ASIO's deputy head, Jack Behm, and Bob Santamaria, the guiding hand behind the Democratic Labor Party, which helped keep the Australian Labor Party out of power until 1972.

Whitlam also knew little about Ted Shackley, even though he headed the CIA's East Asia division, which included Australia, for much of the time Whitlam was prime minister. Shackley was probably the agency's most experienced covert action operator. At age thirty-four he had headed JM/WAVE, a CIA program that conducted worldwide action against Castro's Cuba, and was part of another program that focused on assassinating Castro. Some of the Cubans working for Shackley joined him when he subsequently ran the CIA's 'secret' war in Laos, using mercenaries who were deeply entangled in drug trafficking.[4] More bombs were dropped on Laos than on Germany during World War II.[5] Around 80 million of these bombs did not explode, leaving a terrible legacy that continues to kill Laotians, especially children. The CIA achieved none of its objectives in Laos: the country still has a communist government.

After being promoted to Saigon station chief, Shackley subsequently headed the Western Hemisphere division, where his most important job was to foster the conditions for the removal of President Salvador Allende's elected government in Chile. The intervention culminated in Allende's death during General Augusto Pinochet's military coup in September 1973. Many of Pinochet's opponents were tortured, executed or 'disappeared' in secret prisons. Whitlam's withdrawal of two ASIS officers who had been posted to Chile to help the CIA was one of the many things that upset Shackley about the Labor government. He became head of the East Asia division in May 1973. Frank Snepp, who had worked for him in Saigon, said that when Shackley took over the East Asia division he ordered his staff to 'have no dealings whatsoever with the Australians ... [They] might as well be regarded as North Vietnamese collaborators.'[6]

Shackley's next job, which he took up in May 1976, was as deputy CIA director in charge of covert operations. It later emerged that he was a close friend of Edwin Wilson, a former CIA operative who in 1983 was convicted of illegally selling weapons to the Libyan dictator Muammar al-Gaddafi in the 1970s. A new CIA director, Stansfield Turner, sacked Shackley in 1979. Shackley later wrote a book, *The Third Option*, that made a case for covert action when neither diplomatic nor military efforts would work.

Not surprisingly, Attorney-General Lionel Murphy's 'raid' on ASIO's headquarters on 16 March 1973 greatly agitated Angeleton, who tried to have Whitlam removed shortly afterwards. The raid was prompted by Murphy's concern that the security preparations for the forthcoming visit by the Yugoslav prime minister, Džemal Bijedić, a Serb, were inadequate— the police had received credible threats regarding attempts to assassinate him, and there had been numerous acts of politically motivated violence by Croatians against Serbs, and vice versa, in Australia over many years. Murphy believed the former Coalition attorney-general Ivor Greenwood had prevented ASIO from investigating potentially violent Croatians, and found supporting evidence when ASIO's director-general, Peter Barbour, told him Greenwood had said that the *ASIO Act* stated it 'was only concerned with subversion against Australia and the Croatians were not involved in this'.[7]

An interdepartmental committee heard on 2 March 1973 that a police report said Croatian extremists might make another incursion into Yugoslavia.[8] On 15 March 1973, Murphy received information stating that the interdepartmental committee, including its ASIO representative, did not want to contradict Greenwood's relaxed attitude towards the Croats. He then asked ASIO's Canberra branch for a late-night meeting, where its staff produced a report of the committee meeting that said the briefing for Murphy's statement on the Croats 'should not be contrary or inconsistent to that of the previous government'.[9] The wording gave Murphy reasonable grounds to visit ASIO headquarters in Melbourne the next morning to find out what was going on. He was fully entitled to do so, and to examine files where necessary. Precisely what he authorised the Commonwealth Police to do is unclear, but they turned up at ASIO head-quarters before Murphy, sealed safes and confined staff to the auditorium as they arrived for work. None of this was necessary. Murphy should simply have told Barbour earlier that morning that he would be arriving to discuss Bijedić's visit.

Some senior staff who had been told by ASIO's Canberra office about Murphy's impending visit, however, removed files from the building before he arrived, without Barbour's consent According to confidential sources with an intimate knowledge of what happened, Barbour's deputy, Jack Behm, was involved in storing the files at Melbourne's City and Overseas Club—contrary to the rules about handling classified material. Understandably, the culprits didn't make a note for inclusion in ASIO files about their illicit action.

During the raid Murphy looked only at files he asked for relating to Croatian extremists,[10] but this didn't stop the delusional Angleton claiming in an interview with the ABC that Murphy had 'barged in and tried to destroy the delicate mechanism of internal security which had been built on patiently since World War II … Everything worried us. You don't see the jewels of counter-intelligence being placed in jeopardy by a party that has extensive historical contacts in Eastern Europe, that is seeking roads to Peking, when China used to be one of the major bases of the illegal NKVD [Soviet secret police agency] operations which encompassed Japan, Australia and New Zealand.'[11] Murphy didn't look at any counterintelligence 'jewels'—just skimpy files on Croatian extremists in Australia—and Whitlam, like Nixon, was right to seek a path to China.

After he retired, John Walker, the CIA's station chief in Australia for much of the Labor government's years, and I had lunch in New York in 1981. At that lunch he gave me some background on the attempt to remove Whitlam.[12] Walker was previously the CIA station chief in Israel, where he reported to Angleton instead of the head of the Near East division. He said dissatisfied ASIO staff in contact with Angleton initially suggested the move against Whitlam, and that Angleton, whom Walker greatly admired, considered Whitlam a 'serious threat' to the US. He said Angleton instructed him to get Barbour to publicly state that Whitlam had lied when he told parliament that the ASIO director hadn't complained to him about Murphy's visit; Whitlam would then supposedly be sacked for lying to parliament. Walker said that when asked to do this, Barbour refused. The record of the meeting taken by the head of the PM's Department, Sir John Bunting, contained nothing about a complaint, reinforcing Barbour's refusal to destroy a prime minister he was supposed to serve.

None of those involved in pressuring Barbour seemed concerned that it would be a serious espionage offence for CIA and ASIO officials to interfere in Australian politics in this manner. The job of Australia's counterintelligence organisation is to prevent espionage, not encourage it. The gently spoken Barbour was left in an invidious position where a significant proportion of senior officers strongly opposed his continued leadership. To Whitlam's discredit, he didn't realise that Barbour had acted honourably, unlike other ASIO officials.

Following Barbour's refusal to call Whitlam a liar, some disgruntled ASIO staff and ex-staff put Barbour under surveillance to establish if he was having an affair with a young woman who was his executive assistant.[13] The head of ASIO's Canberra branch, Colin Brown, told the Hope Royal Commission in August 1975 that Barbour's habit of travelling with his secretary was 'ill-advised, indiscreet and I think could well lead to someone asking a question in the House'.[14] Hope added this to other complaints that convinced Whitlam to dismiss Barbour in September 1975. In contrast, Whitlam had quickly rejected concerns that the JIO head, Gordon Jockel, could be a security risk because he lived with a young woman from Indonesia who was supposedly connected to that country's intelligence services.

Brown's concern for the proprieties of Barbour's travelling with his secretary—a common practice at departmental-head level—showed a certain chutzpah. During our lunch in New York, Walker told me that while Brown was head of ASIO's Canberra branch, he had an affair with Walker's wife, Diana.[15] Walker described Diana as very wealthy. She and Brown moved to the US after marrying in Canberra, with several senior ASIO staff as guests at the wedding. Walker, who was wealthy himself, told me 'I was angry about the affair, but found out too late for it to really affect my relationship with ASIO, where Brown was my principal point of contact'.[16] He also told me he was conscious of the irony that Shackley asked him to find out if Junie Morosi was having a relationship with a coalition shadow minister as well as Jim Cairns.[17] Almost no one in ASIO, including those who peddled vindictive rumours about Barbour's more innocuous activities, was concerned about Brown's relationship with the wife of a senior foreign intelligence officer.

Brown could see the problem, though. His former wife, Rosemary, wrote me a letter on 28 June 1981 in which she said the affair had been going on since 1973, but she had waited until the following year to confront her husband. She said she told him she would have to tell Walker about the 'two-edged sword' Brown was holding, but Brown told her she 'would destroy ASIO's relationship with the CIA' if she did.[18] As a result, she said, she did nothing, explaining that 'ASIO wives are very thoroughly brainwashed. So, in the name of the ASIO/CIA cause, a 34-year marriage was dissolved, a family broken and the ex-Mrs Brown left in midair with nothing.'[19]

Whitlam caused US intelligence officials further anxiety after the Soviet Union proposed setting up a joint ground station with Australia to photograph objects in space. In itself, there was nothing wrong with working cooperatively with the Soviets—Nixon had showed the benefits of doing so when he negotiated the SALT agreements. Whitlam strongly resented the pressure from Foreign Affairs and the US to reject the proposal, adding his own defiant caveat to the departmental answer prepared for a parliamentary question. On 3 April 1974 he told parliament: 'The Australian government takes the attitude that there should not be foreign military bases, stations, installations in Australia. We honour agreements covering existing stations. We do not favour extension or prolongation of any of those existing ones.'

Given that notice could be given on 10 December 1975 to terminate the Pine Gap agreement, alarm bells rang in Washington. Ambassador Green told the Foreign Affairs head, Alan Renouf, that, taken at face value, Whitlam's words 'represented a grave threat to the global Western balance against the Soviet Union, and ANZUS would be called into question'.[20] However, shutting Pine Gap would not have threatened the Western global balance against the Soviets, for the good reason that the latter did not even have a signals intercept satellite like Pine Gap's. This imbalance heavily favoured the US. What mattered was nuclear balance—each side had far more than enough weapons to deter the other. Nothing in ANZUS required Australia to host intelligence-gathering bases. Even if Whitlam shut Pine Gap, the US would still have its associated satellites, and they could be linked to ground stations elsewhere, such as Guam.

But once the satisfying taste of his rebellious parliamentary answer faded, Whitlam said the bases could stay. The obvious exception to tolerating the bases would have been if he had discovered that the US was actively undermining his government.

The US concerns about losing Pine Gap produced a serious reaction at the highest level. Before Nixon was forced to resign in August 1974, he commissioned National Security Study Memorandum 204. It was finalised in July. As set out by Curran, the central concern of the memorandum was how to assure the continued presence of the US facilities in Australia. It said Australia's desire for greater self-reliance in foreign policy was characterised by an 'aversion to anything that smacks of the Cold War or superpower condominium and by a desire to associate with the causes of the world's underprivileged'. Curran says James Schlesinger's recommendation, called Option One, took the hardest line. It proposed shifting the US bases out of Australia, reducing the flow of intelligence and the number of joint military exercises, increasing restrictions on US–Australia trade and capital flows, and adopting a 'vigorous reaction' to foreign policy initiatives that undercut the US position. Option One's value was said to be that it 'could undermine [the Labor government] with the Australian people, setting the stage for an opposition victory'.[21] As Curran said, 'It was a remarkable comment: the administration was contemplating what course of action would have the most devastating domestic political effect.'[22]

It's hard to reconcile this proposed foreign interference with some commentators' sneering dismissal of any suggestion the US seriously considered getting rid of the Whitlam Government. Option One was ultimately rejected as Pine Gap could be shut before being replicated elsewhere. The memorandum noted, 'It is less than certain that the government of Australia … will not exercise its option to terminate the existing agreement upon one year's notice after December 1975.'[23] Curran says the White House eventually decided to persevere with the Labor government, 'test and clarify Whitlam's intentions' over the remainder of 1974, and make 'selective use of pressure on Whitlam if necessary'.[24]

31
FRASER'S NARROW ESCAPE

'Disenchanted Australians ... agree with the Prime Minister [Whitlam] and blame the Liberal-Country coalition for the mess ... [Fraser's] ability to force an election has clearly been weakened.'

CIA analyst Dunning Idle IV, 8 November 1975[1]

The historian John Blaxland says that by early 1975, US concerns about the Whitlam Government had become more intense and its embassy officials confided to ASIO that the 'maintenance of the ALP government in power is essential to Soviet planning for this area'.[2] (There are no credible suggestions that the Soviets helped Labor.) In June 1975, US embassy officials issued another warning to ASIO, this time about how Whitlam was allegedly risking the bilateral intelligence relationship.[3] James Curran says a remark by the US ambassador to Australia, Marshall Green, to the US defence secretary in March 1975 'suggests a distinct edginess at the highest levels about the possible revelation of some kind of CIA activity in Australia'.[4]

The CIA had abundant opportunities to damage Whitlam, including the decision by Labor's energy minister, Rex Connor, to use the con man Tirath Khemlani to raise a large loan in the Middle East. In June 1976, an ASIO official told *The Bulletin*: 'Some senior ASIO men suspect ... there was a certain CIA involvement in the loans scandal. Some had expressed the thought that at least some of the documents which helped discredit the Labor government in its last year in office were forgeries planted by the CIA.'[5] The CIA had access to the intercepts of the flurry of telexes that Khemlani and other 'chancers' generated in the hunt for the money; these others included intermediaries with links to the CIA, such as Commerce International. The CIA revealed in answer to a freedom of information request that it held fourteen intelligence reports on this company, but it refused to release a word because of national security exemptions.[6]

By mid–1975 Khemlani had run up large travel expenses but hadn't received a cent from Connor. One well-placed Coalition source told me that the CIA had laundered US$400,000 through an American mining company to pay Khemlani to come to Australia on 14 October 1975 and release damning information about how Connor was still chasing a petro-dollar loan despite the withdrawal of his authority. My source had no obvious motive to lie, but said he couldn't break a confidence about how he knew the money was from the CIA rather than the mining company that stood to gain from Labor's demise.

The Opposition leader, Malcolm Fraser, used Khemlani's revelations to justify his announcement on 15 October 1975 that the Coalition would block the budget in the Senate to try to force an early election. Khemlani's New York associates also told me he had received a large sum of money during the loans affair; however, his lawyer refused a request for me to interview his client about the source of this money.[7] Although plausible, none of these claims show the CIA actually tried to destabilise the government in 1975 after undertaking some planning in 1974.

Whitlam continued to unnerve the White House after Fraser refused to pass the budget. He sacked the head of ASIS, Bill Robertson, on 21 October, prompting Governor-General Sir John Kerr to demand a full explanation. A month earlier, Whitlam had sacked Peter Barbour as head of ASIO after a recommendation from the Hope Royal Commission on Intelligence. In my view, both dismissals were unjustified.[8]

On 2 November, without supporting evidence, Whitlam accused the National Country Party (the junior Opposition partner) of accepting CIA funding. A US author with good intelligence sources said the CIA 'secretly poured money heavily into the opposition Liberal and National Country parties. The CIA wanted Whitlam out.'[9] It wouldn't be surprising if this happened: the CIA told the Pike congressional committee in the mid-70s that 32 per cent of all CIA covert action abroad consisted of 'election support—the largest single category'.[10]

I revealed in the *AFR* on 3 November 1975 that the CIA ran the Pine Gap base near Alice Springs, not the US Defense Department as Australian governments had previously claimed.[11] I reported that its first head was Richard Stallings, a CIA official. After the State Department denied this, the National Country Party leader, Doug Anthony, put a parliamentary question on notice on 6 November challenging Whitlam to confirm that Stallings worked for the CIA. Whitlam intended to do so when parliament resumed on 11 November, but couldn't because Kerr sacked him earlier that day.[12] Kerr's decision was hugely controversial, not least because he violated the fundamental constitutional convention that the leader with the majority in the House of Representatives (Whitlam) should be prime minister.

During the lead-up to these tumultuous events, a CIA analyst in the Canberra embassy, Dunning Idle IV, did a balanced, often insightful job of reporting to Washington. The public learnt what Idle was reporting after the *National Times* published extracts from leaked editions of the *National Intelligence Daily (NID)*, a four-page top-secret newsletter prepared for the president early each morning. Idle had bad news for those National Security Council members who Curran reported had assumed that destabilising Whitlam's government would lead to his defeat. Instead, by October 1975 it seemed US policy-makers might get their worst possible outcome: Fraser's defeat and the loss of Pine Gap.

Idle reported in *NID* on 8 November that the determination of the Australian Opposition to force a general election was weakening. He said Whitlam had managed to raise 'real alarm about the dire consequences of government bankruptcy, which he claims will result from the Opposition's blocking government appropriations. Disenchanted Australians ... agree with the Prime Minister and blame the Liberal–Country coalition for the mess ... Fraser this week offered to delay the election for six months—a proposal quickly rejected by the Prime Minister ... [Fraser's] ability to force an election has clearly been weakened.'[13]

Idle's analysis suggested that if Kerr had not sacked Whitlam on 11 November, the Coalition might have backed down and passed the budget. Idle had earlier reported for *NID*, on 22 October, that many Liberals privately agreed with Whitlam that the upper house had no right to block the budget. He said, 'Fraser has accomplished what no Labor Party leader could ever do. He has united the Labor Party and bound union leaders more tightly to it. Unpopular, weak, and apprehensive that they were losing their grip, party figures overnight had become fiercely angry, solidly united and ready for a fight.'[14] Several Coalition MPs, including the Liberals' deputy leader, Phillip Lynch, told me at the time that a backdown was a distinct possibility. If so, Labor would have been in a better position to perform credibly at the normal election due around

May 1977. It was a much improved government after Whitlam sacked three troublesome Cabinet ministers, Conner, Cairns and Cameron, in mid-1975 and replaced them with highly competent performers such as the new treasurer, Bill Hayden.

In the weeks leading up to 11 November, Whitlam increasingly angered senior members of the US government by speaking out about Pine Gap and the CIA. They realised he only had to stay in power until 10 December 1975 to give notice to end the Pine Gap agreement. Whitlam had given conflicting accounts of whether he would do so. Green told me that the US never knew where Whitlam really stood on this issue.[15] After Idle reported in *NID* on 8 November that Whitlam's prospects had greatly improved, the head of the CIA's East Asia division, Ted Shackley, promptly asked the ASIO liaison officer in Washington to pass on a strongly worded message to his director-general about how 'the CIA feels grave concern' about Whitlam's behaviour.[16] Shackley seemed to assume that Whitlam was to blame for leaks about Pine Gap, but Whitlam certainly had not leaked Stallings' name and occupation to me, while other journalists told me they relied on US sources. Shackley's telex said he wanted an answer from ASIO about whether Whitlam had changed his attitude to the bases, adding that CIA officials 'feel that if this problem cannot be solved, they do not see how mutually beneficial relationships are going to continue ... The CIA does not lightly adopt this attitude.' The telex greatly angered Whitlam, but his dismissal meant he could not give notice on 10 December 1975 to close Pine Gap as US officials had feared.

Given that it was already publicly known that Pine Gap was run by the CIA and linked to signals intelligence satellites, Victor Marchetti, a former senior CIA officer, later said Shackley was probably concerned about something else the CIA was doing in Australia 'that was really sensitive and had to be kept from the Australian people'.[17] A former US military officer with a detailed knowledge of the CIA, William Corson, told me in Washington in 1980 that Shackley had a continuing interest in the drug trade following his time as CIA station chief in Laos and Vietnam, and this was what concerned him about future revelations in Australia.[18] He said that CIA-sanctioned heroin trafficking out of Indochina involved bringing drugs into Australia via big US transport planes that landed at Richmond air force base outside Newcastle en route to Alice Springs, where they picked up large quantities of signals intelligence from Pine Gap. Corson said this made the planes immune to Customs inspection. Shackley was sacked in 1979 for having an unsanctioned relationship with Ed Wilson, who was convicted in 1983 of selling arms to the dictatorial Libyan regime.

Whitlam predominantly blamed Kerr for his demise, but gave a speech in parliament on 4 May 1977 in which he said a disturbing aspect to Shackley's telex was that he described his message as 'an official demarche on service to service link'—in other words, the elected government was not to be informed. Whitlam said, 'Implicit in the CIA's approach to ASIO for information on events in Australia was an understanding that the Australian organisation had obligations of loyalty to the CIA itself before its obligations to the Australian government. The tone and content of the CIA message [were] offensive; its implications were sinister. Here was a foreign intelligence service telling Australia's domestic security service to keep information from the Australian government.' In a follow-up parliamentary speech on 24 May 1977, he said the 'interests of the CIA are not necessarily those of Australia … Australia must be satisfied that American agents are not acting in a manner contrary to our interests as a nation. Are we to let an ally get away with something a rival would not be allowed to get away with?'

Shackley later told me in Washington that he wasn't worried about an adverse reaction from Whitlam—such as shutting Pine Gap—because he never expected ASIO to show the telex to him.[19] Although he denied giving Kerr a copy, he said he expected it would be shared with other members of the intelligence community because this was how things were done. This was true, but ASIO had changed under Barbour's leadership and its acting head, Frank Mahoney, accepted it could not withhold the contents of such a message from the government in a democratic society. Nevertheless, Blaxland maintained that there was no indication in ASIO files for the claim that Shackley's telex suggested that ASIO had obligations of loyalty to the CIA before its obligations to the Australian government. He said the cable was 'not underhanded'.[20] As Whitlam explained in parliament, that is precisely what it was and precisely what Shackley intended.

Blaxland made a more fundamental error when he alleged, 'Without seeking official confirmation [before 11 November] Whitlam declared that Stallings was a CIA operative … in charge of establishing the Pine Gap installation.' In fact, Whitlam had been briefed. Tange had officially informed him of this in October 1975 after the prime minister demanded an answer. It was a belated admission by Tange, who had lied in his first briefing to Whitlam in December 1972 by telling him the Pentagon ran the base. Whitlam only confirmed what I had already made public on 3 November 1975. Apparently, Blaxland didn't understand that only Defence gave briefings on Pine Gap. At that stage, ASIO had not been briefed.

32

SOME DISTINGUISHED GENTLEMEN FROM THE CIA

'The CIA [was involved] in some 900 foreign interventions over the past two decades.'

US journalist and historian Taylor Branch[1]

Bill Morrison, Labor's defence minister in 1975, threw new light on Whitlam's dismissal when he told journalist Andrew Clark, '[Governor-General Sir John] Kerr sought and received a high-level briefing from senior defence officials on a CIA threat to withdraw intelligence coopera-tion from Australia … I don't think it [the briefing] was decisive, but I think it reinforced his position [about sacking the government].'[2] Clark later told me Morrison had been 'completely lucid and his recollection sharp' when he said this.

I share Morrison's view that the briefing would not have been decisive but would have reinforced Kerr's decision to sack Whitlam on 11 November 1975. Morrison's information complements a conversation I had with the chief Defence scientist, John Farrands, at a midmorning function in the Senate gardens in April 1977. Much to the annoyance of Defence head Arthur Tange, Farrands enjoyed talking to journalists, subject to the common proviso that he'd deny saying anything that got him into trouble. (I made a note of the 1977 conversation about ten minutes after it ended.)

Farrands began by asking if I'd read anything good on science recently. When I told him about an article I'd just read in a US Army science journal—a rare occurrence—he laughed and said, 'We'll make a scientist of you yet.'[3] When I asked why he had visited Kerr on 28 October 1975, he said, 'That was just a cup of tea. You'd be much more interested in later on. Looking back, it's hard to understand what all the fuss was about.' He said that following the US complaints about Whitlam and Pine Gap, 'Tange ran around, making calls, meeting military chiefs, ministers and others. He told me to ring Kerr and fill him in.' Farrands did not mention, and may not have known, that according to Morrison, Kerr initiated the request for the briefing. Farrands said he called Kerr on 8 November and gave him a summary of the concerns about Whitlam.

I reported in the *AFR* a brief account of what Farrands had told me, without identifying him, and stated, 'There is no hard evidence that the briefing influenced Kerr's decision.'[4] Yet John Blaxland accused me of claiming that Whitlam's dismissal was the 'result' of Farrands' briefing of Kerr in 1975.[5]

Farrands rang me shortly after publication of my article to say he'd had a 'heated exchange' with Tange and was under intense pressure to deny the report. He said Tange had told him it was 'imperative that no one knows' about the briefing—he was particularly worried that Whitlam would think Tange had 'gone behind his back'. I told Farrands he knew what he'd said, and the call ended amiably. As expected, he subsequently denied the substance of what I reported, but not that we had spoken on each occasion.

Kerr saw himself as commander-in-chief of the Australian military and never hesitated to ask for briefings from Australian or US officials. There were ample opportunities for him to hear about the US concerns regarding Labor before Farrands' briefing. The US's and Tange's concerns were wildly overblown: Whitlam merely said the CIA ran Pine Gap, which was already public knowledge. The Soviet spy Christopher Boyce had answered that question for the Kremlin.

Kerr later denied that the Farrands briefing had occurred. It would have been surprising if he'd confirmed it—he'd copped savage criticism following the dismissal for violating one of the main constitutional conventions and for concealing his thinking from his prime minister. He did not assist his credibility by also denying that he'd had contact with US intelligence officials in the past. He had been president of LawAsia and deeply involved in the Australian Association for Cultural Freedom, each of which had received CIA subsidies, and had visited the US in 1967 to discuss further funding for LawAsia four months after it had been publicly identified as receiving CIA money.[6]

Whitlam's folly in appointing Kerr to the vice-regal post was another example of his appalling judgement of people. He seemed oblivious to the widely known fact that Kerr had been a strong critic of the Labor Party as far back the 1950s and had been involved with covert CIA-funded organisations in the 1960s that amounted to unacceptable foreign influence.

Whitlam's judgement about Tange was no better. Initially, he treated Tange as one of the traditional public servants he admired. But Tange saw himself as the ultimate 'keeper of the secrets'.[7] He deceived Whitlam in his initial briefing by saying that Pine Gap was run by the Pentagon rather than the CIA—something a prime minister had every right to know—and in November 1975, he attempted to bully and intimidate Whitlam.[8] Tange later explained that he didn't want to take defamation action against me over an article relating to November 1975 because he was concerned his case might 'be compromised by evidence that the Defence Department had, from occasional misjudgement rather than any plot, failed to inform its minister of certain things'.[9] Given that he'd deceived the prime minister, his caution was justified.

Andrew Hay, an influential ministerial staff member who had a major role in the Coalition's campaign to bring Whitlam down, told me in 2016 that he knew Tange wasn't loyal to Whitlam. (He called Tange 'Sir After Dark' because that was when Tange 'did his best work'.) Hay, a friend of mine, said Tange was 'operating behind the scenes to see the end of the Whitlam Government and that he [Hay] was hoping to write about it, but didn't have the energy to pull the files out'.[10]

After key US National Security Council documents were declassified, James Curran revealed that senior US policy-makers considered 'some kind of covert CIA activity in Australian domestic politics' in 1974, but apparently abandoned the idea later that year.[11] It's unclear if planning was revived in 1975 when Whitlam was considered a much bigger problem. Although Curran said he found no evidence of involvement in Whitlam's dismissal, he later explained that he meant no documented evidence was available, especially as many CIA documents are unavailable. The expatriate Australian journalist Phillip Knightley, who reported widely on intelligence issues for the London *Times*, said the whole point of a covert intelligence operation is to leave no trace, so there need be 'no paper in the CIA archives setting out how the Whitlam Government could be destabilised'.[12] Moreover, the United States could have used another clandestine agency such as Naval Intelligence Unit Task Force 157, which John Walker told me was doing something in Sydney and Melbourne while he was CIA station chief in Australia, but he didn't know what it was.[13]

Many American politicians and journalists had no trouble acknowledging in the 1970s that the US engaged in unacceptable forms of foreign interference. The CIA was established in large measure to engage in conspiracies on behalf of the US government, and has done so on numerous occasions. The *New York Times Magazine* reported on 13 September 1976 that congressional investigations had shown that the CIA, 'in some 900 foreign interventions over the past two decades, has run secret wars around the globe and has clandestinely dominated foreign governments so thoroughly as to make them virtual client states ... Distinguished gentlemen from the CIA hatched assassination plots with Mafia gangsters.' The revelations largely stopped following Bill Colby's sacking as CIA director on 2 November 1975 for being too willing to comply with congressional requests for sensitive information.[14]

Informed discussion of the Whitlam era deserves a more mature approach than lazy attempts to brand discomforting information as part of a conspiracy theory.[15] In this context, it's worth noting that in August 1978, Richard Holbrooke, the assistant secretary of state who investigated claims that something untoward happened in Australia, said, 'I cannot vouch for the fact that nothing improper was done by the CIA during the Whitlam Government. I can't be sure.'[16] It is also worth remembering that a former US consul general in Melbourne acknowledged that the CIA intervened in Australian politics in the 1960s.[17]

In 1975 the CIA replaced John Walker as its station chief in Canberra with Milton Wonus, from its science and technology division. Wonus, who had a specialised knowledge of Pine Gap, reported to Ted Shackley in Washington. Like other gentlemen from the CIA, he enjoyed partying with an eclectic mix of guests. Walker told me in New York in 1981 that Wonus (who was known by his middle name, Corley) often spent time in Kings Cross where he hung out at a bar and restaurant owned by US businessman Bernie Houghton. Houghton was a key figure in the Nugan Hand Bank, which was notorious for money laundering, drug and arms dealing, and offering to make donations to political parties.[18] Shackley told me in Washington that he had used Houghton to shift money for the CIA when he was in Vietnam and Laos, and that one of the partners in the Nugan Hand Bank, Michael Hand, had worked for him in covert military operations in Laos before becoming a 'banker'.[19] Houghton also had Australian intelligence connections: police investigators found that when he arrived without a valid visa at Sydney Airport on 12 February 1972, an immigration official wrote on his file: 'Vouched for by ... Mr Leo Carter, ASIO'.[20] Carter was ASIO's New South Wales head. Houghton's passport was stamped 'A', allowing him to stay in Australia for as long as he wanted. The Stewart Royal Commission on Nugan Hand stated that Hand was also given special treatment by immigration in 'irregular' circumstances.[21]

Against this backdrop, former CIA officer Kevin Mulcahy phoned me in mid-1981 after I had returned from a Washington posting, saying he wanted me to come back to Washington so he could tell me about a detailed explanation 'Corley' (Wonus) had given him about what the agency had done in Australia in 1975. I explained that my workload meant I couldn't return until later. Mulcahy had earlier told me that he'd become a friend of Wonus while working with him in the CIA's science and technology division. Mulcahy died in October 1981, not long after the phone call, but I have no reason to doubt the official verdict that there were no suspicious circumstances. Without knowing what Wonus had told Mulcahy, I had no article to write.

Seymour Hersh, who'd introduced me to Mulcahy in Washington, said Mulcahy was a prosecution witness who had helped obtain the indictment of Ed Wilson for offences related to the illegal sale of weapons and explosives to the Libyan dictator Muammar al-Gaddafi and providing terrorist training.[22] Formerly a CIA employee, Wilson was a covert operative in Naval Intelligence Unit Task Force 157. In 1979, a new CIA head, Stansfield Turner, sacked Shackley for not reporting his unsanctioned relationship with Wilson. In the same year, Wilson also met with Houghton five times in Switzerland.[23]

33
EMBRACING IGNORANCE

'There are a number of conversations that would make it unwise for his allegations about CIA activity in Australia to be rejected out of hand.'
ASIO officer Mike Leslie[1]

Australian officials did not want to know about Christopher Boyce's claims that he had learnt in a highly sensitive job that the CIA had deceived the Australian government and interfered in Australian politics and unions. The FBI arrested Boyce in the US in January 1977 and charged him with selling secrets to the Soviets. Boyce said that he had found out about the deception and interference while working in the code room at TRW, the Californian firm that basically operated Pine Gap and its associated Rhyolite satellites for the CIA. Although allegations of foreign interference should concern a counterintelligence organisation, senior officials in ASIO, Foreign Affairs and Defence didn't want to find out.

ASIO's Washington liaison officer, Mike Leslie, was the honourable exception. Much to the discomfort of his superiors, he proposed inter- viewing Boyce in jail without anyone from the CIA present. He insisted, 'If it is desired to establish the truth or otherwise of Boyce's allegations, the only course open is for us to ask him questions.'[2] After he told ASIO headquarters, as quoted above, that it would be unwise to reject Boyce's allegations out of hand, he followed up by saying, 'So far, nothing has emerged which renders his allegations incredible.'[3] In addition to Boyce's claims of day-to-day CIA deception of the Australian government and its alleged interference in trade unions, Leslie wanted to know what Boyce had told the Soviets that might affect Australian security.

The telex messages ASIO headquarters sent back to Leslie—reinforced by strong advice from the heads of Defence and Foreign Affairs—urged him to hold off doing the interview. Referring to a redacted section in a 2 May 1977 telex to HQ, however, Leslie argued: 'These and certain other items give the strong impression that [Boyce's] comments on CIA involvement with the trade unions in Australia and his access to KW7 cypher equipment (which would partly account for his knowledge) are not without foundation.'[4]

Following US government claims that former CIA official Victor Marchetti had put Boyce up to making these allegations, Leslie telexed on 13 May, 'There are more corroborative indicators that Boyce did know of CIA activities through his employment at TRW than that Marchetti put him up to it.'[5]

A top-secret telex from ASIO's acting director-general on 16 May 1977 ordered Leslie to delay any interview, saying that he would appreciate that 'This whole concern is a very hot political potato and I think it would be unwise for you to interview Boyce at this time. It could be seen as ASIO interfering, or ASIO trying to paper over alleged cracks, although it would be neither. There would of course be no guarantee that what Boyce told you was the truth and certainly no way of checking out his information.'[6] Equally, there was no way for ASIO to know whether the CIA's denials were truthful.

Leslie was not allowed to read a classified report from the CIA director, Stansfield Turner, to a congressional committee, but he telexed HQ on 22 June 1977: 'There would appear to be no foundation to Boyce's claims.' Nevertheless, the New York Times Los Angeles bureau head, Robert Lindsey, regarded Boyce as credible after getting to know him while working on the book he wrote on the case, The Falcon and the Snowman. Boyce gave the FBI previously unknown details about what he had given the Russians, even though this resulted in him getting a longer sentence. He said he handed over photos he'd taken of encryption ciphers, data on the Rhyolite and Argus satellite programs, message traffic and a study of future intelligence needs—thousands of documents in total.[7] He also told them that messages had sometimes been mistakenly sent about military traffic and other programs.[8] Lindsey said Boyce was disturbed by the US's behaviour when he read CIA telex messages showing its Australian agents had infiltrated the leadership of Australian unions.[9] Using intelligence and other sources, Lindsey discovered that the election of Gough Whitlam's Labor government in December 1972 sent jitters through the CIA, which 'wanted Whitlam out'.[10]

Bill Pinwill, the first Australian journalist to interview Boyce in jail, quoted him as saying that CIA officers had a 'deep distrust of the Whitlam government' and took a close interest in the blocking of the 1975 budget.[11] Pinwill reported in the same article that Boyce said, 'Joe Harrison, the senior CIA "resident" at TRW, described the Governor General as "our man Kerr".' Boyce referred to this alleged CIA description of Kerr in an interview with CBS's *60 Minutes* program on 21 November 1982. He also told Australian journalist Ray Martin that the TRW security head, ex-CIA officer Rick Smith, had explained that he found out from a briefing that the agency withheld information from Australian governments.[12] Referring to late 1975, Boyce said in the Martin interview that CIA officials complained that Whitlam wanted to know what was going on at Pine Gap and by 'publicising it, was compromising the integrity of the system'. It was a typical arrogant presumption that the elected prime minister had no right to know what was happening on Australian soil. Whitlam didn't reveal any secrets. Boyce, not Whitlam, compromised the system's integrity—and he did so right under the nose of the CIA.

So what records did Defence give the NAA about Boyce's activities? After I asked to see the archives, they replied on 29 February 2016 that they had been unable to locate any records relating to this request among the Defence records in their custody. Nor were there any records in the archives from the Foreign Affairs and Prime Minister's departments about Boyce. Only ASIO was forthcoming with the documents quoted above.

The US has long deployed undercover intelligence officers in Australia. But in the 1970s Australian officials didn't want to know about this any more than they wanted to know about Boyce. The CIA's long-serving head of counterintelligence, James Angleton, ran a network of subordinates designated as 'labor attachés' in US overseas posts.[13] Not all were undercover CIA officials, but they all came under Angleton's effective control. The US used these and other channels to fund supportive unions and politicians, and counter communist influence in other unions. It also funded trips to the US for selected unionists. The historian David McKnight found US archival documents revealing that dozens of Australian union leaders took advantage of these 'freebies'.[14] He said the distribution lists for typical cables from the labor attachés in Australia showed that the CIA received over three times more reports from the attachés than the US Labor Department, which supposedly employed them.[15]

Even though some of the US labor attachés were undeclared CIA officers, both the official ASIO history and the Hope Royal Commission stated that there were no undeclared CIA officers in Australia. The denials were naive, although qualified in Hope's case by a statement that ASIO 'had very little information on these matters and still less curiosity'.[16] The official ASIO history states that the royal commission's secretary, George Brownbill, said US senator Frank Church told him that Australia was 'exempt' from US intelligence collection activities.[17] This is demonstrable nonsense. As noted in Chapter 31, in 1975 Dunning Idle IV was collecting and sending back intelligence on Australia's political situation for the CIA's *National Intelligence Daily*, even though collecting intelligence on Australia was not an authorised part of his declared job of liaising with Australia's JIO. Moreover, CIA officials had interfered directly in Australian politics in the 1960s.[18]

Before stating that clandestine US intelligence operations never occurred in Australia, the official historian should also have looked at a December 1973 ASIO minute written after Defence Minister Lance Barnard directed his departmental head, Arthur Tange, to conduct an inquiry on whether there were any US intelligence activities directed against Australia's military interests. The acting director-general, Colin Brown, said in the minute that Tange's inquiries followed the CIA's decision to take court action to prevent publication of the book *The CIA and the Cult of Intelligence* by Marchetti and John D. Marks. Brown said the CIA told Tange that the book's original text made numerous references to Australia and New Zealand. The CIA required all such references to be removed from the draft, with one exception: a statement that US military forces 'used secret agents in Australia for obtaining information'.[19] Tange asked Brown 'whether ASIO had any means of checking on the likelihood of such activities having taken place in the past or currently taking place'.[20] Brown said, 'I pointed out that to identify undercover agents of the US in Australia (if any) would be as difficult as it is to identify Soviet illegal residents since the high standard of training of both make detection difficult.'[21]

Brown, who was an admirer of the CIA and its station chief's wife, with whom he had an affair, said, 'To the best of my knowledge we were unaware of any US intelligence activity directed against Australia.' A more candid answer would have been that ASIO didn't know because it didn't try to find out. Even so, it was hardly a blunt denial.

Because Marchetti had been a special assistant to the CIA's deputy director, Richard Helms, and his co-author, Marks, had a similar job with the State Department's Bureau of Intelligence and Research, they were able to provide a wealth of information in *The Cult of Intelligence*. The CIA initially deleted over 300 sections of the book, and following court action 168 remained redacted.

There is little doubt the US had adequate resources to undertake clandestine operations in Australia. Bill Darcy reported in the Sydney *Sun* on 4 May 1974 that Marchetti had told him the US had twenty to thirty clandestine operatives in Australia. Marchetti also said that his close friend Richard Stallings found out while heading Pine Gap that some of these operations included funding the Liberal and Country parties. Given that the agency's head, Bill Colby, described the election of the Whitlam Government as a 'crisis', it would not be surprising if he allocated ample resources to the 'crisis'.[22]

To my knowledge, one undeclared CIA officer, Claire Hutchings, was in Canberra from early 1974 to late 1977. Now long retired, she held a more senior position than her husband, Burt Hutchings, a declared CIA liaison officer with ASIO. The official diplomatic list for that period simply refers to her as Mrs Hutchings, wife of Burt. The NAA has located records of his arrivals and departures, but none for Claire Hutchings (or Hutchens)— although illegal undeclared officers commonly use an assumed name for travel. Hutchings used her married name in her social activities in Australia. I know that one ASIO officer knew about her clandestine role while she worked as a language specialist at ANU. This officer, who was a friend of both the Hutchings, should have told the director-general that Claire was an undeclared intelligence official of a foreign power. His failure to do so illustrates the difficulties of relying on ASIO to conduct an effective counterintelligence operation against its dominant partner. It also demonstrates why there is no reason to believe ASIO assurances that there are no undeclared CIA officers in Australia. The specifics of Hutchings' undercover work are unclear, but apparently it didn't include spying on ANU academics.

Hutchings conducted a sexual relationship with a senior Whitlam Government minister of interest to the US. Later, in Washington, I confirmed the relationship. The minister told me Hutchings sometimes brought along another woman friend to join these activities, which he described in convincing detail. He also said he was aware, and amused, that Hutchings was married to a CIA official in the embassy. I only learnt later that she was also a member of the CIA, so I couldn't mention this added appeal to the minister. It is not clear if Hutchings' ministerial liaison related to her CIA job or was strictly recreational.

PART 5

AUSTRALIA'S SOVEREIGNTY CLAIMS—THE AMBITIOUS TO THE SUPINE

34

AUSTRALIA'S EXPANSIONIST AMBITIONS

'No nation owns Antarctica. A passport is not required to enter ... [There is] free access for scientific investigation and other peaceful pursuits.'

US State Department[1]

Despite fears that some other country will seize its Antarctic 'territory', Australia doesn't own any part of that continent—never has and never will. Its claims have always lacked international recognition except from a handful of other countries with claims. The reality is that Australia ratified the 1961 Antarctic Treaty that put all territorial claims on indefinite hold, demilitarised the continent, and promotes international scientific cooperation. The treaty, which excludes any new claim, or the enlargement of an existing one, during its unlimited life, was achieved mainly because US president Dwight D. Eisenhower and USSR president Nikita Khrushchev talked to each other in the interests of international cooperation.

Hardly any countries recognised the earlier territorial claims to Antarctica, including Australia's continuing claim to 42 per cent of the continent. Six other nations—Argentina, Chile, France, New Zealand, Norway and the UK—claim a total of around 38 per cent, and about 20 per cent is unclaimed. Australia, Chile and Argentina also claim exclusive economic zones (EEZs) to offshore areas around the Antarctic mainland. Australia's claim to this extra 2 million square kilometres is audacious, avaricious and invalid.

Australia also claims EEZs around Heard Island and McDonald Islands in the sub-Antarctic, about 4100 kilometres south-west of Perth, and around Macquarie Island, about 1500 km south of Hobart. Macquarie Island is closer to New Zealand's Invercargill than to Hobart. When Australia's claims elsewhere are included, it has the largest jurisdictional claim to an area of the earth's surface—around 27.2 million square kilometres. About half of this is over ocean or sea.[2]

The Antarctic Treaty's ban on enlarging an existing claim explains why almost no other country accepts Australia's EEZs. The US State Department sent a formal note to the Foreign Affairs Department on 31 March 1995 pointing out: 'It is a well-established principle that the sovereign rights over an EEZ ... derive from the sovereignty of the coastal state over adjacent land territory ... The US must reiterate its long-standing position that does not recognize any claim to territories in Antarctica.'[3] The US also stated the accepted international position on Antarctica: 'No nation owns Antarctica. A passport is not required to enter ... [There is] free access for scientific investigation and other peaceful pursuits.'[4] These facts did not stop the *Sydney Morning Herald*'s international editor, Peter Hartcher, writing in that paper on 29 January 2019 that Australia 'has sovereignty over 42 per cent' of the Antarctic. The fact that it doesn't have sovereignty suggests the US would not spend blood and treasure to protect Australia's imaginary 42 per cent. It also means that Australia can't stop any other country establishing scientific research facilities there. Australia's own research efforts are meagre, which is why its scientists welcome the chance to collaborate with American, Chinese, Russian, Indian and South Korean research facilities within Australia's defunct claim.

In 1991, the treaty was amended to impose a ban on minerals exploration; this is due for renegotiation in 2048. The widely anticipated outcome is that no country will be able to unilaterally begin mining or petroleum production. If the new agreement doesn't preserve the Antarctic as an international wilderness, it is likely to allow limited commercial development with the proceeds partly shared on a global basis. Australia's chances of reviving its implausible claim to own 42 per cent of the continent are nil.

Australia's claims to waters around islands near Indonesia may be more precarious than many assume. Christmas Island is only 360 kilometres south of Java, but it is 1560 kilometres from the closest part of the West Australian coast, at Exmouth. Once a British colony administered from Singapore, the island was only handed over to Australia in 1958. Its population of about 1400 are mainly descended from indentured labourers brought from Malaya to work in the island's now-depleted phosphate mines. The Indonesian parliament has so far refused to ratify a 1997 treaty to establish an EEZ with Australia, even though the Indonesian government accepted the dividing line back in 1997. Growing Indonesian power suggests the line will eventually be redrawn.

Indonesia accepts Australian sovereignty over the Ashmore and Cartier islands south of the Indonesian island of Rote. These islands are 320 kilometres off Australia's north-west coast and less than 80 kilometres from Rote. In 1933, Britain handed formal administration of them to Australia, which initially allowed controlled access for traditional Indonesian fishers whose forebears had lived there intermittently. The CIA's 2018 *World Factbook* notes: 'Australia has closed parts of the Ashmore and Cartier reserve to Indonesian traditional fishing; Indonesian groups challenge Australia's claim to Ashmore Reef.'[5] Although it might seem to undermine its emphasis on protecting the nation's sovereign borders, the government excised Christmas Island and the Ashmores from our immigration zone in 2001 to prevent anyone who reaches them from claiming asylum in Australia.

The potentially lucrative rights to petroleum resources that Australia won in a favourable seabed agreement with Indonesia in 1972 no longer seem politically viable. Back then, Australia conducted illegal espionage to gain inside information about Indonesia's negotiating position. Although this was not the only factor, the 1972 agreement gave Australia rights to what was on or below the seabed, covering a much bigger area than would have occurred if the boundaries had been based on the median line.[6]

Changes in international law, and the strategic imperative for Australia to get along with Indonesia in future, have altered the negotiating context. An Indonesian push for a boundary that reflects the 1994 Law of the Sea's clear preference for a median line will be hard to resist, especially after Australia was forced to accept a fairer seabed boundary with Timor-Leste following the exposure of our ruthless treatment of that country. Shortly before the fledgling nation gained its hard-won independence in May 2002, Australia behaved like a big power by withdrawing from the Law of the Sea tribunals and other maritime jurisdictions to stop Timor-Leste taking legal action over disputed petroleum fields. (This did not inhibit Australian governments from lecturing China about the importance of adhering to the global rules-based order in that nation's claims in the South China Sea.) In 2004 the foreign minister, Alexander Downer, authorised ASIS to bug East Timor's Cabinet room while it discussed its negotiating position on offshore resource boundaries. The gist of the illegally obtained information was passed to Woodside Petroleum, which had offshore leases near the small island. An ASIS whistleblower exposed the bugging after learning that Woodside had later hired Downer as a consultant. Australia's subterfuge had the perverse result of ensuring that new boundary lines and revenue-sharing arrangements were agreed in 2018.

35

CHAINED TO THE CHARIOT WHEELS OF THE PENTAGON

'It is almost literally true that Australia cannot go to war without the consent and support of the US.'

Gary Brown and Laura Rayner[1]

The republican movement in Australia is irrelevant: Australia could become a republic tomorrow and nothing of substance would change. The British monarchy has no say in Australian government decisions. It's a different story with the head of the American republic. A US president presides over a military-industrial-intelligence complex with a huge say in whether Australian governments go to war, buy particular weapons, host US-run military and intelligence bases, and ban imports from certain countries. The upshot is that Australia has surrendered much of its sovereignty to the US.

Crucially, the US requires almost all countries that buy its weapons systems, including Australia, to send sensitive components back to the US for repairs, maintenance and replacements without the owners being allowed access to critical information, including source codes, needed to keep these systems operating. As far back as 2001, the conclusion of the Parliamentary Library research paper quoted above was that Australia could not conduct operations requiring the use of its advanced weapons platforms for any length of time without US support. Since then, we have become much more dependent on US support for far more complex systems. This means we could be defenceless if attacked, unless the US allows the Defence Force independent access to key operational components of fighter planes, missiles, submarines, surveillance systems and so on. If Australia became involved in a conflict with Indonesia against the wishes of the US, the Americans could refuse to keep the weapons systems operating. This may seem unlikely, but is not implausible.

Israel is the only country to have successfully demanded that it be able to operate key systems independently of the US. Like Australia, Israel has bought the US F-35 fighter plane, whose cloud-based computer 'brain'— the autonomic logistics information system (ALIS)—constantly sends and receives information to and from its manufacturer, Lockheed Martin. The American defence writer Joseph Trevithick reported in 2017, 'Israel has secured unique and unprecedented rights to tinker with its F-35s, operate its ALIS systems outside the centralised network—and possibly operate the F-35s independent of the ALIS totally. It is even developing its own software to sit on top of the existing applications.'[2] Trevithick said this approach could help address the problem that ALIS 'could also offer an incredibly attractive Achilles heel for enemy hackers to sink their teeth into'.[3]

As well as the F-35, Australia depends on continuing access to US systems during a major conflict to operate its Super Hornet fighters, its Growler cyber-warfare planes, its Poseidon maritime-patrol aircraft, its Wedgetail airborne early warning and control aircraft, and its big Triton drones.

Although the ability to operate our major weapons systems independently is crucial to defending Australia, our leaders prefer to ignore this fundamental flaw and become more tightly integrated with US forces. But integration can also undercut Australian sovereignty by reducing Australia's scope for independent military action in other ways.

Shortly after returning from his six-year posting as Australia's ambassador to Washington in 2016, Kim Beazley gave a speech in which he said Americans wanted to move beyond 'interoperability' of the two countries' military forces to 'integration'.[4] He explained that integration meant that what the US would 'actually want of our platforms [ships, planes, etc.] is the performance of tasks that they don't have the resources to do'.[5] He gave the example of how the US Marine Corps in the Pacific wanted to plug a capability gap by using the Australian Navy's new ships equipped with big helicopters for landing troops.[6] Integrating these ships into the US forces could mean that the Australian Navy wouldn't be able to deploy them at short notice to meet Australia's own needs in critical circumstances.

In his speech Beazley welcomed how Australia was much more important to the US in 2016 than when he was defence minister in the Hawke

Government in the 1980s. He said that the US didn't really care what our government did as long as the Americans could use the 'joint facilities' (the intelligence-gathering bases in Central Australia and the communication station at North West Cape in Western Australia) and we contributed to surveillance operations against the Russians' Vladivostok (Pacific) Fleet. He said, 'We would not have been a nuclear target but for those joint facilities. The Americans recognised that ... [so] they put us on a very long leash provided we were prepared to support the facilities.'[7]

Others might see nothing to celebrate in being put on a leash, long or short. But Beazley relished the short leash. He said, 'From being a strategical irrelevancy during the Cold War, we became the southern tier of the global political system which is the East Asian economy. We are actually critical.' In effect, this means Australia has a critical role in the US efforts to increase economic and military pressure on China, and if that fails, in winning the ensuing war against 1.4 billion people.

Tom Nichols, a US professor of national security affairs, put the American alliance in perspective when he wrote: 'In 2014, following the Russian invasion of Crimea, *The Washington Post* published the results of a poll ... The people who thought Ukraine was located in Latin America or Australia were most enthusiastic about using force there.'[8] American enthusiasts for bombing a staunch antipodean ally did not have the advantage back then of Prime Minister Malcolm Turnbull's famous declaration that Australia and the US are 'joined at the hip'.

Labor governments surrendered Australian sovereignty in other ways in 2008 by agreeing to renew the lease on NWC without any conditions on how US nuclear-attack submarines could use the base.[9] This could include undermining China's ability to deter a nuclear war.[10] Labor subsequently agreed to let the US install long-range ground sensors at NWC to help conduct space warfare against Russia and China in violation of Australia's support for a treaty outlawing the militarisation of space. The public were not told about the significance of these developments, nor about similar changes at the Pine Gap satellite base. The NSA essentially runs Pine Gap's role in intercepting a wide range of electronic signals that provide real-time targeting information for battlefield use by US forces.[11] It also helps detect data on heat emissions from missiles, jet engines and ground explosions that feed into military operations, including space warfare, regardless of whether Australia opposes a particular US war.

Australian ministers are sometimes so keen to buy US military equipment that they reject good advice not to do so. For example, they insisted on buying the most important component of the trouble-plagued

Collins-class submarine—the computerised combat data system—from a US firm that had never made one. It was a costly failure. The Howard Government then commissioned Malcolm McIntosh, a former chief of defence procurement in Britain, and John Prescott, a former managing director of BHP, to recommend a replacement. McIntosh and Prescott advised that a proven German system called ISUS rated best in all categories, and senior Australian defence officials agreed.[12] But the Coalition defence minister, Peter Reith, decided in 2000 that he knew better and chose a US company, Raytheon, that had never built a combat data system for a conventionally powered submarine.[13] Integrating the new Raytheon system into the Collins class was a difficult task that would need to be spread over several years. It is due to be included, without a competitive tender, in the big new French-Australian submarines on order.

Australian governments have also trusted Americans rather than experts from elsewhere to advise on decisions about purchasing equipment that is unfamiliar to them. In December 2016, the Turnbull Government appointed a naval shipbuilding advisory board chaired by a former secretary of the US Navy, Donald Winter. Three other board members are former US Navy admirals, and two are US civilians. Winter is being paid $1.468 million for his part-time work on this panel from April 2017 to December 2019; one former US admiral is getting over $964,000 and another almost $600,000.[14] Australia's two board members have no direct experience of shipbuilding, and the nine-member board includes no one from naval shipbuilding countries in Europe or Asia.[15] Because no US ships are considered suitable, Australia is building big new British-designed frigates and extensively redesigning French nuclear submarines to use battery power. Although the US has not built a conventionally powered submarine in living memory, Winter was also appointed to chair the government's expert advisory panel overseeing the competitive evaluation process for the Australian Navy's new submarines.

A decade ago, Australian Defence officials were so keen to buy the US's Lockheed Martin F-35 fighter planes that they ignored Pentagon warnings that more work was needed to fix faults in the aircraft. The defence minister, John Faulkner, announced on 25 November 2009 that the government would pay $3.2 billion for fourteen F-35 fighters, for delivery in 2014. A little over two months later, US Defense Secretary Robert Gates announced that he would extend flight testing of the F-35, delay the purchase of 122 planes, sack the general in charge of the program, and withhold US$614 million from Lockheed Martin because it had failed to meet a number of key goals and benchmarks. Yet Faulkner said in his 25 November announcement, 'Defence has done more analysis on this platform than any other platform in the acquisition history of the Australian Defence Force.'[16] If so, how come it missed repeated warnings from the Pentagon and the US Government Accountability Office about the plane's severe deficiencies?

There was no excuse for not waiting or, better still, for completely re-evaluating the reckless purchase, which Prime Minister John Howard initiated in 2002. It's now clear that the F-35 will be vastly more expensive to maintain than originally promised. When two F-35s visited for the 2017 Avalon Airshow they could not depart Australia on schedule because they were not capable of flying in bad weather. The air show's media release stated, 'It is well documented that the F-35A aircraft requires modifications for lightning protection and these modifications have not yet been completed on the two visiting Australian aircraft.'[17] Despite its stealth capability, the F-35 can be detected by over-the-horizon radars and other radars using different frequencies, and by optical, heat and other sensors.

In another example of misguided decision-making, in 2000 Defence chose the US aerospace firm Boeing to integrate AGM-142 missiles into the F-111 strike aircraft. Boeing fitted the missiles nine years behind schedule, and the F-111s retired a year later, leaving about 100 missiles that Defence said had cost $400 million and were 'disposed of by explosive demolition'.[18]

Australia also seeks to win favour in Washington by buying US equipment on the basis that it is 'interoperable' with the Pentagon's—but in most cases, non-US equipment would also be readily interoperable using a communications data link. The US conducts submarine exercises with a dozen navies without having trouble communicating with them. None, except Australia's, has a US-made computerised combat management system.

Designing and manufacturing all components locally isn't feasible for Australia at present, especially in complex electronic equipment. But costs could be much lower if Australian governments stopped buying equipment designed for participating with the US in high-intensity warfare around the globe. The existing low-cost 4000-tonne Anzac-class frigates have served Australia well. They should have been replaced with similar-sized ships instead of the 7000-tonne British Type 26 frigates now being built for a total cost of $35 billion. Likewise, many Australian observers are mystified by why the government didn't choose twelve high-quality, well-proven German submarines of the kind that are operated by Israel, Singapore and other navies. They would cost around $10–$12 billion compared to the government's $50 billion initial estimate for the twelve big redesigned French submarines, the first of which will not become operational until after 2035 and the last not until 2050. The Collins class is due to retire in 2025.[19] A more realistic cost estimate for this complex project is over $80 billion in 2020 dollars, partly because a new version of the Collins class must be designed and built to avoid a capability gap.

Unlike normal joint exercises, embedding Australian troops, ships and planes in US forces raises serious sovereignty issues. Placing troops under foreign control effectively deprives Australian governments of the ability to pull them out if a conflict suddenly occurs. In 2013 the Gillard Government agreed to embed HMAS *Sydney* for almost two months in a US carrier battle group based at Yokosuka, Japan. The *Sydney* was under US command when Japan's renewed emphasis on its claim to the uninhabited Senkaku Islands became a flashpoint with China.[20] The battle group was widely expected to be the first responder in a clash over these tiny islands that Japan claimed after the 1905 Sino-Japanese war. The Senkaku are 38 kilometres from mainland China, 426 km from Okinawa and only 20 km from Taiwan, which Australia recognises as a province of China.

Similar sovereignty problems apply to Australian troops embedded under the US command in Hawaii. Australian military personnel are also deeply engaged in US war planning and command structures. Defence says there were approximately 450 Australian personnel serving in liaison and exchange positions in the US in April 2018. Approximately 130 were embedded within US command structures, and approximately thirty were employed as liaison officers 'to exchange operational plans, information and concepts'.[21]

Before Australian participation is taken for granted, governments should state clearly that Australian forces will not engage in international aggression in violation of international law and Article 1 of the ANZUS Treaty.

36

SURRENDERING JUDICIAL SOVEREIGNTY

'The significance of the ISDS [investor-state dispute settlement] arbitral
processes is global. They have general implications for national sovereignty,
democratic governance and the rule of law.'
Former High Court chief justice Robert French[1]

The Hawke Government's abolition in 1986 of appeals to the British Privy
Council was widely praised as an overdue move to ensure that the nation's
highest court was no longer subordinate to a court in another country.
Later governments signed trade and investment treaties allowing non-
judicial bodies to overturn High Court decisions by using investor–state
dispute settlement (ISDS) clauses in the agreements. Ceding sovereignty
to international organisations to promote prosperity, human rights and
environmental protection can have clear benefits, as can international laws
prohibiting aggression, inhumane weapons, war crimes, and so on. The
General Agreement on Tariffs and Trade and the World Trade Organization
helped boost prosperity after World War II, but these arrangements have
been largely supplanted by bilateral and regional agreements. Mainstream
economists argue that these only shift trade from one country to another
without increasing global trade.

A former High Court chief justice, Robert French, says, 'Arbitration
tribunals set up under ISDS provisions are not courts. Nor are they required
to act like courts ... Questions have been raised about their consistency,
openness and impartiality.'[2] As well as lacking effective appeal processes,
French says their decisions have implications for 'national sovereignty,

democratic governance and the rule of law'.[3] Even the name of a country where a case is being heard in secret is undisclosed.

These tribunals have a history of imposing hefty penalties on governments pursuing public policy goals in areas such as health, consumer protection and the environment. Unlike foreign corporations, Australian firms can only appeal against these policies in a proper court. Partly for these reasons, John Howard while prime minister resisted intense US pressure to include ISDS clauses in the Australia–United States Free Trade Agreement. Subsequent Coalition governments ignored Howard and included ISDS clauses in several bilateral and regional agreements.

Coalition ministers usually claim they obtain special 'carve-outs' to protect particular programs, such as the Pharmaceutical Benefits Scheme. But Greg Wood, a former deputy head of the PM's Department with extensive trade policy experience, says ISDS clauses constrain the ability of future governments to introduce legislative changes to take account of how 'issues, circumstances and community attitudes shift'.[4]

For example, there was no carve-out to protect Labor's 2011 law requiring plain packaging and health warnings for tobacco. After Philip Morris Asia lost a High Court challenge, it took legal action against the government under an obscure 1993 investment agreement with Hong Kong. The company used the agreement to argue it should be paid vast sums for the 'expropriation' of its Australian investments. Former Labor treasurer Wayne Swan argued in a secret ISDS hearing in Singapore that Philip Morris Asia had only taken over the tobacco giant's Australian operations to create a Hong Kong link to challenge the plain packaging law. The case ended when the tribunal found that the company had contrived its affairs to secure standing under the treaty. Wood said Philip Morris's argument that its intellectual property had been damaged by the plain packaging legislation 'was not put to the test by the tribunal on its merits, and there is no certainty where it would have come out'.[5]

The Comprehensive and Progressive Agreement for Trans-Pacific Partnership (also known as TPP-11) agreement covering Australia and ten other countries contains some ISDS provisions. The full text of TPP-11 (and that of other trade and investment agreements) is long and prolix. It was negotiated in secret, preventing the public from knowing what has being agreed on its behalf until the final version was eventually released.

The lack of proper public scrutiny of TPP-11 could prove extremely costly. Based on overseas examples, Australia could easily be hit with damages of many hundreds of millions of dollars. The prudent course is to reject ISDS clauses in such cases and focus on achieving the real gains available from freer trade.

PART 6
TRYING TO PLUG THE LEAKS

37

INSPECTOR TANGE INVESTIGATES

'I do not consider the full or partial revelation as seriously or irretrievably damaging.'

Bob Hamilton, senior Defence official[1]

It was not until the dying days of the McMahon Government in 1972 that classified information started leaking on a noticeable scale. Before then, leaks rarely disturbed the equanimity of most senior mandarins. In 1976 JIO listed over forty journalists who had published significant intelligence leaks from 1972 to 1975, not counting leaks on defence and non-security issues.[2] This change partly reflected the greater willingness in the West to subject secret institutions to tougher scrutiny following the lies the Pentagon had peddled about the Vietnam War and the congressional exposures of abuses of power by intelligence agencies. A new generation of Australian journalists was replacing an older one who had accepted, for example, that the public need not know about the damage that secrecy concealed during the British nuclear tests in the 1950s and 60s.

Once the leaks gathered pace following the election of the Whitlam Labor government in December 1972, Defence head Arthur Tange's reaction was dysfunctional. His demands to find the leakers chewed up the time of senior officials who had more important things to do than pursue often inept and always futile investigations. Tange, for example, never satisfactorily completed the task set by Defence Minister Lance Barnard when he publicly announced that the department would undertake the first-ever study of how best to defend Australia. Despite being called the Defence Department, it had never done such a study in its seventy-two years of existence.

Unless otherwise stated, the documents quoted below were generated as part of Tange's investigations into the leaks during 1973–79.[3] They show that approximately 350 files were created in pursuing leaks published by me, including lengthy studies of my modus operandi and motives. Many were kept in Tange's office. Given the harmless nature of most of the leaks, Tange's zealotry can be partly be seen as due to his reliance on secrecy to maintain his bureaucratic power.

Initially, many of Tange's underlings made frenzied efforts to meet his demands. He even asked for evaluations of the damage that could be done if documents that hadn't leaked did so in future. One senior official, Bob Hamilton, basically told Tange to calm down. When Hamilton was asked to examine several of these supposedly sensitive documents, he concluded, 'I do not consider the full or partial revelation as seriously or irretrievably damaging to our diplomatic or defence interests or those of our friends and allies, and I consider that further revelations would generally add only marginally to the damage.'[4]

After assessing the consequences of a leak of a three-volume set of briefing papers handed to the new defence minister, Bill Morrison, in June 1975, Hamilton said, 'I do not consider that these disclosures would produce unmanageable strains or protracted ones.' If the Americans expressed concern, he said, the leaking of the *Pentagon Papers* on the Vietnam War should 'especially inhibit an emotional and damaging US reaction'. In Hamilton's assessment, the common interests in Australia's intelligence relationship with the US would 'sweep the eddy of the present away'.

The director of defence security, Commodore P.J. Hutson, also gave a dismissive response after Tange asked him to investigate my publication of a leaked copy of his (Tange's) June 1978 speech detailing cuts to projected defence spending over the following five years.[5] Hutson explained in a brisk minute to Tange that the only copy of the speech that 'has not been fully accounted for' was from his office.[6] He said he did not propose to take the matter any further, as the speech was only classified 'Restricted'.

Defence investigations always came to the strong conclusion that leaks did not come from within the department or JIO. Foreign Affairs expressed similar faith in its staff. In one case, Tange reacted with his usual horror to a news report that the Japanese were replacing insecure diplomatic codes, which the DSD could easily break, with more secure ones. The article, which I wrote from Tokyo in July 1976, noted that Japan's lax approach to communications security had some advantages. I said that cables intercepted in 1973 'showed genuine concern on the part of the Japanese about Rex Connor's attitude as Minerals and Energy minister and this helped convince Whitlam he had a problem in this area'.[7]

In a typical response to a leak, Australia's ambassador to Tokyo, Mick Shann, sent Tange a letter on 3 August 1976 saying he was 'completely confident that no one in the embassy could in any way be involved' and that my disclosures had caused only 'mild' interest in official circles. This was also the response of a recent head of the Japanese Foreign Ministry who invited me and another guest to dine at his home while I was in Tokyo. In his letter to Tange, Shann also said that Whitlam, who was in Tokyo at the time, told him, 'Tange has a fixation about Toohey.' Given the mild Japanese response to the leak, Whitlam's comment suggested he had Tange's 'fixation' in perspective.

After telling Tange that he had a 'possible lead to the source', Shann fingered Greg Clark, whom he described as a 'considerable friend' of mine. Despite Shann's gratuitous 'lead', Clark was not my source. Fluent in Japanese, Russian, Chinese and French, Clark joined Foreign Affairs in 1956 before resigning in 1965 over the Vietnam War and moving to Japan. He briefly joined the Prime Minister's Department under Whitlam in 1973 before returning to Japan, where he became a respected academic and a prolific commentator. He never felt the need to endear himself to Australian ambassadors.

Unlike most of the leaks I reported, Defence was untroubled by one quoting from a National Intelligence Committee (NIC) assessment that helped debunk Defence Minister Jim Killen's extravagant claim on 30 June 1976 that the Soviet Union posed a military threat to Australia. Instead of complaining about the security breach, a JIO minute to Tange merely said that the *AFR* article contained direct quotes from the NIC report that 'were accurate'. JIO was clearly tired of Killen's fact-free rants. The threat didn't last long, prompting the headline 'Russia: The Three-Hour Threat'. This was the time it took for Foreign Minister Andrew Peacock to slap Killen down, bluntly stating, 'We have never been talking about a direct military threat.'[8] Killen then issued a press release to 'amplify' his previous claim. It was a humiliating backdown in which he acknowledged that the government 'did not regard the Soviet Union as a direct military threat'. My article also explained that Killen's initial press conference had been studded with overwrought remarks painting the Soviet Union as bent on world domination through every means at its disposal, ranging from merchant shipping to 'advanced metaphysics'.

Tange was much less alarmed by leaks when he dealt with US or British officials. During a meeting with the British high commissioner, Tange reassured him that there was 'nothing sinister' about anything Clem Lloyd or I had done while on Barnard's staff before we resigned.[9] During a 1976 meeting with the CIA station chief, Corley Wonus, and his military intelligence counterpart, R.C. Nunemaker, Tange said he did not think my 'motive was one of hostility to the US or attempt to do damage to our international situation or theirs'.[10] Although he was trying to smooth the diplomatic waters, that was an accurate statement of my motives, which were about keeping readers informed. At the meeting Tange again stressed that nothing had leaked from his department. Instead, he told the two US intelligence officials that there was a 'lot of evidence' (there was none) that I had obtained a good deal of my information from ministerial offices in the Fraser and Whitlam governments.

Perhaps understandably, Tange focused on me as I had worked as private secretary for Barnard for the first seven weeks after the election until I left to join the *AFR*. With one exception, all the documents subsequently leaked were not even written until after I left, in most cases many years afterwards. The exception was the previous government's 1971 secret study called *The Strategic Basis of Australian Defence Policy*. A rival newspaper published a leaked copy in June 1973. Due to Barnard's casual attitude to handling classified documents, I saw his copy of the 1971 document, which Tange gave him in a secure satchel along with other classified documents. Barnard emptied the contents onto his office settee before leaving one Friday for his Launceston home. Carpenters were working near the settee to install a shower and toilet he'd ordered to rectify what he saw as the previous occupant Doug Anthony's deplorable neglect of his entitlements. Although the carpenters might have enjoyed some additional weekend reading material, I put the contents in the safe.

Tange was initially convinced that my leaks were coming from Labor ministers and staff and would instantly cease with the arrival of the Fraser Government. They didn't—they continued for decades—and Tange never identified any leakers. The primary motivation of all my sources was to reveal information they considered the public should know. As far as I could tell, their political sympathies, if any, ranged across the spectrum.

The *National Times* later reported on other documents that were released under FOI. Those above were deemed exempt.[11] The *NT* said an August 1976 document showed that Defence had recommended putting my movements under surveillance and monitoring my activities in case I tried to blackmail public servants into leaking. It also said the Fairfax group should be investigated to see if it paid people to leak. I don't know if these proposals went ahead, but I do know that Fairfax never paid anyone in Defence to leak to me, and I never blackmailed anyone. Apart from the obvious ethical objections, enough sources came forward of their own volition.

Chapter 14 suggests that as the leaks continued, the deputy head of the PM's department, Mike Codd, in 1978 was probably the last senior official to refuse a Cabinet request to investigate leaks. Nevertheless, Bill Pritchett, who replaced Tange as department head in 1979, did not have the same appetite as his predecessor for relentless investigations into leaks, nor the same volcanic temper. As one observer put it on Pritchett's death, 'Where Tange changed Defence through brains, bile, bluster and bullying, his successor Bill Pritchett did the same job just through the use of his brain.'[12]

Tange never managed to have anyone charged with leaking. In my case, he settled on trying to get the US embassy to refuse to give me a visa. A senior US diplomat told me he warned Tange that if he persisted in his attempts, the diplomat would personally sign my visa application. Soviet officials invited me and another journalist, Paul Kelly, to their embassy in May 1976 to discuss the possibility of one of us visiting Moscow. They chose Kelly, presumably because they thought he was better suited ideologically.

38

LABOR GOES TO COURT

'Oyster reveals much which should concern and alarm us.'

Ian Macphee[1]

After Bob Hawke's Labor government was elected in 1983, it was far keener to take court action to suppress media reporting than Malcolm Fraser's government before it had been. The book of documents compiled by Richard Walsh and George Munster in 1980, *Documents on Australian Defence and Foreign Policy 1968–1975,* was an exception. The Fraser Government succeeded in getting the High Court to prevent Fairfax from publishing extracts, and copies of the book were withdrawn. However, Chief Justice Anthony Mason stated that the court wouldn't automatically prevent publication if it served the public interest by keeping the community informed. This had to be balanced against a competing public interest that could sometimes constrain publication on national security and other grounds. New legislation thirty-five years later explicitly ruled out a public-interest defence in some cases.

Fraser did not resort to the courts after newspapers published several top-secret documents, including material from the Hope Royal Commission, highly sensitive cables between the CIA and ASIO, and an internal defence study on possible threats to Australia (the Hamilton Report). But Hawke didn't shrink from tapping phones to try to discover leakers. He even ensnared one of his senior ministers, Peter Walsh. ASIO tapped my home phone not long after the Labor government was elected in March 1983. The tap picked up a call Walsh made to the phone, and Hawke then reprimanded him for speaking to me.

The *National Times* later published a three-part series called 'The AUSTEO Papers',[2] which revealed abuses and shortcomings involving Australia's intelligence agencies, amid some good work. One article revealed that when China made a military incursion into Vietnam in 1979, the US withheld signals intelligence from Australia despite all the solemn assertions about the intimate relationship between the two countries. Another article in the series revealed that Australia had spent millions of dollars on a joint intercept station in Hong Kong that failed to provide useful intelligence. It also quoted Bob Furlonger, head of the Office of National Assessments in 1978, as saying Australia's intelligence coverage in the South Pacific was limited, but should improve with the installation of a sophisticated phone-intercept system called Reprieve in the Australian High Commission in Port Moresby and the embassy in Jakarta. Another article revealed that ASIO and the CIA regularly met in 'safe houses' to exchange often ill-based claims about individual Australians—for example, that certain Labor politicians were 'communist sympathisers'. ASIO had never told any government about these meetings, and tried unsuccessfully to conceal them from the Hope Royal Commission.[4] Another article praised the quality of an ASIO report, under Director-General Justice Woodward, about Middle East terrorism compared to the shoddy work ASIO had done earlier on Croatian terrorists in Australia.

After the first instalment appeared in some early copies of the 6 May 1983 edition of the *NT*, Hawke announced that the government had obtained a late-night injunction from Chief Justice Harry Gibbs on 5 May prohibiting further publication and ordering the Fairfax group to give the court all classified documents relating to the series. I explained in an affidavit that no one else at Fairfax or elsewhere (other than the government) had copies, and I couldn't hand them over as I'd destroyed them in the interests of good housekeeping.

The case demonstrated Fairfax's strong opposition to government censorship during that period. The company retained Melbourne QC Neil McPhee, an officer in the Army Reserve, but he refused to represent me as he thought I should go to jail and Fairfax should apologise. Although the company chairman, James Fairfax, was rarely involved in court cases, on this occasion he made it plain that the company would not apologise and would strongly resist any attempt to jail one of its journalists. I was given a separate QC, who told me he was on a retainer from ASIO. I said this was fine and never heard from him again. A highly skilled junior barrister,

Richard Refshauge (later an ACT Supreme Court judge), protected my interests.

Another QC, Tom Hughes, was called in after McPhee objected to my argument in a proposed article that the government's plan to use the defence minister's regulatory powers to let the DSD intercept phone calls would be illegal, as only ASIO could lawfully intercept phones. If my argument was valid, it would bolster Fairfax's claim that it was in the public interest to reveal a planned illegal act by a government, and if McPhee, retained by Fairfax, prevailed on this point, it would have weakened the company's defence. To resolve the issue, a meeting was held in Hughes' chambers at 8 a.m. on the Saturday. Hughes said that as a former attorney-general he was familiar with the law applying to phone intercepts. He briskly explained to his Melbourne counterpart why he was wrong: in 1983 only ASIO could legally intercept phones, and it needed a warrant issued by the attorney-general.

Further costs were incurred in moving to Canberra for lively negotiations with the government's lawyers. I had spoken over the years with each of the public servants who had now sworn an affidavit that publication would breach national security. By Sunday evening, a settlement was reached with the government, which agreed to allow publication of the other proposed articles in the series after relatively minor changes. Refshauge objected vigorously to a last-minute attempt by McPhee to put me on the stand before the settlement was formalised in court the next morning. The case began on the Friday morning and was basically settled by the Monday morning, but not before Fairfax had spent tens of thousands of dollars.

The Hawke Government later tried to suppress parts of the book *Oyster: The Story of the Australian Secret Intelligence Service*, co-authored by Bill Pinwill and me. The government took action in the Federal Court after receiving draft copies of eight chapters in highly unusual circumstances that involved fellow journalists. In mid-1988, Pinwill had posted drafts of the chapters to the publisher, who subsequently mailed annotated copies to my address in October. I never received them.

I set out my understanding of what had happened in an affidavit to the court on 28 November 1988.[5] The affidavit said that Channel 10's news editor in Sydney, Des McWilliam, had phoned me on 22 November to say he wanted to hand over some property belonging to me and Bill—namely, the draft chapters. I then got a call from Kerry O'Brien, who worked for Network Ten in Canberra, who said words to the effect of 'I know you had a phone call from Des McWilliam. Why don't you ring him back? You really should do something about this today.' I then met McWilliam, who said a Ten journalist had obtained the material approximately two weeks earlier; he didn't say how. He said there was strong pressure at the station to film the handover of the material to me, but he was resisting.

My affidavit stated that McWilliam then said words to the effect of 'I gave it to Kerry last weekend. He has assured me he hasn't talked about this to anyone. We have photographed some pages on video, but it has been treated as confidential within the station.' He rang later and said words to the effect of 'We will have to go to air with the story. Gareth Evans knows we have something called *Oyster* which appears to be part of a manuscript produced by you and Bill Pinwill. He knows we have handed it over to you.'

The affidavit says that on 24 November 1988 I spoke to Evans, who was responsible for ASIS as the foreign minister, and then voluntarily gave computer discs and printouts of the proposed book to the court after Evans agreed that publication of the book would be negotiated between senior officials and Pinwill and me. Evans said that I would be pleasantly surprised at how little ASIS wanted to cut. After the dust settled, I got a call from a senior journalist at Ten who told me on a non-attributable basis that he'd discovered one of Ten's news staff had given the draft copies to the government. My understanding is that they were given to Evans or Kim Beazley. I am completely confident O'Brien did not hand them over.

After the court hearing began, the government's QC launched into a flamboyant accusation about how we should have produced the draft copies under the discovery process. We didn't include these notated copies in what we handed to the court for the simple reason that we had never received them from the publisher. The government, which had been handed this material, had not produced it, but the QC apparently wasn't aware of this as he attempted to ensnare us. Solicitor-General Tom Sherman, who was sitting alongside him, saw the problem and pulled at the QC by his coat-tails, saying in a stage whisper, 'Sit down, man!'

We then began negotiating with the officials—Kim Jones from Foreign Affairs and a senior ASIS officer—over what could be published. The negotiations were plain sailing. At the conclusion, the ASIS officer said he thought the book was 'fair' even though it gave a detailed account of his service's secretive activities and blunders.

We said in the authors' note at the start of the published book that the negotiations 'were conducted in a sensible and professional spirit and the government responded speedily to the various drafts submitted to it. Apart from one major deletion identifying a public relations firm, we are satisfied that the amendments and rephrasing which resulted from our negotiations have not impaired the overall integrity of the book.'

Ian Macphee, the Coalition's shadow foreign minister, had no qualms about accepting our invitation to launch *Oyster*. He lost the shadow portfolio before speaking, but said the book revealed much that 'should concern and alarm [the Australian public]'.[6] His insightful speech is reproduced as the foreword to the paperback edition of *Oyster*. No subsequent minister or shadow minister has defended the publication of classified material as sometimes a healthy part of our democracy.

Writing in *The Age* later, Robert Haupt revealed the information that had been deleted from the book. The government had accepted that we could include this information as an appendix in the paperback edition of *Oyster*. The appendix explained that Eric White Associates, established in 1947, had a lengthy role, unknown to most of its employees, in providing cover for ASIS's overseas operatives as supposed employees of the firm. Its owner, Eric White, was a close friend of Prime Minister Bob Menzies. White did the government a favour by helping ASIS, but he could expect the government to favour his clients in return. By 1964, he was running the third-largest PR company in the world. Its appointment in the late 1960s to advise Tunku Abdul Rahman's Malaysian government created a well-placed source of information for ASIS; a contract with the Indonesian government followed. White's Bangkok office was opened specifically as cover for ASIS. In 1974, the company, along with its embedded ASIS operatives, was taken over by an American PR conglomerate that was swallowed by another group, which dropped the name Eric White Associates. White left the company in 1986. The sky did not fall in when this deleted information was revealed in newspapers and in the paperback edition of *Oyster*.

Another deletion from the book was merely silly: the government insisted that no previously unnamed ex-ASIS officer could be named.[7] The stated reason was that it might help a country identify the agents (informants) the named ASIS officer ran there. This rigid rule meant we could not name an early ASIS official posted to Indonesia who didn't have any agents and preferred to spend most of his time drinking with fellow expats.

While government censorship was forcing *Oyster* to obey this rule, bookshops were simultaneously selling the memoir of one of ASIS's ex-deputy directors, Harvey Barnett.[8] His book's dust jacket identified every country where he had been posted, including Indonesia, with no concern about the potential to identify his local agents. At least he had some agents, unlike the incompetent officer whose name we couldn't mention.

39

EMBARRASSING THE GOVERNMENT, INFORMING THE PUBLIC

'Why should the public not know ... to what extent the Americans exert influence over Australian decisions?'

Michelle Grattan[1]

The Hawke Government raced into the High Court following revelations in the September 1988 edition of the independent magazine *The Eye* that US Secretary of State George Shultz had dictated a new Australian policy overturning the long-standing position of previous Coalition and Labor governments that nuclear-armed warships could not enter Australian harbours.[2] Shultz intervened after the defence minister, Gordon Scholes, followed departmental advice and announced on 13 December 1983 that the government would apply the existing bipartisan policy and ban the British aircraft carrier HMS *Invincible* from entering Sydney Harbour. Shultz immediately rang Prime Minister Bob Hawke, who told Foreign Minister Bill Hayden to call Shultz.

Shultz told Hayden he would send a new announcement and not only dictated the policy, but also the press release. After seeing the text, senior diplomat Geoff Miller sent Hayden a minute warning: 'It would be most unwise to issue a statement of this sort without detailed consideration.' Negotiations dragged on until Scholes backed down and announced Shultz's policy on 26 February 1984. Warships coming into Australian harbours no longer had to declare whether nuclear weapons were on board. Scholes, a decent and thoughtful man, was demoted to the junior ministry.

The announcement began: 'The Australian Labor Party and this government'—words written by Shultz, not the Australian government. To illustrate the extent to which the US was dictating policy, *The Eye* published extracts from Shultz's text alongside Scholes' near-identical version. The Coalition's acting shadow foreign minister, Alexander Downer, told the ABC's *7.30 Report* on 31 August that it was a 'most extraordinary thing' to allow the Americans to write press releases for the Australian government. The account of the government's backdown was one of a series of short articles that *The Eye* dubbed 'The Hayden Papers'. The series began by saying the magazine had discovered the details of Shultz's intervention among an estimated 10,000 pages of documents and assumed (perhaps wrongly) that Hayden had discarded the documents as of no relevance to his forthcoming job of governor-general.

Following the court case, *The Eye* reported that the government had sought an order from the High Court to search my home in Sydney but it gave the wrong address.[3] Thankfully, Chief Justice Tony Mason refused to grant this rarely used 'Anton Piller' order, which allows the government to ransack the occupants' home.

Mason made separate orders on 1 September 1988 that required me to hand over not only the documents relating to the Hayden Papers, but seemingly any Defence or Foreign Affairs documents, or extracts therefrom, no matter how old or innocuous. In an affidavit to the court, I explained that I couldn't hand over the Hayden Papers because I'd destroyed them (on security grounds). I refused to comply with the rest of Mason's order as the transcript suggested it was not limited to classified documents and could mean I was supposed to hand over any press release, ministerial statement or departmental report I'd obtained going back to the 1940s.[4] Justice Daryl Dawson, who took over when the court resumed on 6 September, said Mason's orders were no longer in force, awarded costs against the Commonwealth and flicked the case to the Federal Court. No further hearing was necessary as the case was settled on 8 September.

The articles in the Hayden Papers series included many revelations apart from those about the government's humiliation over the nuclear ships issue. One article, called 'Holding ONA at bay', gave examples of papers from the Office of National Assessments, which was headed by the hawkish Michael Cook. One of these papers tried to reverse Labor's policy of supporting a Comprehensive Test-Ban Treaty to slow the nuclear arms race. ONA's fatuous argument was that the treaty would 'present the US weapons laboratories with problems in preserving career opportunities to attract good staff'.[5] The article reported that a memo on 8 December 1983 from the Arms Control Branch in Foreign Affairs expressed astonishment that this factor had been mentioned. It also took issue with ONA's reference to the opposition to the treaty as the 'Western arguments', pointing out they were only the arguments of the Reagan administration, and that supporters of the treaty included Germany, Italy, the Netherlands, Norway, Denmark, Canada, Japan, New Zealand and Australia. Hayden never leaked any classified information to me, but he did tell me that Justice Bob Hope had told him that Cook had complained to him that Hayden's 'anti-Americanism' was a problem. Hope, who had conducted the Royal Commission on Intelligence and Security beginning in 1974, looked a little surprised to see me coming in Hayden's door as he was leaving, after imparting this message only a couple of minutes earlier.

One of the government's justifications for taking court action was that the articles would damage relations with Indonesia and Papua New Guinea. They didn't: Indonesia subsequently signed an agreement on offshore oil boundaries that was highly favourable to Australia; and PNG's prime minister, in a droll put-down of Hayden's dismissal of PNG's leaders as 'immature', said he was too mature to bother about it. The government's claim that the article would 'embarrass' Hayden as the governor-general designate was legally irrelevant as well as baseless. Although the leaked documents sometimes put him in a bad light, he happily told me he wasn't bothered. The new departmental head, Dick Woolcott, correctly predicted that the fuss would soon blow over.[6]

Because there was no official collection of documents called the Hayden Papers, the government didn't know which documents it was trying to injunct. The Press Council dryly observed, 'As the Government does not know what was in these papers, other than what was published, the injunctions lack a certain degree of precision.'[7] Referring to the case against *The Eye*, Michelle Grattan, a senior journalist renowned for her unbiased analysis, said the dangers from suppression were greater than those from leaks: 'Why should the public not know … to what extent the Americans exert influence over Australian decisions? … Just because information has a secrets stamp on it, it gains an aura it would not have if it were conveyed verbally, for example, in a ministerial leak.'[8]

Postscript: Bill Hayden's often prickly attitude to some American policies attracted the ire of US intelligence services. A highly placed Australian official with an intimate knowledge of what happened told me on a non-attributable basis that a US agency tried to damage Hayden. The official explained that this agency asked an Australian intelligence officer in Washington in the 1980s to send a damaging transcript of audio recording to the officer's Canberra headquarters. The recording was allegedly of Hayden in bed with a woman in Cairo who was a local CIA contact. The intelligence officer subsequently put the material through his security blender. When I questioned Hayden about this, he said that other than in official meetings, his wife, Dallas, was with him the entire time he was in Cairo.

40

EVANS: A VEXATIOUS LITIGANT UNDONE

'We relied on speculation in mounting the court case.'

Gareth Evans[1]

Less than two months after the government lost the Hayden Papers case about leaked classified documents, Foreign Minister Gareth Evans obtained a special late-night High Court hearing on 8 November 1988. The upshot was that my colleague Bill Pinwill and I were accused of causing the death of Australian spies.[2]

Evans lodged an affidavit with the court claiming to 'verily believe' that the November issue of *The Eye* would carry an article disclosing the identity of an ASIS officer in South-East Asia. The problem for Evans and Justice Bill Deane was that the November 1988 edition was already circulating in Parliament House and contained no such article. Nevertheless, Deane issued an injunction against *The Eye* to prevent publication of this non-existent article. Because the case could have dragged on for many costly months, he should have demanded plausible evidence instead of relying on Evans' flimsy assertions about what he 'verily believed'.

If Evans wanted to establish the truth before rushing to court, he could have phoned me and discovered there was no such article in that edition and none was planned in future. He was unrepentant in the Senate the next day, claiming he had acted on 'a reliable source'. The reliability of this source was never tested in court as the case was settled with costs against the Commonwealth once it became clear that its allegations were totally

false. The Commonwealth also accepted my assurance that I had no intention of ever publishing what it had alleged.

Fortunately for the government, the case ended so promptly that it
couldn't use a Foreign Affairs briefing note that recommended bizarre
points to use in a press conference or a court about the dangers of leaking
the name of an ASIS officer.[3] In one puzzling example, the note warned
about what had happened when the New Zealand government tried to
jail the French secret service operatives who sank the *Rainbow Warrior* in
Auckland Harbour in 1985. It said France had responded with 'threats to
trade access, attacks in international forums, spoiling of export products
and restrictions on embassy access'.[4] What should New Zealand have
done? Apologise for catching murderous terrorists who were intelligence
officers? The note also referred to Indonesia's retaliation against Australia
after David Jenkins published articles in the *Sydney Morning Herald* in April
1986 about President Suharto's immense wealth. No leaked Australian
information was involved, but the briefing note implied that the *SMH*
shouldn't have mentioned the dictator's corruption.

The most astonishing proposal in the Foreign Affairs note was that the
government should say it was common knowledge in major countries
that espionage occurs, but that countries in South-East Asia and the South
Pacific were not aware of this. In essence, Australia's diplomats were saying
that these countries were too backward to realise that espionage occurs.
The note also claimed there had been no repercussions from the publication of the Hayden Papers because they didn't deal with 'espionage
operations conducted against friendly countries'. On the contrary, one of
the articles revealed that a secret memo with the code word 'Spoke' showed
that HMAS *Cessnock* was carrying a team from the DSD to conduct electronic espionage against Indonesia. At the time, Australian newspapers were
hyperventilating about how Russian trawlers can carry eavesdropping gear.
Acting on his own advice, Evans made an emotive claim to the judge that
this article would endanger the life of an ASIS officer and his family. This
officer was near retirement, working in Canberra, not in South-East Asia,
had no family and was not in danger.

Evans later admitted on the ABC's *PM* on 23 November 1988 that he
had relied on 'speculation in mounting the court case' and only a 'bit of
evidence'. Yet he had asked that an injunction give him the right to censor
all references by me to ASIS activities overseas in future, no matter how
outrageous. Evans had been the attorney-general during the scandalous
ASIS 'raid' on Melbourne's Sheraton Hotel in November 1983, but now
was demanding that I be subjected to ongoing censorship about anything

this erratic agency might do. No such constraint would apply to any other journalist.

Rather than showing remorse for stuffing up in the High Court, in the same *PM* interview Evans tried to justify what he had told Justice Deane by saying that two ASIS contacts had been murdered during the past eighteen months in 'circumstances where a connection was easily able to be drawn between them and our operation'. The sensational claim received widespread publicity, with repeated suggestions in the media that people who wrote about ASIS were likely to cause the murder of its agents. The clear inference was that *The Eye* and Bill Pinwill and I, as co-authors of *Oyster*, might be responsible for these deaths. The only known instance where ASIS's local contacts have lost their lives was in Indochina, and no one has ever pretended that the media were responsible for that tragedy. ASIS officers are rarely in danger of being killed. If one is caught in Tokyo receiving confidential information on natural gas negotiations, he or she won't be taken outside and shot.

Grattan wrote shortly after his *PM* interview that Evans had admitted to her that no connection could be drawn between ASIS and the deaths of the two people he had referred to in that interview.[5] On 18 January 1989 he sent Pinwill a letter acknowledging that 'Our working assumption has certainly been that the identity of the ASIS officers in question *as* ASIS officers remains unknown and that the victims were not killed as a result of these contacts.' This was a blunt repudiation of his claim on *PM* on 23 November that the connection could easily be made and the offensive inference that Pinwill and I were somehow responsible for their deaths. ASIS has enough trouble recruiting good contacts overseas without its minister publicly suggesting they could be murdered as a result of their work—a suggestion seemingly prompted by nothing more than Evans' need to justify his reckless accusation about *The Eye*. Unhappily, similar impetuous behaviour sullied Evans' often outstanding contribution to public life.

There is nothing necessarily wrong with naming ASIS officers. Former ASIS officers have done so in books; so have journalists in newspapers. I had long known the identity of the ASIS officer whom Evans said in his affidavit was in danger of being killed, but I never saw any reason to publish his or her name. For legal reasons, the officer is called 'Z' here. I hadn't named Z earlier when someone in ASIS told me he was disturbed that Hayden, while foreign minister, had asked the spy agency to arrange for an officer to approach a young Australian journalist, Gwen Robinson, to become an informant (agent) when they were both working in the same South-East Asian country. Robinson told me that Z had asked her, somewhat hesitantly, to pass on information she picked up on rebels in a dangerous part of the country. As one of the few Western journalists in this country who was invited to parties by the local defence minister, Robinson was well aware that if it became known she was Z's informant, she could face serious harm from the rebels and/or the minister. It was plausible that this link could emerge: an Australian diplomat in the country had been known to mention Z's name and ASIS job during dinner parties with Australian and British journalists.[6] This diplomat also supplied Evans with the 'speculative' information he relied on in court.

ASIS should be required to follow the 1970s US practice of banning the CIA from using journalists as agents. If the connection is exposed, it puts the lives of other journalists serving overseas at risk because they can also be suspected of spying. Today, CIA officers again pose as journalists, while ASIS and Australian paramilitary operatives sometimes pose as aid workers.

There was one final touch to Evans' reckless allegations. Because they overlapped with another legal action involving *Oyster*, the government required Pinwill to give a legally binding undertaking not to reveal Z's name. It feared that I had told Pinwill Z's name; I hadn't. Nevertheless, the government told Pinwill the secret of Z's identity to prevent him revealing a secret he didn't know until the government told him. On 7 November 1988, a Foreign Affairs officer was dispatched with due solemnity to hand Pinwill a copy of an ambassador's message that passed on the erroneous gossip that formed the basis of Evans' High Court affidavit. Pinwill read the message in the Australian Government Solicitor's office in Sydney, returned it on the spot and signed the undertaking never to reveal his newly acquired government secret. Such are the ways of this mysterious beast called national security.[7]

PART 7
LIBERTY LOST

41
DISMANTLING THE MENZIES LEGACY

'A powerful case might be made out for the view that the emotion of fear is the most significant of all the emotions in the field of politics ... Nothing sustains a dictatorship as does fear ... If we look about us, will we be quite satisfied that fear is not an instrument of policy even in a democracy?'

Robert Menzies[1]

Australia's longest-serving prime minister, Bob Menzies, did not shrink from exploiting fear during his sixteen years as Coalition prime minister after defeating Labor in the 1949 election. He repeatedly fanned fears about communism, and tarnished Labor in the process. He tried to outlaw the Communist Party in 1951 and introduced conscription for the Vietnam War. Rigid secrecy concealed the damage done by the British nuclear tests. Nevertheless, he usually showed a genuine commitment to the great English legal traditions protecting individual liberty against intrusions by the state—unlike most Australian prime ministers since 2001.

At the height of the Cold War, Menzies rebuffed attempts in 1952 by his attorney-general, John Spicer, to expand offences relating to espionage and official secrets. In addition to the death penalty for spying, Spicer wanted tough sentences for a wide array of offences, including seven years' jail for anyone who took meteorological observations prejudicial to national defence.[2] Spicer was stymied by Allan McKnight, a member of that near-extinct breed: a fearless official in the Prime Minister's Department. McKnight wrote to Menzies with uncompromising bluntness: 'After studying the bill, one feels that every deed is an offence and whether prosecution will follow, or not, is simply a matter of official discretion.'[3] He said an airline passenger who tried to take a photo of Sydney's Harbour Bridge but accidentally photographed a nearby oil-storage facility would commit a prima facie offence attracting the death penalty, and the onus would be on the accused to prove no crime had occurred. The Menzies Cabinet threw out the entire bill. A later attorney-general, Garfield Barwick, managed to toughen the anti-subversion laws in 1961, but not without extensive amendments to his bill.

Civil society under Menzies was often stultifying. Social norms constrained what was considered acceptable to say or do. The Hope Royal Commission, established by the Whitlam Government in 1974, made damning findings about ASIO's activities despite its limited formal powers in the 1950s and 60s. Speaking at the release of the declassified versions of Hope's reports, the royal commission's secretary, George Brownbill, said, 'We found a security service that had been badly politicised ... The ASIO files disclose numerous cases where gossip and tittle-tattle about people and their so-called "Communist sympathies" was recounted to certain Menzies government figures and then revealed in some cases under parliamentary privilege.'[4] A supplement to Hope's report found that ASIO believed it was entitled to withhold important information from elected governments.[5]

In 1960 Menzies legislated to ensure that ASIO was the only body entitled to obtain a warrant to intercept phones. A further safeguard was that it had no executive powers and was confined to collecting and processing information (or misinformation) under the beguiling name of 'intelligence'. Accountability was also enhanced by the lack of any prohibition on naming an ASIO employee. This changed in 1980. Police can still be named.

The Whitlam, Fraser and Hawke governments mostly held the line against Australia becoming a national security state. The official figures show ASIO was intercepting an average of eighty-five phones a year between 1974 and 1983.[6] However, by 2006–07 police and other bodies, including crime and corruption commissions, received 3280 warrants for intercepts.[7] In another blow to accountability, ASIO no longer releases details of how many authorisations it receives to intercept phones or access telecommunications data. Nor does it release the number of warrants issued under its contentious questioning and detention powers, or how many Special Intelligence Operations it conducts. Whistleblowers who expose abuses of power during these operations now face severe jail sentences.

Sixty-three agencies, apart from ASIO, obtained a staggering 333,980 approvals to access stored telecommunications data in 2015–16.[8] In many cases, this 'metadata' is just as useful as access to the content of a message or phone call. Each agency could self-authorise access to this data provided its intention was to 'enforce a criminal law, impose a pecuniary penalty, or protect the public revenue'.[9] The sixty-three agencies included the RSPCA, the Victorian Taxi Services Commission, the Australian Fisheries Management Commission and some local government authorities.[10]

The number of agencies was subsequently cut to twenty, yet 3717 intercept warrants were issued in 2016–17 along with 300,224 approvals to access telecommunications data stored by phone companies.[11] Of the 4154 publicly revealed warrants for telephone intercepts issued in 2016–17, only 1.56 per cent related to terrorism offences. Although the 4154 did not include the secret total for ASIO, insiders say the total figure showed just how few of the warrants related to the main national security problem used to justify the huge expansion in phone intercepts since the 1980s, let alone the 1960s.

In one example, state police intercepted the phone of a washed-up professional tennis player, Nick Lindahl, during a long investigation by New South Wales and Victorian detectives into whether he stood to gain $3800 by betting on a match he intended losing against an unranked junior in a minor tournament in Toowoomba in Queensland in 2013.[12] If anyone was silly enough to bet on this game, that was their problem, not cause to use phone intercept powers. The *Sydney Morning Herald* reported this incident on 29 January 2016 with the page-one headline 'World tennis in the spotlight as match fixing controversy continues'.

Despite the government's claim to have cut the number of agencies allowed to access stored telecommunications data to twenty, journalist Karen Middleton reported in November 2018 that at least eighty were accessing individuals' data by using loopholes in other laws to request and receive information without a warrant.[13]

The pressure for intrusive laws and repressive powers beyond telecommunications had earlier gathered pace under the Keating Government, primarily at the urging of the irascible foreign minister, Gareth Evans, and the defence minister, Robert Ray. Evans had a quick temper and resented foreign diplomats chewing his ear about an adverse media report. In 1995 Ray, an instinctively secretive Labor right-wing-factional boss, tried to gain support for new laws to force newspaper and magazine publishers to submit articles touching on national security issues for vetting before publication. Media executives, quietly supported by senior Defence offi- cials, succeeded in stopping governments from dictating what they printed or broadcast. Whatever his motivation, Evans introduced a bill to suppress publication of foreign affairs, defence and intelligence material that could allegedly harm relations with other countries, no matter how odious the regimes in those countries. Hitler, Stalin and Pol Pot would have approved.

Both proposals lapsed following the election of the Howard Government in 1996, until revived in various forms after the 11 September 2001 terrorist attacks in the US. Fear was then exploited to justify a massive bipartisan expansion of the powers of the state at the expense of individual liberty, in areas unrelated to terrorism. For example, in April 2008, sixteen police raided the *Sunday Times* office in Perth after it revealed that the state Labor government was planning to spend $16 million on an advertising campaign that would help it electorally. In July that year, the AFP investigated the phone records of the Nine Network's Laurie Oakes following leaks about the government's FuelWatch program.

More government agencies are now exempt from review by courts and tribunals, removing one of the great checks and balances on executive power. The AFP even presumed in August 2016 that it had the right to raid Parliament House, access its IT systems and seize thousands of documents to find the source and the recipient of leaks that told the National Broadband Network's ultimate owners—the public—about problems with rising costs and delays.[14] In the past, police and intelligence agencies would have never tapped phones in Parliament House, let alone raided an institution at the pinnacle of Australia's democratic system of government. This meant that for over a century, parliamentarians and their staff were free to receive information without police swooping on their offices.

The AFP claimed in this case that commonplace commercial documents were secret, even if not classified as such. They relied on a section of the revised *Crimes Act* that refers only to disclosure of official secrets by Commonwealth officials, not to employees of an independent corporation such as the NBN. The parliament should have found the AFP in contempt and repealed the new laws that criminalise the disclosure of information of public importance. It did neither.[15] Instead, the Turnbull Government introduced legislation in 2018 to make it a potential criminal offence to leak or receive a much wider range of documents, classified or not.

No major political party is offering to restore the values of the earlier era, when habeas corpus prevailed, the onus of proof was on the prosecution, the accused was allowed to see the evidence relied on by the Crown, and ASIO officials could not legally kidnap people, or raid a lawyer's offices and seize documents in a commercial case in which the government was a part of the opposing side.[16] The Morrison Coalition government in December 2018 even boasted that a new law made Australia the first

Death of General Gordon at Khartoum, Jean Leon Gerome, print, 1895,
© Wm Finley & Co.

The New South Wales colonial government sent an expeditionary force
to the Sudan war in 1885. While prime minister, Julia Gillard praised the
military campaign in Sudan as one of the colonial wars that was 'not only
a test of wartime courage, but a test of character that has helped define our
nation and create a sense of who we are'. However, the Australian contingent
didn't show any courage on the battlefield in Sudan, as the battle was over
before they arrived. A former British governor general of Sudan, General
Charles Gordon, had already been killed during a popular uprising against
British colonial rule. Although a minor farce, the expedition was a prelude to
Australian participation in much deadlier wars, many as equally unnecessary.

General Sir Ian Standish Monteith Hamilton, Library of Congress Prints and Photographs Division

'Australia—not Empire—is the string we must harp on. We must encourage them to do what they will do willingly and lavishly, namely pay up for safeguarding a White Australia from the cursed Jap', General Hamilton wrote the above to the British Prime Minister, HH Asquith, in February 1914 after he'd faced strong opposition to his attempt to earmark a section of the Australian Army for imperial expeditionary service. By the time World War I broke out later in the year, however, Australians were willing to fight in the Middle East and Europe. As commander of operations at Gallipoli, Hamilton led Australian, New Zealand, British and other forces to a traumatic defeat.

John Burton, photograph supplied by Pamela Burton.

John Burton, head of the External Affairs department between 1947 and 1950, was a deep strategic thinker who wanted Australia to seek its security in Asia after the Pacific war to a greater extent than did most subsequent governments. He was an early supporter of independence for Indonesia and other colonies to counter communism, and saw India as being more important to Australia's future than Britain. Unusually for an Australian diplomat at that time, he had a PhD in economics, and developed a keen interest in conflict resolution.

General Curtis LeMay, United States Air Force, 1950s.

'We went over there, fought the war and eventually burned down every town in North Korea [largely by napalm bombing]', stated General Curtis LeMay, Commander, US Strategic Air Command, 1948–1957. When asked at a congressional hearing in June 1951 if North Korea had been virtually destroyed, the Far East Air Force Bomber Commander General Emmett O'Donnell replied, 'Everything is destroyed. There is nothing standing worthy of the name.' As the reliance on missiles increased, LeMay was renowned for supporting a continuing role for bombers as 'manned perpetrators'.

Plutonium blowin' in the wind. Staff Sergeant Frank Smith of the Australian Health Physics Team, February 1957.

After a secret report showing that the British nuclear tests had scattered highly dangerous plutonium around parts of South Australia was leaked on 4 May 1984, the Hawke government began remedial action neglected by the Menzies government.

G.R. Richards (Deputy of ASIO) and Brigadier Charles Spry (ASIO Head), National Archives of Australia, 1954.

Urged on by US authorities, ASIO spent almost twenty years trying to identify Australians who spied for the Soviet Union in the 1940s. This effort was sparked by a US–UK codebreaking program, which revealed that the Soviets had local agents in several countries. The US never told ASIO head, Sir Charles Spry, that US citizen William Weisband was the most important Soviet agent. Weisband had told Moscow in 1948 that the US had broken its codes—the Soviets switched to more secure versions.

General Lloyd Fellenz (left), US Army, Professor Sydney Sunderland (right) photo courtesy Media and Publications Unit Photographs Collection, University of Melbourne Archives. Photographer Norman Wodetski, BWP22197.

While Dean of Medicine at Melbourne University from 1953 to 1971, Sydney Sunderland was a secret advisor to the Defence Department on chemical and biological warfare. In the early 1960s, he produced top secret reports strongly supporting tests of nerve agents in Australia as requested by the United States. As a neurologist, Sunderland had an acute understanding of the extreme toxicity of VX, the main nerve agent to be tested in Australia for potential use in the Vietnam War. Sunderland attended a top-secret meeting with the head of the US chemical and biological weapons testing program, General Lloyd Fellenz, who arrived in Australia in early 1963 to discuss the proposed trials. Fellenz candidly acknowledged, 'The scale and type of trials now necessary are such that these cannot be conducted inside the US due to the dangers involved'. Rigid secrecy ensured that the public was given no inkling of the proposal for the United States to test VX in tropical North Queensland. After much delay, the Menzies government refused in June 1965 to let the trials go ahead. The proposed tests were not revealed until they were leaked in May 1988. Sunderland received many honours during his life for his contributions to science, government and society. This book is the first public acknowledgement that he actively supported using nerve agents to kill people.

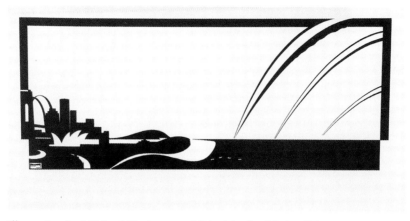

Illustration by Michael Fitzjames published in the *National Times*.

After the *National Times* reported in February 1985 that the Hawke government had agreed to help the US test the splashdown of new missile warheads in the Tasman Sea, the Labor Party revolted. The decision, taken in secret by only three ministers, was overturned.

Harry S Truman, Frank Gatteri, United States Signal Corps, c. November 1945, Harry S Truman Library & Museum.

Although the Soviet Union had not fought in the Korean War, the benign looking President Truman seriously contemplated its nuclear destruction in an extract from a note he wrote in 1952: 'This means that Moscow, St Petersburg, Mukden, Vladivostok, Peking, Shanghai, Port Arthur, Dairen, Odessa, Stalingrad and every manufacturing plant in China and the Soviet Union will be eliminated. This is the final chance for the Soviet government to decide whether it desires to survive or not.'

The bombs used in 1952 would have been much more devastating than the one that Truman ordered to be dropped on Hiroshima in 1945.

Contrasting approaches to the rule of law involving the encryption legislation.
Michael Pezzullo, Fairfax Media/Alex Ellinghausen.

Michael Pezzullo, Secretary, Home Affairs Department told a parliamentary
committee on 19 October 2018, 'If we were to say to you a notice is a
warrant, and through an incantation and the sprinkling of some magic dust
on it, all of a sudden greater oversight is achieved—it's the same person.
It's the attorney general of the Commonwealth rigorously discharging their
ministerial responsibilities.'

Margaret Stone, Auspic Collection.
Photographer: David Foote. Copyright
© 2015 Commonwealth of Australia.

Margaret Stone, Inspector General of
Intelligence and Security, told the same
committee on 16 November 2018,
'[The authorisation of notices] is not
abracadabra. It's not an incantation.
It has to be real.'

country in the world to force tech companies to help the state access encrypted messages on mobile phones and other personal devices and install various forms of malware.

Many supporters of these new laws call themselves 'conservatives'—but conservatives once prided themselves on their opposition to the growth of the state's power over the individual. It was Lord John Acton, a conservative, who famously warned that 'power tends to corrupt and absolute power corrupts absolutely'.[17] Some recent Coalition politicians, who embrace the shift in power to the state, shamelessly claim to support the same freedoms as Menzies championed. Malcolm Turnbull, who strongly endorsed the expansion of government powers while prime minister, gave an address to the Menzies Research Centre on 22 May 2017 in which he quoted Menzies as saying, 'The greatest tragedy that could overcome a country would be for it to fight a successful war in defence of liberty and lose its own in the process.'

42
SEVENTY-FIVE NEW LAWS AGAINST MURDER

'I'm old enough to remember that one of the reasons why we could be sure during the Cold War that the Soviets were the "bad guys" was because they were the ones who tapped their citizens' phones and read their mail, who could arrest their citizens without charge and detain them indefinitely without needing to prove them guilty of any crime—and "we", by contrast, did not do any of those things … Now we do.'

Saul Eslake[1]

Terrorism has been used to justify many of Australia's repressive new laws. Murdering people has long been a crime; so has conspiracy to murder and failing to tell the police what you know about a crime. These existing laws applied to terrorism (politically motivated violence) before new legislation made being murdered by a terrorist much more important than being murdered by anyone else.

Before the attacks in the US on 11 September 2001, terrorism was more prevalent than is now commonly realised, but politicians saw no reason to respond with draconian new laws. Nor did they exploit fears of terrorism. George Williams, the dean of law at the University of New South Wales, says the federal parliament has introduced seventy-five new terrorism laws since September 2001.[2] That number is far greater if state and territory parliaments are included.[3]

A list compiled from official and semi-official sources shows that there were 154 acts of politically motivated violence in Australia between June 1966 and September 2001, including bombings, stabbings and shootings.[4]

The targets included American, Yugoslav, Soviet, Mexican, Indian, Italian, Iranian, French, Turkish, Israeli, Indonesian, South African and Vietnamese diplomatic premises. Other targets included Serbian Orthodox churches, synagogues and mosques. Terrorists assassinated a Coptic Christian leader, a Church of Christ minister and a Turkish consul general. In July 2001, an anti-abortionist campaigner killed a security guard outside a Melbourne family planning clinic. Croatians attacked Serbian people and property, and vice versa. Croatian expatriates mounted armed incursions into Yugoslavia to try to spark a rebellion in 1963 and 1972.[5]

The absence of explicit anti-terrorism laws did not stop ASIO or the police from gathering intelligence on dangerous groups or individuals before an attack occurred. Police could lay conspiracy charges before a crime occurred. ASIO could have given more help if it had allocated fewer resources to building files on large numbers of harmless Australians. Some modest changes to the law might also have helped.

Despite the scale of politically motivated violence before 2001, political parties did not compete on who was toughest on terrorism. In February 1978 a bomb killed two garbage collectors and a policeman and injured eleven people after exploding in a garbage truck's compactor. The bomb had been placed in a garbage bin at Sydney's Hilton Hotel where a Commonwealth Heads of Government Meeting was being held. Despite the presence of twelve foreign leaders, the Fraser Government did not introduce special terrorism legislation after the incident.[6]

Murderers with no political, religious or ideological motivation also terrorise people, sometimes on a horrific scale. In April 1996, a mentally disturbed Hobart man, Martin Bryant, killed thirty-five people and wounded another twenty-three with a semi-automatic rifle at the historic convict jail Port Arthur. The Howard Government tightened gun-control laws, but did not start monitoring the mentally ill as potential criminals.

Terrorism should not be ignored, but much more could be done to reduce the large number of avoidable deaths from road accidents, domestic violence and other causes. One quarter of all homicides in Australia are committed by a current or former partner of the victim—the latest available report from the Australian Institute of Health and Welfare records 512 victims in the two years from 1 July 2012 to 30 June 2014. Many of these domestic violence incidents had multiple victims.[7] Since 2001, annual spending on ASIO has grown by a staggering 10.7 per cent; ASIS by 10.6 per cent; the AFP by 4.2 per cent; and Defence by 3.7 per cent—higher in every case than the average increase by governments on their other responsibilities.[8]

Compared with Bryant's horrendous toll in a few hours and the domestic violence toll of around 260 deaths a year, terrorists killed eight people between 1966 and September 2001 and injured at least thirty-five others. At the time of writing, terrorists had killed three people in Australia since September 2001;[9] no one was seriously injured in these incidents. More might have died if ASIO and the police had not prevented other planned attacks occurring.

Highlighting the heinous nature of terrorist violence and imposing heavy jail terms is meant to act as a deterrent, but governments and the media often promote a sensationalist treatment of terrorism that can have a perverse appeal for potential perpetrators. This is one reason intelligence officials such as former MI5 head Dame Eliza Manningham-Buller object strongly to US references to 'waging a war' on terrorism. Manningham-Buller said in her Reith Lectures, 'I have never thought it helpful to refer to a "war" on terror, any more than to a war on drugs. For one thing that legitimises the terrorists as warriors … What happened was a crime and needs to be thought of as such.'[10]

Terrorism doesn't pose an existential threat to Australia. Unlike an occupying military power, terrorists cannot take over and run the country. Nor can they kill more than a tiny proportion of the population. World War II killed 70 million people. A nuclear war could kill hundreds of millions. A serious breach of the quarantine safeguards could do more harm than terrorists.

The Howard Government went much further than was justified when it introduced a bill in 2002 to give ASIO detention and questioning powers that let it hold people in secret custody, including those who were not suspected of committing a crime. Detainees could be held incommunicado for seven days, couldn't contact their families or employers, couldn't be told why they were being held, could be denied normal access to lawyers, and could face five years' jail if they refused to answer questions or told anyone what happened for up to two years after their release. Amendments incorporated in the 2003 *ASIO (Terrorism) Act* softened some aspects of these powers. Innocent detainees can now have limited contact with their families and a lawyer, but their 'captors' decide when this occurs. Detainees can still be asked to reveal the location of an overseas acquaintance. If they do, they can reasonably fear that the information will be used to kill people if shared, as commonly occurs, with Australia's intelligence partners who engage in extrajudicial executions. No one should be required to answer such a question in these circumstances. Three legal scholars say the 2003 Act 'remains unique in the Western democratic world in that it establishes a system ... whereby an intelligence agency may coercively question and detain a non-suspect citizen'.[11] Yet John Howard signed up to George W. Bush's 2003 invasion of Iraq, 'Operation Enduring Freedom', while simultaneously curtailing freedom in Australia.

Federal police were later given powers to take people into 'preventative detention' for up to two weeks and subject others to 'control orders' that effectively put them under house arrest for up to twelve months. In his 2012 annual report, the independent national security legislation monitor, Bret Walker SC, recommended repealing these detention and control orders as unnecessary to keeping Australians safe. Subsequent governments have ignored his recommendations, although Walker warned that the control orders could continue to restrict a person's liberty after a prosecutor lost in court. A Sydney lawyer, Michael Bradley, commented, 'I do not trust the AFP to be a better judge of who should be locked up than our criminal courts. That is the definition of a police state.'[12] A joint state–Commonwealth review committee said the law reminded some people of the 'sudden and unexplained disappearance of citizens ... the fearful rule of discredited totalitarian regimes'.[13]

George Brandis was often disturbingly ignorant about the legislation he introduced while he was attorney-general. When unveiling a thick new terrorism bill in July 2014, he said, 'The *ASIO Act* is largely the 1979 *Act* and is in some respects obsolete—it predates the internet age.'[14] The 1979 *Telecommunications (Interception) Act* has been 'updated more than 50 separate times in the past two decades',[15] as reported by Melbourne academic Chris Berg. Berg says, 'The debate over national security powers is always held under a veil of ignorance. The democratic accountability problem is enhanced even further by the fact that—as Edward Snowden's leaks demonstrate—Western governments have repeatedly lied about their national security actions and have kept hidden evidence of their own wrongdoing.'[16] Berg argues that 'Any proposal by the government to increase its own power should be treated with scepticism. Double that scepticism when the government is vague about why it needs extra powers. Double again when those powers are for law and order. And double again every time the words "national security" are used.'[17]

Brandis further dismembered essential checks and balances in September 2014 when he introduced a new law making it a criminal offence for anyone to reveal anything about a 'Special Intelligence Operation', even though this law allows ASIO and its 'affiliates' to commit criminal acts other than murder and serious violent offences. There is no way for journalists, or anyone else, to find out if they might be breaking this law by checking with ASIO about whether a stuff-up was part of an SIO. Yet they could face five to ten years in jail for reporting something the public has every right to know. In a rare admission that a law went too far, the Turnbull Government partially exempted 'outsiders', such as journalists, from the law in 2016. But an 'inside' whistleblower who reveals that a suspicious death occurred during a botched operation could still face a savage jail sentence.

ASIO behaved impeccably during the AFP's wrongful arrest and charging of Mohamed Haneef with terrorism offences, telling the government there was no evidence the Gold Coast doctor was involved in terrorism. Shortly afterwards, the Director of Public Prosecutions (DPP) recommended the charges be dropped. But the government stubbornly backed the AFP's $8.2 million pursuit of Haneef until it admitted after twelve months that he was no longer a suspect. No AFP personnel were disciplined for confusing a gut instinct with evidence.

Nor do NSW counterterrorism police have a reassuring record. A University of NSW student spent a month in a high-security prison after police charged him with serious terrorism offences on 31 August 2018. The next day, the front page of Sydney's *Daily Telegraph* featured a photo-shopped image of the young Sri Lankan man wearing an Arab headdress, with the headline 'Poster boy for terror'. The charges were dropped a month later after two handwriting experts said it was unclear if he had written the note central to the case. The police initially refused to apologise.[18] Someone else was later charged.

Successive governments have also failed to protect the right of Australian citizens not to be tortured or wrongly imprisoned by the US. American agents detained Egyptian-Australian citizen Mamdouh Habib in Pakistan in October 2001 and interviewed him in the presence of officials from the AFP and ASIO. The CIA then 'rendered' him to Egypt, where he was tortured over several months before being transferred to the US military jail at its Guantánamo Bay naval base—located on territory the US seized from Cuba in a war in 1898 and never gave back. In January 2005, the US released Habib from Guantánamo without charge. The prosecutors explained that they lacked evidence, but this didn't stop Howard Government ministers continuing to imply that Habib was a terrorist.

In contrast, Stephen Harper's Conservative Canadian government conducted a thorough review after the CIA kidnapped one of its citizens, Maher Arar, and rendered him to Syria for torture by the government of the US's then friend President Bashar al-Assad. After the review established that Arar had been the innocent victim of false intelligence, he was awarded AU$11.4 million. In 2010, when Habib sued the Australian government over his detention and torture, the parties eventually agreed to an out-of-court settlement for an undisclosed sum.

The US treatment of a young Australian rural worker, David Hicks, also violated the Magna Carta's principles. A local warlord captured Hicks in Afghanistan in late 2001 and sold him for US$1000 to US troops, who transferred him to Guantánamo in early January 2002, where he was kept shackled in a cage.[19] The then attorney-general, Daryl Williams QC, described Hicks as 'one of the 10 most dangerous men in the world'.[20] The claim was ludicrous. Hicks consistently claimed he had been subjected to extended beatings, long interrogations, sleep deprivation and anal rape—treatment that was widely reported to be commonplace for supposedly dangerous prisoners. In early 2007, the then attorney-general, Philip Ruddock, responded to concerns about Hicks' deteriorating health by saying people in Australia didn't claim to be unfit to plead 'simply because they've been detained'.[21]

In March 2007, over five years after his capture, Hicks entered a pretrial plea to a single charge of providing material support for terrorism. He returned to Australia in May 2007. The US Court of Appeals ruled in October 2012 that the charge was invalid as his offence didn't exist in law when he allegedly committed it.

The Australian watchdog—the Inspector-General of Intelligence and Security—appears to have done a reasonable job of trying to tackle abuses of power, despite a tiny staff. However, no one scrutinises the quality of the secret reports from intelligence agencies. Many politicians and journalists simply assume that a 'Top Secret' stamp always transforms dross into gold. Respected economist Saul Eslake says, 'When it comes to matters of "security" any idea of close scrutiny or proper appraisal seems to go entirely out the window.'[22] The reality is that secrecy often hides incompetence and rewards conformity. Given the history of faulty reasoning and disastrous mistakes by our governments and security agencies, a separate oversight body is essential for maintaining quality control.

43

AUSTRALIA'S OWN NATIONAL SECURITY STATE

'The fact that the attorney-general of the day has the ultimate discretion about whether to launch a prosecution only adds to the concern.'
Paul Murphy, CEO of the Media, Entertainment and Arts Alliance[1]

It would be a brave soul who argued that the people of the former Soviet Union gained from the secrecy surrounding its national security agencies. The power of Australia's national security establishment has grown enormously in recent years, as has its protective wall of secrecy. A succession of new laws is turning Australia into a national security state. Even if parliament moderates a particular bill, the text gives a good guide to what the national security officials will later resurrect.

The Turnbull Coalition government went much further than any predecessor when it introduced two new bills in December 2017—the Espionage and Foreign Interference Bill and the Foreign Influence Transparency Scheme Bill. The first incorporated such a broad definition of espionage that it effectively suppresses public discussion on an unprecedented scale. A joint media organisations submission to the Parliamentary Joint Committee on Intelligence and Security on 22 January 2018 said the bill '[would criminalise] all steps of news reporting, from gathering and researching information to publication/communication, and [would apply] criminal risk to journalists, other editorial staff and support staff [who] know of the information that [would now be] an offence to "deal" with, hold and communicate'.[2] The submission quoted the bill as saying it could apply to the release and reception of 'information of any kind, whether true or false and whether in a material form or not, and includes (a) an opinion; and (b) a report of a conversation'.[3] When the amended bill became law, it retained this catch-all clause. The bill also made it an offence to leak, receive or publish 'inherently harmful information' and says that the prosecution does not have to prove it is national security classified information.[4]

Another new offence would be to publish anything that could 'harm or prejudice relations between the Commonwealth and a state or territory' or cause a 'loss of confidence or trust' in a state or Commonwealth government, however justified the loss of trust.[5] This would potentially criminalise a vast range of media reporting on everyday politics. The espionage bill provided a fifteen-year jail sentence for a new offence of publishing or broadcasting anything for an Australian audience concerning national security that could be available to a 'foreign principal' who read, listened to or watched what was reported. As the media has no control over who reads, sees or hears what it produces, this clause covers just about everything it produces. There would be almost no public interest defence.[6] The clause could apply to normal reporting and commentary that exposes stuff-ups by the intelligence services, scandalous behaviour in the defence forces, or the rising cost of weapons acquisitions.

The Law Council of Australia's submission to the same committee expressed its concern about another clause that would make it a national security offence to cause intangible damage or prejudice to Australia's international relations, 'including political, military, and economic relations'.[7] This offence is another that shouldn't exist in an open society— it could apply to criticism of US trade barriers, Indonesia's destruction of rainforest, or an arms build-up by China or India.

Not long after the harsh new laws to stop critical media report-ing on national security issues were introduced, the then chair of the Parliamentary Joint Committee on Intelligence and Security, Coalition MP Andrew Hastie, made a spirited defence of free speech in February 2019. His unusual behaviour was triggered by a court awarding the Chinese-Australian businessman Chau Chak Wing just under $800,000 including costs in a defamation case after Fairfax Media in 2015 accused him of bribing the president of the UN General assembly. The media group, which is now part of the Nine Network, said it would appeal the court's finding that it had not established its defence that the article was true. Hastie said he was concerned about the impact of the defamation laws: 'The ability to report freely and fairly on national security is a vital part of our democracy.' Never mind that he has been one of the most fervent supporters of new national security laws that provide severe jail sentences for journalists even if they report accurately on reprehensible behaviour by the security agencies.[8] Hastie seemed unconcerned that the court found serious errors in Garnaut's article.[9] Prime Minister Malcolm Turnbull commissioned Garnaut in 2016 to head a secret ASIO enquiry into Chinese influence in Australia. At the time of writing, the outcome of an appeal is not known and the report remains secret, so it is not possible to assess its overall accuracy.

Amid the proliferation of new offences, it is worth remembering that there has never been a classic espionage operation in which an Australian has divulged military or other governmental secrets of any significance to a foreign intelligence official.[10] Instead of spies on the ground, many espionage attempts these days rely on hacking into computers and databases from offshore locations. Encryption and protection of computer systems, not new laws, should prevent hacking of sensitive government information.

In discussing the bill, ministers didn't explain why espionage is fine when Australian spies do it overseas. Nor did they acknowledge that espionage can help prevent wars by providing information that convinces each side that the other has no aggressive intentions. No Australian politician has ever acknowledged the damage secrecy can cause. President John F. Kennedy, however, admitted he shouldn't have intervened to prevent the *New York Times* publishing sensitive details about the imminent invasion of Cuba by CIA-sponsored exiles in April 1961. The failed assault contributed to Cuba's decision to host Soviet nuclear-armed missiles, almost culminating in a nuclear war with the USSR in 1962. *Times* executives said Kennedy later told them, 'If you had printed more about the [CIA] operation, you would have saved us from a colossal mistake.'[11]

Leaks to the Australian media have never killed anyone. The US relies heavily on secret intelligence from Pine Gap in Central Australia to identify targets for bombing in the Middle East or for drone attacks elsewhere, often resulting in the death of civilians. Well-timed leaks about the phoney intelligence on Iraq's weapons of mass destruction might have prevented the 2003 invasion and its disastrous consequences. Official secrecy repeatedly conceals the killing of innocent people.

Two academic lawyers make a strong case that the 'lack of formal protection for free speech and other human rights has allowed Australia's federal parliament to enact many laws in response to terrorism that would be unthinkable in other [democratic] countries'.[12] They also note that the metadata laws requiring telecommunications companies to retain customers' digital information for two years can expose the identity of sources such as government officials. In late 2017 the government introduced Journalist Information Warrants, which agencies need from an issuing authority comprising lawyers approved by a minister before they access a journalist's metadata. Journalists can't contest the validity of a warrant because they are not told about it.

Some journalists find it much easier to toe the official line and stay 'on the drip' from ministers and security officials. A low point came when the ABC boasted in late January 2018 that it had received hundreds of highly classified Cabinet documents in a government filing cabinet that had been sold to a second-hand shop. It was an unwelcome gift. The ABC published a small number of bland stories before handing the lot to ASIO, and stressed that it had refused to report anything bearing a national security stamp in case it endangered public safety. Cabinet submissions never contain that sort of detail. If they did, you just don't report those aspects. In explaining its pathetic behaviour, the ABC implicitly condemned many journalists whose disclosure of highly classified material has served the public interest without hurting national security or any person.

It beggars belief that nothing in the hundreds of classified documents in the filing cabinet, including many below the classification 'Top Secret', could have been reported responsibly if the ABC had behaved more like a public broadcaster and less like an East German state broadcaster. A former senior Defence official, Patrick Gourley, said it was a 'gutless effort' by the ABC, adding, 'It is difficult to think of a single instance of a national security leak that has done any great harm.'[13]

Amendments to the espionage and foreign influence bills modified some of the problems before they became law on 28 June 2018. Maximum sentences for some offences were reduced and the attorney-general had to approve some prosecutions—but this is of scant value if the politician holding the office of attorney-general never rejects any request from intelligence officials that could help his or her party.

The Law Council remains unhappy with several clauses. It criticises the continued inclusion of reporting and commentary on 'economic and political relations with another country' in the definition of 'national security offence'.[14] The head of the Media, Entertainment and Arts Alliance, Paul Murphy, said, 'It took enormous effort by us and other media organisations to get amendments removing some of the [bill's] worst elements. But the legislation that eventually passed is still quite dangerous. It remains unclear at what point a journalist might cross the line and commit an offence under its provisions.'[15] He added, 'The fact that the attorney-general of the day has the ultimate discretion about whether to launch a prosecution only adds to the concern.'[16] Referring to the approval of bugging Timor-Leste's Cabinet offices for purposes that harmed that struggling country, Murphy said, 'The attorney-general Christian Porter's approval of the prosecution of "Witness K" and his lawyer Bernard Collaery is alarming.'[17]

44

FIGHTING A PHANTOM CALLED FOREIGN INFLUENCE AND THE ENCRYPTION DEMONS

'A proposal to break the security architecture of the Internet is so blindingly misconceived that the standards body that oversees the whole medium has told the government in writing to shelve it.'

Scott Ludlam[1]

The cross-fertilisation of ideas and influences from multiple sources, both foreign and local, greatly benefits science, the arts, business and public discussion. Yet Malcolm Turnbull's government in December 2017 introduced the Foreign Influence Transparency Scheme (FITS) Bill, which threatened these gains. A wide range of Australian people and organisations would potentially commit a crime unless they registered as an 'agent'. They would have to register if they acted for a foreign government, foreign public enterprise, foreign political organisation or foreign business that seeks to affect the Australian political system and government decisions. The bill's 1781-paragraph-long explanatory memorandum said failure to register would constitute a new criminal offence punishable by up to seven years' jail, and the head of the Attorney-General's Department would decide who should have registered but didn't.

There is no excuse for criminalising anything in this area beyond the standard US definition of an 'agent of influence' as a person who is 'directed by an intelligence organization to use his position to influence public opinion or decision-making in a manner that will advance the objective of the country for which the organization operates'.[2] ASIO has long had the power to deal with such agents. No Australian has ever been shown to meet this definition.

If new legislation can stop any country from covertly influencing Australian policy or elections, fine. Constraints on freedom of expression are different. With rare exceptions, it should be a fundamental democratic right for people to try to influence the opinions of others about all sorts of topics, including public policy. Bret Walker, a former independent monitor of Australia's national security laws, wrote, 'Much foreign influence is benign ... [including] support for increased trade, travel and cultural understanding ... Our politics would be devalued by the implication that good ideas come only from Australia.'[3]

Science is a standout example of the benefits of openness—but some commentators want Australian universities to cut joint scientific research with Chinese universities.[4] According to a January 2018 US National Science Foundation report, 23 per cent of US international articles in science and engineering are co-authored with Chinese collaborators. Australia's share is only 6 per cent.[5]

Apart from America's impact on Australia's defence and national security policies, the predominant influences on our governments are companies, lobbyists, journalists, think tanks, academics, churches and others wanting to sway government policy. Party discipline over how parliamentarians vote on legislation is often crucial—and responsive to campaign donations. The *Foreign Influence Transparency Scheme Act* banned foreign donations to political parties, but any ban should include the much more influential donations from Australian corporations and unions. Public disclosure should apply to behind-the-scenes approaches to governments and politicians, except perhaps from individuals acting on their own behalf. Others who publicly advocate policy changes should reveal any funding they receive from vested interests. Journalists and academics usually do this, but other commentators and think tanks should be far more transparent about their funding, as should lobbyists not covered by narrow existing regulations.

It's no secret that the US influences Australia's national security policy, even if the full extent of that influence remains behind closed doors. There is nothing necessarily unacceptable about this, but it would be surprising if much has changed in this regard since a congressional committee concluded that during the 1960s the CIA 'developed a worldwide system of standby covert assets, ranging from media personnel to individuals said to influence the behaviour of governments'.[6] As mentioned in Chapter 28, research by a Carnegie Mellon scholar, Dov Levin, found that the US intervened in eighty-one foreign elections between 1946 and 2000 while the Soviet Union/Russia did so in thirty-six.[7] The US also succeeded in overthrowing governments, while the Soviets tried and failed.[8] If Russia tried, there is no evidence it succeeded.

Like other countries, China is entitled to put its views to Australian governments through its representatives and media outlets. There is little convincing evidence that China exercises undue covert influence on government policy. Whatever influence it has didn't stop Prime Minister Turnbull repeatedly criticising China. When announcing the new legislation at a press conference, however, he stressed that China was not the sole target: 'Interference is unacceptable from any country, whether considered friend or foe.'[9] He added that there was no 'stain' in registering as a foreign agent. Some journalists' questions suggested there should be a 'stain' if China were involved. China undoubtedly tries to influence or bully people in Australia who have a Chinese background, but there are no significant examples of this changing government policies. In any event, all Australian citizens should be entitled to advocate policy changes, provided they don't accept clandestine inducements from any quarter.

Previously, Australia's intelligence agencies weren't as eager as they are today to exaggerate a possible threat. JIO head Gordon Jockel sent Prime Minister Malcolm Fraser a stinging analysis of a draft speech Fraser was due to deliver on 1 June 1976, saying, 'No service is done to the nation by those who portray an exaggerated spectre of Soviet power and of American weakness … The Soviet Union remains far behind the US and our allies in any overall assessment.'[10]

Former Labor prime minister Paul Keating won a quick retraction of the offensive imputations in a *Sydney Morning Herald* article that said confidential sources had suggested if the FITS Bill were to become law he would have to register as an 'agent of foreign influence' because he sat on the advisory council for the China Development Bank.[11] There is not a jot of evidence that Keating, who received a US$3000 annual board fee, acted as an agent of influence for China. Yet the article implied he should register because he had recently said Australia's 'foreign policy should be more independent of the US'. Expressing a view that millions of Australians share does not make Keating a Chinese agent of influence. Others who have served on this board include Henry Kissinger, former governors of central banks and development banks, and former managing directors of the International Monetary Fund. A healthy public debate means all Australians, including Keating, should be free to advocate a wide range of policies without attracting implicit slurs about their loyalty.

Few believe that an intense effort will go into examining the large number of Australian politicians, academics, think-tank members and journalists who have spoken in support of the United States, accepted US study grants or been on US-paid trips to America. Other problems arise when government insiders become clandestine sources for another country. WikiLeaks published cables in 2010 showing the US State Department had repeatedly stated that the identity of a Labor minister, Mark Arbib, as a 'protected source' must be 'guarded'.[12]

The government watered down the FITS Bill after it realised that dozens of vocal businesses, think tanks, lobbyists, law firms, charities and advocacy groups would have been caught in its net. The revised bill excluded charities, arts organisations, most think tanks and lobby groups, among others, but many of the original clauses suppressing freedom of expression were barely changed in the legislation that passed on 28 June 2018.

The flood of new laws did not stop with the passage of this law. Complex draft legislation, blandly named the 'Assistance and Access' Bill, was released in August 2018 that would allow the authorities to 'add, copy, delete or alter' data after people had been forced to hand over their phones and computers in defined circumstances.[13] Tech companies would have to comply with similar requests about their customers' data. If they refused, they would be subject to a jail sentence of up to five years, or a fine of up to $10 million. Individuals could face a fine of up to $50,000.

The barely amended bill was passed in December 2018 after only four days of parliamentary scrutiny, with the Morrison Government boasting that the new law was a world first. But beating China and the US in these stakes is nothing to boast about. The new law lets ASIO and eleven other agencies issue 'technical assistance notices' and 'technical capability notices' to a wide range of technology companies, including manufacturers of smart phones and other devices, internet service providers, social media platforms, software developers and many others. The notices can force these companies to help the agencies access their customers' encrypted messages surreptitiously, sometimes prior to encryption; remove electronic protection; alter or remove data; build in new technology to gain entry; and insert software to conduct covert surveillance of the devices' owners.

A politician (the attorney-general) usually authorises technical assistance notices. The Law Council of Australia has been concerned that it is unclear whether the more intrusive technical capability notices require a warrant from a court.[14] The council's 2018 president, Morry Bailes, said it is also seriously concerned that the new law allows the agencies to detain individuals to provide compulsory assistance without them being allowed to contact a lawyer.[15] Some tech employees are concerned that the agencies could compel them to do things without telling their employer.[16]

The government insisted it won't build vulnerabilities into communication systems, but a wide range of knowledgeable opponents of the bills, including tech giants, say this is unavoidable.[17] One concern is that introducing flaws into systems could damage Australia's $3.2 billion IT export industry.[18] As well as weakening the overall system, the problem with inserting malware or a virus is that it can escape and end up in the hands of criminals, as happened with the NSA's malware called WannaCry, which in 2017 was used in ransomware attacks on hundreds of thousands of systems.[19] It is not publicly known what malware or viruses the Australian agencies will insert on devices under the new encryption law, but there is a good chance that the NSA will supply them.

Scott Ludlam, a tech-savvy commentator and former Greens senator, noted that the Internet Engineering Task Force, which is responsible for setting key technology standards, 'has rejected the development of any system designed to aid state actors [to] compromise the security of Internet communications'.[20] He said that a proposal to break the security architecture of the internet is 'so blindingly misconceived that the standards body that oversees the whole medium has told the government in writing to shelve it'.[21]

The Morrison government stressed that the new law will help catch terrorists and paedophiles, but it also covers minor offences that are normally dealt with in local courts. This is because it applies to offences with a maximum sentence of three years' jail where convictions often lead to little or no jail time. If terrorists and paedophiles were really the main target, the threshold could have begun with offences having a maximum sentence of over ten years.

The twelve agencies can act on requests from foreign countries, with no apparent safeguards about whether the information can be used for sinister activities such as extrajudicial executions. The law's purposes, including the protection of Australia's 'foreign relations' and 'national economic well-being', are so broadly defined that a request for access would be hard for a court to deny.

It takes a special kind of arrogance for Australia's political leaders and their intelligence bosses to presume they know better than most international specialists. At the time of writing, it is unclear what amendments the winner of the 2019 federal election might make to this law, which has all the hallmarks of a modern police state. The only safe option is to scrap it.

45
THE NATIONAL SECURITY SUPREMO

'The state has to embed itself invisibly into global networks and supply chains, and the virtual realm, in a seamless and largely invisible fashion, intervening on the basis of intelligence and risk settings, increasingly over a super scale and very high volumes.'

Michael Pezzullo, head of Home Affairs[1]

Ignoring the dangers, the Turnbull Government created an overarching new bureaucratic structure to run the nation's immensely powerful security apparatus. Called the Home Affairs Department, it incorporates ASIO, the Australian Federal Police, the Australian Border Force, the Australian Criminal Intelligence Commission, and the Australian Transaction Reports and Analysis Centre. It also has responsibility for immigration; border control; transport, cyber and critical infrastructure security; and countering foreign interference, among other duties.

The creation of the new department was not recommended by an independent report. A former senior Defence official and Immigration Department head, Michael Pezzullo, drove its formation; he also happened to be its first head. Labor has supported the new departmental structure, if not all the details. ASIO was previously an independent agency within the attorney-general's portfolio, while the AFP had earlier been in the former Justice Department. While the attorney-general (AG) has retained responsibility for issuing warrants for phone intercepts, four junior ministers in the Home Affairs portfolio have gained the power to approve requests for control orders that can put people under house arrest, including those who haven't been convicted of a crime. Although all the agencies are supposed to remain independent within Home Affairs, the decision to put so much power in the hands of one Cabinet minister, initially Peter Dutton, and a single departmental supremo, Pezzullo, weakened the checks and balances inherent in the previous portfolio arrangements.

ASIO is already too powerful, having been transformed into a formidable arm of executive government—a process that began when John Howard was prime minister. The AFP has also accrued more powers, and an appetite for using them. Instead of being placed in a new department eager for them to exercise their authority, ASIO and the AFP should be in separate departments, have fewer powers and face much better resourced external scrutiny. The changes are an emphatic illustration of how far the nation has moved from the days when Prime Minister Robert Menzies scrapped proposed espionage and secrecy laws in 1952.[2]

The day before George Brandis left the AG's job in February 2018, journalist Karen Middleton reported that he had told a closed meeting of ASIO officers that he feared the new departmental structure could make the intelligence organisation vulnerable to political interference.[3] She said Brandis quoted from the Pezzullo speech cited above where he said that the state had to embed itself invisibly into global networks and supply chains, and the virtual realm, in a seamless and largely invisible fashion. Pezzullo's words gave scant comfort to those concerned about growing totalitarian tendencies in Australia. However, we are yet to reach the American situation, where a two-year investigation concluded that 1271 US government organisations and 1931 private companies work on programs related to counterterrorism, homeland security and intelligence in about 10,000 locations across the country.[4]

Pezzullo, a passionate Catholic, said globalisation had created a 'dark universe [in which] evil is becoming much more manifest … You can never stop thinking about how to improve your security settings [because] homes are no longer sealed off from the outside.'[5] A former senior Defence official, Paddy Gourley, responded to Pezzullo's almost apocalyptic vision of the future by noting that murder rates have gone down in Australia (as have overall crime rates). He said, 'The main danger for people in their houses comes from their inhabitants; in the last 50 years, thousands of women in Australia were murdered in their homes by their partner.'[6]

Pezzullo also said, 'The very architecture of security has to be re-engineered. This Home Affairs enterprise will, in effect, create the third force of security, the third pillar … [Its] security power is designed to protect the home front acting on a global scale, organised into a single enterprise to deal with the interconnected globalised threats that we face at home, recalling that home is not what it used to be.'[7] It's unclear what the second pillar is, but he says the first is Defence, which projects hard power abroad. Pezzullo set out what he saw as the seven major threats to Australia in the speech in March 2019. The list included Islamic terrorists, but not white supremacists.[8] Two days later, an Australian white supremacist murdered 50 people praying in two Christchurch mosques in New Zealand.

Home Affairs has not merely overseen the existing security laws: it has taken the lead role in creating new legislation to feed new forms of multifaceted information about individuals into its centralised databases. It led the push to adopt new 'identity matching' legislation that lets it amalgamate and disseminate a wide range of biometric and other identifying information on most Australians. Although not always accurate, facial-recognition technology is applied to photos from passports, drivers' licences, and so on.[9] The program is expected to incorporate other biometric and fingerprint data. No warrant is needed for approved agencies to gain access.

A researcher with Human Rights Watch warns that Home Affairs has broad powers to add and share new identity-matching information,[10] while the Law Council cautions that a strict line should be drawn between using identity matching to investigate serious crimes, such as terrorism, and using it to fine jaywalkers and litterers. Otherwise, the council says, the system could 'creep towards broad social surveillance of Australia's citizens'.[11]

Home Affairs was instrumental in introducing the draft bill in August 2018 to greatly expand the ability of security agencies and police to force people and companies to give them access to encrypted messages on their electronic devices and computers.[12] The bill became law on 6 December 2018, with almost no time for proper parliamentary scrutiny of the final version. No other country has gone to such extreme lengths to force companies to alter their systems to facilitate access by the security agencies, and, as noted earlier, such alterations could potentially introduce damaging weaknesses.

Middleton reported that when Pezzullo was giving evidence to the Parliamentary Joint Committee on Intelligence and Security, he downplayed concerns about the lack of external warrants to approve notices to companies to help an agency gain access to encrypted data. He gave a dismissive answer to the committee hearing on 19 October 2018: 'If we were to say to you that a notice is a warrant, and through an incantation and the sprinkling of some magic dust on it, all of a sudden greater oversight was achieved—it's the same person. It's the attorney-general of the

Commonwealth rigorously discharging their ministerial responsibilities.'[13] However, it would be different if a court had to issue a warrant to make a company do something it insisted would introduce a weakness into its system. This would not be the same as letting a politician called an attorney-general sprinkle magic dust to ensure it was all legal and above board.

On 16 November 2018, the inspector-general of intelligence and security, Margaret Stone, told the same committee when referring to the authorisation of notices, 'This is not abracadabra. It's not an incantation. It has to be real.'[14] Stone also said she was 'very concerned that the inspector-general's office doesn't appear in the legislation' it was expected to oversight. Middleton made the point that the other members of the Five Eyes intelligence club (the US, UK, Canada and New Zealand) all received the draft encryption bill and were kept informed about what was happening, unlike Stone or the Commonwealth ombudsman, Michael Manthorpe. Apparently, Pezzullo's priorities were to keep this Anglo-Saxon club happy rather than giving timely information to the Australian watchdogs whose responsibility it is to oversee the conduct of our intelligence and security agencies.

When Pezzullo moves on, it seems highly likely that he will be replaced by someone with a similar mindset. There is almost no example since 1952 of an Australian government repealing a national security law without replacing it with a tougher version, but the growth of ever more powerful intelligence and law enforcement agencies must be reversed if Australia wants to restore the individual liberties that have been lost.

In an open society, the media would act as a check on Home Affairs' excessive use of its powers. But Australia is no longer an open society. As noted, unlike the legal situation throughout the twentieth century, it is now a criminal offence to receive leaked government information and some non-government material. When this new offence is combined with the national security state's ability to access encrypted digital data, it becomes much easier to keep the public in the dark, because the state will know who has been in contact with journalists.

In these circumstances, investigative journalist Andrew Fowler will have warned in vain: 'Unless there is a concerted effort by the West to abandon the surveillance state into which we are all being drawn, it is highly likely that the journalism that relies on dissent to expose the great injustices perpetrated by governments, particularly when they hide behind the cloak of national security, will be journalism of the past. It won't disappear over-night, but will fade slowly over the years, like the democracy it defends.'[15]

PART 8

THIRTEEN WARS—ONLY ONE A WAR OF NECESSITY FOR AUSTRALIA

46

THE FOUNDATION MYTH OF
OUR FOUR COLONIAL WARS

'Not only a test of wartime courage, but a test of character, that has helped define our nation and create the sense of who we are.'

Prime Minister Julia Gillard[1]

Opposition to Australian participation in nineteenth-century colonial wars in New Zealand, Sudan, South Africa and China was strongest when memories of those wars were freshest immediately after Federation in 1901. Many considered the country's leaders had been much too willing to send troops overseas to fight in places that posed no threat to Australia.

Following the vicious Boer War in South Africa, most leading political figures strongly opposed further expeditionary campaigns at the behest of the British 'protector'. Once it became clear that Australia needed no protection from minor 'enemies', fears were put aside with a maturity lacking in many modern Australian leaders keen to embark on more expeditionary wars. Three-time prime minister and Protectionist/Liberal Party leader Alfred Deakin was one of the strongest opponents of participating in more expeditionary wars, but he had taken a different view in the 1880s, when he wanted an imperial role for Australia in the South Pacific. The Queensland premier, Thomas McIlwraith, even took possession of eastern New Guinea and its offshore islands in the name of Queen Victoria, but was overruled by Britain.[2]

After World War I, most Australians seemed content to forget about the colonial wars. It wasn't until Julia Gillard became Labor prime minister in the twenty-first century that any leader tried to instil a sense of pride in Australia's contribution to these wars. In a speech in April 2011, quoted above, she called our participation in the colonial wars a 'test of wartime courage and character' that had helped define our nation. She said in the same speech, 'We live in a free country, and in a largely free world, only because the Australian people answered the call when the time of decision came.' The extravagance of Gillard's rhetoric was rivalled only by her ignorance.

The 1885 expedition to Sudan had nothing to do with Australia's freedom, let alone Sudan's: Britain wanted to secure its colonial control of Sudan via British-occupied Egypt. Nor did the expedition create an enduring 'sense of who we are'—unless Gillard meant that we are always willing to go to war, no matter how irrelevant the conflict might be to Australia.

While the Sudan expedition was underway, many Australians did not share Gillard's later fervour. The Australian War Memorial's online history of the expedition says, 'Meetings intended to launch a patriotic fund and endorse the government's action were poorly attended in many working-class suburbs, and many of those who turned up voted against the fund. In some country centres there was a significant anti-war response, while miners in rural districts were said to be in "fierce opposition".'[3]

Far from being a noble chapter in Australian history, the Sudan adventure was a minor farce. Gillard's stirring tale of valour in battle is unrecognisable in any account of what happened. In 1885, the New South Wales government sent a contingent of 758 soldiers to Sudan to avenge the death of General Charles Gordon during a popular uprising against British control. He had been dubbed 'Chinese' Gordon for his exploits in China, where he had helped suppress an uprising against European control of Shanghai as a trading centre. In Sudan's case, the British didn't even ask its colonies for help—the NSW government offered the troops, and the British accepted provided NSW paid for them and they were under British command. It rejected offers from other states.

Britain's goals in Sudan were to exclude its French rivals and (half-heartedly) avenge the death of the eccentric and unmanageable general. Gordon, who had previously been governor-general of Sudan, had been sent back in 1884 to evacuate Egyptian troops who had been defeated during the local uprising in Khartoum. Disobeying orders, he used some of the Egyptian troops to attack the Sudanese insurgents and died in the failed attack.

The NSW contingent sailed on 3 March 1885. Instead of a chance to display the 'wartime courage' that Gillard later found so inspiring, the action was over by the time the contingent arrived on 29 March. The War Memorial says, 'Far from the excitement they had imagined, the Australians suffered mostly from the enforced idleness of guard duties.'[4]

Two new colonial wars beckoned—one in South Africa and one in China. In the latter case, Australia answered the call from Britain by sending ships and soldiers to help suppress the Boxer Rebellion. The Boxers (a European term) were members of one of several secret societies rising against Western intruders who had successfully demanded the right to large tracts of land and other concessions, including exemption from Chinese law. Australians knew little of the background beyond reports that the Boxers were attacking Westerners. Initially, our troops were sent to help capture a Chinese fort at Pei Tang, but in an echo of the Sudan campaign, by the time they got there the battle was over. Other Australian troops joined an international contingent to take another fort, only to find the town had already surrendered. The War Memorial history says, 'The international column then marched back to Tientsin [Tianjin] leaving a trail of looted villages behind them.'[5]

Again, this doesn't support Gillard's claims about how the colonial wars helped Australians to show 'courage on the battlefield' and create a 'sense of who we are', unless she meant looters. This aggressive Western intervention and the earlier wars promoted by British officials, corporations and traders to force China to open its borders to the opium trade help explain why the leadership in Beijing today is determined never to suffer such humiliation again.[6]

Gillard also supported the 1899–1902 Boer War, although there was little to celebrate in this conflict. No courage on the battlefield was needed when Australian soldiers shot unarmed civilians who'd surrendered. The British and the Dutch had earlier dispossessed the indigenous population of some of their lands in what is now South Africa. It was a brutal war between the British-led troops and descendants of Dutch settlers called Boers over control of territory. After the British raided a Boer state in an attempt to seize recently discovered goldmines, the Boers declared war. Queensland offered to send troops before Britain asked, but when the other states were asked, they all sent contingents as well. NAA records show that a total of 10,000 soldiers or more served in the Australian contingents; over 500 of them died.[7]

As the conflict dragged on, Australians at home became disenchanted, especially as the effects on Boer civilians became known.[8] After the initial stage, each side turned to guerilla warfare and the conflict became nastier. Over the next two years the British set up what they initially called refugee camps but later described as concentration camps. Similar camps were established in other wars, including the 1898 US invasion and occupation of the Philippines.[9] A Boer War historian says that the South African camps included women and children who had been forced from their homes by Britain's scorched earth policy, 'in which thousands of homesteads were burnt and food supplies, livestock and crops destroyed'.[10]

A War Memorial backgrounder for voluntary guides discussed the number of people who had died of starvation, disease and exposure in the concentration camps, noting that the precise number of deaths of black Africans in concentration camps is unknown as little attempt was made to keep any records of the black Africans who were interned.[11] Another historian says that no fewer than 145,000 Boers and 140,000 black Africans were interned. Of these, at least 27,927 white people (including 22,074 children) and at least 23,000 ('probably many more') black people died in the camps.[12]

In early 2019, the War Memorial removed the backgrounder from its website because parts of it were inaccurate; there are no plans to replace it with other information on the use of scorched earth policies and concentration camps in the Boer War.[13]

Although Gillard's speech praised all the colonial wars, she didn't specifically mention the sporadic New Zealand wars from 1845 to 1872. Given the inducement of being allowed to settle on confiscated Maori land, about 2500 Australian volunteers answered the call. In part, the New Zealand conflict paralleled the Frontier Wars already underway in Australia, where white settlers and police, sometimes aided by British troops, suppressed Aboriginal efforts to prevent further dispossession of their land. A common estimate is that 20,000 Indigenous people and 2000 white people died in the Frontier Wars. More recent research concludes that over 60,000 died in Queensland alone.[14] An even larger number of Aboriginal people died due to introduced diseases and starvation after being evicted from their hunting grounds. In comparison, the War Memorial says that from 1860 to the time of writing, 102,868 Australians have died in overseas wars.[15]

47

WORLD WAR I: LABOR'S SECRET PLANS FOR AN EXPEDITIONARY FORCE

'Australia—not Empire—is the string we must harp on. We must encourage them to do what they will do willingly and lavishly, namely pay up for safeguarding a White Australia from the cursed Jap.'

General Sir Ian Hamilton[1]

Following Federation, the British initially struggled to rekindle Australian support for new expeditionary wars. Reflecting this disenchantment, the 1903 *Defence Act* authorised the government to call up males only for home defence in times of war, but not overseas service. After World War I broke out in August 2014, referendums to boost troop numbers by introducing conscription were lost in 1916 and 1917.[2]

A letter discovered by historian Greg Lockhart in the archive of British general Sir Ian Hamilton's papers in London gives a striking insight into the depth of Australians' feelings. Hamilton wrote to the British prime minister, H.H. Asquith, saying that when he arrived in Australia in early 1914 to earmark a section of the Australian Army for expeditionary Imperial service, he found the country stood firm against this proposition until he appealed to old fears. He said they would 'pay up for safeguarding a White Australia from the cursed Jap. When the time comes, and when we are fighting for our lives in India or elsewhere, I for one am confident the whole military force of Australia will be freely at our disposal.'[3]

Hamilton was right about Australians' fear of Japan, although that country was a British ally at the time. Labor's leader, Andrew Fisher, was deeply disturbed by the ease with which Japan had won the 1904–05 war with Russia. While he was PM in 1909, Fisher ordered three torpedo destroyers to help defend against a Japanese invasion. The Opposition leader, Alfred Deakin, had long warned about the Japanese danger, but he maintained the strong opposition to expeditionary wars he had earlier expressed as prime minister.

Lockhart notes that another historian, John Mordike, discovered in another secret War Office archive that Labor's defence minister, George Pearce, offered to establish an expeditionary force during a meeting of the June 1911 Imperial Conference in London, provided the ultimate intention was kept completely secret.[4] In 1909, Pearce referred to the threat the Japanese posed to Australia, and more generally the threat from the "'hordes of semi-barbarians" to the north'.[5]

Following this meeting, Lockhart says the necessary preparations began for Australia to develop an expeditionary force without any publicity about its purpose. This made a crucial difference to how quickly the government was able to send volunteer forces overseas after the war began in July 1914.

As former army officers, Lockhart and Mordike reject the official war historian C.E.W. Bean's claim that the 20,000-man Australian Imperial Force was raised and ready to be sent to war in six weeks. According to Lockhart, 'No one builds an army of that size and quality from nothing in that time. It overlooks the myriad requirements—planning, organisation, tactical doctrine, training, supply, equipment and transport—without which the raising of such a force would have been impossible.'[6]

Contrary to the common assumption, Lockhart says, the British were not arguing in 1911 that Germany was any threat to Australia. Instead, a report that year by the Committee of Imperial Defence concluded, 'With no more than 2500 German troops sprinkled between German colonies in Africa and China, a German landing in Australia was "to the last degree improbable".'[7]

Lockhart's conclusion to his essay is that the sentimentality of the dominant historical literature still protects the imperial ascendency of 1911–14 in the culture as well as the politics of the nation. He says, 'That is the great deception: Australians still have as little idea of why they were fighting in World War I as of why they are fighting in Afghanistan. The deception has nurtured the autocratic war-making powers of a few ministers each time they decide to send off an expedition. The expeditionary strategy and related culture [have] saved us from nothing, caused great grief and could cause more.'[8]

Writer Paul Daley says the war was only a horrific beginning for many of the injured: 'The shell-shocked, like the limbless and disfigured, were kept from view while the nation mourned its lost generation and stoically got on with the task of building the nation. The front doors were bolted shut—hiding the domestic violence, the untouched dinners, the terrified kids, the countless suicides, the rampant alcoholism and the morphine addiction.'[9]

Journalist Tony Stephens interviewed many Gallipoli veterans before they died and said they used their ebbing years 'to stress that battlefields are unsatisfactory places to resolve arguments'.[10] Albert White, a veteran who had never been previously interviewed about the war, told Stephens, 'Gallipoli was a bastard of a place. I never understood what we were fighting for. All I could think of is I never wanted to go back to the bloody place.'[11] Alec Campbell, the last survivor to die, was more sanguine, telling Stephens that Gallipoli took less than a year, or 1 per cent of his life: 'It's not all that important personally.'[12] Campbell went on to be president of the Launceston Trades Hall Council, complete an economics degree when he was over fifty years old, and campaign with Lady Jessie Street for peace.

Australian governments spent hundreds of millions of dollars more than the British did in commemorating the 100th anniversary of World War I. Unfortunately, they rarely mentioned that New Zealand was part of the ANZAC forces. Stephens mused on what those who served in Gallipoli would make of it all: 'It's not just the ceremonies but what David Stephens of the Honest History Coalition calls Anzackery—the luxury cruises to Gallipoli, music and television shows, stubby holders, plethora of children's books, T-shirts, the Anzac Day display in the fruit and vegetable pavilion of Sydney's Royal Easter Show and Woolworths' attempt to keep Anzac "Fresh in Our Memory".'[13] In Stephens' view, 'Many of the old soldiers ... would agree with the idea that Anzac Day be reinvented as a day for all victims of war.'[14]

One of the great lessons of World War I is that it started for no rational reason.[15] Australian politicians sent young people off to a horrendously wasteful war when the nation's security was not at risk. But it's now common to hear young people interviewed on Anzac Day say how proud they are that their great-grandfather or great-uncle served at Gallipoli to defend Australia. They weren't defending Australia: they were helping to invade Turkey, a country that posed no threat to us.

Much has also been written in recent years about the undoubted skill and endurance shown by horses and riders during the Australian cavalry charge in 1917 during the battle for Beersheba, which was then in Turkish-controlled Palestine and is now in Israel. There is rarely any mention of the part that the capture of Beersheba played in furthering the goals of the secret 1916 Sykes–Picot Agreement between Britain and France on how to share spheres of influence in territory taken from the Ottoman Empire. Often, the new borders created ongoing problems by ignoring existing divisions on ethnic, religious and linguistic grounds. In a crime that was covered up for decades, Australian and New Zealand troops massacred all the Bedouin males in a camp at Surafend in Palestine shortly after the 1918 Armistice began. As many as 100 were killed and the camp burnt.[16]

Instead of letting the dead rest in peace, some distant descendants of 200–300 Australian and British soldiers killed in France convinced the Australian government in 2007 to undertake a multimillion-dollar project to dig up the remains at a 1916 group burial site, do DNA tests where possible, and then re-bury them in individual graves in a newly built cemetery. The simplest option—and the most respectful, in the view of many correspondents to newspapers—would have been to erect a commemorative plaque at the site.[17] But others successfully argued that identifying the remains was essential to their getting 'closure' about the deaths of grand-uncles they never knew.[18]

Recent political leaders have been keen to rekindle the pride in an Australian warrior culture built around the landing at Gallipoli in April 1915 and later battles in the trenches in France. Prime Minister Julia Gillard claimed in an Anzac Day address, 'This was our first act of nationhood before the eyes of a watching world.'[19] However, the former Coalition prime minister Malcolm Fraser said it was absurd for a country to claim it became a nation by answering the call from another nation to go to a war where its troops were under the ultimate command of generals of that other nation (Britain).[20]

Australia has been a nation since Federation in 1901, and would have remained one if it had avoided World War I and the terrible suffering that did not stop with the end of the war. Paul Keating gave a powerful rebuttal to Gillard's claim that World War I made Australia a nation. Speaking at the War Memorial on 11 November 2013, he said, 'There was nothing missing in our young nation that required a martial baptism of the European cataclysm to legitimise us … We were moving through the processes of Federation to new ideas of ourselves. Notions of equality and fairness, suffrage for women, a universal living wage, support in old age, a sense of inclusive patriotism.' He said this sense of nationhood brought new resonances—Australian stories and poetry—and new ideas such as Federation architecture.

These were real national achievements, unlike participating in a war where at least 60,000 Australians were officially killed and 156,000 were wounded out of a population of under five million. More recent estimates of the overall casualty numbers are much higher.[21]

48

WORLD WAR II: NO SOVEREIGN INTEREST IN THE INTEGRITY OF AUSTRALIA

'The United States was an ally whose aim was to win the war [and who had] no sovereign interest in the integrity of Australia. [Its purpose] in building its forces in the Commonwealth was not so much from an interest in Australia but rather from its utility as a base from which to hit Japan … The US would be doing it irrespective of the American relationship to the people who might be occupying Australia.'
John Edwards quoting what General Douglas MacArthur told Prime Minister John Curtin in a meeting in Melbourne on 1 June 1942[1]

The most important theatre for Australia in World War II was the Pacific, not Europe, but we agreed to send expeditionary forces to Europe and the Middle East immediately World War II formally began in September 1939. Unlike earlier expeditionary wars, this contribution could be justified initially as a response to Hitler's invasion of Austria, Czechoslovakia and Poland—later reinforced by details about his slaughter of six million people in gas chambers.

The Soviet Union played the dominant role in defeating Hitler after he invaded Russia while trying to finish his conquest of Europe and much of the Middle East. The supply of American arms and, eventually, troops also helped. British historian Richard Evans says, 'The sheer scale of the conflict between the Wehrmacht and the Red Army dwarfed anything seen anywhere else during World War II. From 22 June 1941, the day of the German invasion, there was never a point at which less than two-thirds of the German armed forces were engaged on the eastern front. Deaths on the eastern front numbered more than in all the other theatres of war put together, including the Pacific.[2] Hunger inflicted a horrific toll during the 872-day siege of Leningrad. A book by highly regarded Russian historian Sergey Yarov states, 'While the exact number who died during the siege ... will never be known, available data point to 900,000 civilian deaths, over half a million of whom died in the winter of 1941–42 alone[3] ... When the military deaths in three years of fighting in or near Leningrad are added, the total death toll may have been as high as two million.'[4] Soviet soldiers and civilians are commonly estimated to have accounted for over 80 per cent of all German military casualties in World War II, at the enormous cost of at least 26 million Soviet civilians and soldiers dying.

In an essay on the origins of the Pacific War, veteran journalist Max Suich said, 'Australia was at the very centre of the inflammatory issues that led to war with Japan: disputes over access to raw materials; competition for markets that became a trade war; hostile denunciations and diplomatic exchanges arising from racial pride and imperial alliances.'[5] He said Australia was overtly antagonistic to Japan on the international stage as early as 1919, when Prime Minister Billy Hughes publicly humiliated the Japanese government at the postwar Paris Peace Conference by vetoing its request to be formally acknowledged as an equal with the white Anglo-Saxon empires. Suich warned, 'The hostile, clumsy and rarely coherent polices Australia adopted towards Japan after World War I are exhibiting faint but disturbing parallels with our policies towards China, the new rising Asian giant ... China is not the dissatisfied militaristic nation that glorified war and pursued expansionism that Japan was. However, some of the forces at work at that time have their counterparts today.'[6]

Initially, the Japanese advanced rapidly after their December 1941 invasion of South-East Asia and their attack on Pearl Harbor on 7 December that year. After the US commander, General Douglas MacArthur, was forced out of the Philippines, he set up a more secure headquarters in Australia. As quoted above, he left no doubt that his primary mission was not to save Australia's neck.

Biographer John Edwards says that MacArthur told Prime Minister John Curtin on 1 June 1942 that any appeal now 'should not be for forces for offensive action but for those necessary to ensure the security of Australia by adequate defence'—a line of thought that Edwards says probably encouraged Curtin to warn of the threat of invasion long after it receded.[7]

The historian Clem Lloyd reported in the *National Times* in 1983 that a young historian, David Wilde, had discovered archival records indicating that Curtin deliberately magnified the threat of a Japanese invasion to ensure the survival of his government and boost the bedraggled morale of the Australian people. Lloyd said Wilde's interpretation was confirmed in part by the newspaper's own research in the US National Archives in Washington, DC. Wilde concluded that Curtin's government received highly accurate intelligence 'which indicated that invasion of Australia was never a probability, even in the early months of 1942 ... and never part of Japan's initial war plans'.[8]

The notion that the US set out to rescue Australia remains a powerful influence on national thinking, although MacArthur told Curtin on 1 June 1942 that the US was 'not interested in preserving the sovereign integrity of Australia'.[9] Japan's success in catching the Americans off-guard and the speed of its initial advance have lodged in the minds of many Australians, but big improvements in surveillance technology over the seventy-five years since then should provide ample time to bolster defences against a similar downward thrust in the future.

Australian politicians and war planners relied on British assurances that its large naval base in Singapore would defend Australia. Hindsight is not needed to conclude that the planners recklessly ignored the obvious: defending Singapore would not be a British priority once Britain faced a serious threat in Europe. The War Memorial's summary of World War II says that over 130,000 troops on Singapore surrendered on 15 February 1942, including 15,000 Australians; 7000 of those captured died before the war's end.[10] The collapse of the Singapore garrison was a stunning failure of Australia's doctrine of forward defence. Had our troops been kept at home for deployment in the South Pacific, far fewer would have been taken prisoner and endured the horrors of the Sandakan death march and the Thai–Burma Railway.

The War Memorial says thousands of Australian airmen continued to serve in Europe and the Middle East after Japan entered the war. Although more RAAF members fought against the Japanese, losses among those flying against Germany were far higher. Some 3500 Australians were killed in this German campaign, making it the costliest of the war.[11] These aircrew could have been brought home immediately after Pearl Harbor to reinforce the Australian troops that had been withdrawn from the Middle East.

A total of 39,000 Australian servicemen and women died in World War II. Over 30,000 were taken prisoner, and two-thirds of these were captured by the Japanese in the first weeks of 1942. While those who became prisoners of the Germans had a strong chance of returning home, 36 per cent of prisoners of the Japanese died in captivity.[12]

By 1944, the Japanese navy was almost destroyed and its air force had been crippled, but forty army divisions were still tied down in China and Manchuria by local resistance fighters, compared to twenty-three divisions trying to resist the American advance through the Pacific, and another nineteen divisions that were occupied in South-East Asia.[13] Without the efforts of the resistance fighters in China and Manchuria in particular, the Japanese could have put up a far more formidable fight against the advancing Americans. This tremendous contribution from Japan's Asian opponents is often overlooked in discussions about the role the US and Australia played.

Almost one million Australian men and women served in World War II out of a population of seven million. Australian industry supplied huge quantities of food, medicine, clothing and other support to Australian and American troops. Although US naval and air support was valuable in securing supply lines in the south-west Pacific, Defence analyst Andrew Ross makes a strong case that Australia's own forces would have mounted a formidable defence against any feasible Japanese invasion.[14] Referring to the Allied war effort in a report to Congress in December 1946, President Harry S. Truman said, 'On balance, the contribution made by Australia, a country having a population of about seven million, approximately equaled [that of] the US.'[15] An impressive industrial base in 1942 quickly began mass-producing ammunition, explosives, rifles, machine guns and big artillery pieces, as well as large numbers of fighter planes and ships. By the end of the war, local industry had built 2000 combat aircraft.

It's debatable whether Australian industry today could produce an equivalent effort, particularly when modern fighter planes are so complex.[16] However, with a current population of 25 million, claims that Australia couldn't raise sufficient troops to defend the country make little sense, particularly as modern surveillance techniques should be able to provide a much longer warning time than in 1942.

Following the war, External Affairs Minister Bert Evatt and his departmental head, John Burton, wanted a bigger diplomatic and economic focus on Asia, but in 1949 this held no appeal for the incoming Coalition PM, Bob Menzies. Burton, the son of a Methodist minister and a Christian himself, headed External Affairs between 1947 and 1950. He was a significant strategic thinker who opposed communism and supported independence for Indonesia and other colonies as being in Australia's long-term interest. The historian David Fettling says, 'Burton became the foremost champion in Australian government of a national reorientation to Asia ... [His] strongly pro-Republican stance to the Indonesian crisis was coupled to a vision of Asia-wide political independence combined with economic growth and state-centred development ... Burton's fundamental objective was to attain security and stability in Australia's immediate region, including from communist insurrections: in this way he was an exemplar of, not an exception to, the long Australian "search for security".[17]

After Burton died in 2010, the ANU professor of strategic studies Des Ball smeared him and Evatt as Soviet spies. Without any supporting evidence, Ball wrote in 2011 that he was more than ever convinced that 'Evatt and Burton were witting parties to the Soviet espionage operations in Australia'.[18] He stated unequivocally that Burton had 'lied' to the Petrov royal commission about the date he first met Jim Hill, who had been accused of spying. When one of Burton's daughters, Pam, correctly told Ball that the date he was citing from the royal commission transcript referred to something else, he switched to saying his source was 'too secret' to be revealed.[19] She then pointed out that Ball had quoted from the public transcript of evidence, and noted that the head of MI5, Roger Hollis, had recorded in the file that Burton was not an espionage agent and had been very cooperative (in helping to improve security).

A lawyer and former senior public servant, Ernst Willheim, also rebutted Ball's claims in detail and asked, 'Would Dennis Richardson, as head of DFAT and the former ASIO head, have provided a glowing tribute on Burton's death if he had harboured the slightest suspicion Burton was a traitor?'[20] Willheim says David Horner, who wrote Volume 1 of the official ASIO history, told him he had found no evidence that Burton was a spy.

Despite his ideas being rejected by Menzies, Burton's diplomatic legacy didn't vanish without trace, not least because it reflected the reality of Australia's geographic location. Bill Pritchett, who joined External Affairs in 1945 and retired as Defence head in 1984, wrote that it would have been better when World War II ended 'if we had not become caught up with Britain and the US, but had to make our own way in Asia'.[21] Paul Keating, as Labor PM in the mid-1990s, argued that Australia should seek its security in Asia, not from it. Nevertheless, the dominant policy thrust since 1949 has been to seek security in ever-closer ties with the US.

49

KOREA: BARBARISM UNLEASHED

'Three months after it started, the North Korean invasion had been repulsed and the mandate of the UN achieved. The war should have been over ... Washington's ideological and military enthusiasm ensured a wider and more substantial conflagration—continuing the war for nearly three more years. Civilian deaths are estimated to have been over 3 million.'

Michael Pembroke[1]

Korea suffered terribly during the twentieth century. First, Japan brutally occupied it from 1910 until surrendering in 1945. Then, although the Korean people wanted to remain a unified country, World War II's victors presumed the right to divide it among themselves. The Soviet Union became responsible for administering north of the 38th parallel and the US below that line, based on the understanding that a unified Korea would be able to govern itself in a few years. Soviet troops withdrew in 1948, never to return, leaving Kim Il Sung as dictator. In the south, Syngman Rhee was a slightly less repressive dictator. US troops withdrew in 1949, but returned in 1950 and remain there.

There were cross-border raids by each side before 1950, but the Soviet dictator Joseph Stalin was reluctant to back Kim's proposals to reunify the country by invading the south. He eventually agreed on the condition that no Soviet troops be involved. The northern forces crossed the 38th parallel into the south on 25 June 1950, but the Soviets didn't veto a UN Security Council resolution on the same day calling on the north to withdraw. Two days later the UN recommended the South be given assistance 'to repel the armed attack and restore international peace and security to the area'. It passed two resolutions in July to establish what was later called a UN Command to conduct the military operation, but gave no authorisation to invade the north once North Korea's troops were pushed back to the 38th parallel.

In his 2018 book on Korea, historian and NSW Supreme Court judge Michael Pembroke says the sole purpose of the UN's collective intervention 'was to rebuff the invasion … to restore the integrity of the border. The appropriate legal and moral response, and the only one authorised by the UN, was to stop North Korean aggression, halt and defeat it, but not to become an aggressor oneself.' [2] However, the US had no intention of stopping at the 38th parallel when it saw an opportunity to prise North Korea away from the Sino-Soviet bloc.

On 28 June 1950, only three days after the initial invasion, the Menzies Government became the second nation to commit naval, army and air units to the conflict. The external affairs minister, Percy Spender, pushed Australian participation through Cabinet 'while Menzies, who at that stage opposed sending troops, was incommunicado on the high seas between London and Washington'.[3] The NAA's notes on Australia's prime ministers say, 'In the privacy of Cabinet, Menzies conceded that while the electorate was being told the troops were being sent to assist the UN, in fact they had been committed to secure Australia's relationship with the US.'[4] As has become standard practice, Australia went to war to please the Americans.

Pushing the North Koreans back to the 38th parallel was clearly justified under the UN Charter's prohibition of aggression, but once the US took the war above the 38th parallel, it was a different matter. Yet the Menzies Government never reviewed its initial commitment.

On 7 October 1950, the UN passed a resolution that the head of Australia's External Affairs Department, Alan Watt, warned was so loosely worded that it could be interpreted as allowing UN forces to go past the 38th parallel.[5] The headstrong General Douglas MacArthur, who led the UN command, soon did so, pushing on to Yalu on the border with China. Despite China's desperate poverty, Mao Zedong was determined to stop what he saw as a US attempt to threaten his country by controlling North Korea. At the time, the Soviets were still confronting the devastation of World War II, in which 26 million Russians had died. Stalin still refused to provide any troops, but later supplied some MiG-15 fighter planes and lent China money to buy other weapons.

China initially infiltrated 200,000 troops into North Korea without the US detecting what was happening. Many more would soon join them.

The troops lacked air cover much beyond the Chinese border and had only basic weaponry and flimsy boots in freezing cold, but the US soon learnt that the Chinese troops did not lack courage, endurance or ingenuity. They routed the US-led forces, forcing them back below the 38th parallel.

Bewildered Americans accused their troops of being unmanly, but the blame lay largely with President Harry S. Truman and MacArthur. Headquartered in Tokyo, MacArthur was ill-served by poor military intelligence and his own sense of invincibility. Pembroke records that the Australian mission in Tokyo reported bluntly on 7 November 1950 that 'MacArthur believed that it was time for a showdown with Communism [and] the British war correspondent Reg Thompson said he nursed "dreams of the conquest of Asia"'.[6] In Washington, the leadership had refused to believe that China would be willing to fight the US. Pembroke says, 'It was blinded by disdain for enemy it did not know or respect.'[7]

The stalemate on either side of the 38th parallel presented another opportunity to end the war that should never gone beyond the first three months. Instead, the US chose revenge and its retreating army adopted a scorched earth policy.

However, this was nothing compared to the carnage its air force unleashed against the north. America had a chemical weapon that was almost as terrifying as nuclear weapons: napalm, the phosphorus and gasoline gel that spread rapidly after igniting at 1150°C and that had been used extensively against Japanese cities in 1945. The firebombing of Tokyo in March 1945 destroyed the city and killed over 100,000 people—more than were killed initially by either of the atomic bombs later dropped on Hiroshima and Nagasaki. Curtis LeMay, the air force general responsible for the fire-bombing in Japan, led the bigger onslaught with napalm against North Korea. Almost every city, town and village was destroyed by napalm or high explosives, as were basic infrastructure, dykes and dams. Australian Mustang fighter planes also dropped napalm on targets in North Korea, including Chinese troops.[8] The war cost the lives of 339 Australian soldiers and pilots.

By 1951, even MacArthur couldn't stomach what was happening, saying, 'The war in Korea has already almost destroyed that nation of 20 million people. I have never seen such devastation ... After I looked at the wreckage and those thousands of women and children and everything, I vomited ... If you go on indefinitely, you are perpetuating a slaughter such as I have never heard of in the history of mankind.'[9]

This damning statement to a congressional hearing was delivered by MacArthur after Truman sacked him in April 1951 for wanting to expand the war into China, but LeMay had no qualms about continuing to pound and burn North Korea from the air until shortly before the armistice on 23 July 1953. Nor did moral concerns inhibit those who ordered soldiers to kill civilians and directed navy ships to use their 5-inch guns to kill refugees.[10] The American historian Bruce Cummings described an encounter he had in the South Korean city in 1968: 'On the street corner stood a man who had a peculiar purple crust on every visible part of the skin—thick on his hands, then on his arms, fully covering his entire head and face. He was bald, he had no ears or lips, and his eyes, lacking lids, were a greyish-white with no pupils … This purplish crust resulted from drenching with napalm, after which the untreated victim's body was left to somehow cure itself.'[11]

Pembroke says the US considered using germ warfare against Korea and China in 1952, citing documented evidence that it had developed large quantities of biological weapons and was planning air-drops.[12] He says there's no documented evidence that US planes delivered them, although some accounts make a distinction between operational and experimental use. He also points out that 9500 declassified documents were reclassified in subsequent decades.

To Pembroke, the most disturbing consequence of the war is that it led to a state of permanent militarism in the US, where military spending now accounts for 54 per cent of discretionary budget spending.[13] He says in an earlier age it was thought that 'only fascists and socialists celebrated war; that only they glorified the armed struggle … that only they believed that power grows out of the barrel of a gun. The civilised world regarded armed conflict as barbarism, brutality, ugliness and sheer waste … Now, no nation has more guns, weapons, ships and aircraft [than the US].'[14]

Journalists covering Foreign Minister Don Willesee's 1975 visit to North Korea, including myself, confronted a suffocating cult of personality surrounding Kim Il Sung. It was worse even than the cult of Mao in China, which we had just visited. Nevertheless, glimpses of a common humanity were occasionally available.[15]

Following a prime ministerial visit to the Korean demilitarised zone in April 2011, Julia Gillard said she wanted more Australians to know what their country was fighting for. She said, 'We fought for democracy.'[16] But Australia did not fight for democracy. It fought on the side of the brutal, corrupt dictator Syngman Rhee against a marginally worse dictator in the north. South Korea did not become a democracy until 1988. At the time of writing, North Korea remains a totalitarian dictatorship and a peace treaty is long overdue.

Although North Korea is often described as communist, it has removed all references to Marxism in its constitution and may now be closer to a cult built around a hereditary leader. Knowledge of the outside world is severely restricted, but if Gillard's ignorance is any guide, so too is Western understanding of the horrors of the Korean War.

50
OFF TO WAR AGAIN: MALAYA AND INDONESIA

'The battalion conducted extensive operations on both sides of the border [in the secret war].'

Australian War Memorial[1]

In May 1950, Australia agreed to a British appeal for expeditionary forces to help fight a communist insurgency in Malaya. Britain had declared an emergency in June 1948 after the guerilla wing of the Malayan Communist Party (MCP) shot dead three British planters, a Chinese rubber contractor and a Chinese foreman in the north of the country.[2] The 'emergency' was really a protracted war against the guerillas, who had fought the Japanese occupation before Britain resumed control of its Malay colony and its rubber and tin resources.

The War Memorial's brief history says, 'Despite having no more than a few thousand members, the MCP was able to draw on the support of many disaffected Malayan Chinese, who were upset that British promises of a path to full Malayan citizenship had not been fulfilled.' In *Dangerous Allies* Malcolm Fraser says there is no doubt the communists were heavily involved, but Britain 'contributed to the problem by not consulting or accommodating different ethnic groups within Malaya over the future status of their nation'.[3] Malaya gained independence in 1957, but the war wasn't over.

Initially, Australia contributed a significant deployment of destroyers, frigates, aircraft carriers, and bomber and transport aircraft, plus artillery and two army battalions. By the war's end in 1963, thirty-nine Australian servicemen had been killed and twenty-seven wounded.

The Malaya commitment had barely ended before Australia again dispatched expeditionary forces—this time to a secret war against Indonesia, which had adopted a policy of 'Confrontation' against what it considered a British Imperial policy of encirclement using the new federation called Malaysia. Indonesia's President Sukarno claimed Britain had pressured Malaya into joining this federation with Singapore and the newly independent British colonies of Sarawak and Sabah in the non-Indonesian side of Borneo. Confrontation was mostly confined to boisterous Indonesian propaganda and military harassment and incursions, rather than a full-scale war against the new federation of Malaysia.

Prime Minister Robert Menzies wanted to send troops to Borneo after Britain called for a military commitment, but he held back initially because of the attitude of his own diplomats and the US. Conscious of the long-term need for good relations with Indonesia, Australian diplomats counselled caution. As discussed in Chapter 25, President John F. Kennedy bluntly told Menzies in July 1963 that the US would not supply ground troops to support the Australians. Following this humiliating lesson on the limits of ANZUS, the government waited until 1965 before secretly participating in what remained an undeclared war against Indonesia.

The public was told almost nothing about what was happening. The fact that Australian and New Zealand forces were under British command did not help rebut Sukarno's claim that he was reacting to a form of neo-colonial encirclement. Although the Australian and New Zealand troops were based in Sarawak on the Malaysian side of the border with Indonesia, they conducted deadly cross-border raids.[4] The potential for a more difficult conflict was real, especially if Indonesia extended the war to its border with Papua New Guinea, for which Australia still had territorial responsibilities. Instead, Confrontation fizzled out after General Suharto took power from Sukarno amid horrific communal violence sparked by military action in October 1965. Indonesia and Malaysia negotiated an end to hostilities in August 1966, Indonesia having achieved one of its aims when Singapore left the Malaysian federation in August 1965.

Australia's cross-border raids remained classified until 1996, but Coalition ministers still publicly refused to admit Australian troops had crossed the border to fight Indonesians. In March 2005, Veterans' Affairs Minister De-Anne Kelly was the first government minister to commemorate the sacrifices of Australian troops in Borneo forty years earlier. However, *Age* journalist Mark Forbes noted on 23 March that year that

Kelly still maintained the official fiction about their role by saying, 'The soldiers patrolled the jungle areas to intercept enemy incursions', without referring to the fact that they made combat incursions into Indonesia.

That conflict cost twenty-three Australians their lives. Meanwhile, another war, this time in Vietnam, was underway.

51

VIETNAM: STOPPING AN ELECTION, THEN LOSING AN UNNECESSARY WAR

'Yes, we did kill teachers and postmen. But it was the way to conduct the war. They were part of the Vietcong infrastructure ... Everyone goes over the speed limit from time to time.'

Brigadier Ted Serong[1]

When Australian troops first arrived in Vietnam in 1962, they joined a war in which resistance groups had long opposed foreign occupiers, the latest being the French, Japanese and Americans. France's colonial presence in Vietnam began in Da Nang in 1858 and expanded to include much of present-day Vietnam as well as Cambodia and Laos (collectively called Indochina). The French crushed successive rebellions until the Japanese replaced them between 1940 and 1945. The Japanese met serious opposition from the Viet Minh, a coalition of communist and nationalist groups led by Ho Chi Minh, who had spent thirty years in exile.

The US supported the Viet Minh against the Japanese and briefly rejected restoration of French colonialism. In January 1943, President Franklin D. Roosevelt told his secretary of state, Cordell Hull, 'France has had the country—thirty million inhabitants—for nearly a hundred years and the people are worse off than they were at the beginning.'[2] This approach didn't survive Roosevelt's death in April 1945. Undeterred, Ho Chi Minh declared independence in September. Postwar, the French resumed both their colonial role and their fight with the Viet Minh. Ho Chi Minh again declared independence in 1950, releasing a constitution that drew directly on the US Declaration of Independence.

Looking through a Cold War lens, America saw Ho Chi Minh solely as a communist, not a strong nationalist as well.

In 1950, the US announced it would provide military aid and advisers to help the French. The historian Fredrik Logevall says that in April 1954, the Menzies Government rejected a US request to help provide naval support for the French, followed shortly afterwards by a noncommittal response to a question about a possible military contribution in Vietnam—prompting President Dwight Eisenhower to complain that 'the Menzies government seemed unwilling to act independently of London'.[3] In his Cabinet submission opposing the assistance, External Affairs Minister Richard Casey said, 'Australia's destiny was not so completely wrapped up with the United States as to support them in action which Australia regarded as wrong.'[4] Despite their supposed 'special relationship' with the US, successive British governments refused to become militarily involved in Vietnam.

Under the military leadership of General Vo Nguyen Giap, the Viet Minh ultimately won a decisive victory at the Battle of Dien Bien Phu in 1954. The French surrendered and left. Later that year, an international conference adopted the Geneva Accords that divided Vietnam at the 17th parallel between the north and the south and specified that a general election to unify the country be held no later than 1956—a commitment that reflected the UN Charter's support for self-determination. But the US and South Vietnam never signed the Accords. With US encouragement, prominent warlord Ngo Dinh Diem, a fervent Catholic in a predominantly Buddhist country, took over as the south's leader in 1955. With the CIA's Colonel Edward Lansdale as adviser, Diem accepted US advice not to participate in the election, which even Eisenhower conceded Ho Chi Minh would have won.[5]

US intervention prevented the scheduled 1956 election being held at all—an extreme action in comparison with the alleged Russian interference in the 2016 US presidential election. Had Ho Chi Minh won, the country might have been reunified without a protracted war involving foreign intervention. Denied the promised elections, the Viet Minh started a guerilla insurgency in the south, where the local insurgents were known as the Vietcong.

Australia and the US began discussing a small contribution of Australian military instructors in 1961. However, the defence minister, Athol Townley, told the external affairs minister, Garfield Barwick, in March 1962 that the initial reaction from the American generals in Saigon 'was rather unenthusiastic' as they considered they had sufficient troops of their own.[6] The US had at least 11,000 advisers in Vietnam and more rapidly arriving.

The Australian Army was not desperate to go—it offered ten officers and possibly a few non-commissioned instructors.[7]

The State Department wanted to avoid the appearance of unilateral US action and the offer of instructors was accepted. Townley announced in parliament on 24 May 1962 that Australia would commit thirty military instructors 'to assist in the training of the ground forces of South Vietnam'. It's unclear whether Cabinet was told that some members of the Australian Army Training Team Vietnam (usually known as 'the Team') would come under the direct control of the CIA rather than the Australian Army. A small number of the Team later joined the CIA's notorious Phoenix program that assassinated suspected supporters of the Vietcong. This was kept secret from the Australian public.

Colonel Ted Serong promptly put his hand up for the job of leading the Team—a job for which he was disturbingly unsuited. He wrote to the chief of the general staff (CGS), General Reg Pollard, in February 1962 suggesting that Australia needed the shooting practice. He said, 'The only Australian shooting is me [an exaggeration]. We must keep in the action, or we will be also-rans. I would lead them myself. The advantages are obvious—continued operational experience, prestige and a gesture of Allied solidarity.'[8]

Historian and Vietnam War veteran Bruce Davies' detailed outline of Serong's career contains nothing to suggest Serong was a counterinsurgency expert, as widely described, partly due to his own self-promotion and tireless networking. The hype continued after his death. An obituary in *News Weekly* in October 2002 said Serong shared the view of his close friend Bob Santamaria, the leading Catholic political activist, about the importance of the struggle against communist totalitarianism: 'The final resolution of the struggle—the defeat of communist insurgencies in Asia—owed much to the efforts of Brigadier Serong over many years.' Apparently *News Weekly* was under the delusion that Serong defeated the communist insurgency in Vietnam.

Davies says Serong had spent most of World War II in Australia, with brief periods in Port Moresby where he was a staff officer in the administration. He didn't engage in combat. Surprisingly, for someone so keen to take the fight up to the communists, he didn't serve in Korea or Malaya, nor gain any counterinsurgency experience. It was not taught when he was at the Canungra jungle warfare training base in south-east Queensland—rather, Australian soldiers were taught how to fight a conventional war in a jungle environment.[9] Moreover, the Australian trainers who were sent to Vietnam agreed to follow US training methods.

In her 2001 biography of Serong, written with what she called a 'generous' Australian Army history grant, Anne Blair says US Secretary of State Dean Rusk asked Australian ministers to make Serong the Team's first commanding officer.[10] Davies says Serong then put a lot of time into networking among US military, diplomatic and CIA officials in Saigon and elsewhere. After reading a cutting about Serong being in Munich, new CGS General Wilton asked an aide, 'What on earth is the bloody man up to now?'[11]

As well as instruction in jungle warfare, training in clandestine operations occurred at the ASIS base on Swan Island near Geelong. Some army officers, including Serong, were told they would be working as part of ASIS. Meanwhile, ministers were kept in the dark. Although Barwick had ministerial responsibility for ASIS, he later told Blair he did not know of Serong's connection with ASIS. Its director, Major General Walter Cawthorn, had a background in military intelligence in Egypt and India, but there was no obvious reason why Team members should be working for ASIS. The rationale was that some members would operate under CIA control—but ASIS did not decide what they could do in Vietnam while they were working for the CIA.

Blair wrote that Serong, who gave her unfettered access to his private diaries, recorded that Cawthorn instructed him to 'Get me 10 years'—a reference to the time needed to stop a communist victory.[12] Cawthorn was usually regarded as much less gung-ho than this. Even if Serong's account is accurate, which is most unlikely, the instruction was fanciful: the Team never had more than 100 men, and Cawthorn wasn't in a position to give Serong instructions. The CIA did that.

Serong was a contentious choice. He was a Catholic zealot who—in common with Santamaria—ignored the church's teachings on what constituted a just war. Unlike many members of the Team, he had no qualms about assassinating unarmed people. After he was replaced as the Team's commanding officer in early 1965, he was seconded to the CIA.[13] Frank Walker says he joined the CIA's Phoenix program, where he dismissed moral concerns about killing civilians, later telling *Time* magazine, 'Yes, we did kill teachers and postmen. They were part of the Viet Cong infrastructure ... Everyone goes over the speed limit from time to time.'[14]

Serong was not simply a motorist. Until he resigned from the Australian Army in 1968, it had a responsibility to ensure he did not breach the rules of war. It failed, not least because it lost control over his behaviour. The ASIO liaison officer in Saigon, Mike Leslie, reported that the CIA decided in March 1967 not to extend Serong's contract 'because he sought out journalists to generate publicity for himself and declared that he was an intelligence officer rather than an army officer'.[15] It seems he never mentioned this failure to renew his contract to his biographer. Nor is it clear when, or if, he told the Australian Army that the CIA had dropped him.

Although Blair admired Serong in many ways, she noted that he was a fierce opponent of communism and a defender of what he saw as 'civilisation', but that he did not see political democracy as central to this fight.[16] After returning to Australia he became patron of a militia group called the AUSI Freedom Scouts, which the federal and state police believed had hidden large numbers of high-powered rifles on several properties in underground ammunition caches with camouflaged steel trapdoors. Its leader, Ian Murphy, was another devout Catholic, who believed the church 'had been largely taken over by Communist sympathisers'.[17]

Fortunately, Serong was not typical of most Team members. In his official history of the Team, Ian McNeill said that while some Australian soldiers had been seconded to the CIA from the start of the deployment, the majority worked with the South Vietnamese Army under the operational control of the American Military Assistance Advisory Group.[18] Other Team members, such Barry Petersen, who came under the direct control of the CIA, wanted nothing to do with assassinations. McNeill, who also served in the Team, acknowledged that abuses did occur and that they were not confined to the Phoenix program: 'Assassinations, false accusations by which private scores were settled, the indiscriminate rounding-up of suspects, and torture, particularly in the early years, were included in the repertoire of some connected with Phoenix.'[19] Although other estimates are higher, McNeill gives official figures showing that over 20,000 individuals were victims of Phoenix's targeted killings program; however, 'The Viet Cong infrastructure remained largely intact.'[20]

In 1964, the job of those Team members involved in training was changed to let them accompany South Vietnamese forces during operations and engage in combat themselves. Former diplomat Garry Woodard, who studied the official papers while a visiting fellow at the NAA, showed that this new role went beyond the more limited task Barwick had envisaged in 1962.[21] After stressing that the Vietnamese people in both north and south were intensely nationalistic, McNeill said, 'It is well to remember too that what is being discussed is the will of brother to kill brother and sister to kill sister. In the circumstances, a lack of will would seem a virtue.'[22] Unlike Serong, many members of the Team shared McNeill's assessment.

McNeill saw a deeper cause for the ultimate defeat of the south and its allies, saying, 'North Vietnam could demonstrate a greater legitimacy to be the future of a united Vietnam. By its efforts, French colonial rule had been terminated and independence reached. Under the venerated Ho Chi Minh the claim by the North Vietnamese to represent the abiding aspirations of all Vietnamese was more convincing than the counter-claim by the shifting junta in Saigon.'[23]

There was no excuse for policy-makers to pretend they didn't know about the force of Vietnamese nationalism—it was well documented by the early 1950s. Nor was there any excuse for rejecting the 1956 election required by the Geneva Accords and UN principles supporting self-determination. Secrecy, ignorance, incompetence and brutality combined to produce malign consequences. The US, with Australia tagging along, brought horrific devastation to a small developing country. In addition to the war crimes, torture, assassinations and widespread use of toxic herbicides, the US dropped over six million tonnes of bombs on Vietnam—more than the combined total it dropped in World War II and Korea.

And it still suffered a dishonourable defeat.

52

TESTIMONY FROM THOSE WHO WERE THERE

'One American soldier hit ... one poor woman who had a thin nylon dress and a little baby on her chest. The flame missed the woman's face but completely burnt the baby to an ash. Why do that?'
Bevan Stokes, Australian Army Training Team, Vietnam[1]

SBS in 2016 gave viewers a new insight into the war in Vietnam when it broadcast a three-part television documentary series that let members of the small army group called 'The Team' tell the Australian public in disturbing detail about their experiences.

Only about 100 Team members served at a time. Of the total 990 Team members who were deployed through to December 1972, thirty-three died and 122 were wounded.

Called *Vietnam: The War that Made Australia*, the TV series shows that many members of the Team managed to retain their humanity despite intense American pressure to carry out orders they regarded as morally repugnant.[2] When the Team were first deployed as trainers in 1962, some members were secretly assigned to the CIA—a practice that continued with subsequent deployments. The series shows that some Team members developed a genuine rapport with the Vietnamese and hill tribespeople they trained. The narrator explains that they soon discovered that the CIA was ordering some Team members to train their students to assassinate unarmed people. In one case, Barry Petersen said his CIA controller ordered him to create teams of assassins 'to attack and kill and mutilate people who are enemy agents or informants and sometimes cut off their heads and leave messages to terrorise these people who are prone to be agents for the enemy'.[3] Much to the anger of the CIA operative, Petersen said, 'I can't do that. It's just too easy to have … innocent people knocked off.'

Apart from these requests, which went far beyond what the Australian government had told the public would be a training role, other changes soon saw Team members fighting alongside South Vietnamese government forces in battles. Some members joined the CIA-sponsored Political Action Teams (PATs) seeking to win villagers' support through aid, while killing any Vietcong they encountered. Don McDowell, an early participant in the PAT tactics, said it soon became 'pretty obvious that the program had run off the rails. People started to be targeted although they might not have been VC.' He said, 'Unless you're a robotic twerp, you absorb a great deal of stress. I'd take a break of two or three days and sit by a beach and ruminate on how life was unfair for the poor bloody Vietnamese.' Ian Teague was another Team officer assigned to the CIA's PAT units. He said he wouldn't let the members of the units become assassins instead of killing people in what was usually considered fair fighting.

The narrator says that as the massive use of US firepower increased in 1965, Team members such as Charles Emery found the American approach to war hard to stomach. Emery accompanied American task forces that called in air power to destroy entire villages. He said, 'They were in their own villages doing naught, but they were classified as Vietcong. After the strafing and the napalming, I was told that we had killed the Vietcong and that's troubled me all my life. It was impossible to identify them as being the enemy.' Another Team member, Bevan Stokes, said, 'The Vietcong might go and kill two or three villagers, but the Americans are killing the whole village.' He said he went on one operation where the Americans used flamethrowers to burn huts: 'One American soldier hit … one poor woman who had a thin nylon dress and a little baby on her chest. The flame missed the woman's face but completely burnt the baby to an ash.'

Team member Bruce Davies said he was on patrol with a South Vietnamese battalion that came under fire from a hamlet when supporting American tanks blew it away.[4] He said, 'I was aghast. That's not warfare, that's almost like murder.' He was equally enraged by how the Vietcong had left one of its young fighters chained to a machine gun so he couldn't run off. Shortly afterwards, Davies came across a wounded Vietcong soldier, raised his rifle and came within a millimetre of shooting him. He said, 'I realised that, whoa stop … this is just murder.' Reflecting on his experiences, he said, 'You really take your soldier shell and put it to one side and say, "My God, what have we done?"'

The team had to face the reality that it wasn't only the Vietcong who could kill them. The CIA could also do so, as testified in Frank Walker's book *The Tiger Man of Vietnam*. Team member Jack Leggett told Walker how close he had come to being murdered by a CIA operative, B.J. Johnson, whom he angered by refusing to assassinate four unarmed women suspected of carrying documents and food for the Vietcong.[5] Walker said the CIA had appointed Leggett to run a Provincial Reconnaissance Unit that was part of the Phoenix program, but he insisted his unit would have to stay within the Australian Army's rules of engagement. Shortly afterwards, Johnson, who worked for the CIA-run Vietnamese Police Special Branch, told Leggett to assassinate the four women. Leggett said there was no need to kill them when it would be easy to arrest them instead. He said, 'I told him I had not trained for years as an army officer to assassinate unarmed women. He hit the roof.' He told Johnson that even if he agreed, 'It would not make one iota of difference to the outcome of the war.'

Leggett told Walker that at around eleven that night Johnson turned up at his house pointing a pistol at him and said, 'I am going to blow your fucking head off.' Leggett said he had no doubt that Johnson would have done it and believed he was only saved by the unexpected arrival of two armed Vietnamese members of his unit.

Thanks to the SBS documentary series, we now know that many of the Team's highly professional soldiers, who witnessed the conduct of the war at close quarters, responded with a level of human decency not shared by some covert action enthusiasts, such as Team leader Ted Serong. The Team members' accounts of US conduct in the war add to the reasons why no Australian troops should have been sent to Vietnam.[6]

The effects of war on the Team and other Australian troops did not always stop with their return. Apart from psychological and other effects, they had to deal with the possibility that they had been poisoned by the dioxin contained in Agent Orange—the most common defoliant the US used to destroy vegetation, including crops, to deny cover and food to the Vietcong. In effect, the US was denying food not just to the Vietcong, but to anyone in Indochina who relied on those crops. The US sprayed 45 million litres of dioxin-containing Agent Orange out of a total of 75 million litres of defoliant used between 1961 and 1971.[7]

The US also sprayed insecticides, such as DDT and the carcinogenic dieldren, that can seriously damage human health. With alleged use of chemical weapons in the news these days, it shouldn't be forgotten that the US engaged in chemical warfare in Vietnam, where its effects persist.

The US tried to keep the spraying across Indochina a secret in the Western world until at least 1965. It was no secret for the locals, who could not fail to notice when a plane was spraying them and their crops with herbicides. In a cable to the State Department in 1965, the US ambassador to Laos, William Sullivan, said, 'We can carry on these efforts only if we do not, repeat do not, talk about them, and when necessary, if we deny that they are taking place.'[8]

The Australian military used defoliants in Vietnam, but its instructions were to stay clear of food crops and rubber trees. The military also knew from a secret report written by Major K.J. Maxwell in December 1963 that the Americans engaged in 'Crop destruction to deny foodstuffs to insurgents' as well as camouflage cover.[9] It is not known if the Australian military or government objected to the US about this form of chemical warfare.

Although destroying about 20 per cent of South Vietnam's forests, the spraying failed to deny the Vietcong adequate jungle camouflage. It left a terrible legacy of dioxin contamination that can lead to cancer and birth defects in the grandchildren of the people who were exposed during the war, predominantly those who were allied to the US 'protector'. Dioxin is an extremely toxic chemical that remains in Vietnam's water tables and soil and still enters the food chain today. A powerful photojournalism essay in 2015 said, 'Nearly 4.8 million Vietnamese people have been exposed, causing 400,000 deaths … One million people are currently disabled or have health problems due to the dioxin in Agent Orange, 100,000 of whom are children.'[10] A University of Newcastle researcher says the US military was allegedly told that trials showed dioxin to be toxic.[11]

Although US and Australian governments spent years denying there was any problem with the defoliants, eventually they had to acknowledge authoritative studies showing that the incidence of cancer among veterans was shockingly high—50 per cent higher than rates in the general population, and higher still for particular cancers.

No Australian minister today could dismiss a similar problem with a sick joke as the Coalition's defence minister, Jim Killen, did in 1980. Killen, who prided himself on his wit, told parliament on 27 March 1980 that his department had given him the names of herbicides used in Vietnam: Reglone, Gramoxone, Tordon and Hyva. He added that as far as he was concerned 'they could be four horses running at Rosehill on Saturday'. This is the same man who opposed adding fluoride to water because he 'knew' it to be terribly dangerous.[12]

53

A DEFEAT BORN OF SECRECY, IGNORANCE, ARROGANCE AND BRUTALITY

'War is not hell. It is fun.'

Nora Ephron[1]

In 1964, Robert Menzies' government followed its worst political instincts and decided to boost Australia's small expeditionary forces in Vietnam by 1000. These numbers grew to over 7600 before the war ended in defeat. The decision resulted in the needless deaths of over 520 Australian soldiers, and over 3000 were wounded in a war that inflicted terrible suffering on the Vietnamese people.

Estimates of the number of Vietnamese killed vary from about 1.2 million to over three million, with civilians making up the majority of the higher estimates. These figures do not include deaths in Laos and Cambodia, nor in the war against the French. About 58,000 US soldiers died, 4000 South Koreans and almost forty New Zealanders. Many surviving Allied soldiers, as well as large numbers of Vietnamese, suffered prolonged illnesses.

In committing the initial battalion after sending a small training team in 1962, the government didn't invoke the ANZUS Treaty. Nor was it acting on a US request for this many troops or an invitation from the South Vietnamese government.[2] The Cabinet wasn't advised by departmental officials: it chose to rely mainly on its own blinkered view of the world and that of the hawkish Air Chief Marshal Frederick Scherger.

Unlike some of his ministers, Menzies was notoriously uninterested in Asia. When announcing the battalion's deployment on 29 April 1965, he said, 'The takeover of South Vietnam would be a direct military threat to Australia and all the countries of South and South-East Asia. It must be seen as part of a thrust by Communist China between the Indian and Pacific oceans.' This reasoning, dubbed the domino theory, assumed that monolithic communist aggression would spread from Indochina to topple all the countries along the path to Australia. The communists won, but the dominoes never fell. If an excuse for not intervening were needed, Admiral Grant Sharp, the head of US forces in the Pacific, acknowledged on a visit to Canberra in October 1964 that Australia's commitment to Indonesia–Malaysia might preclude it from deploying troops further north.[3]

Cabinet's Foreign Affairs and Defence Committee had made the decision on 17 December 1964 to send the army battalion to Vietnam, although Menzies did not tell parliament until 29 April 1965. The committee considered a letter from President Lyndon Johnson requesting 200 more combat advisers, but not combat troops. But the committee decided on a full battalion, provided the South Vietnamese government made a request. It didn't. Former diplomat Garry Woodard said the decision was strongly advocated by the new foreign minister, Paul Hasluck. His predecessor, Garfield Barwick, had warned that Australia needed to be careful not to be seen, in Woodard's summation, as the 'US deputy sheriff' in Asia, but unlike Barwick, Hasluck shunned advice from his own department.[4] Malcolm Fraser, who was defence minister between January 1966 and March 1971 and had earlier been army minister for two years, said in his 2014 book *Dangerous Allies* that Air Chief Marshal Scherger basically wrote the key Cabinet submission.[5] However, in sharp contrast to current military planning, Lieutenant General Sir John Wilton insisted that the Australian Army must not be integrated with US forces but instead should operate separately in Phuoc Tuy Province.[6]

Labor leader Arthur Calwell replied to Menzies' 29 April announcement with an exceptional speech on 4 May 1965, written by Graham Freudenberg. Calwell told parliament there was a 'civil and guerilla war in South Vietnam, aided and abetted from the north'. He said there had been eight or nine governments involved in the South Vietnam president Diem's murder in 1963, and none had popular support. Calwell correctly predicted that sticking to the existing course 'would surely and inexorably lead to American humiliation in Asia'.

Contrary to Menzies' core premise, Calwell rightly argued that the nationalistic communist regime in the north was not a Chinese puppet but part of a country 'with a 1000-year history of hostility towards China'. In 1948, Ho Chi Minh had warned colleagues against seeking Chinese help to combat the French, saying he would 'sooner sniff French shit for five years than eat Chinese shit for the rest of my life'.[7] (Since winning the war in 1975, successive communist governments in Vietnam have largely remained antipathetic to China.) Calwell concluded that Labor would oppose a 'cruel, costly and interminable' war that would 'prolong and deepen the suffering' of the Vietnamese people and possibly see troop numbers rise to 8000 and the use of 'voteless, conscripted 20-year-olds'. It was a prescient call. Troop numbers reached a peak of 7672 in 1968 and a total of 19,000 conscripts were sent, plus naval and air force units.

Labor's principled stand hurt it badly at the 1966 election, but became an asset in subsequent elections. However, Julia Gillard as PM trashed Labor's opposition to the war in her address to the US Congress on 10 March 2011. She sought to gain US favour by stating: 'We have stuck together. In every major conflict. From Korea and Vietnam to the conflicts in the Gulf.' On the contrary, Labor is entitled to be proud of its opposition to the war in Indochina.

Indochina's impoverished populations were no threat to the US or Australia, but the US and other foreign forces subjected them to death and disfigurement from carpet bombing, napalm, dioxin and prolonged torture. Some were massacred in villages, like in My Lai in March 1968. In that case, the head of US forces in Vietnam, General William Westmoreland, initially congratulated the killers on an 'outstanding action'.[8] The truth emerged only because some American soldiers refused to stay silent and Seymour Hersh, then a freelance journalist in the US, in November 1969 revealed the slaughter of several hundred unarmed villagers by US forces.

Fraser later slammed the US for initiating the 1963 assassination of President Ngo Dinh Diem, whom it had installed, and his brother Dình Diem Nhu. He warned that the decision was a 'pointer to the character of American governments … [yet no high-level Australian official in Washington] asked whether the US had the right to order the removal of the head of a country with whom they were an ally, fighting this difficult war. They implicitly assumed that they did.'[9] The assassinations followed French president General Charles de Gaulle's call earlier in 1963 for Vietnam to be unified and neutralised. Diem's brother Nhu had reportedly opened direct links with de Gaulle. Fraser said, 'One of the most serious blunders of the US at this time was that it made no effort to explore de Gaulle's option.'[10]

Fraser said he did not believe that any Australian government would have sent troops to Vietnam in 1965 'if they had known what the CIA and [Defence Secretary Robert] McNamara both believed at the time—that the cause for which America was fighting was hopeless ... Either the Americans were derelict in their duty to tell an ally or they were deceitful.'[11] However, while he was prime minister from 1975 to 1983, Fraser accepted the US's insistence that Australia recognise Pol Pot's Khmer Rouge regime, which killed 1.8 million Cambodians during its genocidal reign from 1975 to 1979. This recognition continued after the Khmer Rouge was no longer the government.

Australian author Paul Ham says the Saigon press corps tended to ignore stories about Americans killing Vietnamese civilians. The war 'rarely impinged' on the average reporter's mind above the level of 'a great story'.[12] Although the ABC generally gave a fuller picture, he says the controller of news destroyed a reporter's tape of an interview with journalist Wilfred Burchett because he saw Burchett as a traitor. Ham is no admirer of Burchett, but says Burchett had had unrivalled access to the highest levels of the Vietnamese communist hierarchy: 'This idiotic act of editorial vandalism served neither the public interest nor the historical record.'[13]

Ham refers to Australian wire service reporter Jan Graham's description of a common journalistic view of the war as being 'like a big Luna Park every day of the week. Let's try a new ride. Let's jump out of a chopper ... Let's watch people getting blown up by mines. Let's shoot a few gooks.'[14] Ham says old media hands eschewed the terms 'war crime' and 'atrocity' as quaint, morally earnest phrases that had lost meaning in one vast war crime: 'In time language itself became a casualty of war.'[15]

Gullible journalists were in for another surprise following the war. Saigon's Hotel Continental, which opened in 1880, now displays photos and brief notes on famous guests such as Graham Greene, who wrote the classic novel *The Quiet American* while staying there. Greene's photo is next to one of a lesser-known figure—Pham Xuan An. During the war, An reported for *Time* and other publications while befriending a wide circle of South Vietnamese officials and influential Americans, such as the CIA's station chief, William Colby, and its renowned military adviser, Edward Lansdale. None realised that An was a spy smuggling information to the Vietcong in messages inside egg rolls.

As the war intensified, so did heroin addiction among US troops. Because Sydney was designated a US R&R city, heroin use increased sharply in Kings Cross and spread to other parts of Australia. It is well established that the CIA facilitated the heroin supply after becoming deeply involved in the drug trade in its 'secret' war in Laos. Although secret in the West, it was no secret to the people of Laos, who were subjected to heavy bombing. The CIA's proprietary airline, Air America, flew the drugs out of Laos and nearby countries to the global marketplace.[16] The flights allegedly helped fund the CIA's mercenary troops who grew opium poppies, but the secrecy also ensured that corrupt CIA operatives could help themselves to the proceeds. The CIA was also associated with Sydney's Nugan Hand Bank, which financed drug trafficking, money laundering and international arms dealing (see Chapter 32).[17]

Even before Labor was elected in 1972, Coalition governments had accepted that the war in Vietnam was a strategic mistake. In August 1969, at the height of the nation's participation in the war, Defence Minister Allen Fairhall announced a 5 per cent cut to military spending. He told parliament he could safely cut spending because the lack of any early threat to the nation's security provided a 'breathing space'.[18] Goodbye, domino theory! Instead, Fairhall accepted that a communist victory in Vietnam posed no threat to Australia. The new focus on defending the nation closer to home remained until John Howard's government restored the forward defence doctrine by joining the illegal 2003 invasion of Iraq.

Meanwhile, communist-led Vietnam has now given de facto support to the American policy of 'containing' China. In 1986, it adopted a market-oriented economy under a policy called Doi Moi, with many enterprising Vietnamese embracing the opportunities. Poverty remains and political freedom is constrained, but the country has become much more prosperous in recent years.

Although the US and Australia never paid reparations for the damage they caused, the Vietnamese now welcome almost all visiting Australians. Yet in August 2016 some Australians loudly denounced the Vietnamese for exercising their sovereign right to decide how many foreign visitors could crowd onto the congested Long Tan battlefield site on a farmer's land. Much to the anger of some who enjoy this form of military tourism, the Vietnamese decided that the 3000 Australians who turned up wanting to celebrate the Long Tan 'victory' were unmanageable, and enforced an earlier policy of only allowing small groups around the site's commemorative cross. Malcolm Turnbull and other ministers brusquely demanded that more Australians be allowed to celebrate/commemorate a 'victory' in a minor battle in a war that killed up to three million Vietnamese.

An Australian company commander at the Long Tan battle, Harry Smith, said in 2016 that if 3000 Japanese demanded the right to visit Darwin to commemorate its wartime bombing, 'We'd be up in arms too.'[19] Greg Dodds, a Vietnam veteran, said the local people were sick of a crowd of Australians arriving each year: 'We are the people, after all, who killed their brothers, fathers, cousins and sons. Let's just leave the Vietnamese to enjoy the peace. And the gains of that peace are not slight.'[20]

Tourists could have shared that peace ever since 1956, when the internationally agreed election to unify Vietnam was promised. Instead, the US intervened, stopping an almost-certain Ho Chi Minh victory. Vietnam would have been unified and there would have been no war, no military tourism, no commemorative crosses, no napalm and no dioxin deformities.

54

AUSTRALIAN TROOPS SHOULD HAVE LEFT AFGHANISTAN WITHIN A FEW MONTHS

'For more than one hundred years Australian defence strategy has been based on "expeditionary" operations. If we are going to learn anything from the disasters of the last fifty years in Vietnam, Iraq and Afghanistan, it should be that this model has failed politically, socially, militarily and ethically. Simply put, the era has gone in which predominantly white, predominantly European, predominantly Christian armies could stampede around the world invading countries their governments either don't like or want to change ... Without exception, wars lead to injustice and depravity.'

Williams Foundation policy paper[1]

Australia sent an expeditionary force to the civil war in Somalia in the early 1990s as part of an almost impossible UN-sanctioned attempt to enforce a peace and deliver humanitarian assistance. The Australian Army arrived in 1992 and left in 1994. A total of 1500 served; four were injured and one was killed. The Australians left when it was clear that it was time to go—unlike what later happened in Afghanistan.[2]

The US, Australia and other countries began an expeditionary war against Afghanistan after nineteen al-Qaeda terrorists flew planes into American buildings on 11 September 2001. None of the terrorists were Afghans—fifteen were Saudis—and their flying training had occurred in the US. But Afghanistan copped the brunt of the military response because al-Qaeda's Saudi leader, Osama bin Laden, had established training camps there. The military response should have concentrated on capturing bin Laden rather than subcontracting the job to Afghan warlords who were more intent on seizing territory for themselves.[3]

The Taliban religious movement, supported by Pakistan's Inter-Services Intelligence (ISI) agency, had been largely in control of Afghanistan since 1996. The Mujahideen, a group supported by the CIA, ISI and Saudi intelligence, had earlier won a 'holy war' against the Soviet-supported secular government based in the capital, Kabul. Bin Laden, with the CIA's support, had provided logistics and other help to the Mujahideen.

While in power, Taliban leader Mullah Mohammed Omar imposed a severe form of Islamic law but failed to provide government services to make the lives of the Afghans, especially women, slightly less miserable. However, he showed no interest in undertaking global terrorist acts, correctly seeing bin Laden's support for international terrorism as endangering the Taliban. His government contacted US officials offering to hand bin Laden over before 11 September,[4] but President George W. Bush made it plain he was only interested in revenge. Bin Laden escaped from Afghanistan not long after the US-led forces invaded on 7 October 2001. The US's puzzling priority on regime change in Kabul facilitated bin Laden's escape with a hard-core group of 200 al-Qaeda members.[5] A few remained, but there is no evidence they engaged in international terrorism.

With bin Laden gone and the Taliban showing no sign of turning to international terrorism, the original rationale for the presence of foreign troops in Afghanistan vanished. Western troops stayed to kill Afghans as US presidents continued to treat the Taliban as synonymous with al-Qaeda. Toppling the Taliban wasn't difficult, but a competent and honest government didn't replace it in Kabul and the Taliban soon led an effective insurrection. The US assassination of bin Laden in his home in Pakistan in 2011 without bothering to interrogate him for intelligence purposes made no difference to the insurrection or global terrorism.

Prime Minister John Howard quickly dispatched an Australian special forces contingent to Afghanistan in line with the UN resolution authorising this action after the terrorist attack of 11 September. The usual difficulties for foreign forces fighting amid a civilian population soon emerged. On 17 May 2002, Australian SAS troopers mistakenly caused the death of at least eleven civilians they had wrongly assumed to be al-Qaeda members. Defence Minister Robert Hill was confident they were al-Qaeda, telling me, 'There are well-defined personnel identification matrices used by our special forces to identify al-Qaeda. In general, the tactical behaviour and the weapons and equipment they are carrying are quite distinct from the behaviour and weapons carried by the local Afghan people.'[6] But they weren't al-Qaeda: a *New York Times* report on 3 June 2002 established that the SAS had been sent to the area on the basis of false intelligence.[7] The report said two tribes opposed to the Taliban had been battling for control of the area for several years. When one villager raised his rifle at the Special Air Service (SAS) soldiers, they shot him dead. Members of both villages then opened fire on the SAS soldiers, who killed another three people before American air support killed at least eight more and wounded sixteen others.[8]

Howard withdrew the 200-strong Special Operations Task Group (SOTG) in November 2002 to prepare for the impending invasion of Iraq. In August 2005 he sent them back, followed by a small construction group. The deployment eventually reached 1550, supported by another 800 personnel in the region. All combat troops had been withdrawn by December 2013, but 300 advisers and trainers remained at the end of 2018.

Although the Taliban was armed with little more than man-made roadside bombs and old AK-47 semi-automatic rifles, a US victory was never likely while it adopted tactics that caused heavy civilian casualties from bombing and ground assaults, often based on false intelligence. As a Williams Foundation paper said, 'The deployment of expeditionary forces to invade another country immediately alters the dynamics of war. The land component of those forces has to fight amongst the people of the invaded country—a circumstance which almost invariably creates profound social, cultural, and political tensions.'[9] US libertarian advocate and author Scott Horton makes another point about Afghans: 'Their religion is not why they fight … Virtually all men of any culture would fight back against a foreign army occupying their country.'[10]

Many Afghans were disaffected under the Western-supported government because they became victims of police corruption, violence and government neglect, particularly outside Kabul. In contrast, the Taliban offered a quick resolution of disputes over stolen goats and so on.[11] In government, the Taliban had largely eradicated the opium-based drug trade, but under the new government the trade again flourished after CIA-supported drug barons ignored the US Drug Enforcement Administration's anti-drug efforts. The insurgents adjusted to the change by embracing opium growing to assist in funding the Taliban.

With the war floundering, the chairman of the chiefs of staff, Admiral Mike Mullen, told Congress in 2008, 'We can't kill our way to victory.'[12] But the military upped the tempo of the killing. The Afghan government complained, with good reason, that ill-conceived home invasions to kill or capture alleged Taliban members only produced more recruits, particularly when the accusations were false.

Australia was already outwearing its welcome. During a night-time operation in the Oruzgan province in November 2008, Australian special forces wrongly identified a fiercely anti-Taliban district governor, Rozi Khan, as an enemy and killed him. The Australian Defence Force (ADF) never explained how it made the damaging error.[13]

General Stanley McChrystal, who became chief of the US forces in Afghanistan in 2009, acknowledged, 'The Afghan people are the insurgency.'[14] He said if US forces killed one insurgent, relatives would supply ten new recruits, and 'We've shot an amazing number of people [at roadblocks]. None was proven to have been any real threat.'[15]

McChrystal's point was illustrated on 12 February 2009 when a group of Australian commandos made a night-time raid on an Afghan home. The pre-raid surveillance was sorely deficient, failing to detect the presence of children. The commandos threw grenades into the home, killing five children. In September 2010, the director of military prosecutions, Brigadier Lyn McDade, charged two commandos with manslaughter by negligence, but the military judge heading the court-martial did not proceed to trial because he decided the charges were wrong in law. The prosecutor, who had come under intense public criticism, did not pursue the issue. However, Defence was keen to clarify that the prosecutor's decision didn't mean there was never a duty of care to civilians. A spokesperson said, 'The Law of Armed Conflict imposes obligations to take "constant care" when conducting military operations to minimise causing harm to civilians.'[16]

At Defence Minister Stephen Smith's request, McDade submitted an account of why she had laid the charges. She said that on the weight of the evidence, the Afghan man killed in the raid was 'not an insurgent but an Afghan national defending his home and his family from attack'.[17] The ADF revised its initial description of the man as an insurgent to 'an Afghan fighting male', but has never explained why the compound was raided.[18]

Labor PM Julia Gillard retained her enthusiasm for this doomed expeditionary war and the continued presence of the 1500 Australian troops in Oruzgan Province. Speaking in parliament on 19 October 2010, she said Australia would stay 'for at least another decade'. In contrast, Democratic US president Barack Obama famously declared he would not stay another decade, nor spend another trillion dollars.

During 2011, Western special forces conducted night-time raids on more than 1000 homes a month, despite the military estimating that only

14 per cent of them had any real links to the insurgency.[19] The Australian government let its special forces increase the tempo and the risks by undertaking targeted assassinations of nominated individuals—a practice that doesn't fit the traditional view of how the ADF fights a war.

In a detailed investigation, ABC journalists Dan Oakes and Sam Clark reported that classified documents showed there was a growing sense of unease at the highest Defence levels about the 'desensitisation' of some members of the special forces who kill insurgents but also unarmed men and children.[20] They also reported that a decorated special forces soldier, who could not be named, said, 'Ultimately, the behaviour of some elements of SOTG led to the indiscriminate, reckless and avoidable deaths of innocent civilians, caused by an institutional shift in culture that contributed to the decay of moral and ethical values towards armed conflict.'[21] A former Australian soldier, August Elliott, wrote that a former task-group member told him new fly-in fly-out missions using Black Hawk helicopters 'saw the entire concept of operations switch from "clear, hold and build territory" to "land, kill and leave".'[22]

Fairfax Media journalists Nick McKenzie and Chris Masters went much further in a series of reports in June 2018. They said a report commissioned by the ADF had found that some special forces soldiers allegedly committed war crimes in Afghanistan amid a 'complete lack of accountability'.[23] They said some troops embraced warrior culture but others loathed it. This culture included a devotion to the Hollywood movie *300*, which glorifies the fighting prowess of the ancient Spartans. Legal action precludes giving details of serious allegations and denials here.

The Afghanistan war has been lost. A pro-Western government might control some territory around Kabul, but it's unlikely that it can rely on Western security assistance as a form of unending welfare dependency. At a minimum, the Taliban is likely to consolidate its control of the south and probably negotiate a role in the central government. Foreign terrorist groups might expand, but the Taliban won't want to tolerate their presence if it attracts heavy air strikes.

The historian Andrew Bacevich says avoiding war was once a US national priority: 'In Washington, war has become tolerable … War now serves as a medium through which favours are bestowed, largesse distributed and ambition satisfied.'[24] Similar concerns apply to Australia. The goal of ridding Afghanistan of al-Qaeda was achieved in late 2001, and that's when the troops should have been withdrawn.

We have spent over $8.3 billion on a futile expeditionary war that by the end of 2018 had killed forty-two Australian soldiers and wounded 261.[25]

55

HOWARD AND IRAQ: KNAVE OR NAIF?

'The Australian government knows Iraq still has chemical and biological weapons ... that pose a real and unacceptable threat to the stability and security of our world.'

John Howard[1]

When Prime Minister John Howard made this statement in parliament on 4 February 2003, his government knew no such thing. Nor did he. Yet he was about to publicly commit Australia to another expeditionary war when the nation's security was not threatened. It was a war of aggression that breached Article 1 of the ANZUS Treaty prohibiting using force without UN approval, and it led to continuing death, turmoil and suffering in the Middle East.

When Howard spoke, Iraq had not possessed WMDs for over ten years. Given the magnitude of his blunder, his speech is worth a closer look. He said, 'Iraq continues to work on developing nuclear weapons. Uranium has been sought from Africa.' However, UN pressure had already forced Iraq to abandon its nuclear weapons program, and the International Atomic Energy Agency announced in March 2003 that the uranium-from-Africa story was based on a crude forgery.

A parliamentary committee on the WMD intelligence, chaired by Liberal backbencher David Jull, concluded in its March 2004 report that the Defence Intelligence Organisation had 'always expressed doubts about the production of biological or chemical weapons beyond 1991'.[2] DIO also said that if Iraq still had any functioning WMDs their use was likely to be 'defensive rather than offensive'.[3] The committee found that other assessments by Australian agencies didn't support the government's suggestion that the Iraqi 'arsenal' represented a 'grave and immediate [or] real threat'.

WMDs were central to Howard's case for war. He told the National Press Club on 14 March 2003 that Iraq's WMDs were the only sufficient justification for war—unlike regime change, human rights abuses or spreading democracy.

As the invasion was underway on 20 March, Howard gave a televised address to the nation that upped the threat from Iraq's chemical and biological weapons: 'Even in minute quantities [they] are capable of causing destruction on a mammoth scale.' This was demonstrable nonsense. Australian weapons inspectors who had tested Iraqi nerve agents after the 1991 Gulf War found these agents could not cause destruction on a mammoth scale. The deputy director of the UN's Organisation for the Prohibition of Chemical Weapons, Dr John Gee, told me in 1998 that the Iraqi nerve agents (sarin and VX) were of a much poorer quality than those the West produced. Gee, who had been an Australian weapons inspector, said, 'The Iraqi compounds degrade very rapidly due to contaminants which speed up decomposition.'[4] Western forces also inoculate their troops against the effects of nerve agents before entering a danger zone, and antibiotics can treat infections from biological weapons such as anthrax.

Although the US, UK and Australian governments treated the weapons inspectors contemptuously (and the Iraqis sometimes obstructed them), most did an outstanding job in Iraq after 1991. Helped by tough import bans on sensitive equipment and materials, the inspectors and the Iraqis destroyed all WMD stocks that were left. The inspectors also ensured that attempts to resurrect the previous WMD programs would be detected by ground, air and space-borne sensors.

In a submission to Jull's committee, former Defence Department head Bill Pritchett said that even if Saddam Hussein still had some WMDs, it was hard to believe he wouldn't be deterred from attacking his neighbours by the overwhelming US response to his 1990 attack on Kuwait. Pritchett, who had provided Australian governments with strategic guidance over many years, said the US plans against Iraq 'broke far away from our own national interests and the urgent task of dealing with terrorist movements'.[5] He also cautioned against letting US intelligence shape Australian policy.

Howard said in his 20 March address that Australia's security alliance with the US was another reason for participating in the invasion, but his careful placement of Australia's troops in Iraq meant that none died. Pentagon figures show almost 4500 US soldiers had died by the end of 2017. Estimates vary, but hundreds of thousands of Iraqi fighters and civilians also died and millions more were injured or displaced. A future president is unlikely to consider that the US owes Australia a big debt for deploying troops to a debacle in 2003 where no Australian soldiers died.

Howard also said on 20 March that the supply of intelligence was a 'priceless component' of our relationship with the US and the UK. Far from being priceless, the WMD intelligence was worse than useless: it provided the rationale for a disastrous invasion. Yet he persisted with this claim in his 2010 autobiography, *Lazarus Rising*.[6] He also implied in his address that joining the invasion was crucial to obtaining 'timely and accurate intelligence' on terrorism—but the US swapped intelligence on terrorism with dozens of countries that didn't participate in the invasion.

Before the invasion, the Australian media was mostly content to treat government claims about WMDs as true, while denigrating the inspectors. The ABC's *Four Corners* broadcast a *Panorama* program the BBC aired on 23 September 2002 called 'The Case against Saddam'. *Four Corners* deleted some of the more outrageous errors, but the program still promised 'hard evidence of what Hussein's actually got today and what he stands a good chance of getting in the not-too-distant future'. *Panorama* had no evidence, hard or otherwise—just government propaganda. When I asked *Panorama*'s reporter Jane Corbin detailed questions about specific errors in her program, she gave a comprehensive reply saying that when she used the words 'hard evidence' she did not mean 'proof', and continued in that vein without addressing the core problem that she had no hard evidence, let alone proof, for the program's claims.[7] Despite this travesty, the BBC sacked its director-general for allowing a radio journalist to report correctly that UK prime minister Tony Blair had used 'sexed-up' intelligence.

Most Australian newspapers displayed pictographs showing Iraq's military assets as roughly comparable to those of the invaders, but Iraq didn't have a functioning air force or navy by 2003, and its army was in no condition, or mood, to fight. One of the ABC *7.30 Report*'s 'expert' panellists during the war, retired brigadier Jim Wallace, suggested Saddam could detonate large conventional bombs that were 'dirty with chemical or biological agents'.[8] He ignored the point that the intense heat from detonating high explosives would kill biological agents and degrade any chemical weapons. The program also stated that the Iraqis had fired nine Scud missiles—but none were fired because none existed, as the weapons inspectors had made plain. The Defence Department was little better: it released a report claiming that the SAS had 'neutralised' Iraq's ability to fire WMD-armed Scuds into Israel. There were no Scuds to neutralise.[9]

One senior Australian official who was intimately involved in the prewar discussions told me on a non-attributable basis, 'It didn't matter that Saddam hated Islamic extremists. The Americans just wanted to see body parts flying through the air somewhere in the Middle East.'

Some commentators tried to resuscitate the nonsense that Saddam was in league with al-Qaeda. Former intelligence officer turned commentator Paul Monk bluntly stated that a meeting in Prague between the al-Qaeda terrorist Mohamed Atta and an Iraqi intelligence official had taken place.[10] It hadn't. FBI director Robert Mueller proved Atta, who led the 11 September hijackers, had been in the US at the time of the alleged Prague meeting. Monk even suggested in the same article that the 11 September mastermind, Khalid Sheikh Mohammed, was really a deep-cover Iraqi intelligence officer and not a Kuwaiti. If true, the US would eagerly have told the world after repeatedly waterboarding the boastful Mohammed following his capture.

As late as July 2003, one gullible Australian journalist was still swallowing the fairytale spun by his US contacts. Under the headline 'WMD Doubts Are Ludicrous', Greg Sheridan quoted US Under Secretary of State for Arms Control and International Security Affairs John Bolton as saying the evidence that Saddam had WMDs 'is so overwhelming, he can barely understand how it is doubted'.[11] At the time of writing, Bolton is President Donald Trump's national security adviser.

When the final report of the US presidential commission on the intelligence about WMDs was released in March 2005, it demolished the rubbish peddled by George W. Bush, Blair and Howard. But Howard has insisted with each passing year that he made the right decision to participate in the illegal invasion. Never mind that it spawned a horrendous new terrorist threat where none existed before; nor that the US installed a corrupt and incompetent government influenced by Tehran's Islamic revolutionary regime; nor that the Iraqi government approved a new constitution recognising Islam as the source of law in the once-secular nation.

By 2010 the Islamic State (IS) terror group had occupied large parts of Iraq and Syria. It faced almost no resistance from Iraqi forces that had received billions of dollars of US assistance, which had created a dangerous form of welfare dependency. Although Labor prime minister Kevin Rudd withdrew Australian forces in 2008, Australian fighter planes returned to help the US bomb IS-occupied cities, causing heavy civilian casualties. Countries in the region with bigger air forces than Australia's did not contribute. IS eventually lost its Iraqi territory, but it can still conduct terrorist atrocities around the globe. Australian jets also bombed suspected IS targets in Syria, without the Syrian government's approval.

Australia did not join the US–French decision to bomb yet another country, Libya, in 2011 to help overthrow yet another dictator. The target was Libya's Colonel Muammar al-Gaddafi, although he had abandoned his WMD programs and support for terrorism. Gaddafi was murdered after being anally raped with a knife.[12] US Secretary of State Hillary Clinton later gloated, 'We came. We saw. He died.' She didn't mention that Libya was left in chaos: slave markets prospered, terrorist groups and army factions took control of large parts of the country, and a huge flood of refugees swamped Europe.[13]

Howard was so confident of his own judgement that he did not seek the normal public-service advice before joining the invasion. He took strategic advice from a staff member, Peter Jennings, who later became the director of the Australian Strategic Policy Institute, which is funded by the government and arms manufacturers. A department head with intimate knowledge of the prewar decision-making process later said, 'It was not really a matter of advising on the strategic pros and cons, only what to do if the word was "Go".'[14] The debacle reinforces the case for parliament to decide whether Australia should go to war, not prime ministers whose decision is ticked by a Cabinet subcommittee.

Howard has repeatedly tried to justify himself by saying that he 'genuinely believed' Iraq had WMDs,[15] but personal belief is no way to make public policy, particularly when the believer is eager to believe. Even after Sir John Chilcot's highly critical 2016 official report on the British involvement in the war concluded that the action was based on flawed intelligence, Howard told journalists he wouldn't 'retreat from' his decision to invade.[16] Chilcot said the benefit of hindsight was not needed to understand that the intelligence was flawed. He also said, 'The risks of internal strife, active Iranian pursuit of its interests, regional instability and al-Qaeda activity were each explicitly identified before the invasion.'[17]

Although Howard is widely considered a shrewd observer, he failed to notice, in the memorable words of MI6 head Sir Richard Dearlove, that the 'intelligence and the facts were being fixed around the policy [to invade]'. Demonstrating how a leak to a journalist can be in the public interest, Richard Smith quoted Dearlove's words from a secret memo and Foreign Secretary Jack Straw's remark that the case for military action was 'thin'.[18] Despite his intimate participation in the inner circle, apparently Howard was not told about the contents of this devastating memo.

Perhaps he knew, but couldn't reveal the grubby reality because he wanted to participate in the invasion. Alternatively, he was just another Australian politician mesmerised by high-level access in Washington and London.

Either way, Howard is responsible for one of the most shameful and damaging decisions in Australian political history. He should have admitted his blunder long ago—a blunder based on his ignorance and phoney 'intelligence' stamped 'Top Secret'.

PART 9
NUCLEAR RISKS ARE EVER PRESENT

56

THE DEPRAVITY OF
NUCLEAR WAR PLANNING

*'A defective computer chip … had generated the erroneous warning.
The chip cost forty-six cents.'*

Eric Schlosser[1]

Nothing so starkly illustrates the depravity of nuclear war planning as the targeting list for the US's Single Integrated Operational Plan (SIOP). Nothing so bleakly illustrates the irresponsibility of the planners as their continued refusal to install self-destruct devices that activate when missiles are launched by accident. The war plans have changed over time, but the number of anticipated deaths remains unconscionable. The 1962 version of the SIOP envisaged killing an estimated 108 million Soviet citizens, 104 million Chinese and 2.6 million Poles.[2] A later version planned to strike Moscow with 400 warheads as part of 12,000 targets in the USSR; China would also be attacked even if it wasn't threatening the US.[3] By the latter half of the 1980s, the US still planned to use 12,000 warheads launched from land, submarines and heavy bombers.[4]

This level of death and destruction was calmly and secretly planned in the name of national security by respectable members of the US national security state. Using 400 warheads on Moscow, each much more powerful than those dropped on Hiroshima, meant a great city and its inhabitants would be killed in horrific explosions, monstrous fires and dust storms. Planning to use 400 warheads to keep pummelling the radioactive rubble long after almost all life was extinguished would have displayed a level of depravity never before experienced in human history.

During the Cold War, Australian leaders relied on the SIOP to shelter under the US nuclear umbrella when the number of USSR and US strategic nuclear warheads reached a peak of 31,000 each. The total number has fallen, but how many are still targeted on Russia and Moscow is secret. Australia still relies on the US nuclear umbrella, and is also directly complicit. The Pine Gap intelligence-gathering base helps identify nuclear targets, and the North West Cape communications base is linked to US submarines that can be tasked to detect and destroy Chinese and Russian ballistic-missile submarines, potentially undermining deterrence because they are in a strategically weaker position geographically than the US.

Unlike the US submarines, the noisy Soviet submarines during the Cold War didn't have ready access to open ocean. Those based at Murmansk had to make a long transit through multiple choke points before reaching their patrol areas in the Atlantic Ocean. Those based at Vladivostok also faced barriers before reaching open waters in the Pacific. The Soviet submarines were all relatively easy to detect with a wide range of overhead and underwater sensors, and could then be trailed by US nuclear-attack submarines, often for an entire trip.[5] In 1985, Navy Secretary John Lehman confirmed that US nuclear submarines would attack Soviet ballistic-missile submarines 'in the first five minutes of a war'.[6] This meant that the US could sink the supposedly invulnerable submarines intended to deter a US first strike. Australia's submarines played an important detection role in what was called Gateway operations near Vladivostok, without any apparent consideration of how this could undermine nuclear deterrence. The USSR had so many land-based ICBMs that enough would survive to retaliate to a first strike.

Russia might just have enough today, but China almost certainly doesn't. The Pentagon reported in 2018 that China now has seventy-five to a hundred ICBMs and four nuclear submarines.[7] Each submarine carries twelve nuclear-armed ballistic missiles. These submarines are confined behind natural underwater obstacles plus a vast array of US, Japanese and other sensors.[8] Given that it would be relatively easy to detect and sink the submarines and destroy China's small number of land-based missiles, China doesn't seem to have enough missiles to deter a nuclear attack.

After the Cold War ended, US officials involved in nuclear policy interviewed many of their Soviet counterparts at length and, contrary to the general expectation, a picture emerged of extremely conservative Soviet leaders who refused to endorse a first-strike option. John Battilega, who studied the interview transcripts for a US Army War College project, says it appears that the Soviet military command was intent on preventing a catastrophic war after it concluded that 'nuclear weapons were a political tool, with very limited military utility'.[9] Almost all interviewees from the Soviet side perceived the US as preparing for a first strike. This was based on Soviet intelligence about the SIOP and the US's multiple new independently targeted missile warheads.

While the leaders' conservatism was reassuring, the common expectation after the USSR collapsed in 1991 was that there would no longer be any prospect of a full-scale nuclear war. This was illusory. US policy today retains two options: a first-strike use of nuclear weapons is one; the other is to 'launch on warning'.[10] Russia's stance is unclear, but possibly less conservative than it was under the cautious communists.

What is clear is that the risk remains of an accidental nuclear war started by missiles launched in error. Eric Schlosser, an American authority on the subject, gives one example of what could go wrong: 'On 3 June 1980, at about 2:30 in the morning, computers at the national military command headquarters … issued an urgent warning: the Soviet Union had just launched a nuclear attack on the US.'[11] A massive retaliatory strike was only minutes away when the Pentagon acknowledged it was a false alarm. Schlosser says, 'An investigation later found that a defective computer chip in a communications device at NORAD [North American Aerospace Defense Command] headquarters had generated the erroneous warning. The chip cost forty-six cents.'[12]

Schlosser says another false alarm occurred in 1979 when someone mistakenly inserted a training tape into an early-warning computer that showed a highly realistic simulation of an all-out Soviet attack.[13] During the Cold War, he says false alarms were triggered by the moon rising over Norway, the launch of a weather rocket from Norway, a solar storm, sunlight reflecting off high-altitude clouds, and a faulty telephone switch in Colorado.[14]

The Union of Concerned Scientists (UCS) points out that nuclear war was also narrowly averted when a Soviet officer, Lieutenant Colonel Stanislav Petrov, was confronted with early-warning data indicating that the US had launched five nuclear missiles. Instead of notifying his superiors, Petrov decided it was a false alarm and took no further action. The UCS says, 'If a different officer had been on duty, the false alarm could easily have turned into a catastrophe.'[15]

The UCS also notes a long list of accidents involving nuclear-armed bombers. On 24 January 1961, five of the six safety devices on a nuclear bomb failed in a crash after a bomber lost a wing over North Carolina. A bomber carrying four nuclear weapons crashed in Greenland in 1968, contaminating the surrounding area with plutonium, and a B-52 bomber collided with a tanker over Spain in 1996, scattering plutonium over nearby fields after two of its hydrogen bombs hit the ground.[16]

The 1983 NATO exercise Able Archer, which simulated a nuclear response to a conventional Soviet invasion of Europe, is one of the best-known examples of unnecessary secrecy almost resulting in a nuclear catastrophe. The Soviets were about to respond with nuclear weapons when a spy in NATO's headquarters told them it was only an exercise.[17] The danger would never have arisen if NATO had informed the Soviets about the exercise.

Human error is ever present. Despite strict safety protocols, the UCS says six nuclear-armed cruise missiles were mistakenly loaded onto a B-52 bomber at Minot Air Force Base in August 2007. The plane sat on the tarmac unguarded overnight and then flew 2400 kilometres to another base where it was nine hours before a maintenance crew realised the weapons were live.[18] Another concern is that illicit drug taking remains a problem among ICBM launch crews.[19]

The US and Russia could equip their missiles with self-destruct devices to abort a mistaken launch, but they give no satisfactory explanation for their refusal to do so. Many also warn that missile control systems can now be hit by a wide range of previously unknown cyber-warfare tools available to terrorists, hoaxers and governments.

US presidents retain the sole right to launch nuclear missiles, regardless of their sobriety or mental stability. Other officials may try to intervene but don't have the formal authority to prevent a determined president inflicting horrendous havoc on the world.

57

THE WEST'S RECKLESS RUSSIAN POLICIES

'Expanding NATO would be the most fateful error of American foreign policy in the post-Cold War era.'

George F. Kennan[1]

Russia has a large nuclear arsenal and a relatively small economy. Its conventional military forces are no match for those of the US, but they are also far from impotent. Apart from the presidency, Russia's political institutions are mostly weak. Even the president can't run everything in a sprawling, shambolic country where bureaucracies, interest groups, oligarchs and the Russian Orthodox Church also compete for power.[2] Some aspects of civil society remain vibrant, particularly in Moscow, where the arts and entrepreneurial start-ups thrive.[3]

Because Australia is enmeshed in the US's nuclear war fighting machinery, Russia matters to it, but there is no realistic way that Russia will regain the Soviet Union's status as a superpower whose conventional forces might have been able to advance across Western Europe—if neither side used nuclear weapons. No mainstream Russian politician shows any sign of wanting to use nuclear weapons, but this could change in response to a perceived existential threat, including a false alarm that triggers a nuclear launch during a time of high tension.

Given that NATO's military spending is over twelve times bigger than Russia's, Moscow couldn't invade and occupy Western Europe, let alone start a world war.[4] Although Russia has long been able to occupy the Baltic States should it wish to, it hadn't done so at the time of writing.

In June 2018, Russia had about 1440 deployed strategic nuclear war-heads on long-range missiles and bombers with a total of 6850 warheads that could be deployed, while the US had 1360 missiles deployed out of a total of 6550 warheads it could use.[5] Adding to this potential volatility, a large proportion of the population in the two countries is deeply nationalistic. The other nuclear-armed nations have far fewer warheads in total, and not all are deployed. France has 300, China 280, Pakistan 140–150, India 130–140, the UK 120, Israel 80 and North Korea 20.[6]

It didn't have to be like this. When Mikhail Gorbachev presided over the dissolution of the Soviet Union, many Russians looked forward to becoming closer to the West. Instead, US-dominated institutions such as the International Monetary Fund (IMF) insisted the Russian economy needed harsh medicine to facilitate the transition to a market economy. When implemented, this predictably produced a deep economic depression—hardly the best way to reward the Russians for abandoning communism. The economy shrank by 40 per cent, which was more than during the 1930s Depression in the West; male life expectancy declined; and poverty rose.[7] US leaders reneged on their clear promise not to expand NATO to include former Soviet countries on Russia's border. Despite denials, the US National Security Archive in 2018 released declassified documents clearly showing such a commitment was made to Gorbachev and his successor, Boris Yeltsin.[8]

Many Western strategists made powerful critiques of this policy. George F. Kennan, the architect of the US Cold War doctrine of containment, wrote: 'Expanding NATO would be the most fateful error of American foreign policy in the post-Cold War era … which may be expected to inflame the nationalistic, anti-Western and militaristic tendencies in Russian opinion [and] have an adverse effect on the development of Russian democracy.'[9] The conservative Australian analyst Owen Harries said that the USSR 'voluntarily gave up its Warsaw Pact empire, collapsed the Soviet system upon itself, and then acquiesced in its own demise—all with virtually no violence … The regime could have resisted the forces of change, thus either extending its life or going down in a welter of blood and destruction.'[10] Instead, Gorbachev chose to support the reunification of Germany within NATO, after the West promised it would not expand the military pact any further. Today, NATO are close to St Petersburg—a city whose population suffered terribly during the protracted Nazi siege in World War II, but never surrendered.

Yeltsin was a drunken buffoon who became Russia's first elected president in 1991. He let the economy fall apart, enriched oligarchs by selling them state assets at ridiculously low prices, and failed to stop criminal gangs extorting crippling sums of money from small and medium-sized businesses. With his approval ratings in single digits, a reinvigorated Communist Party looked like winning the 1996 election, but the US intervened to keep Yeltsin in power, as the 15 July 1996 edition of *Time* magazine detailed in a cover story headed 'Yanks to the Rescue—The Secret Story of How American Advisers Helped Yeltsin Win'.

Shortly before the 2000 election, Yeltsin handed the baton to Vladimir Putin, his dull-looking deputy. Initially, Putin wanted closer ties with Europe, telling the BBC: 'Russia is part of European culture and I do not consider my own country in isolation from Europe.'[11] He also suggested Russia should join NATO. The US would never have allowed this, but a more far-sighted European leadership could have reduced future tensions by inviting Russia to join the European Union.

After being rebuffed, Putin sought support from the Russian Orthodox Church and the nationalists. Russian incomes improved along with Putin's popularity, despite his increasingly autocratic rule.[12] Incomes then declined. One reason for this was a fall in prices for Russian oil; another was that the West imposed sanctions after Putin's 2014 reincorporation of Crimea into Russia. Crimea and its important naval base had been part of Russia from 1783 until 1954, when Nikita Khrushchev handed it to Ukraine, which was then part of the USSR.

Unlike the continuing catastrophe triggered by the 2003 US-UK-Australian invasion of Iraq, the reincorporation of Crimea occurred with little violence. A large majority of Crimea's population wanted to rejoin Russia, following what they saw as the installation of a hostile US-backed government in Ukraine. A BBC analysis of a leaked phone call between US secretary of state Victoria Nuland and the US ambassador to Ukraine in 2014 clearly shows she intervened heavily in decisions about who should hold key positions in the new government following the overthrow of the elected pro-Russian president.[13] One year after the annexation, *Forbes* magazine said, 'Poll after poll shows the locals there—be they Ukrainians, ethnic Russians or Tatars—are mostly all in agreement: life with Russia is better than life with Ukraine ... At some point, the West will have to recognise Crimea's right to self-rule.'[14]

In another source of tensions, George W. Bush gave formal notice on 1 July 2002 that the US would unilaterally abandon the Nixon–Brezhnev landmark Anti-Ballistic Missile Treaty. US leaders had previously considered this treaty essential to maintaining nuclear deterrence because it guaranteed that each side could retaliate if attacked. As well as deploying anti-ballistic missiles on air warfare destroyers, Bush announced in 2007 that the US would install an ABM system in Poland and associated radars in the Czech Republic to counter a possible attack by Iran. However, the location meant Russia, not Iran, would be the target. The Obama administration added a second ABM site in Romania.[15] Russia reacted by saying it would stick to the existing New START arms control agreement but not cut any further. So did the US. It now seems that each will deploy more nuclear weapons. If so, they will breach their undertaking in the Nuclear Non-Proliferation Treaty to move towards eliminating nuclear weapons.

During the 2018 election campaign, Putin said Russia was developing supposedly invulnerable delivery systems for nuclear weapons. He later released a video of a supposed prototype being tested. Fortunately, most of these systems are unlikely to materialise because Russia can't afford them; however, it could afford to smuggle warheads into target countries. The US is deploying a nuclear-armed, precision-guided missile on fighter jets. Called the B61-12, the weapon has variable explosive yields. The lowest is 600 times bigger than a conventional bomb. A supporter of the new weapon, retired air force general James Cartwright, said on US television that the lower yield could make nuclear weapons 'more usable'.[16] He didn't explain why nuclear-armed opponents wouldn't respond with existing higher-yielding weapons until the situation escalated into a full-scale nuclear war.

President Donald Trump has repeatedly said he wants the US to have more nuclear weapons than anyone else. He approved the 2018 Nuclear Posture Review, which emphasises the integration of nuclear and non-nuclear warfare in the US military's doctrine, training and exercises,[17] and announced that the US would abandon the Intermediate-Range Nuclear Forces Treaty, which would allow it to put these weapons in Western Europe as well as much closer to China. Many Europeans had earlier welcomed the treaty as reducing the chances that they would be directly involved in a nuclear war between the US and Russia.

To avoid a calamity, the US and Russia must lower the temperature. But the mood has been so poisonous in Washington that any official who speaks to a Russian risks being hauled before a grand jury. Part of the overheated atmosphere stems from a willingness by many journalists and politicians to demonise Putin, although he is not as repressive as the supposedly moderate Soviet leaders who followed Stalin (Gorbachev excepted). In 2016, Nuland told a Senate committee that the US had spent $100 million on an anti-Putin propaganda campaign in and around Russia.[18] This is rarely mentioned amid claims that Putin interfered in the

2016 US election campaign without spending nearly as much. In a rare exception, the *New York Times* acknowledged that Russia's efforts were no different from those of the US.[19]

Lowering the temperature will require many Western politicians and journalists to be less eager to assume that Putin personally authorised atrocities such as the use of an old Russian-made anti-aircraft missile to kill all 298 people on a Malaysian airliner on 17 July 2014. The missile was fired by one of the dozens of often-fractious, often-drunk separatist militia groups in East Ukraine, possibly with the help of an experienced Russian operator. Apparently, those responsible mistook the airliner for a hostile Ukrainian plane. In a similar tragedy, the US warship *Vincennes* shot down an Iranian airliner on 3 July 1988 after it took off from Tehran Airport, killing all 290 people on board. The *Vincennes*, which was inside Iranian territorial waters, was equipped with the highly sophisticated Aegis radar system, yet it somehow mistook the big passenger airliner for a much smaller US-made Iranian F-14 fighter jet whose radar profile was well known to the *Vincennes'* crew. US president Ronald Reagan didn't authorise the captain's actions; nor is Putin is likely to have authorised the destruction of the Malaysian plane.

There is no reason for tensions to be higher now than during the Cold War. Nuclear war was averted during the 1962 Cuban missile crisis after President Khrushchev sent a message to President Kennedy suggesting a way out. Kennedy told his brother Robert to talk to the Soviet ambassador, and swift negotiations resulted in the USSR withdrawing its missiles from Cuba and the US promising to withdraw its missiles from Turkey six months later. Khrushchev trusted Kennedy to deliver on his promises.

Trust and a willingness to discuss new arms-control agreements covering all nuclear weapons are certainly needed now. Russia, unlike the US, no longer has a surveillance satellite to give it twenty to thirty minutes' warning of a nuclear launch—it relies instead on radar that gives only three or four minutes' warning. It's unclear if Russia has a 'launch on warning' policy. If it does, it would have so little time to detect a false alarm that a horrendous retaliatory launch could easily occur accidentally.

58

DESTRUCTION IS ONLY
A TANTRUM AWAY

'The proposition that nuclear weapons can be retained in perpetuity and never used—accidentally or by decision—defies credibility.'
Canberra Commission on the Elimination of Nuclear Weapons[1]

The Labor prime minister Paul Keating put Australia at the forefront of arms-control efforts in November 1995 when he established the Canberra Commission on the Elimination of Nuclear Weapons to recommend a path to a nuclear-free world. Keating attracted leading international specialists to participate in the commission, including Nobel-winning scientist Joseph Rotblat, ex-US secretary of defence Robert McNamara, ex-French prime minister Michel Rocard, and ex-head of the US Strategic Air Command General George Butler.

After the commission released its report in August 1996, the new Coalition government presented it to the UN in September that year and to the annual Conference on Disarmament in Geneva in 1997. The report concluded, 'The proposition that nuclear weapons can be retained in perpetuity and never used … defies credibility. The only complete defence is the elimination of nuclear weapons and the assurance that they will never be produced again … The only apparent military utility that remains for nuclear weapons is in deterring their use by others. It would disappear completely if nuclear weapons were eliminated.'[2] The commission also stressed that a strong international verification regime would be needed to convince the existing nuclear powers to disarm.

Former Labor minister for foreign affairs Gareth Evans co-chaired another high-quality commission in 2009 that stressed: 'Nuclear weapons are the only ones ever invented that have the capacity to wholly destroy life on this planet.'[3]

After Labor lost the 1996 election, Keating and Evans' former colleague Kim Beazley told a parliamentary committee that he accepted Australia could be a nuclear target because it hosted US installations.[4] The risks were not trivial. An ex-deputy head of Defence, Paul Dibb, wrote in 2005, 'We judged that the SS-11 ICBM site at Svobodny in Siberia was capable of inflicting one million instant deaths and 750,000 radiation deaths on Sydney. And you would not have wanted to live in Alice Springs, Woomera, Exmouth or even Adelaide.'[5] Keating didn't share Beazley's seemingly sanguine acceptance of the potential death of 1.75 million Sydneysiders.

Coalition prime minister John Gorton in the late 1960s was the most senior politician to want Australia to get nuclear weapons. Journalist Tom Hyland reported that declassified documents obtained by the National Security Archive in Washington show that Gorton bluntly told US Secretary of State Dean Rusk in a Canberra meeting on 6 April 1968 that he did not trust the US to defend Australia and that he wanted the option to develop nuclear weapons because Australia 'could not rely upon the US for nuclear weapons [protection] in the event of nuclear blackmail or an attack on Australia'.[6] After Rusk said the US wanted Australia to commit to the Nuclear Non-Proliferation Treaty, Gorton explained that he was concerned that Japan and India would go nuclear and that signing the NPT would prevent Australia doing likewise for the next twenty-five years. Gorton eventually signed the NPT in February 1970, and the newly elected Whitlam Government promptly ratified it in January 1973.

Preliminary work on an Australian bomb was already underway in Sydney in 1968 at the Lucas Heights headquarters of the Australian Atomic Energy Commission. Its chair, Sir Philip Baxter, passionately backed Gordon's ambitions. The US was sufficiently concerned to place air-sampling sensors on the ground, and on planes that overflew Lucas Heights, to detect isotopes associated with the weapons program.[7]

Gorton was right to doubt that the US would always come to Australia's aid with nuclear weapons. It's hard to believe the US would risk the obliteration of one or more of its major cities if it agreed to use nuclear weapons to help Australia. Take the case of a nuclear-armed state that was attacking Australia, but only with conventional weapons. In one scenario, the US could use a low-yield nuclear weapon in what it described as a one-off action to destroy a target in the attacking country. The adversary might then retaliate with a nuclear attack on a small Australian target, such as Launceston, and insist this was also a one-off action. In another scenario, instead of being the first to use nuclear weapons since 1945, a rational US president would reasonably refuse to use them because the conflict could escalate into a full-scale nuclear war that killed millions of Americans.

Nothing has changed about the advantages of non-proliferation. If more countries acquire nuclear weapons, the risk increases that they will be used (accidentally or otherwise) to kill millions of harmless people. But Australia's ingrained fear of a threat from Asia has resurfaced as China's growing power attracts more attention. Calls for Australia to consider developing nuclear weapons have re-emerged, this time among think tanks and academics, although not yet senior politicians. ANU scholar Stephan Frühling sees several advantages of going nuclear, but not yet.[8] Doing so could easily encourage others, such as Indonesia, to follow. The possession of nuclear arms would not prevent Australia and Indonesia from becoming involved in conventional war, as happened between India and Pakistan in 1999.

Coalition governments since 2007 have bluntly refused to push for nuclear disarmament, preferring to rely on the dubious protection of a US 'nuclear umbrella'. They should revisit the explanation US officials gave to their Australian counterparts during negotiations in 1974: 'The threat of massive retaliation, with all its catastrophic risks, was essentially a bluff.'[9] The Coalition prime minister Malcolm Turnbull didn't support a UN conference resolution on 7 July 2017 to establish a legally binding treaty prohibiting the development or possession of nuclear weapons. There were 122 votes in favour and one opposed. Australia was one of thirty-five to abstain, claiming the treaty had imperfections.

Supporters of the UN resolution aren't pretending more work isn't needed to address the difficulties. One acknowledged problem is how to get the existing nuclear-weapons states to agree. No country has followed President F.W. de Klerk's moral lead when his South African apartheid government voluntarily dismantled its nuclear weapons in the early 1990s. Part of the solution is to develop an international verification authority that can provide the strong level of trust needed for the nuclear-armed powers to agree to relinquish their weapons.

The International Campaign to Abolish Nuclear Weapons (ICAN) has gathered support since Australian activists established it in 2007. After it was awarded the Nobel Peace Prize in December 2017 in Oslo, its leader, Beatrice Fihn, said, 'The only rational course of action is to cease living under conditions where our mutual destruction is only one impulsive tantrum away.'[10] The Turnbull Government refused to congratulate the Australian-led organisation on its award.

Nothing will be achieved until international leaders start talking calmly to each other in an effort to make progress. Nixon and Brezhnev did so, as did Reagan and Gorbachev. William Perry, a former US secretary of defence, gives another compelling example of the value of talking rather than trying to prove who's toughest. After observing the 1962 Cuban missile crisis from inside the White House early in his career, Perry was dismayed by the American media's triumphal 'crowing that Khrushchev had "blinked"'.[11] He said this was specious: 'Not only because Khrushchev's decision to back down spared the world from an unprecedented catastrophe, but because the [crisis] … accelerated the nuclear arms race already underway'.[12]

Before Australian policy-makers again extol the value of sheltering under the US nuclear umbrella, they should heed Perry's advice: 'A lifetime in which I had first-hand experience and special access to top-secret knowledge of strategic nuclear options has given me what may be a unique, and chilling, vantage point from which to conclude that nuclear weapons no longer provide for our security—they now endanger it.'[13]

PART 10
THE CHANGING OF THE GUARD

59

THE RISE OF CHINA, INDIA AND INDONESIA

'A country where the strong prey on the weak, where a burgeoning middle class opposed to free multi-party elections is willing to stand up ... for more accountable government, a place where money-making is called socialism.'

John Keane[1]

Great powers rise and fall, regardless of Australia's wishes. There is no inherent reason why we must be worse off if the relative economic and strategic power of China, India and Indonesia keeps rising while that of the US declines. Ever since World War II, Australian business has coped with political upheavals, decolonisation, wars, economic crises, disruptive technologies and policy changes while welcoming the opportunities created by China over the past forty years.

Australia's national security establishment, however, refuses to welcome China's rise. It wants to damage China's economy, although this would make Australia worse off economically but no safer.[2] Australia's two-way trade with China was worth over $183 billion in 2017—more than the total with Japan, the US and India.[3] Faced with change, many in the media and the wider population have also reverted to a reflex fear of China. Australians' earlier fear was that China's hungry hordes would pour down and eat their lunch. The new fear is that China can buy enough weapons and political influence to reduce Australia to a puppet state. Terrible images may even arise of the prominent politician Peter Dutton pulling a fat Chinese general in a rickshaw across the Sydney Harbour Bridge.

Precise predictions can be wrong, but the overall message is that the economic power of China, India and Indonesia will dwarf Australia's in future decades, notwithstanding periods of slower growth.[4] The world already depends on China for much of its prosperity: it contributed 32.5 per cent to world GDP growth in 2017 compared to 9.6 per cent contributed by the US.[5] Forecasts in the Australian government's 2017 Foreign Policy White Paper show the Chinese economy well ahead of the US's by 2030.[6] The big accounting firm PwC's projections to 2050 are even more sobering. They show the size of Australia's economy dropping from nineteenth in the world to twenty-eighth while many Asian countries forge ahead. According to PwC, China's economy will be largest by 2050, followed by India, the US and Indonesia.[7] China's middle class is forecast to expand to 850 million people by 2030.[8] If this happens, it will create tremendous opportunities for a wide range of Australian industries, as will the growth of the middle class in India and Indonesia.

Although Australia's relative economic and strategic clout is projected to shrink sharply, the 2017 White Paper seems incapable of recognising that Australia is in no position to keep insisting that everyone must obey the US-led rules-based international order that has supposedly kept the peace and delivered prosperity since 1945.[9] Never mind that the US repeatedly engages in illegal wars of aggression, breaks trade rules and abandons nuclear arms control treaties. The most likely outcome is that China will be the dominant power in its immediate region, and India and Indonesia will be increasingly powerful in their neighbourhoods. China will have no motive to invade Australia and probably not the military capability for decades. It won't be able to dominate Europe or North America.

A leading Asia scholar, Kishore Mahbubani, says that Chinese president Xi Jinping's accumulation of enormous political power has been taken in the West as a harbinger of armed conflict. But he says it has 'not fundamentally changed China's long-term geopolitical strategy … [of] avoiding unnecessary wars … Quite remarkably, of the five permanent members of the UN Security Council, China is the only one that has not fired a single shot across its border in thirty years since a brief naval battle in 1988. By contrast, even during the relatively peaceful Obama Administration, the American military dropped 26,000 bombs on seven countries in a single year.'[10]

Nothing is certain. China could collapse economically and politically or continue to thrive and revert to its earlier commitment to live in Confucian harmony with its neighbours. It is unlikely to become a democracy while its population fears this form of government would be as divisive as it is in the US. Even less likely, it might become a democracy and seek global dominance, as the US has done. Many outsiders, including myself, prefer to change governments in free and fair elections, but support for liberal democracy is waning in the West.[11]

Only the most curmudgeonly Sinophobe could dismiss former World Bank president Jim Yong Kim's statement that China has lifted over 800 million people out of poverty. As Kim said, 'This is one of the great stories in human history.'[12] It reflects favourable policy settings and the hard work and enterprise of the Chinese people. However, income distribution remains badly skewed.

When I covered Foreign Minister Don Willesee's visit to China in 1975, people dressed in drab Mao suits had no choice about where they lived or worked, and still suffered from the madness of Mao Zedong's Cultural Revolution. Severe poverty was entrenched. Today, people are much freer to dress fashionably and buy or rent their own homes, although many struggle to afford to do so close to their jobs in city centres. In 2018, 134 million Chinese holidayed overseas and millions more studied abroad.[13]

Under Mao, there was no private sector. Today, it comprises about 70 per cent of the Chinese economy. Further expansion is expected to slow under President Xi, but it's likely that many high-tech companies could still thrive and start-ups will abound, unless US policies block their export markets. China's Communist Party rejects the Marxist goal of imposing complete public ownership of the means of production, distribution and exchange, and punishes Marxist labour activists who try to improve wages by forming militant unions.[14] It could easily, and just as inaccurately, be called the Capitalist Party or even the Confucian Party.

The political scientist John Keane says of modern China, 'Contradictions are found in all the leading institutions, at every street corner, in every nook and cranny of its vibrant multimedia scene ... a country where the strong prey on the weak, where a burgeoning middle class opposed to free multi-party elections is willing to stand up ... for more accountable government, a place ... where there are more billionaires, skyscrapers and card-carrying communists than in the rest of the world.'[15]

The 2018 announcement that President Xi would hold his post for life is troubling. Philippa Jones, a former Australian diplomat turned Beijing publisher, told me in 2016 that policy formation in the one-party state had been far less monolithic than often portrayed. She said sanctioned contention about broad economic and social policy was often a check on the government, and that she feared that although the party used extensive polling to keep in tune with public sentiment, party panels set up by Xi would 'overtake the role of the technocratic agencies in decision-making'.[16] Xi has cracked down particularly hard on Communist Party corruption in a popular campaign that has punished over 1.5 million party members, including some of his main party rivals, but not his family or factional allies. There is no guarantee he will survive—widespread public anger could erupt if his provocative boasts about China's growing power rebound or anger grows at his attempts to control the personal behaviour of the Chinese people.

Human rights abuses are the biggest blot on modern China. Although 50,000 protests are held each year, they can be controlled or banned and political dissidents can be jailed.[17] Tibetans and the Islamic Uighur minority in Xinjiang Province receive the harshest treatment. There are credible reports that the Chinese government has interned one million Uighurs in 're-education' camps out of a population of 10 million.[18] This is a hugely disproportionate reaction to the Uighur terrorist attacks in Tiananmen Square in 2013 and at Kunming railway station in 2014.

The government plans to roll out a 'social credit' system covering the entire population by 2020. It will use massive databases from private and public sector sources to grade citizens on their social behaviour, rewarding those who do well.[19] Punishments for those who rate badly will range from minor to much more onerous. Australia has cashless debit cards that control what items some welfare beneficiaries, mainly Indigenous people, can buy. Single parents must follow a prescribed plan of behaviour called ParentsNext or lose their welfare payments. A system like China's may never be accepted in Australia, but many traditional civil liberties have been scrapped here with little fuss.

In 2018, the US imposed high tariffs on Chinese imports and pressured its own firms to stop producing goods more cheaply in China. It also complains that China has stolen patents to help it grow, as Japan and South Korea did—but earlier, the US allegedly stole British technology.[20] Mainstream economics regards patents and copyright as initially needed to entice industrial inventors or artistic creators to produce. Beyond that level, protection increases consumer prices unduly and prevents firms using the lowest-cost inputs. In its (misnamed) free trade agreement with the US, Australia foolishly agreed to extend the copyright on products of the entertainment, software and similar industries to seventy years after the death of the creator—far longer than Lennon and McCartney needed to write songs for the Beatles. Damaging trade flows will erode an important source of ballast in the US–China relationship. Unlike China's ineffi-cient, but heavily subsidised, state sector, its private sector accounts for about 85 per cent of total industrial production, yet receives significantly less budget assistance than its much smaller Australian counterpart.[21]

The US National Research Council says the federal government has played an integral role in the early development of numerous strategic industries—'Telecommunications, aerospace, semiconductors, computers, pharmaceuticals and nuclear power are among the many industries that were launched and nurtured with federal support.'[22] But in June 2018 the United States stated that it considered China's high-tech goals to pose an unprecedented national security threat.[23] This is implausible. The US will long remain the most militarily secure nation on earth. Its commercial concern is that some Chinese companies are gaining an edge over their US rivals by spending huge sums on original research. Staff-owned high-tech firm Huawei is a particular target because it creates cutting-edge communications and information technology at attractive prices. Huawei allocates at least 10 per cent of its revenue to research and development in thirty-seven joint centres around the globe. In late 2018, it sold more smart phones than Apple (whose phones are assembled in China).[24]

Australia stopped Huawei supplying routers to the NBN in 2012, supposedly to protect its top-secret national security communication system. But that system can't be accessed from the NBN, especially from the sections Huawei would supply. In 2018, Australia banned Huawei's advanced and competitively priced new 5G equipment that has a wide range of benefits in areas such as business, medicine, education and the remote operation of infrastructure, as well as for personal usage, but high-grade encryption can ensure important information remains secret. The Australian Signals Directorate expects 'these new technologies will provide new ways [for the ASD] to detect and track threats'.[25] China could do the same, regardless of whether Huawei supplied Australia's network. The Chinese government can order companies to hand over domestic data, just as the Australian government can and does. It would make no sense for a Chinese government to order Huawei to misuse its technology overseas, as the international reaction could destroy the financial viability of one of its leading high-tech companies. It has other ways to conduct electronic espionage. Without a convincing public explanation, it is hard to see the justification for completely banning Huawei's 5G equipment, which Optus and TPG intended using, while Telstra preferred Ericsson's 5G system. The government could have mandated the use of Telstra's system for the remote operation of critical infrastructure, in conjunction with additional protection against cyber attack. Optus and TPG could have still used Huawei's 5G equipment to provide serious competition in the rest of the market.

The different systems would sometimes need to interact, but critical infra-structure could still be protected. Highly classified information would still use the government's secure network, which is inaccessible by 5G.

After Britain decided in April 2019 to allow Huawei to supply part of its 5G networks, subject to tests of the equipment, *The Economist* said Australia's policy was 'wrongheaded', partly because there was no public evidence of spying by Huawei. It said, 'If an open system for global com-merce is to be saved, a framework has to be built for countries to engage economically even if they are rivals.'[26] The highly regarded commentator Jeffrey Sachs has noted that the US government has provided no evidence that Huawei has engaged in spying.[27]

But Australian journalists described approvingly how members of the Anglo-Saxon 'Five Eyes' intelligence club ate a lobster dinner at a Nova Scotia resort in July 2018 while devising a campaign to destroy Huawei by warning everyone to boycott its equipment. The increasingly hubristic heads of the agencies at the dinner actively conduct illegal electronic espionage themselves.

Australia's national security zealots also try to attack China's economy by advocating bans on Chinese foreign investment, often on spurious national security grounds. The campaign against a Chinese company leasing a commercial wharf in Darwin's port included warnings that US and Australian warships would have to get Chinese permission to enter the port.[28] However, the ADF and ASIO stated that there would be no national security problems as all foreign ships need government permission to enter Australian ports.[29]

Another false alarm occurred after the Australian Bureau of Statistics' census website collapsed on 9 August 2016 because it couldn't cope with the volume of census forms submitted. Yet the ABC repeatedly reported the next day that the crash had been due to a foreign 'denial of service' cyber-attack, despite the fact that reliable information was widely available that morning showing that no such attack had occurred.[30] Peter Jennings, the director of the Australian Strategic Policy Institute, which is partly funded by the US arms industry, wrongly told the ABC's *7.30* pro-gram that night that China's government was most likely responsible. The following day Prime Minister Malcolm Turnbull publicly acknowledged that the crash had been due to a failure by the ABS and IBM.

In 2017 the media made repeated claims that Chinese students in Australia were berating university lecturers for criticising China, but gave few examples. Christopher Kremmer, who teaches Chinese students in a postgraduate class at the University of New South Wales, says, 'I generally find them extremely respectful of their teachers. They are mainly interested in passing their courses and having fun.'[31] Another lecturer, David Brophy, said that in his Chinese history courses at Sydney University, 'I regularly touch on sensitive issues, including Tibet and Xinjiang. My students from China have never been anything but respectful and engaged.'[32] In contrast, one University of Sydney tutor relinquished his teaching duties after Chinese students complained he'd called them 'pigs' and cheats 'due to low IQs'. He kept his research job.[33]

The accusations against China multiplied in Clive Hamilton's 2018 book *Silent Invasion*. The ABC reported that Hamilton said, 'Thousands of agents of the Chinese state have integrated themselves into Australian public life—from the high spheres of politics, academia and business all the way down to suburban churches and local writers groups.'[34] Hamilton, a professor of ethics, presented no evidence for this wild assertion. None of the 300 Chinese entities in the China Chamber of Commerce in Australia have made donations to political parties, and only 2 per cent of campaign donations come from any foreign source.[35]

There is no evidence of an Australian government succumbing to clandestine Chinese influence. But any attempts by Beijing to bully Chinese Australians are unacceptable. So are evidence-free media accusations that Chinese Australians are effectively fifth columnists.

The media went into overdrive on 8 February 2019 after presiding officers calmly announced that an unknown source had made a cyber-attack on the parliamentary computer network, but that it had been swiftly blocked and there was no evidence it had been an attempt to influence parliamentary processes or the forthcoming federal election. The officers also made plain that the attack had not affected the computer systems of government ministers and their staff, which are heavily protected against hacking. This did not stop the ABC reporting that a Canberra University 'expert' said that Parliament House contains the 'crown jewels' for those looking for state secrets.[36] Why this expert's demonstrable nonsense was reported is a mystery. It is widely known that access to classified ministerial communications, let alone the 'crown jewels', is not possible via the parliamentary computer system.

The media quickly concluded that China was responsible. Perhaps it was, but attributing responsibility is no longer easy when intelligence agencies can make it wrongly appear that cyber-attacks come from their adversaries.

There is a good chance India will flex its muscles as it becomes stronger. Nor should an increasingly powerful Indonesia, the country with the world's largest Muslim population, be ignored. Indonesia is a lively democracy and is well located to attack or harass Australia. It is not a threat on present indications. That could change if Australians continue to ignore its sensitivities—for example, by loudly demanding it immediately release drug dealers from jail. Shortly after becoming prime minister, Scott Morrison, in a failed effort to win a by-election in October 2018, proposed shifting Australia's embassy in Israel from Tel Aviv to Jerusalem. The proposed shift was a hot issue in Indonesia, but Morrison showed no sign he'd given this a moment's thought. The Australia–US decision to use Papua New Guinea's Lombrum naval base for their ships also drew criticism in Indonesia.[37]

Future leaders should be reminded that past Defence Department strategists such as Bill Pritchett made a convincing argument that Australia could not be confident the US would come to Australia's aid in a clash with Indonesia.[38] Nothing has changed in that regard.

60
GOING TO WAR AGAINST CHINA

'The US has used force 160 times since the Cold War ended in 1991.'
US Congressional Research Service[1]

No iron law states that the current arms build-up in the Asia–Pacific must trigger a clash between a rising and a declining power that escalates until it kills millions. It's much too glib, however, to assume that more military spending will always minimise the risks of a catastrophe.

The core strategic reality is that the US doesn't need to be the dominant power in Asia to maintain its own national security. Unlike the US, China must remain part of Asia. Although China's growing economic and military power gives it added clout in its neighbourhood, it could never pose a serious military threat to the US homeland. Even if the US cut its own military spending by two-thirds, it would still be higher than the combined total for China and Russia.[2]

Strategic studies professor Hugh White says, 'America has no real reason to fight China for primacy in Asia, shows little real interest in doing so, and has no chance of succeeding if it tries.'[3] But many American politicians want the US to remain militarily dominant in the Asia–Pacific and seem to assume that 'boots on the ground' won't be needed in any conflict.

China, unlike the US, is strategically weak. Much of China's trade, including 80 per cent of its oil imports, goes through the easily blockaded Strait of Malacca, and it's surrounded by potential adversaries, such as India, Japan, Vietnam, South Korea and possibly Russia and North Korea. Although its forces are improving, it will be decades before China has anything like the US's ability to project power around the globe (even if it chooses to). Its last prolonged military experience was in the Korean War in the early 1950s. The US has fought numerous wars since then. Admittedly, the US fared badly in Afghanistan against ragged bands of peasants equipped with clapped-out rifles and homemade explosive devices.

Now US military planners believe its forces would be better suited to high-end warfare against China. This was the premise of its publicly announced 2010 AirSea Battle plan. Apart from a total trade embargo that would devastate Australian exports, the plan included deep missile strikes into China, guaranteeing the conflict would escalate. A serving American naval officer, Commodore Matthew Harper, warned that it would quickly collapse the global economy, saying, 'Focusing solely on Chinese military capabilities clouds the critical challenge of preventing a catastrophic Sino-American conflict.'[4] When I mentioned this article to a senior Australian naval officer, he asked for a copy and then sent a note saying, 'Anyone contemplating a war with China is insane.' This perspective hasn't stopped successive governments secretly authorising the Australian military to help with planning for participating in such a conflict.[5] A tight blockade on Australian exports to China remains in the plans.

Despite its immense power, the US could struggle to win an ultimate victory over China. It would be fighting far from home against a nation with impressive cyber-warfare capabilities, and anti-shipping missiles and torpedoes that could sink US carrier battle groups. Even if China lost the initial battle, it would be highly likely to rebuild its strength before resuming hostilities. The only way for the US and its allies to achieve an enduring victory would be to invade China, occupy hundreds of major cities for decades, and win a relentless guerilla war. A nuclear war might circumvent an invasion but could kill huge numbers of Americans and Chinese.

It is doubtful if China's relatively small nuclear forces could survive a US attack. The US has a total of 6550 warheads—1350 deployed on long-range missiles and bombers—compared to China's total of 280.[6] Ever since George W. Bush unilaterally abandoned the Anti-Ballistic Missile Treaty, the US has deployed conventional missiles on ships and land that can destroy nuclear-armed ballistic missiles. Its attack submarines can track and sink China's four ballistic-missile submarines.[7] This means China must expand its nuclear forces to ensure that enough retaliatory missiles would survive to deter a first strike.

Taiwan and the South China Sea are usually considered potential flashpoints for a war. Almost all countries, including the US and Australia, recognise China's sovereignty over Taiwan, but the US also remains committed to defending Taiwan. China tolerates the offshore island having its own armed forces and a democratic political system and welcomes its big investments on the mainland, but is adamant it will never accept a formal Taiwanese declaration of independence. For China, using force against one of its own provinces is not the same as attacking another country. There is no requirement under ANZUS for Australia to join this fight, and it shouldn't do so, particularly if Taiwan provokes a war.

Ideally, whether a province gains independence should depend on a referendum, which China would not accept. Likewise, the US wouldn't allow a referendum for the indigenous population of Guam, its Pacific Island territory/colony that hosts big air-force and navy bases.

China's abrasive behaviour in the South China Sea has aroused concerns about its intentions, although its activities are more limited than often assumed. The disputes are between littoral states that claim territorial waters in a sea covering about 3.5 million square kilometres of the Pacific Ocean's 162 million square kilometres. Former Australian Navy captain Sam Bateman, an eminent scholar on the subject, says, 'It's simply not true to say that Beijing claims almost all the South China Sea and islands within it as sovereign Chinese territory. It may claim all the "features" [uninhabited rocks, shoals, islets and reefs etc.], but only claim sovereign rights over resources of the sea. These rights are not to be confused with the sovereignty a country exercises over its land territory and territorial sea.'[8]

In pursuing its claims, China hasn't killed anyone or invaded another country, unlike the US, the UK and Australia when they invaded Iraq in violation of all the rules. Nevertheless, China should have accepted the 2016 international tribunal ruling in The Hague against its claim to an exclusive economic zone (EEZ) around some 'features' near the Philippines. The tribunal applied the treaty resulting from the 1994 UN Convention on the Law of the Sea (UNCLOS) to deny EEZ claims by littoral states to small offshore features. It didn't consider the building of artificial islands.[9] Unlike the US, China has ratified the treaty, but it behaved like a great power by rejecting the 2016 ruling. The US lost an international case after illegally dropping mines in Nicaraguan harbours in the 1980s, but ignored the ruling. Australia is not without sin: when Timor-Leste became independent, Australia withdrew from international maritime jurisdictions to try to stop it taking legal action over disputed petroleum fields.[10] The tribunal in the Philippines–China case also ruled that UNCLOS extinguished all historic claims.

Britain continues to assert its historic claims to the Falkland Islands, 13,000 kilometres from the UK. In March 2016, a UN commission on continental shelves expanded Argentina's maritime territory to include the Falklands, which are only 480 kilometres from its shoreline. Britain rejects the commission's finding.

Because it is a major beneficiary of trade, China doesn't deny freedom of commercial navigation in the South China Sea. Most of Australia's trade with China and North Asia doesn't even go through that sea.[11] US Freedom of Navigation patrols assert a right of passage for warships within 12 nautical miles of Chinese-claimed reefs and rocks in the South China Sea. Bateman says for Australia to conduct similar patrols 'as a push-back against China would serve no useful purpose. Rather these operations could help destabilise a situation that is looking increasingly more stable.'[12] He also says the South China Sea is not 'international waters' as it is almost entirely covered by the littoral states' EEZs for exploiting natural resources. Rules apply to passage through these zones.[13]

The Chinese government is under intense nationalistic pressure to keep asserting the same claims that Chiang Kai-shek's US-supported Nationalist government made in the 1940s. Chiang fled to Taiwan in 1949, and Taiwan still makes these claims today without attracting the same opprobrium as China. Taiwan has a military presence on Pratas Island, 850 kilometres from its capital, Taipei. Taiwanese patrol boats trying to land activists on disputed islands between Japan and China bumped into Japan Coast Guard vessels in July 2012.[14] Japan is not blameless: it has an implausible claim to an EEZ around Okinotori, a scattering of tiny rocks in the Philippine Sea, 1700 kilometres from Tokyo. The Japan Coast Guard clashed with Taiwanese fishing boats there in 2016.

China's land-reclamation works in the South China Sea to create sand islands are highly contentious. Vietnam and the Philippines also put military forces on disputed islands and engage in minor land reclamation. Although China can use these small platforms for military purposes, they are hard to defend against nearby Filipino or other forces. Admiral Dennis Blair, a former head of the US Pacific Command, says resolving the disputes calls for 'coordinated diplomacy rather than a military response'.[15] At the time of writing, the Association of Southeast Asian Nations (ASEAN) countries and China are working on a code of conduct to set a framework to resolve disputes.[16]

One diplomatic solution would be for all parties directly involved to freeze their claims and agree to share any resources in a sustainable manner. It's not impossible. Presidents Eisenhower and Khrushchev jointly promoted the much tougher 1961 Antarctic Treaty, which put all territorial claims on indefinite hold, banned militarisation and encouraged scientific cooperation anywhere on the continent.

Despite the near-impossibility of a long-term victory in a catastrophic conventional or nuclear war with China—a war with no bearing on US security—Australia's 2017 Foreign Policy White Paper wants the US to take a bigger military role in the Indo [Asia] Pacific.[17] It also hopes an increasingly powerful India would be a counterweight to China.[18] However, if Australia expects India to be its next big protector, it's likely to be disappointed. India had long been a culturally rich and prosperous civilisation before it was plundered during almost two centuries of British rule that left it impoverished and de-industrialised.[19] The Indian economist Ulsa Patnaik calculates that India lost over £9 trillion to Britain between 1765 and 1938, the bulk of it from the heavily taxed Indian peasantry.[20]

Alexander Davis, who researches Indian foreign policy, says, 'India desires a multipolar or polycentric world order, which is fundamentally different to the current (post) imperial "liberal international order" in which the US underwrites most of the rules.'[21]

Nevertheless, India is worth appreciating by Westerners, regardless of its strategic utility. It has much to offer visitors, usually tolerates freedom of expression, and produces a rich English-language literature. It is also a democracy where corruption is rife, leaders ignore widespread poverty, women are badly treated, the caste system survives, and Hindu militancy promotes violence against Muslims. It also oppresses the Kashmiri population.

India might reach a tacit understanding with China in which each has its own sphere of influence. Hugh White says neither would have the power to contest the other's sphere 'except at immense cost, and it is not clear why either would choose to do so'.[22] Australian foreign policy makers would then have to live with two headstrong rising powers, not just one.

The White Paper acknowledges that the risk of a direct threat to Australia is low, but frets about the future. Apart from its primary goal of maintaining internal security, China's military forces have been designed to stop a potential enemy getting close to the mainland rather than for fighting far away. So were Australia's. Their primary job was to control access to the sea–air gap around the nation, but they are now increasingly integrated into the US's more wide-ranging forces.[23] Rather than global domination, the Pentagon sees China as having a limited goal of being able to 'ultimately re-acquire regional pre-eminence'.[24] This requires China to project power relatively long distances from its coast—the Australian Navy has been able to do this since 1913. Two former Defence heads, Allan Hawke and Rick Smith, have explained why China has no motive to undertake the extremely costly endeavour of trying to invade Australia. They say, 'Global markets provide a far more cost-effective means of obtaining resources than military force.'[25] No one has identified any other plausible motive for China to attack Australia, unless we were participating in a US war against China. The joint US–Australian SIGINT bases in Australia already put a big effort into identifying targets for conventional and cyber warfare against China.

In the meantime, we should restore diplomacy to the pinnacle of our foreign relations, while maintaining forces to deter and, if necessary, defeat aggressive military action against the nation. As well as being able to defend the approaches to Australia through the island chains to its north, some of our forces should be able to operate beyond that barrier and defend against missile attacks that stop short of an attempted invasion. Australia is far from helpless. When its population was only seven million during World War II, there were a million people in uniform and many more in support roles. The population is now 25 million and the economy much bigger. Unlike the rapid Japanese advance in the Pacific War, modern surveillance tech-nology should give Australia ample warning of hostile preparations to acquire the necessary forces for a major attack.

No prime minister should proclaim, as Malcolm Turnbull did in 2017, that Australia is militarily 'joined at the hip' to the US.[26] During his February 2018 visit to Washington, he even claimed that Australia and US had been 'mates' ever since their armies fought together in a three-hour battle at Fromelles in 1916. But the two 'mates' didn't even establish diplomatic relations until 8 January 1940. Instead of fumbling for a non-existent security blanket, a little dignity wouldn't go astray.

Australia is one of the most secure countries on earth. It doesn't share land borders with any country, let alone any country with a history of ethnic, religious or other hatred stretching back centuries. It has not been invaded since 1788. Foreign Minister Julie Bishop said in January 2018, 'We do not see Russia or China as posing a military threat to Australia.'[27] It would be good if the US became less belligerent and China didn't behave like the kind of hegemonic power it once decried. But we have to deal with the world as it is—a world with almost no threat to Australia but a genuine risk of a military conflict between the US and China.

To keep Australians safe, political leaders should avoid participating in wars that pose no direct threat to the nation. The exception might be to help respond if one country clearly invades another. However, the comforting policy assumption seems to be that not many Australian troops would be killed or maimed by participating in a conflict with China. Nothing is inevitable, but twelve of the last sixteen major occasions where a rising power has challenged a declining power have resulted in war.[28] As cited above, a Congressional Research Service study shows that the US has used force 160 times since 1991. If war again erupts and Australian troops end up helping to invade China, they could be fed into the greatest human mincing machine the world has ever seen.

Alternatively, a full-scale nuclear war can't be ruled out while the necessary weapons exist. If one occurs, a nuclear warhead could obliterate Sydney or Melbourne. Some people will become scorch marks etched into the pavement. The heat will vaporise others, leaving no trace. The blast will dismember many more, while the radioactive fallout slowly kills over decades.

Nuclear war is one of the great threats to human existence. Global warming is another, as is the severe loss of biodiversity threatening the world's food supply. Avoiding catastrophe requires co-operation not mindless confrontation; dialogue not constant exploitation of unfounded fears. Fears spread by journalists in thrall to the national security state. This juggernaut has already shredded civil liberties in Australia. Now it is steering the country towards a cataclysmic, but unnecessary, war. All in the name of 'making Australians safe'!

ACKNOWLEDGEMENTS AND OBSERVATIONS

Many people and cultural institutions have helped with the research, writing and production of this book. The National Library, the NSW State Library and the Sydney City Council libraries provided essential support. The National Archives of Australia, especially its senior reference officer Andrew Cairns, made an invaluable contribution. Historian Philip Dorling pointed me towards helpful archival material. Unhappily, the archives are not easy to search.

The archives are more important to Australia's history than the War Memorial, which covers only one aspect of the nation's story. They should be funded at least as well as the War Memorial. Unfortunately, the way the archives are currently organised makes them difficult to use. A user, for example, can provide the name of an official report by a particular organisation, plus the date and other identification, but it can't be found in the archives. Most archival documents should be digitised in a word searchable form and available online. The cost would be minor compared to the money wasted on defence equipment that is of little operational utility.

Paul Malone helped with research and read and improved all chapters, as did my wife Sue. Liz Tynan read the chapters on the British atomic tests, Scott Burchill read those on the intelligence organisations and Australia's thirteen expeditionary wars, and Keiran Hardy read the 'Liberty Lost' chapters.

Louise Adler commissioned the book for MUP, whose executive publisher Sally Heath, senior editor Louise Stirling and the copy editor Katie Purvis were a joy to work with.

Most authors make little money. The task for authors of general non-fiction books could be simplified by including sufficient information in the text to let readers themselves use search engines to look up some sources rather than referring to endnotes with lengthy URLs. No sane person would try to type some of the more convoluted URLs into a search engine. The existing rules for endnotes would not be out of place in the Glass Bead Game. (Google it!)

NOTES

Preface

1 Quoted in W. Macmahon Ball (ed.), *Press, Radio and World Affairs: Australia's Outlook*, MUP, 1938, p. 157.

Chapter 1: The security scandal that the US hid from the newborn ASIO

1 David A. Hatch with Robert Louis Benson, *The Korean War: The SIGINT Background*, Center for Cryptologic History, NSA, 2000.

2 Some lack the full context because the messages were only partly deciphered or poorly translated. Code words still hid the real names of agents after decryption, making it hard to be sure of their true identities.

3 The transcripts can be found at https://www.nsa.gov/news-features/declassified-documents/venona/.

4 These papers are items 13 and 14 in a large document in the UK National Archives at http://discovery.nationalarchives.gov.uk/details/r/C9191674.

5 Apostolia Papadopoulou, 'Soviet intelligence on Barbarossa', Institute of International Relations, Athens, 25 February 2015.

6 Items 13 and 14 in a large document in the UK National Archives at http://discovery.nationalarchives.gov.uk/details/r/C9191674.

7 Australian figures from National Archives of Australia, 'Conflicts: World War II'. <http://www.naa.gov.au/collection/explore/defence/conflicts.aspx>, accessed 6 March 2019.

8 David Horner, *The Spy Catchers: The Official History of ASIO, 1949–1963*, Allen & Unwin, 2014, p. 60.

9 Adam Hughes Henry, email to the author, 29 June 2017.

10 The single abbreviation 'KGB' is used in this book to denote the various arms of Soviet intelligence in the 1940s.

11 Horner, p. 298.

12 Ibid., p. 299.

13 Brian Toohey, 'The security scandal that led to ASIO', *NT*, 26 April 1980.

14 Ibid.

15 Horner, p. 79.

16 Ibid., pp. 79–80.

17 Ibid., pp. 68, 76.

18 Hatch and Benson, ibid.

19 Horner, p. 87.

20 National Archives of Australia, email to the author, 10 August 2017.

Chapter 2: ASIO struggles with change

1 Harvey Barnett, post-retirement conversation with the author about the Combe affair.
2 Robert Manne, 'ASIO's hunt for spies and communists shows flawed intelligence', *SMH*, 17 January 2015.
3 David Horner, *The Spy Catchers: The Official History of ASIO, 1949–1963*, Allen & Unwin, 2014, p. 90.
4 Apart from a general concern with civil liberties, Evatt was defending the reputation of his private secretaries Alan Dalziel and Albert Grundeman, who had been widely accused of being Soviet agents. No supporting evidence was found by the Royal Commission on Intelligence and Security (RCIS) or ASIO.
5 George Brownbill, 'The RCIS: An insider's perspective', speech notes, NAA, 27 May 2008.
6 Horner, p. 362.
7 Ibid., p. 203.
8 John Blaxland, *The Protest Years: The Official History of ASIO, 1963–1975*, Allen & Unwin, 2015, p. 65.
9 Ibid.
10 *NT*, 19 March 1973.
11 Blaxland, p. 68.
12 John Blaxland and Reece Crawley, *The Secret Cold War: The Official History of ASIO, 1975–1989*, Allen & Unwin, 2017, p. 183.
13 Ibid.
14 Ibid.
15 Ibid., p. 262.
16 Quoted in Brian Toohey, 'Principles of liberty treated with disdain', *AFR*, 21 December 2007.
17 Elly (Bill Pinwill), *The Eye*, September 1988, p. 23.
18 Gerard Walsh, 'Threats to Australia's security interests', speech at a Canberra security conference, 1 November 1995.
19 Ibid.
20 Brian Toohey and William Pinwill, *Oyster: The Story of the Australian Secret Intelligence Service*, William Heinemann Australia, 1989, p. 57.
21 Blaxland and Crawley, p. 412.
22 *Wilderness of Mirrors* is the title of David Martin's 1980 book on James Angleton, the CIA's long-term counterintelligence head who branded an ever-widening circle of patriotic Americans as Soviet agents.

Chapter 3: An information gatherer mutates into a secret police agency

1 Judgment in *R v Ul-Haque* [2007] NSWSC 1251.
2 George Brownbill, 'The RCIS: An insider's perspective', speech notes, NAA, 27 May 2008.
3 Judgment in *R v Ul-Haque* [2007] NSWSC 1251.
4 See Brian Toohey, 'Our very own police state', in Eric Beecher (ed.), *Best Australian Political Writing*, MUP, 2009.
5 Brian Toohey, *AFR*, 23 July 2011.
6 Paul O'Farrell, 'ASIO "special intelligence operation" not reported to the watchdog for 10 days', *The Guardian*, 4 November 2016.

Chapter 4: ASIS: The government agency you pay to break the law

1 Justice Robert Hope, *Royal Commission into Intelligence and Security: Fifth Report*, 1976. NAA Series A8908.

2 Unless otherwise stated, what follows is from Brian Toohey and William Pinwill, *Oyster: The Story of the Australian Secret Intelligence Service*, William Heinemann Australia, 1989, p. 15.

3 Christopher Moran, *Classified: Secrecy and the State in Modern Britain*, Cambridge University Press, 2012, p. 122.

4 Ibid., p. 125.

5 Cited in John Dinges and Saul Landau, *Assassination on Embassy Row*, Pantheon, 1980, p. 51.

6 Hope, op. cit.

7 Smith wrote a three-part series for the *Canberra Times*, the *SMH* and *The Age* starting on 14 January 1989.

8 Hope, op. cit. See also Toohey and Pinwill, ch. 11.

9 *Report on the Sheraton Hotel Incident*, Australian Government Publishing Service, February 1984. This report was the basis for much of Toohey and Pinwill's Chapter 11 on the raid.

10 Toohey and Pinwill, p. 248.

11 Bill Pinwill, 'This costly toy', *The Eye*, March Quarter, 1990, p. 11.

12 Alan Fewster, 'We must be careful to avoid seeking intelligence simply for its own sake', *Inside Story*, 1 August 2014.

13 Brian Toohey, *AFR*, 18 February 2006.

14 Leonie Wood and Michelle Grattan, 'Cole report urges criminal charges', *The Age*, 28 November 2006. (AWB claimed the payments were unwitting.)

15 See Chapter 54 in this book.

16 Mark Thomson, *The Cost of Defence: ASPI Defence Budget Brief 2017–18*, Australian Strategic Policy Institute, 2017, p. 37.

17 Dan Oakes and Sam Clark, 'The Afghan Files: Defence leak exposes deadly secrets of Australia's special forces', ABC News, 11 July 2017.

18 Email from Dreyfus to the author, 22 August 2018.

19 Tony Eastley, 'Brandis orders ASIO raids related to East Timor spying case', *AM*, ABC Radio, 4 December 2013.

Chapter 5: ASD/NSA: The Five Eyes club shows the Stasi how it's done

1 James Glanz, 'US can spy on Britons despite pact, N50 memo says', *NYT*, 20 November 2013.

2 Martin Brady was an honourable exception. While DSD head, he gave substantive written answers to questions from Mark Coulthart for the Nine Network's *Sunday* program episode called 'Big Brother Is Listening', which aired on 23 May 1999. ASD's 2019 head, Mike Burgess, is committed to further openness,

3 Paul Farrell, 'History of 5-Eyes: Explainer', *The Guardian*, 2 December 2013.

4 Gwen Robinson and Gina Schien, 'Australia in spy pact, but leaders not told', *NT*, 6 November 1982.

5 Peter Cronau, 'The Base: Pine Gap's role in US war fighting', *Background Briefing*, ABC Radio National, 20 August 2017; attachment 'NSA intelligence relationship with Australia', Top Secret, April 2013.

6 'NSA's foreign partnerships', electrospaces.net, 4 September 2014.

7 See Chapter 15 in this book.

8 Brian Toohey, 'The Austeo Papers: Listening in—DSD's illegal activities in Australia', *NT*, 20 May 1983.

9 Ibid.

10 Brian Toohey and Marian Wilkinson, *The Book of Leaks: Exposés in Defence of the Public's Right to Know*, Angus & Robertson, 1987, p. 140.

11 Toohey, 'The Austeo Papers', op. cit.

12 Ibid.

13 Brian Toohey, 'Huawei ban won't stop hackers', *AFR*, 31 March 2012.

14 For details see p. 319 of this book.

15 A Canadian public interest group has compiled a database of everything the media published about Snowden's revelations as well as the documents. See Snowden Surveillance Archive, https://snowdenarchive.cjfe.org/greenstone/cgi-bin/library.cgi.

16 Morgan Marquis-Boire, Glenn Greenwald and Micah Lee, 'XKEYSCORE: NSA's Google for the world's private communications', *The Intercept*, 2 July 2015.

17 Glenn Greenwald, 'NSA collecting phone records of millions of Verizon customers daily', *The Guardian*, 6 June 2013.

18 Michael Brissenden, 'Australia spied on Indonesian president Susilo Bambang Yudhoyono, leaked Edward Snowden documents reveal', ABC News, 5 December 2014.

19 Philip Dorling, 'Edward Snowden leak: Australia spied on Indonesian phones and data', *SMH*, 17 February 2014.

20 'UK mass interception violates human rights', Privacy International, 13 September 2018.

21 James Ball, 'US and UK struck secret deal to allow NSA to "unmask" Britons' personal data', *The Guardian*, 21 November 2013.

22 Glanz, op. cit.

23 Laurel Poitras et al., 'How the NSA helped Turkey kill Kurdish rebels', *The Intercept*, 31 August 2014.

24 Although it's unclear how the SIGINT was obtained, Pine Gap and its UK counterpart, Menwith Hill, have the leading role in intercepting mobile phone conversations, emails and texts for targeting purposes.

25 Matt Burgess, 'Hacking the hackers: Everything you need to know about Shadow Brokers' attack on the NSA', *Wired*, 18 April 2017.

26 See for example Costas Pitas and Alistair Smout, '"Massive ransomware attack" hits companies, hospitals, schools', *SMH*, 13 May 2017.

27 'Vault 7: CIA hacking tools revealed', WikiLeaks press release, 7 March 2017. <https://wikileaks.org/ciav7p1/?#PRESS>, accessed 14 February 2019.

28 Reuters/AP, 'CIA aware in 2016 of Vault 7 leak that led to WikiLeaks release', ABC News, 9 March 2017.

Chapter 6: The uses and abuses of intelligence

1 Malcolm Fraser with Cain Roberts, *Dangerous Allies*, MUP, 2014, p. 283.

2 Jann S. Wenner, 'Daniel Ellsberg: The Rolling Stone interview', *Rolling Stone*, 8 November 1973.

3 Fraser, op. cit.

4 Brian Toohey, 'Assessing the intelligence of nations', *AFR*, 8 October 1996.

5 Andrew Fowler, *Shooting the Messenger*, Routledge, 2019, p. 147.

6 Nicky Hager, *Secret Power*, Craig Potton Publishing, 1996, p. 24.

7 Michael Burgess, 'Offensive cyber and the people who do it', Speech, Lowy Institute, 27 March 2019.

8 Frank Snepp, *Decent Interval*, Vintage Books, 1978, p. 13.

9 Rod Barton, *The Weapons Detective*, Black Inc., 2006, pp. 22–42.

10 For further details see Brian Toohey, 'Arms aid adds to Timor terror', *West Australian*, 6 September 1999; John Lyons, 'The secret Timor dossier', *The Bulletin*, 12 October 1999, p. 27; *Final Report, East Timor: Senate Foreign Affairs, Defence and Trade References Committee*, Parliament of Australia, December 2000, pp. 174–94; 'Companion to East

Timor: Leaks', School of Humanities and Social Sciences, UNSW; 'The death of Mervyn Jenkins', Nautilus Institute, 11 May 2009.

11 Submission by W.B. Pritchett to the Parliamentary Joint Committee on Intelligence, 13 August 2003.

12 John Howard, *Lazarus Rising*, HarperCollins, 2010, p. 447.

13 Richard Smith, 'The secret Downing Street memo', *The Times*, 1 May 2005.

14 Bob Drogin, *Curveball*, Ebury Press, 2007, p. 279.

15 Michael Wesley, 'Spying scandal: A little snooping is actually a good thing', *SMH*, 19 November 2013.

16 'OPCW issues Fact-Finding Mission reports on chemical weapons use allegations in Douma, Syria in 2018 and in Al-Hamadaniya and Karm Al-Tarrab in 2016', OPCW, 6 July 2018.

17 'Opening statement by the Director-General to the Executive Council at its Eighty-Seventh Session', OPCW, 13–16 March 2018, Paragraph 8.

18 Danielle Ryan, 'WikiLeaks' CIA dump makes the Russian hacking story even murkier—if that's possible', *Salon*, 13 March 2017.

19 Brian Toohey, 'Trump is a fool, but not a traitor', *AFR*, 17 July 2017.

20 Glenn Greenwald, 'Empowering the "Deep State" to undermine Trump is a prescription for destroying democracy', *Democracy Now*, 16 February 2017.

21 Glenn Greenwald, 'CNN journalists resign: Latest example of media recklessness on the Russian threat', *The Intercept*, 27 June 2017.

22 Glenn Greenwald, 'Yet another major Russia story falls apart. Is scepticism permissible yet?', *The Intercept*, 29 September 2017.

23 Greenwald, 'CNN journalists resign', op. cit.

24 'Report on the Investigation into Russian Interference in the 2016 Presidential Election', US Department of Justice, p. 2.

25 More detail in Chapter 59 in this book.

26 Armin Rosen, 'Here's how David Petraeus got off with only a misdemeanour', *Business Insider*, 28 January 2016.

27 Jane Norman, 'South China Sea: Former CIA director David Petraeus says Australia must "be firm" with China', ABC News, 24 June 2017.

Chapter 7: Medical support for trials to keep the Asian hordes at bay

1 Brendan Nicholson, 'Burnet's solution: The plan to poison S-E Asia', *Sunday Age*, 10 March 2002.

2 Churchill used chemical weapons against Russia in 1919: see Giles Milton, 'Winston Churchill's shocking use of chemical weapons', *The Guardian*, 2 September 2013.

3 Mark Weber, 'Churchill wanted to "drench" Germany with poison gas', *Institute for Historical Review*, Winter edition, 1985–86, pp. 501–50.

4 Barton Bernstein, 'Why we didn't use poison gas in World War II', *American Heritage*, August–September 1985.

5 Mark Weber, 'American leaders planned poison gas attack against Japan', *Journal of Historical Review*, May–June 1997, pp. 1, 13.

6 Ibid.

7 Michael Pembroke, *Korea: Where the American Century Began*, Hardie Grant, 2018, p. 143.

8 Richard Overy, 'China's war with Japan, 1937–1945', *The Guardian*, 6 June 2013.

9 These include Sheldon Harris's book *Factories of Death: Japanese Biological Warfare, 1932–45, and the American Cover-up*, Routledge, 1995, and Hal Gold's *Unit 731: Testimony*, Tuttle Publishing, 2004.

10 Ibid.

11 Brandi Altheide, 'Biohazard: Unit 731 and the American cover-up', University of Michigan-Flint, n.d.
12 Bernstein, op. cit.
13 Pembroke, pp. 172, 173.
14 Russell Working, 'The trial of Unit 431', *Japan Times*, 5 June 2001.
15 Much has been published on this. As well as Pembroke, examples include Stephen Endicott and Edward Hagerman, *The United States and Biological Warfare: Secrets from the Early Cold War and Korea*, Indiana University Press, 1999; Julian Ryall, 'Did the US wage germ warfare in Korea?', *The Telegraph*, 10 June 2010; and 'No US biological warfare in Korean War, Soviet documents show', CNN, 11 March 1999.
16 This topic is covered extensively in Geoff Plunkett, *Chemical Warfare in Australia*, Leech Cup Books, 2013.
17 Nicholson, op. cit.
18 Ibid.
19 Ibid.
20 Ibid.
21 Willy Bach, 'Britain, Australia, the United States and Agent Orange in the Indochina Wars: Re-defining chemical biological warfare', *Honest History*, 6 March 2015.
22 'US projects: Chemical warfare testing in Australia', NAA Series A1838, TS 694/7/37.
23 Ibid.
24 Ibid.
25 Nicholas M. Horrock, 'Colby describes CIA poison work', *NYT*, 17 September 1975.
26 Madeleine Kalb, 'The CIA and Lumumba', *NYT Magazine*, 2 August 1981.
27 Deborah Smith, 'Australia aided toxin research', *NT*, 11 April 1982. Smith reported that Defence scientist Dr Shirley Freeman published a paper on shellfish toxin in 1970 comparing its toxicity with that of blue-ringed octopus toxin.
28 John Playford, 'CBW research in Australia', *Australian Left Review*, June–July 1969.
29 Cited by Playford, ibid.
30 Ibid.
31 Ibid.
32 Kate Robson, 'Deans of a distant past', medicine150.mdhs.unimelb.edu.au (accessed 14 April 2015).
33 Ross L. Jones, 'Sunderland, Sir Sydney (1910–1993)', *Australian Dictionary of Biography*, ANU, 2017. <http://adb.anu.edu.au/biography/sunderland-sir-sydney-syd-26721/text34360>, accessed 6 March 2019.

Chapter 8: The best place to test the deadliest nerve agents

1 'US projects: Chemical warfare testing in Australia', NAA Series A1838, TS 694/7/37.
2 Unless otherwise stated, the information in this chapter comes from 'US projects: Chemical warfare testing in Australia', NAA Series A1838, TS 694/7/37.
3 These JIC quotes come from extracts cited in 'US projects: Chemical warfare testing in Australia', ibid. The NAA could not locate the full JIC reports.
4 Jeffrey Lockwood, *Six-legged Soldiers: Using Insects as Weapons of War*, OUP, 2009, p. 193.
5 'VX nerve agent in North Korean murder: How does it work?', *Scientific American*, 24 February 2017.
6 Hanson Baldwin, 'The Pentagon states the case for CB in Vietnam', *NYT*, 25 September 1966.
7 Brian Toohey, 'Just between friends', *The Eye*, May 1988.
8 Letter from Jim Dollimore to the author, Public Affairs Branch, 23 March 1988.

9 'US military planned nerve gas test on Aust troops', ABC News, 6 July 2008. Coulthart told me the Nine Network has sold its archives, which are no longer readily available for citation.

Chapter 9: Fighting the good fight against chemical and biological warfare

1 Gareth Evans, 'Weapons of mass destruction: Maintaining the rage', Dr John Gee Memorial Lecture, ANU, 16 August 2007.
2 Scott Shane, 'FBI laying out the evidence, closes anthrax case', *NYT*, 20 February 2010.
3 Ibid.
4 'Iran–Iraq War (1980–1988)', GlobalSecurity.org, n.d. <https://www.globalsecurity.org/military/world/war/iran-iraq.htm>, accessed 13 June 2017.
5 Evans, op. cit.
6 Ibid.
7 Ibid.
8 Paul May, 'Novichok, the notorious nerve agent', Molecule of the Month, August 2018.
9 Ryan De Vooght-Johnson, 'Iranian chemists identify Russian chemical warfare agents'. SpectroscopyNOW.com, 1 January 2017.
10 Jamie Dettmer, 'Russian nerve agent scientist admits selling deadly toxin to Chechen gangsters', *Voice of America*, 23 March 2018.
11 'VX nerve agent in North Korean murder: How does it work?', *Scientific American*, 24 February 2017.
12 'Skripal suspects confirmed as GRU operatives: Prior European operations disclosed', Bellingcat, 29 September 2018.

Chapter 10: Menzies' gift

1 Menzies speaking in parliament, 21 October 1953.
2 Unless otherwise stated, basic information on the tests in this and subsequent chapters comes from James McClelland, *The Report of the Royal Commission into British Nuclear Tests in Australia*, AGPS, 1985; Elizabeth Tynan, *Atomic Thunder: The Maralinga Story*, NewSouth, 2016; Frank Walker, *Maralinga*, Hachette Australia, 2014; and Robert Milliken, *No Conceivable Injury*, Penguin, 1986.
3 Arthur Macey Cox, *The Myths of National Security*, Beacon Press, 1975, pp. 75–85.
4 Quoted in Brian Toohey, 'Killen warns on plutonium', *AFR*, 5 October 1978.
5 Tynan, p. 87.
6 Sue Rabbitt Roff, 'The dark side of the nuclear family', *New Statesman*, 13 January 1999.
7 Milliken, pp. 87–90.
8 McClelland, p. 413.
9 Ibid., p. 393.
10 Fission bombs release energy by using high explosives to split heavy atoms of plutonium or highly enriched uranium. Thermonuclear weapons fuse together isotopes of light elements (hydrogen and lithium) to briefly create temperatures of over 10 million degrees Celsius. A fission reaction is required to trigger the fusion reaction.
11 Tynan, p. 87.
12 Gallup opinion poll, *The Sun*, 1 June 1957.
13 Tynan, ch. 10 gives a fuller account of the media shortcomings.
14 Walker, p. 190.
15 Ibid., p. 191.
16 Ibid., pp. 192–5.
17 Milliken, p. 94. See also Sue Davenport, Peter Johnson and Yuwali, *Cleared Out: First Contact in the Western Desert*, Aboriginal Studies Press, 2005.

18 W.A.S. Butement, Native Patrol Officer Files, Department of Defence, 14 March 1956; reported in *Canberra Times*, 27 May 1984.

19 H.J. Brown, Memorandum for Chief Scientist re Welfare of Aborigines: Maralinga Project Meteorological Station etc., 7 March 1956, Native Patrol Officer Files, Department of Defence.

20 W.A.S. Butement, Welfare of Aborigines: Maralinga Project Meteorological Station etc., 16 March 1956; reported in *Canberra Times*, 27 May 1984.

21 Milliken, pp. 272–3.

22 Patrick Barkham, 'Britain accused of using troops for nuclear tests', *The Guardian*, 12 May 2001.

23 Walker, pp. 218–30.

24 Walker, ch. 12 gives more information.

25 Alan Parkinson, 'Maralinga: The clean-up of a nuclear test site', *Medicine and Global Survival*, 7(2), February 2002, pp. 77–81.

26 Arjun Makhijani, 'A readiness to harm: The health effects of nuclear weapons complexes', *Arms Control Today*, 29 August 2008.

27 For further detail see Walker, Chapters 10, 13 and 15.

Chapter 11: The deceptively named minor trials

1 James McClelland, *The Report of the Royal Commission into British Nuclear Tests in Australia*, AGPS, 1985, p. 405.

2 Ibid., p. 415.

3 Ibid.

4 Brian Toohey and Deborah Smith, 'Still in the dark on Maralinga', *NT*, 25 May 1984.

5 Robert Milliken, *No Conceivable Injury*, Penguin, 1986, p. 241.

6 More detail on this problem is given in the next chapter.

7 J.L. Symonds, *A History of British Atomic Tests in Australia*, AGPS, 1985, pp. 501–2. For more, see John R. Walker, *British Nuclear Weapons and the Test Ban 1954–1973*, Routledge, 2010.

8 Symonds, p. 406.

9 Elizabeth Tynan, *Atomic Thunder*, NewSouth, 2016, p. 122.

10 NAA Series A6648, 17, McClelland Royal Commission transcript, p. 6352.

11 Ibid., p. 6304.

12 McClelland, p. 413.

13 Ibid., p. 414.

14 Ibid.

Chapter 12: British perfidy, Australian timidity

1 Robert Oppenheimer, speech to the Association of Los Alamos Scientists, New Mexico, 2 November 1945.

2 Elizabeth Tynan, *Atomic Thunder*, NewSouth, 2016, p. 244.

3 Brian Toohey, 'Plutonium on the wind: The terrible legacy of Maralinga', *NT*, 4 May 1984.

4 Brian Toohey and Deborah Smith, 'Still in the dark on Maralinga', *NT*, 25 May 1984.

5 Brian Toohey and Deborah Smith, 'Secrecy muscles science', *NT*, 8 June 1984.

6 Robert Milliken, *No Conceivable Injury*, Penguin, 1986, p. 321.

7 Tynan, p. 122.

8 Ibid., p. 87.

9 Ian Anderson, 'Britain's dirty deeds at Maralinga', *New Scientist*, 12 June 1993.

10 Tynan, pp. 274–96.

11 Alan Parkinson, 'Maralinga: The clean-up of a nuclear test site', *Medicine and Global Survival*, 7(2), February 2002, pp. 77–81.

12 Milliken, p. 270.
13 Alan Parkinson, *Maralinga*, HarperCollins, 2016, p. 60.

Chapter 13: The struggle to reveal Maralinga's malign secrets

1 Brian Toohey, 'Killen warns on plutonium pile: Terrorist threat to British atomic waste', *AFR*, 5 October 1978.
2 Frank Walker, *Maralinga*, Hachette Australia, 2014, p. 197.
3 'Nuclear waste dump in SA: Ex-RAAF man', *The Advertiser*, 3 December 1976.
4 Walker, p. 198.
5 Robert Milliken, *No Conceivable Injury*, Penguin, 1986, p. 263.
6 Ibid., p. 264.
7 Brian Toohey, 'Tighter security wanted at Maralinga', *AFR*, 16 December 1976.
8 John Farrands, Secretary [Arthur Tange], 'Article by Toohey, Financial Review, December 16, 1976', NAA Series A10060.
9 NAA Series A6648, 17, McClelland Royal Commission transcript, pp. 6325, 6304.
10 Ibid.
11 Toohey, 'Killen warns on plutonium pile', op. cit.
12 Ibid.
13 Brian Toohey, 'Maralinga: The "do nothing" solution', *AFR*, 11 October 1978.
14 Chapter 13 in this book shows that Killen simultaneously denied a media report while privately confirming its accuracy in correspondence with the US.
15 Milliken, p. 269.

Chapter 14: A wise mandarin ignores leaks

1 Mike Codd, rejecting a prime ministerial request to investigate a leak: 'Leak of classified documents', NAA Series A937/1992/5814.
2 The account that follows, including quotes from documents in this chapter, is from NAA Series A937/1992/5814.

Chapter 15: How Australia joined the nuclear war club

1 Clark speaking on 16 September 1967 at the official opening of the North West Cape base.
2 Brian Toohey, 'Menzies and the US envoy's sweetheart deal', *NT*, 4 May 1980. Unless otherwise stated, all quotes from cables to and from the US embassy in Canberra are from originals held in the Kennedy Library, as are all quotes from White House briefing papers and correspondence.
3 The 10 July 1963 memo to Kennedy's national security adviser, McGeorge Bundy, from William Brubeck attached briefing and background papers for the meeting, plus a CIA biographical sketch of Calwell.
4 Desmond Ball, *A Suitable Piece of Real Estate*, Hale & Iremonger, 1980, p. 50.
5 'Naval Communication Station Harold E. Holt (North West Cape)', Nautilus Institute, 8 March 2011.
6 'NAVSECGRU stations past and present', NavyCTHistory.com. <https://navycthistory.com/CI_Stations_past_and_present_alphabetical_3b.html>, accessed 2 February 2019.
7 'Uncle Sam and his 40,000 snoopers', *Nation Review*, 5 October 1972.
8 Frank Cranston, 'Value of base to US operations', *Canberra Times*, 12 April 1973.

Chapter 16: Dangerous advice from ignorant Australian officials

1 Congressional testimony from Schlesinger, 11 September 1974.
2 See Chapters 19 and 20 in this book.
3 Brian Toohey, 'Barnard's doomed mission on NW Cape', *AFR*, 3 April 1973.

4 J.R. Walsh and G.J. Munster (eds), *Documents on Australian Defence and Foreign Policy, 1968–1975*, self-published, 1980, p. 34.
5 Ibid., p. 49.
6 Ibid., p. 41.
7 Ibid., p. 51.
8 Philip Dorling, 'Secret's out: Soviets did not target cities', *SMH*, 6 August 2012.
9 Walsh and Munster, p. 54.
10 Brian Toohey, 'America's secret nuclear strategy', *AFR*, 31 August 1976.
11 Ibid.
12 See Part 9 of this book.
13 Walsh and Munster, p. 65.
14 Ibid.
15 NAA Series A10060, p. 146.
16 Ibid., p. 147.
17 'Executive summary', *Report of the Canberra Commission on the Elimination of Nuclear Weapons*, Department of Foreign Affairs and Trade, 1996, p. 1. The Keating Government set up the commission.

Chapter 17: Bluster and belligerence

1 NAA Series A10060, Freedom of Information request: Brian Toohey, p. 50.
2 Chapter 13 in this book noted that Killen publicly denied that plutonium was buried at Maralinga after the *AFR* published an accurate report that it was—a reality he knew the government would have to acknowledge.
3 Brian Toohey, 'Australia gets new US defence station', *AFR*, 8 May 1978.
4 Military construction appropriations for fiscal year 1978 [1977]: Hearings before a subcommittee of the Committee on Appropriations, US Senate 95th Congress First Session. Part 2, pp. 182–3.
5 NAA Series A10060, op. cit., p. 50.
6 Ibid, pp. 53, 54.
7 Ibid., pp. 55–7.
8 Brian Toohey, 'Russell Hill kept the ball', *AFR*, 23 May 1978.
9 NAA Series A10060, pp. 108–10.
10 Ibid., pp. 96–7.
11 Ibid., p. 91.
12 Ibid.
13 Ibid., pp. 76–7.
14 Ibid., p. 70.

Chapter 18: North West Cape: More dangerous than ever

1 Joel Fitzgibbon, Minister for Defence, media release, 18 July 2008.
2 Kim Beazley, 'North West Cape: The joint facility that changed Australian politics', *The Strategist*, 20 December 2017.
3 Hamish MacDonald, 'The wired seas of Asia: China, Japan, the US and Australia', *Asia-Pacific Journal*, April 2015.
4 See chapters on the risk of nuclear war.
5 Cheryl Pellerin, 'US to locate key space systems in Australia', American Forces Press Service, 14 November 2012.
6 'Australia-United States Space Situational Awareness Partnership AUSMIN 2010', DFAT, n.d.
7 Richard Tanter, 'North by North West Cape: Eyes on China', Austral Policy Forum 10-02A, 14 December 2010.

8 'Donald Trump launches new military "Space Force"', ABC News, 19 June 2018.
9 'Donald Trump sets goal to create US military space force by 2020', ABC News, 10 August 2018.

Chapter 19: The man who thought he owned the secrets
1 Robert Lindsey, *The Falcon and the Snowman*, Simon & Schuster, 1979, p. 69.
2 This, and most of what follows, is now in the public domain, or is based on confidential sources.
3 Snowden Surveillance Archive. <https://snowdenarchive.cjfe.org/greenstone/cgi-bin/library.cgi>, accessed 2 February 2019.
4 Arthur Tange, *Defence Policy-Making*, ANU Press, 2008, p. 75.
5 Testimony of Professor Des Ball to the Joint Standing Committee on Treaties, Reference: Pine Gap, Hansard, Parliament of the Commonwealth of Australia, 9 August 1999, p. 3.
6 Author's conversation with Marshall Green, Metropolitan Club, Washington, DC, 12 January 1981. Shortly after the *AFR* published these priorities, Green gave the same list to the *SMH*'s foreign affairs writer, Peter Hastings.
7 D.W. Argall, 'US installations in Australia', 31 August 1973, departmental reference 694/7/47.
8 I worked for Barnard for the first seven weeks he was a minister.
9 Kim Beazley, 'Thinking security: Influencing national strategy from the Academy—an Australian experience', Coral Bell Lecture, Lowy Institute for International Policy, March 2008.
10 Stephen Stockwell, 'Beyond conspiracy theory: US presidential archives on the Australian press, national security and the Whitlam government', Journalism Education Association Conference, Griffith University, 29 November 2005, p. 23.
11 See Chapter 21 in this book.
12 Brian Toohey, 'The arms control myth', *NT*, 4 July 1986.
13 Tange, p. 72.
14 Ibid.
15 Defence paid Edwards $355,000 to write Tange's biography, edit the memoir and prepare his personal archives for deposit in the National Library, as well as paying Allen & Unwin $30,000 to publish the book: Defence Media email to the author, 4 November 2015.
16 Brian Toohey, 'Pointers from Turkey on what the US bases really do', *AFR*, 31 July 1975.
17 Tange, p. 74. A more junior officer, Dennis Argall, had been briefed; so had some JIO officers.
18 Tange, p. 73.

Chapter 20: The man who thought he owned a prime minister
1 Quoted in Paul Kelly, *The Unmaking of Gough*, Allen & Unwin, 1994, p. 32. Tange was referring to Whitlam's intention to confirm the publicly known fact that Richard Stallings worked for the CIA.
2 The second volume of the official ASIO history says Stallings had contacted me with allegations of CIA activities in Australia in the 1960s (John Blaxland, *The Protest Years: The Official History of ASIO, 1963–1975*, Allen & Unwin, 2015, p. 446). I did speak to Stallings, but he was not my source.
3 Unless otherwise stated, this chapter's account of what happened is based on my observations as a journalist at the time and on confidential sources.
4 Brian Toohey, 'Anthony's CIA connection', *AFR*, 3 November 1975 and 'CIA man's wide contacts', *AFR*, 4 November 1975.

5 Paul Kelly and Troy Bramston, *The Dismissal*, Penguin, Melbourne, 2016, p. 164.
6 Brian Toohey, 'The CIA and Whitlam's dismissal', *AFR*, 5 December 1975.
7 Jeffrey Richelson, 'The CIA and Signals Intelligence', US National Security Archive, 20 March 2015, p. 15.
8 'NSA intelligence relationship with Australia', a Top Secret information paper distributed to all Five Eyes members, dated April 2013, p. 2. First publicly quoted by Radio National's *Background Briefing* program 'The Base: Pine Gap's role in US war fighting', 20 August 2017. Snowden supplied the document.
9 Robert Lindsey, *The Falcon and the Snowman*, Simon & Schuster, 1979, p. 260.
10 Quoted by William Pinwill, 'Just who betrayed whom?', *The Australian*, 19 September 1981.
11 Edwards, email to the author, 30 December 2015.
12 Kelly and Branston, p. 264.
13 Arthur Tange, *Defence Policy-Making*, ANU Press, 2008, p. 94.

Chapter 21: The men who spread the fairytale about arms control

1 Quoted in Amy Woolf, 'The New START Treaty: Central limits and key provisions', Congressional Research Service, 11 October 2016.
2 Herbert Scoville, 'The SALT debate: Why Iran doesn't matter', *New York Magazine*, 18 June 1979.
3 Amy Woolf, 'Monitoring and verification in arms control', Congressional Research Service, 21 April 2010, p. 18.
4 Jeffrey Richelson, email to the author, 2 February 2017. Richelson is a leading US researcher on signals intelligence.
5 Eric Schlosser, 'World War Three by mistake', *New Yorker*, 23 December 2016.
6 Other satellite sensors have a peripheral role in detecting electromagnetic pulse from a nuclear explosion.
7 'Verification regime', CTBTO.org, n.d. <https://www.ctbto.org/verification-regime/>, accessed 2 February 2019.
8 Kim Beazley, 'Winning the peace: Australia's role in arms control', speech given at Murdoch University, 12 June 1986.
9 Brian Toohey, 'The arms control myth', *NT*, 4 July 1986.
10 William Burr, 'US Cold War nuclear target lists declassified for the first time', National Security Archive, Washington, 22 December 2015; updated 4 April 2016.
11 Brian Toohey, 'Sydney role in US missile tests', *NT*, 1 February 1985.
12 Brian Toohey, 'Pine Gap prepares to spy on Greece', *NT*, 29 March 1985.
13 Brian Toohey and Marian Wilkinson, 'Preparing For Teal Ruby', *NT*, 10 May 1985.
14 Brian Toohey, 'Weapons blast from space', *NT*, 30 March 1980.
15 NAA Series A14370, JH1977/423.
16 Peter Hartcher, 'The year in review', 2015 Sir Herman Black Lecture, Royal United Services Institute of New South Wales, 16 November 2015.
17 Spencer Ackerman, '41 men targeted but 1147 people killed: US drone strikes—the facts on the ground', *The Guardian*, 24 November 2014.

Chapter 22: The men seduced by the secrets

1 Joint Committee on Foreign Affairs and Defence, Parliament of the Commonwealth of Australia, *Threats to Australia's Security: Their Nature and Probability*, AGPS, Canberra, 1981, p. 18.
2 Kim Beazley, 'Des Ball: A personal recollection', *The Strategist*, 27 October 2016.
3 Kim Beazley and Gareth Evans, memorial service for Des Ball, 22 November 2016.
4 Desmond Ball, *A Base for Debate*, Allen & Unwin, 1987, pp. 147–8.

5 See Chapter 21 in this book.

6 Richard Tanter, 'The "joint facilities" revisited: Desmond Ball, democratic debate on security, and the human interest', NAPSNet Special Report, 11 December 2012.

7 Arthur Tange, *Defence Policy-Making*, ANU Press, 2008, p. 70.

8 Andrew Clark, *NT*, 17 November 1975.

9 Joint Committee on Foreign Affairs and Defence, *Threats to Australia's Security*, p. 18.

10 Kim Beazley, 'Thinking security: Influencing national strategy from the Academy—an Australian experience', Coral Bell Lecture, Lowy Institute for International Policy, March 2008, footnote 14.

11 Ball, p. xii.

12 Testimony of Professor Desmond Ball to the Joint Standing Committee on Treaties, Pine Gap, Hansard, Parliament of the Commonwealth of Australia, August 1999.

13 Duncan Campbell, 'Somebody's listening', *New Statesman*, 12 August 1988. See also Nicky Hager, *Secret Power*, Craig Potton Publishing, 1996, and European Parliament, *Report of the Temporary Committee on the ECHELON Interception System*, 2001.

14 Testimony of Professor Desmond Ball to the Joint Standing Committee on Treaties, op. cit.

15 Peter Cronau, 'The Base: Pine Gap's role in US war fighting', *Background Briefing*, ABC Radio National, 20 August 2017.

16 Ibid.

17 Ibid.

18 Ibid.

19 Ryan Gallagher, 'Inside Menwith Hill, the NSA's British base at the heart of US targeted killing', *The Intercept*, 6 September 2016.

20 Ibid.

21 Richard Tanter, Desmond Ball and Bill Robinson, 'The militarisation of Pine Gap: Organisations and personnel', Nautilus Institute, 14 August 2015.

22 Desmond Ball, Bill Robinson and Richard Tanter, 'The antennas of Pine Gap', NAPSNet Special Report, 21 February 2016. This report says Pine Gap's conventional ground stations for intercepting communication satellites began operating in 1999. They are part of a global network of collection stations, including NSA stations at Misawa in Japan, Menwith Hill and Bude (in Cornwall) in the UK, Cyprus, Oman, Ontario, Geraldton in WA, Shoal Bay in the NT, and Waihopai in New Zealand.

23 Kim Beazley, Lockheed Martin Vernon Parker Oration, Canberra, 22 June 2016.

Chapter 23: The difficult birth and early years of a treaty

1 Graeme Dobell, 'The Downer legacy: The US alliance', *The Interpreter*, 30 January 2009.

2 John Edwards, *John Curtin's War, Vol. 2*, Viking, 2018, p. 75.

3 Quoted by Lachlan Strahan, *Australia's China: Changing Perceptions from the 1930s to the 1990s*, Cambridge University Press, 1996, p. 147.

4 Roger Holdich, Vivianne Johnson and Pamela Andre (eds), *The ANZUS Treaty 1951*, Department of Foreign Affairs and Trade, 2001, p. 1.

5 Ibid., p. xviii.

6 Ibid., p. 56.

7 Dobell, op. cit.

8 Holdich et al., p. 64.

9 Ibid., p. 68.

10 '60 per cent say Japan's pacifist constitution should stay unchanged: Poll', *South China Morning Post*, 22 July 2015.

11 David Horner, 'Shedden, Sir Frederick Geoffrey (1893–1971)', *Australian Dictionary of Biography*, MUP, 2002.
12 Arthur Tange, *Defence Policy-Making*, ANU Press, 2008, pp. 3, 7–8.
13 Brian Toohey, 'The Menzies man who exasperated Washington', *NT*, 6 April 1980.
14 Ibid.
15 Ibid.
16 Ibid.
17 Ibid.
18 Garry Woodard, 'Should Australia do more on the South China Sea?', Australian Institute of International Affairs panel discussion, 10 March 2016.

Chapter 24: Foreign bases and foreign political interference
1 Visit of Australian Prime Minister Menzies, Washington, 17–20 June 1962, Position Paper, drafted by Mr Ingraham.
2 'US National Security Study Memorandum 127', 27 May 1971, Box 183, NSC Institutional Files.
3 Luncheon conversation with Marshall Green, Washington, DC, 12 January 1981.
4 Desmond Ball, *A Suitable Piece of Real Estate*, Hale & Iremonger, 1980, p. 99.
5 Ibid.
6 Brendan Nicholson, 'Revealed: Secrets of the spies in our skies', *The Age*, 10 September 2005.
7 Brian Toohey, 'Menzies and the US envoy's sweetheart deal', *NT*, 4 May 1980.
8 Extract from JIC (AUST) report (61) 50, September 1961, quoted in an official report on 'US projects: Chemical warfare testing in Australia' referred to Chapters 7 and 8 in this book. The NAA was unable to locate a copy of the JIC report despite a diligent search.
9 Brian Toohey, 'CIA funded covert action against Australian critics of Vietnam war', *NT*, 28 June 1980.
10 Ibid.
11 Brian Toohey, 'How the US backed Billy McMahon', *NT*, 26 October 1980.
12 Ibid.

Chapter 25: Enduring faith in a guarantee that doesn't exist
1 J.R. Walsh and G.J. Munster (eds), *Documents on Australian Defence and Foreign Policy, 1968–1975*, self-published, 1980, p. 20.
2 Brian Toohey, 'The Menzies man who exasperated Washington', *NT*, 6 April 1980.
3 Ibid.
4 Brian Toohey and William Pinwill, *Oyster*, William Heinemann Australia, 1989, p. 72.
5 Fletcher Prouty in the 1983 film *Allies*, transcript pp. 9–11.
6 R.G. Casey, Diaries, 15 March 1958, NLA MS 6150.
7 Ibid., 3 September 1957.
8 Quoted in Gregory Pemberton, *All the Way: Australia's Road to Vietnam*, Allen & Unwin, 1987, p. 78.
9 Toohey and Pinwill, p. 94.
10 James Curran, 'A brutal lesson in politics from John F. Kennedy', *The Australian*, 22 November 2013.
11 Ibid.
12 Walsh and Munster, p. 20.
13 Quoted later in *SMH*, 2 April 1965.
14 Curran, op. cit.

15 Ibid.
16 Ibid.
17 Graeme Dobell, 'The Downer legacy: The US alliance', *The Interpreter*, 30 January 2009.

Chapter 26: How New Zealand has survived without ANZUS

1 Nicky Hager, *Secret Power*, Craig Potton Publishing, 1996, p. 24.
2 A.F. Catalinac, 'Why New Zealand took itself out of ANZUS', *Foreign Policy Analysis*, 6(3), 2010, p. 317.
3 Ibid., p. 318.
4 Hager, p. 24.
5 Ibid., p. 23.
6 Ryan Gallagher and Nicky Hager, 'Documents shine light on NZ's shadowy New Zealand surveillance base', *The Intercept*, 8 March 2015.
7 Ryan Gallagher and Nicky Hager, 'NSA and NZ SIGINT agency spying on the communications of Chinese diplomats', *New Zealand Herald*, 19 April 2015.
8 Ryan Gallagher and Nicky Hager, 'Snowden revelations: NZ's spy reach stretches across globe', *New Zealand Herald*, 11 March 2015.
9 Geoff Kitney and Wendy Bacon, 'Rainbow Warrior: French spies on Norfolk Island', *NT*, 11 October 1985.
10 Mark Keenan and Colin Richardson, 'Differences of perspective', Centre for Defence and Strategic Studies, Australian Defence College, March 2011.

Chapter 27: The lonely death of a good policy

1 Minister for Defence, *Australia's National Security: A Defence Update 2007*, released 5 July 2007.
2 'Downer denies Taiwan blunder', AAP, 20 August 2004.
3 Philip Dorling and Richard Baker, 'Missile defence language aimed to deceive Labor Left', *SMH*, 9 December 2010.
4 Michael Danby, 'Defence blunder sends wrong signal', *The Australian*, 16 June 2014.
5 See Chapter 35 in this book.
6 See Chapter 6 in this book.
7 Garry Woodard, 'What we now know about going to war in Iraq', APSNet Special Report, 22 November 2007, p. 56.
8 Ibid. Woodard quotes parliamentary research scholar June Verrier as quoting Hudson.
9 Ibid., p. 13.

Chapter 28: What to do about a bellicose ally

1 Morton Abramowitz, 'How American exceptionalism dooms US foreign policy', *National Interest*, 22 October 2012.
2 Congressional Research Service, 'Instances of use of United States Armed Forces abroad, 1798–2016', 7 October 2016.
3 Scott Shane, 'Russia isn't the only one meddling in elections. We do it too', *NYT*, 17 February 2018.
4 Nuland's reply to a question from Senator Jeanne Shaheen during the Senate Committee on Foreign Relations Hearing: Russian Violations of Borders, Treaties, and Human Rights, 6 July 2016.
5 Address by Nuland to the 'Ukraine in Washington' conference, US-Ukraine Foundation, 13 December 2013.
6 Jonathan Marcus, 'Ukraine crisis: Transcript of leaked Nuland–Pyatt call', BBC News, 7 February 2014.

7 Barbara Kingsolver's novel *The Poisonwood Bible* (Harper, 1998) gives a harrowing account of the consequences for Congolese who were outside the power structure.

8 Stephen Weissman, 'The CIA, the murder of Lumumba, and the rise of Mobutu', *Foreign Affairs*, July/August 2014, pp. 14–24.

9 'Timeline of US covert actions', VOA News, 30 March 2011. Although government-owned, the VOA often provides independent analysis.

10 Charles F. Andrain, *Political Power and Economic Inequality*, Rowman & Littlefield, 2015, p. 88.

11 Walter Laqueur et al., 'Coups d'état, lessons of the past, prospects for the future and a guide for action', Centre for Strategic and International Studies, Georgetown University, sponsored by the Office of the Secretary of Defense, 1 January 1984, p. 18.

12 Abramowitz, op. cit.

13 Ibid.

14 Richard Tanter, 'Tightly bound: The US and Australia's alliance-dependent militarisation', *Asia-Pacific Journal*, 1 June 2018.

15 Garry Woodard, 'What we now know about going to war in Iraq', APSNet Special Report, 22 November 2007, p 13.

16 This figure is based on the program costs for the Reaper announced by Defence Minister Christopher Pyne at a press conference in Adelaide on 16 November 2018.

17 Lockheed Martin Vernon Parker Oration, Naval Institute of Australia, Canberra, 22 June 2016.

18 Ibid.

19 'GDP Forecasts to 2030', Figure 4.2, Foreign Policy White Paper, November 2017. The figures are in terms of purchasing-power parity.

20 'The Long View: How will the global economic order change by 2050?', PwC (PricewaterhouseCoopers), 2017.

21 Malcolm Fraser with Cain Roberts, *Dangerous Allies*, MUP, p. 283.

22 William Pritchett, 'The US and us', Pacific Security Research Institute, 1992, p. 26.

23 Geoff Barker, 'Has ANZUS passed its use-by date?', *Inside Story*, 13 June 2011.

24 For more analysis and detail, see Clinton Fernandes, *What Uncle Sam Wants: US foreign policy objectives in Australia and beyond*, Palgrave Pivot, 2019 and Bob Carr, *Diary of the Foreign Minister*, NewSouth, 2014.

Chapter 29: The irrational US hatred of Whitlam

1 James Curran, *Unholy Fury*, MUP, 2015, p. 204.

2 Unless otherwise noted, the information and analysis in this chapter rely on my work as a journalist in Canberra after I resigned as a staff member for Whitlam's deputy, Lance Barnard, soon after the election. Back then I was more critical of Whitlam than I am now.

3 Curran, 157.

4 Ibid., p. 164.

5 Transcript of Reel 4 of the 1983 documentary *Allies*, p. 33.

6 *The Eye*, July 1987, p. 14.

7 J.R. Walsh and G.J. Munster (eds), *Documents on Australian Defence and Foreign Policy, 1968–1975*, self-published, 1980, p. 228.

8 Ibid., pp. 229, 230.

9 John Blaxland, *The Protest Years*, Allen & Unwin, 2015, pp. 343–4.

10 Curran, p. 204.

11 Luncheon conversation in Washington, DC, 2 January 1981.

12 Extracts from the official record of the Schlesinger–Barnard talks in Washington, DC, 10 January 1974, pp. 12, 13.

13 Ibid., p. 13.
14 Curran, p. 256.
15 Ibid., pp. 304–5.
16 Walsh and Munster, p. 220.
17 The *NT* used leaked top-secret US intelligence reports in 1982 to give a two-part account on 30 May and 6 June of what happened in East Timor.
18 Curran, p. 31.
19 Brian Toohey, 'Marshall Green: A pro in the Canberra embassy', *NT*, 21 March 1982.
20 Brian Toohey and Clem Lloyd, 'The Loans Affair tapes', *NT*, 14 November 1982 and 'The Loans Affair', *NT*, 21 November 1982.
21 Brian Toohey, 'Khemlani squeals on Mafia mates', *NT*, 6 August 1982.

Chapter 30: Punishing an innocent ally

1 James Curran, *Unholy Fury*, MUP, 2015, p. 282.
2 Ibid., p. 260.
3 William Colby, *Honorable Men*, Simon & Schuster, 1978, pp. 364, 365, 396.
4 For more details, see Chapter 53 in this book.
5 'Laos: Obama regrets biggest bombing in history', BBC News, 7 September 2016.
6 Transcript of Reel 4 of the 1983 documentary *Allies*, p. 34.
7 John Blaxland, *The Protest Years*, Allen & Unwin, 2015, p. 323.
8 In response to the Croatian extremists' incursions into Yugoslavia, Murphy drafted a bill making it a criminal offence for people living in Australia to travel overseas to help overthrow a foreign government. The Coalition blocked it in the Senate, but the subsequent Fraser Government ensured it became law.
9 Blaxland, p. 331.
10 Confidential sources who were present during the search of the files.
11 Interview with James Angleton by Ray Martin for ABC-TV's *Four Corners* and *Correspondents' Report*, 12 June 1977.
12 Luncheon conversation with Walker at the Union Club, New York, 22 January 1981.
13 Confidential source.
14 Blaxland, p. 442.
15 Luncheon conversation with Walker at the Union Club, op. cit.
16 Ibid.
17 His account of how he established that the politician was 'active' with Morosi lacked any semblance of logic. His 'source' was a woman professor whom he asked about the shadow minister and Morosi over lunch at the ANU. He took her furious response to his question as proof that she was also 'active' with the politician. This didn't mean that this flimsy 'evidence' wouldn't be treated as accurate 'intelligence' in an attempt to damage someone Shackley disliked.
18 Letter from Rosemary Brown to the author, 28 June 1981.
19 Ibid.
20 Curran, p. 268.
21 Ibid., p. 282.
22 Ibid.
23 Ibid.
24 Ibid., p. 283.

Chapter 31: Fraser's narrow escape

1 More detail is in Brian Toohey and Dale Van Atta, 'New light on the CIA role in 1975', *NT*, 21 March 1982; and Toohey and Van Atta, 'How the CIA saw the 1975 crisis', *NT*, 28 March 1982.

2 John Blaxland, *The Protest Years*, Allen & Unwin, 2015, p. 445.

3 Ibid., p. 446.

4 James Curran, *Unholy Fury*, MUP, 2015, p. 287.

5 'The CIA, Labor and ASIO', *The Bulletin*, 6 June 1976.

6 Brian Toohey and Marian Wilkinson, *The Book of Leaks*, Angus & Robertson, 1987, p. 88.

7 Brian Toohey, 'Khemlani squeals on Mafia mates', *NT*, 6 August 1982.

8 The chapter 'The Unjust Dismissals' in Brian Toohey and William Pinwill, *Oyster*, William Heinemann Australia, 1989, sets out the case against both sackings.

9 Ibid., p. 74.

10 Quoted in William Pinwill, 'The CIA nexus', *NT*, 9 November 1980. The Pike Committee was established in February 1975 to investigate illegal activities by the CIA, the FBI and the NSA; it was chaired by Congressman Otis G. Pike from July 1975 to January 1976, when its mandate expired.

11 Brian Toohey, 'Anthony's CIA connection', *AFR*, 3 November 1975.

12 For more background on events before the sacking, see Chapters 16, 19 and 20 in this book.

13 More detail is in Toohey and Van Atta, 'New light on the CIA role in 1975' and 'How the CIA saw the 1975 crisis', op. cit.

14 Ibid.

15 Luncheon conversation, Washington, DC, 12 January 1981.

16 The full text of Shackley's telex was available in *AFR*, 29 April 1977, and Whitlam read it into Hansard on 4 May 1977.

17 Transcript of Reel 4 of the 1983 documentary *Allies*, p. 41.

18 Corson, who mixed socially with high-ranking US officials such as George Shultz, wrote the 1977 book *The Armies of Ignorance: The Rise of the American Intelligence Empire* (Dial Press).

19 Luncheon conversation with Shackley at La Bagatelle, Washington, DC, February 1981.

20 Blaxland, p. 452.

Chapter 32: Some distinguished gentlemen from the CIA

1 Taylor Branch, 'The trial of the CIA', *New York Times Magazine*, 13 September 1976.

2 Andrew Clark, 'Kerr briefed on CIA threat to Whitlam', *Sunday Age*, 15 October 2000.

3 Quotes are from a note I made of the conversation about ten minutes after it ended.

4 Brian Toohey, 'Pine Gap mystery deepens', *AFR*, 28 April 1977.

5 John Blaxland, *The Protest Years: The Official History of ASIO, 1963–1975*, Allen & Unwin, 2015, p. 449.

6 Andrew Clark and Clem Lloyd, *Kerr's King Hit*, Cassell Australia, 1976, p. 37.

7 See Chapters 19 and 20 in this book.

8 See Chapter 31 in this book.

9 Peter Edwards, *Arthur Tange: The Last of the Mandarins*, Allen & Unwin, Sydney, 2006, p. 240.

10 Note of a phone conversation I had with Hay not long before died from cancer in November 2016.

11 James Curran, *Unholy Fury*, MUP, 2015, p. 260.

12 Quoted by Clark in 'Kerr briefed on CIA threat to Whitlam', op. cit.

13 Luncheon conversation with Walker, Union Club, New York, 22 January 1981.

14 William Colby, *Honorable Men*, Simon & Schuster, 1978, pp. 14, 15.

15 Curran initially took at face value claims about my involvement in a conspiracy theory, but later checked what I had written. He then emailed me to say he was happy to correct his error.

16 William Pinwill, 'Just who betrayed whom?', *The Australian*, 9 September 1981.

17 Brian Toohey, 'CIA funded covert action against Australian critics of Vietnam war', *NT*, 28 June 1980.

18 For more detail, see Brian Toohey and Marian Wilkinson, *The Book of Leaks*, Angus & Robertson, 1987, pp. 197–220. The Nugan Hand Bank collapsed in the 1980s leaving a trail of links to the CIA, arms dealing and the drug trade. According to the Commonwealth–New South Wales Joint Task Force on Drug Trafficking report (Vol. 2, Part 1, June 1982), the small Australian investment bank appointed these Americans to roles in the organisation: Rear Admiral Earl P. Yates as its first president; Brigadier General Edwin F. Black as its representative in Hawaii; army officer Dale O. Holmgren as its Taiwan representative; air force lieutenant general Leroy J. Manor as its representative in Manila; Dr Guy Pauker, a CIA operative, as a consultant; Rear Admiral Lloyd R. Vasey in an unofficial role; General Erle Cocke in an executive position; CIA economist Walter McDonald as a consultant; and William Colby, the head of the CIA from 1973 to 1976, as a legal adviser in Washington after 1979.

19 Luncheon conversation with Shackley at La Bagatelle, Washington, DC, February 1981.

20 Toohey and Wilkinson, p. 198.

21 Ibid., p. 214.

22 Mulcahy was also a key source for two long articles Hersh wrote for the *NYT* in June 1981 about Wilson and his former CIA colleague, Frank Terpil, on the Libyan case.

23 Toohey and Wilkinson, p. 219.

Chapter 33: Embracing ignorance

1 'Records relating to the arrest, investigation and prosecution in the US of Christopher John Boyce and/or Andrew Daulton Lee', NAA Series A6122, 2404, p. 91.

2 Ibid., p. 93.

3 Ibid., p. 91.

4 Ibid., p. 101.

5 Ibid., p. 91.

6 Ibid., p. 86.

7 Robert Lindsey, *The Falcon and the Snowman*, Simon & Schuster, 1979, p. 260.

8 Ibid., p. 259.

9 Ibid., p. 75.

10 Ibid., p. 74.

11 William Pinwill, *The Australian*, 19 September 1981.

12 Ray Martin on *60 Minutes*, Nine Network, 23 May 1982.

13 See Chapter 30 in this book.

14 David McKnight, 'The quiet Americans' *SMH,* 20 February 2003.

15 Ibid.

16 RCIS Top Secret Supplement to the Fourth Report, NAA Series A8908, 4D; and John Blaxland, *The Protest Years*, Allen & Unwin, 2015, p. 454.

17 Blaxland, ibid.

18 Brian Toohey, 'CIA funded covert action against Australian critics of Vietnam war', *NT*, 29 June 1980.

19 C.H. Brown, Minute to Director-General, ASIO, 19 December 1973, NAA Series A6122.

20 Ibid.

21 Ibid.

23 William Colby, *Honorable Men*, Simon & Schuster, 1978, p. 368.

Chapter 34: Australia's expansionist ambitions

1 *United States Antarctic Program: Participant Guide, 2018–2020 Edition*, National Science Foundation, p. iv.

2 Sam Bateman and Anthony Bergin, 'Sea change: Advancing Australia's ocean interests', Australian Strategic Policy Institute, 18 March 2009.

3 'Territory: Australian Antarctic Territory—Australian Claim to Sovereignty—Exclusive Economic Zone', *Australian Year Book of International Law* 15, 1996. <www.austlii.edu.au/au/journals/AUYrBkIntLaw/1996/15.pdf>, accessed 6 February 2019.

4 *United States Antarctic Program: Participant Guide*, op. cit.

5 'Ashmore and Cartier islands: Transnational issues', *World Factbook*, CIA, 2018. <https://www.cia.gov/library/publications/the-world-factbook/geos/at.html>, accessed 6 February 2019.

6 For more details on the Indonesian and Timor-Leste boundaries, see Kim McGrath, *Crossing the Line*, Schwartz Publishing, 2017.

Chapter 35: Chained to the chariot wheels of the Pentagon

1 Gary Brown and Laura Rayner, 'Upside, downside: ANZUS after fifty years', Parliamentary Library Research Paper, 28 August 2001.

2 Joseph Trevithick, 'Lockheed made a three minute long cartoon just to explain F-35's ALIS', *The War Zone*, 23 June 2017.

3 Ibid.

4 Kim Beazley, Lockheed Martin Vernon Parker Oration, Naval Institute of Australia, Canberra, 22 June 2016.

5 Ibid.

6 It is hard to believe there is any capability gap when the US military budget was over US$700 billion in 2018. Based on Stockholm International Peace Research Institute figures, that is well over double the combined estimate for the military budgets of China and Russia.

7 Beazley, Lockheed Martin Vernon Parker Oration, op. cit.

8 Tom Nichols, 'How America lost faith in expertise', *Foreign Affairs*, March/April 2017.

9 See Chapter 18 in this book.

10 For an earlier example of this problem, see 'Cold War strategic ASW' in the official US Navy magazine, *Undersea Warfare*, Spring 2005, and Melissa Healy, 'Lehman: We'll sink their subs', *Defense Week*, 13 May 1985, p. 18.

11 See Chapter 22 in this book.

12 Derek Woolner, 'The lessons of the Collins submarine program for improved oversight of defence procurement', Research Paper, 18 September 2001, Parliamentary Library, Canberra.

13 Ibid.

14 Answer to Parliamentary Question on Notice 116 from Senator Kim Carr, 25 October 2017.

15 Defence Media, email to the author, 12 September 2018.

16 Brian Toohey, 'Faulkner splurges on sub-par fighters', *AFR*, 27 February 2010. This article is the basis of much of this chapter's other information on this topic.

17 'Weather concerns deny final Avalon Airshow F-35 appearance', Australianaviation.com.au, 6 March 2017.

18 Brian Toohey, '$400m worth of missiles up in smoke', *AFR*, 10 October 2014.

19 The German company gave a guarantee it could design and produce much bigger, unproven submarines for $20 billion.

20 *The Australian* headlined its report on 25 April 2013 'Warship to join US fleet in hot zone'.
21 Defence Media, email to the author, 24 April 2018.

Chapter 36: Surrendering judicial sovereignty
1 R.S. French, 'Investor state dispute settlement: A cut above the courts', paper delivered at the Supreme and Federal Court Judges Conference, Darwin, 9 July 2014, p. 3.
2 Ibid., p. 1.
3 Ibid.
4 Greg Wood, 'The TPP-11: Discarding Australia's sovereignty', *Pearls and Irritations*, 31 January 2018.
5 Ibid.

Chapter 37: Inspector Tange investigates
1 NAA Series A10060.
2 Attachment to a letter from Commodore K.G. Gray, acting JIO director, to the Hope Royal Commission on Intelligence, 20 May 1976. NAA Series A6122.
3 The documents were collated into a large file following a freedom of information request from me in 1983, but not released until the archives made redacted versions available in late 2013. Freedom of Information Request: Brian Toohey, NAA Series A10060.
4 'Publication of specified classified material', Minute, R.W. Hamilton, Strategic and International Policy Division, September 1976. NAA Series A10060.
5 Brian Toohey, 'Defence program slashed', *AFR*, 9 October 1978.
6 P. J. Hutson, Minute to the Secretary [Tange], 16 October 1978, Subject: *AFR*, 9 October 1978 'Defence program slashed' by Brian Toohey.
7 Brian Toohey, 'Australia loses its Japan bug', *AFR*, 30 July 1976.
8 Brian Toohey, 'Russia: The three-hour threat', *AFR*, 1 July 1976. Peacock had earlier made his view of Killen plain when I was chatting in his office and his ministerial colleague walked in. Seeing me, Killen pointed and said, 'Either he goes or I go.' Peacock replied, 'Off you go, then.'
9 Record of conversation, meeting, 21 February 1973.
10 Record of conversation, meeting, 31 August 1976.
11 Brian Toohey, 'Behind the bugging', *NT,* 30 November 1984.
12 Graeme Dobell, 'To think and to do in Defence', *The Strategist*, 6 February 2014.

Chapter 38: Labor goes to court
1 Ian Macphee, Coalition frontbencher, launching Brian Toohey and William Pinwill, *Oyster: The Story of the Australian Secret Intelligence Service*, William Heinemann Australia, 1989; his speech was later published as the foreword to the paperback edition (Mandarin Australia, 1990).
2 Brian Toohey, 'Bureaucrats stay silent on phone issues', *NT*, 7 December 1984.
3 Part 1 was published on 6 May 1983; Part 2, after a delay for the court case, on 20 May; and Part 3 on 27 May. AUSTEO is a code word indicating that the documents should be read by Australian eyes only.
4 Justice Robert Hope, Royal Commission on Intelligence and Security, Supplement to the Fourth Report (re ASIO), 1976, p. 30. NAA Series A8908, 4D.
5 Affidavit by Brian Toohey 28 November 1988, Commonwealth of Australia (Applicant) and Brian Toohey (Respondent), No. G1350 of 1988, Federal Court Registry NSW Division.
6 Macphee, op. cit.

7 Usually, the presence of an ASIS officer is declared to the government of the country where he or she is posted, but their local agents are never declared.
8 Harvey Barnett, *Tale of the Scorpion*, Allen & Unwin, 1988.

Chapter 39: Embarrassing the government, informing the public

1 Michelle Grattan, 'No smiles in government ranks as Cheshire cat vanishes', *The Age*, 11 September 1988.
2 'George Shultz writes a press release for Bill', *The Eye*, September 1988, p. 7. This article is the source of what follows on Shultz's intervention. (I edited *The Eye*.)
3 What follows on the court case is based on the account in Brian Toohey, 'Shooting the messenger', *The Eye*, October 1988, pp. 8–11.
4 Ibid.
5 'Holding ONA at bay', *The Eye*, September 1988, pp. 9–10.
6 Keith Scott, 'No lasting damage with neighbours', *Canberra Times*, 7 September 1988.
7 'Status of injunctions against Brian Toohey', *Australian Press Council News*, May 1989, p. 3.
8 Grattan, op. cit.

Chapter 40: Evans: A vexatious litigant undone

1 Gareth Evans, *PM*, ABC Radio National, 23 November 1988.
2 This account draws on reporting in Brian Toohey, 'Gareth goes to court', *The Eye*, February 1989 and Brian Toohey and William Pinwill, *Oyster: The Story of the Australian Secret Intelligence Service*, William Heinemann Australia, 1989.
3 NAA Series A463, 1988/4879.
4 Brian Toohey, 'Gareth goes to court', pp. 12–15, and Toohey and Pinwill, *Oyster*, pp. 265–8.
5 Michelle Grattan, *The Age*, 26 November 1988.
6 Toohey, 'Gareth goes to court', op. cit., and Toohey and Pinwill, op. cit.
7 The barrister John Basten, later a NSW Supreme Court judge, and the solicitor Roger West skilfully defended *The Eye* in court cases described in this chapter.

Chapter 41: Dismantling the Menzies legacy

1 Robert Menzies, 'Freedom from fear', 2UE radio broadcast, 24 July 1942. Transcript from 'The Forgotten People' series, Menzies Virtual Museum. Menzies was PM from April 1939 to August 1941 and from December 1949 to January 1966.
2 Official Secrets: Legislation and Policy, NAA Series A47 94/C 645.
3 Ibid.
4 George Brownbill, 'The RCIS: An insider's perspective', speech notes, NAA, 27 May 2008.
5 RCIS Top Secret Supplement to the Fourth Report, NAA Series A8908, 4D, p. 34.
6 A federal Labor parliamentarian, Daryl Melham, supplied these figures, which were used in Brian Toohey, 'Our very own police state', *AFR*, 10 October 2008.
7 *Telecommunications (Interception and Access) Act 1979: Annual Report for the Year Ending 30 June 2007*, Department of Home Affairs, Australian Government.
8 Ibid.
9 Brian Toohey, 'Security label often a pretense', *AFR*, 22 June 2013.
10 Ibid.
11 *Telecommunications (Interception and Access) Act 1979: Annual Report for the Year Ending 30 June 2017*, op. cit.
12 Brian Toohey, 'A lot of spin in much-fixing talk', *AFR*, 1 February 2016.

13 Karen Middleton, 'Exclusive: Metadata requests top 350,000', *Saturday Paper*, 24–30 November 2018.
14 Brian Toohey, 'Putting the AFP back in its box', *AFR*, 29 August 2016.
15 Ibid.
16 In the case of the raid on the lawyer's office, the lawyer was acting for the Timor-Leste government after a Coalition government authorised ASIS to bug its Cabinet offices. For more details, see Chapter 34 in this book.
17 See the Acton Institute's mission statement and Gertrude Himmelfarb, 'Acton and Burke: For the conservative wisdom of history and tradition', Acton Institute, 18 November 2015.

Chapter 42: Seventy-five new laws against murder

1 Saul Eslake, 'The quest for "security": Is it rational, has it made us safer, and at what cost?', address to the Royal Society of Tasmania, 14 November 2017.
2 George Williams, email to the author, 11 February 2019.
3 George Williams, email to the author, 13 December 2018.
4 'Politically motivated violence in Australia: 1966–2009', in Appendix 1 of Clive Small and Tom Gilling, *Blood Money*, Allen & Unwin, 2011.
5 A well-regarded journalist, Hamish Macdonald, concludes in his self-published book, *Reasonable Doubt: Spies, Police and the Croatian Six*, 2019, that a group of Croatians was wrongly convicted in the 1980s of trying to set off bombs against Yugoslav targets in Sydney and that the key Crown witness allegedly worked for UDB (Yugoslav intelligence).
6 Evan Pederick, an Australian member of the Indian movement called Ananda Marga, was convicted and spent eight years in jail. The case remains contentious.
7 *Family, Domestic and Sexual Violence in Australia, 2018*, Australian Institute of Health and Welfare, 2018, p. 72.
8 Mark Thompson, *The Cost of Defence: ASPI Defence Budget Brief 2017–18*, Australian Strategic Policy Institute, May 2017.
9 Man Haron Monis, a notorious attention seeker and self-proclaimed terrorist, killed a hostage during the December 2014 stand-off at the Lindt Cafe in Sydney. In October 2015, a fifteen-year-old terrorist shot dead a civilian employee of the NSW Police. In 2017, an alleged terrorist, Yacqub Khayre, killed a man in Melbourne before police shot him. In November 2018, a Melbourne man was killed in a knife attack; it's unclear if the attacker was primarily a terrorist or mentally ill.
10 Eliza Manningham-Buller, 'Securing Freedom', Lecture One, Reith Lectures, BBC Radio 4, 6 September 2011.
11 Lisa Burton, Nicola McGarrity and George Williams, 'The extraordinary questioning and detention powers of the Australian Security Intelligence Organisation', *Melbourne University Law Review*, 36(2), 2012, p. 417.
12 Michael Bradley, 'Anti-terror laws: Control order plan takes us closer to a police state', *The Drum*, ABC News, 15 October 2015.
13 *Council of Australian Governments Review of Counter-terrorism Legislation*, Australian Government, 2013, p. 68.
14 Cameron Stewart, 'We need new laws for a more dangerous world', *The Australian*, 19 July 2014.
15 Chris Berg, 'Security bill widens government surveillance powers', *SMH*, 3 August 2014.
16 Ibid.
17 Chris Berg, 'Be sceptical of vague new "national security" powers', *The Drum*, ABC News, 17 July 2012.

18 Michael Safti, 'University of NSW student wrongly accused of terrorism offences plans to sue police and media', *The Guardian*, 23 November 2018.
19 Alfred McCoy, 'The outcast of Camp Echo', *The Monthly*, June 2006.
20 Jenny Hocking and Colleen Lewis, *Counter-Terrorism and the Post-Democratic State*, Edward Elgar Publishing, 2007, p. 58.
21 'Hicks just not handling it well: Ruddock', *SMH*, 31 January 2007.
22 Eslake, op. cit.

Chapter 43: Australia's own national security state
1 Email to the author from Paul Murphy, CEO of the MEAA, 10 July 2018.
2 Joint Media Organisations Submission to the Parliamentary Joint Committee on Intelligence and Security on National Security Legislation Amendment (Espionage and Foreign Interference) Bill 2017, 22 January 2018, pp. 1, 2.
3 Ibid., p. 2.
4 Ibid., pp. 2, 3.
5 Ibid., p. 4.
6 Ibid., pp. 7, 8.
7 Law Council of Australia Submission to the Parliamentary Joint Committee on Intelligence and Security on National Security Legislation Amendment (Espionage and Foreign Interference) Bill 2017, 22 January 2018, p. 61.
8 Chris Merritt, 'Defamation payout to hit Nine', *Weekend Australian*, 23–24 February 2019.
9 Colin Hawes, 'Why defamation lawsuits are crucial for protecting the rule of law: a comment on the Chau Chak Wing case', *Pearls and Irritations*, 19 March 2019.
10 Chapter 1 in this book explains why the information the Canberra spies sent to Moscow in 1945 was trivial.
11 Jann S. Dunlap, '1961: The CIA readies a Cuban invasion, and the Times blinks', *NYT,* 26 December 2014.
12 Keiran Hardy and George Williams, *Free Speech and Counterterrorism in Australia*, forthcoming book.
13 Brian Toohey, 'The ABCs gutless kowtow over lost Cabinet papers', *AFR*, 7 February 2018.
14 'Espionage report a step in the right direction', Law Council of Australia press release, 8 June 2018.
15 Email to the author from Paul Murphy, op. cit.
16 Ibid.
17 Ibid.

Chapter 44: Fighting a phantom called foreign influence and the encryption demons
1 Scott Ludlam, 'National security is a government strength—so Labor will let them be reckless with it', *The Guardian*, 6 December 2018.
2 *Counterintelligence Glossary: Terms & Definitions of Interest for CI Professionals*, Homeland Security Digital Library, Washington, DC, 1 July 2014, p. 9.
3 Bret Walker, 'What problem, exactly, would a foreign agency law fix?', *The Interpreter*, Lowy Institute, 29 November 2017.
4 James Laurenceson, 'China zealotry comes at a cost, if it stops shared university research', *AFR*, 26 February 2018.
5 Ibid.
6 *Church Committee: Book I—Foreign and Military Intelligence*, Select Committee to Study Governmental Operations with Respect to Intelligence Activities, US Senate, 1976, p. 158.

7 Scott Shane, 'Russia isn't the only one meddling in elections: We do it too', *NYT*, 17 February 2018.

8 Examples are given in Chapter 28 in this book.

9 See 'Transcript of joint press conference, Parliament House, Canberra, 5 December 2017: Foreign interference; foreign donations; same-sex marriage; citizenship', parlinfo. aph.gov.au.

10 Brian Toohey, 'How JIO tore into Fraser', *NT*, 27 May 1983.

11 David Wroe and Mark Kenny, 'Foreign interference laws: Paul Keating may have to declare as foreign agent', *SMH*, 6 December 2017.

12 Philip Dorling, 'Arbib revealed as secret US source', *The Age*, 9 December 2010.

13 *Exposure Draft: Telecommunications and Other Legislation Amendment (Assistance and Access) Bill 2018*, House of Representatives, Parliament of the Commonwealth of Australia, 14 August 2018.

14 'Rushed encryption laws create risk of unintended consequences and overreach', Law Council of Australia media release, 7 December 2018.

15 Ibid.

16 David Swan and Primrose Riordan, 'Encryption bill "a gut punch" to the tech sector', *SMH*, 15 December 2018.

17 Christopher Knaus, 'Google and Facebook join rights groups to fight Australia's encryption bill', *The Guardian*, 3 October 2018.

18 Paul Karp, 'Australia's war on encryption: The sweeping new powers rushed into law', *The Guardian*, 8 December 2018.

19 Andy Patrizio, 'Microsoft to NSA: WannaCry is your fault', *Network World*, 17 May 2017.

20 Ludlam, op. cit.

21 Ibid.

Chapter 45: The national security supremo

1 Michael Pezzullo, 'Secretary's remarks to the Trans-Tasman Business Circle', Department of Home Affairs, Australian Government, 13 October 2017.

2 Official Secrets: Legislation and Policy, NAA Series A47 94/C 645.

3 Karen Middleton, 'George Brandis' secret ASIO speech', *Saturday Paper*, 24 February 2018.

4 Dana Priest and William Arkin, 'A hidden world, growing beyond control', *Washington Post,* 19 July 2010.

5 Pezzullo, op. cit.

6 Paddy Gourley, 'Mike Pezzullo's Department of Home Affairs belongs in a dark galaxy far, far away (from reality)', *Canberra Times*, 7 November 2017.

7 Pezzullo, op. cit.

8 Michael Pezzullo, 'Seven Gathering Storms—National Security in the 2020s', Australian Strategic Policy Institute, Canberra, 13 March 2019.

9 Nigel Gladstone, 'State intensifies citizen tracking', *Sun Herald*, 4 November 2018.

10 Cynthia Wong, 'We underestimate the threat of facial recognition technology at our peril', *The Guardian*, 17 August 2018.

11 'Identity matching bill must clearly define the line between appropriate and illegitimate use', Law Council of Australia media release, 3 May 2018.

12 See previous chapter.

13 Karen Middleton, 'Metadata requests top 350,000', *Saturday Paper*, 24 November 2018.

14 Ibid.

15 Andrew Fowler, *Shooting the Messenger*, Routledge, 2018, p. 230.

Chapter 46: The foundation myth of our four colonial wars

1 Julia Gillard, speech at the opening of the Chinese-Australian War Memorial, Sunnybank, Queensland, 6 April 2011.

2 Judith Brett, 'Alfred Deakin and the roots of Australian foreign policy', *Pearls and Irritations*, 15 September 2017.

3 'Sudan (New South Wales Contingent) March–June 1885', Australian War Memorial, n.d. <https://www.awm.gov.au/articles/atwar/sudan>, accessed 11 February 2019.

4 Ibid.

5 'China (Boxer Rebellion), 1900–01', Australian War Memorial, n.d. <https://www.awm.gov.au/articles/atwar/boxer>, accessed 11 February 2019.

6 Amitav Ghosh, the novelist who wrote the Ibis trilogy about the Opium Wars, told an interviewer that during his research he discovered a diary in which a pious British opium trader wrote, 'Please forgive me, God. I was too busy selling opium today, I forgot to pray.' Michael LaPointe, 'The Opium Wars, revisited', *The Tyee*, 12 November 2008.

7 Craig Wilcox, 'The Boer War: Australians and the war in South Africa, 1899–1902', National Archives of Australia Research Guide, 2001.

8 'Australia and the Boer War, 1899–1902', Australian War Memorial, n.d. <https://www.awm.gov.au/articles/atwar/boer>, accessed 11 February 2019.

9 Jason Ditz, 'The Philippines: Remembering a forgotten occupation', *Huffpost*, 18 June 2013.

10 Fransjohan Pretorius, 'The Boer Wars', BBC History, March 2011.

11 'Scorched earth and guerrilla warfare', in *Voluntary Guides Backgrounder 004: Boer War*, Section 9, December 2010; 'Australia and the Boer War, 1899–1902', Australian War Memorial, n.d. <https://www.awm.gov.au/articles/atwar/boer>, accessed 11 February 2019. See also G.N. van den Bergh, 'The British scorched earth and concentration camp policies in the Potchefstroom Region, 1899–1902', *Scientia Militaria: South African Journal of Military Studies*, 40(2), 2012, pp. 72–88; James Robbins Jewell, 'Using barbaric methods in South Africa: The British concentration camp policy during the Anglo-Boer War', *Scientia Militaria: South African Journal of Military Studies*, 31(1), 2003. pp. 2–18.

12 Andre Wessels, *The Anglo-Boer War 1899–1902*, Sun Press, 2011, p. 78. Thanks to AWM historian Thomas Rogers for pointing to this source.

13 Phone conversation with AWM's media manager, 4 March 2019.

14 For a summary of this discussion see Paul Daley, 'Why the number of Indigenous deaths in the frontier wars matters', *The Guardian*, 15 July 2014.

15 'Deaths as a result of service with Australian units', Australian War Memorial, 2018. <https://www.awm.gov.au/articles/encyclopedia/war_casualties>, accessed 11 February 2019.

Chapter 47: World War I: Labor's secret plans for an expeditionary force

1 Quoted in Greg Lockhart, 'Race fear, dangerous denial', *Griffith Review* 32, May 2011.

2 The *Defence Act* was changed in 1943 to allow conscripts to serve in the south-west Pacific, and in 1964 to allow them to serve in Vietnam and elsewhere.

3 Lockhart, op. cit.

4 John Mordike, *An Army for a Nation: A History of Australian Military Developments, 1880–1914*, Allen & Unwin, 1992; John Mordike, *We Should Do This Thing Quietly: Japan and the Great Deception in Australian Defence Policy 1911–1914*, RAAF Aerospace Centre, 2002.

5 B. Beddie, 'Pearce, Sir George Foster (1870–1952)', *Australian Dictionary of Biography*, ANU, 2017. <http://adb.anu.edu.au/biography/pearce-sir-george-foster-7996/text13931>, accessed 7 March 2019.

6 Lockhart, op. cit.

7 Ibid.

8 Ibid.

9 Paul Daley, 'Australia spares no expense as the Anzac legend nears its century', *The Guardian,* 15 October 2013.

10 Tony Stephens, 'Anzac 100: The legend has outgrown the men who fought', *SMH,* 22 April 2015.

11 Tony Stephens, 'Last Anzac is dead', *SMH,* 17 May 2002.

12 Tony Stephens, 'Alec Campbell, the adventurous one 1899–2002', *SMH,* 18 May 2002.

13 Stephens, 'Anzac 100', op. cit.

14 Ibid.

15 For one assessment see Douglas Newton, 'Armistice Day: Narrow nationalist naiveties and voodoo vindications of war', *Pearls and Irritations,* 13 November 2017. See also Marilyn Lake and Henry Reynolds, *What's Wrong with Anzac? The Militarisation of Australian History,* UNSW Press, 2010.

16 Paul Daley, 'The moment that forever changed my perspective on Anzac mythology', *The Guardian,* 9 December 2018.

17 See for example Anne Glenday, 'Digging up the truth about Fromelles, not the bodies, is what counts', *SMH,* 14 July 2008.

18 Josephine Cafagna, 'Closure for the relatives of the Fromelles dead', *7.30 Report,* ABC-TV, 20 March 2010.

19 AAP, 'Did Gallipoli make the Australian nation?', SBS News, 25 March 2014.

20 Malcolm Fraser with Cain Roberts, *Dangerous Allies,* MUP, 2014, p. 38.

21 David Noonan, 'Why the numbers of our WWI dead are wrong', *SMH,* 30 April 2014.

Chapter 48: World War II: No sovereign interest in the integrity of Australia

1 John Edwards, *John Curtin's War, Vol. 2,* Viking, 2018, p. 75.

2 Richard Evans, 'Why Hitler's grand plan during the Second World War collapsed', *The Guardian,* 8 September 2009.

3 Sergey Yarov, *Leningrad 1941–42: Morality in a City Under Siege,* Polity Press, Cambridge, 2017, p. vi. This quote is from the preface by Peter Barber, a historian at King's College, Cambridge.

4 Ibid., p. x.

5 Max Suich, 'Diplomacy that led to human catastrophe', *The Australian,* 23 June 2012. Suich expanded his argument in 'The1930s couldn't happen again—could they?', *The Australian,* 30 June 2012.

6 Suich, 'Diplomacy that led to human catastrophe', ibid.

7 Edwards, pp. 5–76.

8 Clem Lloyd, 'Curtin and the invasion threat', *NT,* 27 April 1983.

9 Edwards, p. 75.

10 'Second World War, 1939–45', Australian War Memorial, n.d. <https://www.awm.gov.au/articles/second-world-war>, accessed 11 February 2019.

11 Ibid.

12 Ibid.

13 Gavin Long, *The Final Campaigns,* AWM, 1963, p. 18.

14 A.T. Ross, *Armed and Ready,* Turton & Armstrong, 1995, p. 427.

15 Ibid.

16 Some complex high-tech weapons and electronic systems may have to be imported, but local industry could make many weapons platforms and systems.

17 David Fettling, *Encounters with Asian Decolonisation*, Australian Scholarly Publishing, 2017, pp. 189–90.

18 Desmond Ball, 'The moles at the very heart of government', *Weekend Australian*, 16 April 2011.

19 Pam Burton, 'John Burton: Undermined by dishonest history', Honest History lecture, Manning Clark House, Canberra, 18 August 2014.

20 Ernst Willheim, 'Sex, spies and lies? The spurious case against ex-department head John Burton', *Canberra Times*, 6 November 2014.

21 William Pritchett, 'The US and us', Pacific Security Research Institute, 1992, p. 26.

Chapter 49: Korea: Barbarism unleashed

1 Michael Pembroke, *Korea*, Hardie Grant, 2018, p. xvi.

2 Ibid., p. 72.

3 Tim Colebatch, 'Menzies and the making of postwar Australia', *Inside Story*, 17 September 2016.

4 'Robert Menzies in office: The Menzies era 1949–66', Australia's Prime Ministers, NAA, n.d. <http://primeministers.naa.gov.au/primeministers/menzies/in-office.aspx>, accessed 21 February 2019.

5 Pembroke, p. 79.

6 Ibid., p. 107.

7 Ibid., p. 83.

8 'Flying Mustangs over Korea was a hazardous occupation', The Anzac Portal, Department of Veterans' Affairs, Australian Government, n.d. <https://anzacportal.dva.gov.au/history/special-features/veterans-stories/great-search-stories/flying-mustangs-over-korea-was>, accessed 21 February 2019.

9 Darien Cavanaugh, 'Why the Korean War was one of the deadliest wars in modern history', *Public Interest*, 2 May 2017.

10 David Morgan, 'Report: Korean War-era massacre was policy', AP, 14 April 2007.

11 Bruce Cummings, *North Korea: Another Country*, New Press, New York, 2003, p. 16.

12 See Pembroke, ch.12, 'Secrets and lies', pp. 170–83 and Chapters 7 and 8 in this book.

13 Pembroke, p. 221.

14 Ibid., p. 225.

15 Min Jin Lee's 2017 saga *Pachinko* (HarperCollins) gives a compelling portrayal of life for those with little power in Japanese-occupied Korea and afterwards.

16 Transcript of doorstop interview, Kapyong, 24 April 2011, PM Transcripts, Australian Government.

Chapter 50: Off to war again: Malaya and Indonesia

1 'Indonesian Confrontation, 1963–1966', Australian War Memorial, n.d. <https://www.awm.gov.au/articles/event/indonesian-confrontation>, accessed 21 February 2019.

2 'Communist gangs kill three British planters, two Chinese in Malaya outrages', *SMH*, 16 June 1948.

3 Malcolm Fraser with Cain Roberts, *Dangerous Allies*, MUP, 2014, p. 108.

4 'Indonesian Confrontation, 1963–1966', op. cit.

Chapter 51: Vietnam: Stopping an election, then losing an unnecessary war

1 Quoted in Frank Walker, *The Tiger Man of Vietnam*, Hachette Australia, 2016, p. 283.

2 Barbara Tuchman, *The March of Folly*, Abacus, 1984, pp. 289, 290.

3 Fredrik Logevall, *Embers of War*, Random House, 2012, pp. 470, 565, 553.

4 Gavan Hogue, 'Australia did say no to the US on Vietnam 1954', *Pearls and Irritations*, 16 February 2017.

5 Dwight D. Eisenhower, *Mandate for Change, 1953–1956*, Doubleday, 1963, pp. 337–8.

6 Bruce Davies with Gary McKay, *Vietnam: The Complete Story of the Australian War*, Allen & Unwin, 2012, p. 64.

7 Ibid.

8 Ibid., p. 62.

9 Ibid., pp. 70–8.

10 Anne Blair, *There to the Bitter End*, Allen & Unwin, 2001, p. 23.

11 Davies, p. 101.

12 Blair, p. 238.

13 Ibid., p. 106.

14 Quoted in Walker, p. 283.

15 John Blaxland, *The Protest Years*, Allen & Unwin, 2015, p. 284.

16 Blair, p. 237.

17 William Pinwill and Brian Toohey, 'Armed and ready', *The Eye*, June/July 1989, p. 9.

18 Ian McNeill, *The Team*, University of Queensland Press, 1984, p. 71.

19 Ibid., p. 408.

20 Ibid., p. 411.

21 Garry Woodard, 'Asian alternatives: Going to war in the 1960s', public lecture at the NAA, 30 May 2003.

22 McNeill, p. 482.

23 Ibid.

Chapter 52: Testimony from those who were there

1 Transcript, *Vietnam: The War that Made Australia*, SBS Television. Darren Hutchinson was the development producer/director and Mike Bluett the series director. The series was made by Joined Up Films in association with SBS and with the assistance of Screen Australia, Screenwest and Lottery West. All quotes from the series are from the transcript the producers provided to the author.

2 Ibid.

3 Ibid.

4 Davies is the author, with Gary McKay, of the 2012 book *Vietnam: The Complete Story of the Australian War* (Allen & Unwin).

5 Frank Walker, *The Tiger Man of Vietnam*, Hachette Australia, 2016, pp. 270–4.

6 Chapter 54 in this book shows that a minority of the Australian special forces in Afghanistan did not share the values of many Team members.

7 Jason von Meding, 'Agent Orange, exposed: How US chemical warfare in Vietnam unleashed a slow-moving disaster', *The Conversation*, 4 October 2017.

8 Cable from US Embassy, Vientiane to State Department, 30 November 1965, quoted by Andrew Wells-Dang in 'Agent Orange in Laos: Documentary evidence', August 2002. <http://www.agentorangerecord.com/images/uploads/resources/studies/Agent OrangeLaos.pdf>, accessed 11 February 2019.

9 AWM115 A305/83/24.

10 Ash Anan, 'Vietnam's horrific legacy: the children of Agent Orange', 25 May 2015, news.com.

11 Jason Von Meding, 'Agent Orange, exposed: How US chemical warfare in Vietnam unleashed a slow-moving disaster', *The Conversation*, 4 October 2017.

12 Among the many outstanding articles written on dioxin, one of the best is Christopher Hitchens, 'The Vietnam syndrome', *Vanity Fair*, 26 March 2007.

Chapter 53: A defeat born of secrecy, ignorance, arrogance and brutality

1 Nora Ephron, 'The war followers', *New York*, 12 November 1973.
2 The first documented evidence that Menzies had not received an invitation from South Vietnam is in Michael Sexton, *War for the Asking*, Penguin, 1981.
3 Garry Woodard, 'Asian alternatives: Going to war in the 1960s', public lecture for the NAA, 30 May 2003.
4 Ibid.
5 Malcolm Fraser with Cain Roberts, *Dangerous Allies*, Melbourne University Press, 2014, p. 144.
6 Fraser, p. 143.
7 Jeffrey Hays, 'Vietnam's relations with China', Facts and Details, 2014. <http://factsand details.com/southeast-asia/Vietnam/sub5_9f/entry-3455.html>, accessed 11 February 2019.
8 Drew Lindsay, '"Something dark and bloody": What happened at My Lai?', *MHQ*, 7 August 2012.
9 Fraser, p. 129.
10 Ibid., p. 125.
11 Ibid., pp. 146–7.
12 Paul Ham, *Vietnam: The Australian War*, HarperCollins, 2007, p. 405.
13 Ibid., p. 414.
14 Ibid., p. 405.
15 Ibid., pp. 409–10.
16 For more details, see Christopher Robbins, *Air America: The Story of the CIA's Secret Airlines*, Putnam, 1979 and Alfred McCoy, *The Politics of Heroin: CIA Complicity in the Global Drug Trade*, Chicago Review Press, 2003.
17 Jonathan Kwitny, *The Crimes of Patriots: A True Tale of Dope, Dirty Money, and the CIA*, W.W. Norton, 1987.
18 Brian Toohey, 'Defence cuts cancel nothing that matters', *AFR*, 7 November 2012.
19 David Wroe, 'Long Tan battle commander Harry Smith says Vietnamese sensitivity must be respected', *SMH*, 19 August 2016.
20 Greg Dodds, 'Let's do without the Vietnam trip', *AFR*, 23 September 2016.

Chapter 54: Australian troops should have left Afghanistan within a few months

1 This policy paper was issued in September 2010 by the Williams Foundation, whose board comprises senior retired military officers. The paper named World War II as probably the only necessary war, but it was removed from the foundation's website following a change in the composition of the board. Alan Stephens was the unnamed author.
2 'Our stories: Somalia', Australian Army, December 2016. <https://www.army.gov.au/our-stories/operations/somalia>, accessed 7 March 2019.
3 Scott Horton, *Fool's Errand*, CreateSpace, 2017, pp. 59–62.
4 Ibid., pp. 49–52.
5 Ibid., pp. 63–8.
6 'Operation Slipper questions', fax from Hill to the author, 21 May 2002.
7 Brian Toohey, 'Don't shoot until you know who they are'. *AFR*, 15 June 2002.
8 For further details see Brendan Nicholson, 'In the line of duty', *The Age*, 2 June 2005 and Rory Callinan, 'In the valley of death', *Time*, 30 May 2005.
9 Quoted in Brian Toohey, 'War leader', *Inside Story*, 5 May 2011.
10 Horton, p. 109.
11 For example, John Braithwaite and Ali Wardak, 'Crime and war in Afghanistan, Part I: The Hobbesian solution', *British Journal of Criminology*, 53(2), 1 March 2013, p. 187.

12 David Morgan, 'Pentagon admits Afghan strategy not succeeding', Reuters, 11 September 2008.

13 Paul McGeough, 'Botched mission costs life of chief', *SMH*, 29 November 2008.

14 Horton, p. 180.

15 Ibid., p. 195.

16 Email from Defence Media Operations to the author, 25 May 2011.

17 Sharon Davis and Helen Grasswill, 'Australian commandos' role in the deaths of five Afghan children questioned', ABC News, 22 May 2016.

18 Ibid.

19 Horton, p. 184.

20 Dan Oakes and Sam Clark, 'The Afghan Files: Defence leak exposes deadly secrets of Australia's special forces', ABC News, 11 July 2017.

21 Dan Oakes and Sam Clark, 'Death in Kandahar', ABC News, 10 July 2017.

22 C. August Elliott, '"Land, kill and leave": How Australian special forces helped lose the war in Afghanistan', ABC News, 12 July 2017.

23 Nick McKenzie and Chris Masters, 'SAS soldiers committed war crimes: Secret report', *SMH*, 8 June 2018.

24 Andrew Bacevich, 'The never-ending war in Afghanistan', *NYT*, 13 March 2017.

25 Mark Thomson, *The Cost of Defence: ASPI Defence Budget Brief 2017–18*, Australian Strategic Policy Institute, 2017, p. 201.

Chapter 55: Howard and Iraq: Knave or naif?

1 Howard in parliament, 4 February 2003.

2 Parliamentary Joint Committee on ASIO, ASIS and DSD, *Intelligence on Iraq's Weapons of Mass Destruction*, 1 March 2004, Chapter 5.

3 Ibid.

4 Brian Toohey, 'Saddam's poison power: The inside story', *AFR*, 14 February 1998.

5 Submission by W.B. Pritchett to the Parliamentary Joint Committee on ASIO, ASIS and DSD, 13 August 2003.

6 John Howard, *Lazarus Rising*, HarperCollins, 2011, p. 462.

7 Fax to the author from Jane Corbin, 29 September 2002.

8 Transcript, *7.30 Report*, ABC-TV, 8 April 2003.

9 *The War in Iraq: ADF Operations in the Middle East in 2003*, Department of Defence, 2004, pp. 21–4.

10 Paul Monk, *AFR*, 21 March 2003.

11 Greg Sheridan, 'WMD doubts are ludicrous', *The Australian*, 10 July 2003.

12 Tracy Shelton, 'Gadhafi sodomised: Video shows abuse frame by frame', *GlobalPost PRI*, 24 October 2011.

13 Glenn Harland Reynolds, 'Africans are being sold at Libyan slave markets. Thanks, Hillary Clinton', *USA Today*, 27 November 2017.

14 Brian Toohey, 'How shock and awe turned to fear and loathing', *AFR*, 18 March 2006.

15 See for example Latika Bourke, 'John Howard "embarrassed" by failed WMD intelligence on Iraq', *SMH*, 22 September 2014.

16 David Wroe and Deborah Snow, 'Chilcot Inquiry: Former prime minister John Howard defends 2003 Iraq decision', *SMH*, 7 July 2016.

17 Paul McGeough, 'Chilcot Report: The mind-boggling incompetence of Bush, Blair and Howard laid bare', *SMH*, 7 July 2016.

18 Richard Smith, 'The secret Downing Street memo', *Sunday Times*, 1 May 2005.

Chapter 56: Nuclear war: The risks are real

1 Eric Schlosser, 'World War Three by mistake', *New Yorker*, 23 December 2016.

2 William Burr, 'US war plans would kill an estimated 108 million Soviets, 104 million Chinese, and 2.6 million Poles: More evidence on SIOP-62 and the origins of overkill', Unredacted: The National Security Archive Blog, 8 November 2011.

3 Schlosser, op. cit.

4 Amy Woolf, 'Nuclear weapons in US national security policy: Past, present and prospects', Congressional Research Service, 28 January 2008.

5 For more details, see 'Cold War strategic ASW' in the official US Navy magazine, *Undersea Warfare*, Spring 2005.

6 Quoted in Melissa Healy, 'Lehman: We'll sink their subs', *Defense Week*, 13 May 1985, p. 18.

7 Office of the Secretary of Defense Department, *Annual Report to Congress: Military and Security Developments Involving the People's Republic of China 2018*, Department of Defense, 16 August 2018, p. 38.

8 See Hamish McDonald, 'The wired seas of Asia', *Asia-Pacific Journal*, 20 April 2015.

9 J.A. Battilega, 'Soviet views of nuclear warfare: The post-Cold War interviews', in Henry D. Sokolski (ed.), *Getting MAD: A Nuclear Mutual Assured Destruction, Its Origins and Practice*, Strategic Studies Institute, US Army War College, 2004, pp. 156–7.

10 Fred Kaplan, 'Nuclear posturing', *Slate*, 22 January 2018.

11 Schlosser, op. cit.

12 Ibid.

13 Ibid.

14 Ibid

15 Union of Concerned Scientists, 'Close calls with nuclear weapons' fact sheet, 2015. <www.ucsusa.org/weaponsincidents>, accessed 12 February 2019.

16 Ibid.

17 *1983: The Brink of Apocalypse*, Channel 4, 5 January 2008.

18 Union of Concerned Scientists, op. cit.

19 Schlosser, op. cit.

Chapter 57: The West's reckless Russian policies

1 George F. Kennan, 'A fateful error', *NYT*, 5 February 1997.

2 Andrew Higgins, 'How powerful is Vladimir Putin really?', *NYT*, 23 March 2019.

3 Christian Neef and Mathias Schepp, 'Vibrant, noisy, and booming: Welcome to the new Moscow', *Spiegel Online*, 22 April 2016.

4 *SIPRI Military Expenditure Database 2017*, Stockholm International Peace Research Institute.

5 'Nuclear weapons: Who has what at a glance', Arms Control Association, 21 June 2018.

6 Ibid.

7 Larry Elliott, 'Russia and economic warfare: RIP the free market new world order', *The Guardian*, 31 August 2014.

8 Svetlana Savranskaya and Tom Blanton, 'NATO expansion: What Gorbachev heard', 12 December 2017 and 'NATO expansion: What Yeltsin heard', 16 March 2018, National Security Archive.

9 Kennan, op. cit.

10 Owen Harries, 'The dangers of expansive realism', *National Interest*, 1 December 1997.

11 Transcript, BBC *Breakfast with Frost* interview with Putin, 5 March 2000.

12 For a nuanced view of Putin, see the Russian-born American writer Keith Gessen, 'Killer, kleptocrat, genius, spy: The many myths of Vladimir Putin', *The Guardian*, 22 February 2017.

13 'Ukraine crisis: Transcript of leaked Nuland–Pyatt call', BBC News, 7 February 2014.

14 Kenneth Rapoza, 'One year after Russia annexed Crimea, locals prefer Moscow to Kiev', *Forbes*, 20 March 2015.
15 Steven A. Hildritch and Carl Ek, 'Long-range ballistic missile defense in Europe', Congressional Research Service, 23 September 2009.
16 Julian Borger, 'America's new, more "usable" nuclear bomb in Europe', *The Guardian*, 11 November 2015.
17 For a succinct analysis, see Fred Kaplan, 'Nuclear posturing', *Slate*, 22 January 2018.
18 Nuland in reply to a question from Senator Jeanne Shaheen during the Hearing of the United States Senate Committee on Foreign Relations: Russian Violations of Borders, Treaties, and Human Rights, 6 July 2016.
19 Scott Shane, 'Russia isn't the only one meddling in elections. We do it, too', *NYT*, 17 February 2018.

Chapter 58: Destruction is only a tantrum away

1 Report of the Canberra Commission on the Elimination of Nuclear Weapons, DFAT, 1996, p. 9.
2 Ibid., pp. 9, 10.
3 Gareth Evans and Yoriko Kawaguchi, *Eliminating Nuclear Threats: A Practical Agenda for Global Policymakers*, Report of the International Commission on Nuclear Non-Proliferation and Disarmament, Canberra, 2009, p. 3.
4 Joint Standing Committee on Foreign Affairs, Defence and Trade, *ANZUS after 45 Years: Seminar Proceedings, 11–12 August 1997*, Parliament of Australia, 1997.
5 Paul Dibb, 'America has always kept us in the loop', *The Australian*, 10 September 2005.
6 Tom Hyland, 'When Australia had a bombshell for US', *SMH*, 6 July 2008.
7 Brian Toohey, 'US monitored "our bomb"', *NT*, 14 December 1980.
8 Stephan Frühling, 'A nuclear-armed Australia: Contemplating the unthinkable option', *Australian Foreign Affairs*, October–November 2018, pp. 71–91.
9 Brian Toohey, 'America's secret nuclear strategy', *AFR*, 31 August 1976.
10 Ben Dougherty, 'Nuclear annihilation only a tantrum away, Nobel Prize winner warns', *The Guardian*, 11 December 2017.
11 William Perry, *My Journey at the Nuclear Brink,* Stanford University Press, 2015, p. 4.
12 Ibid.
13 Ibid., p. xiv.

Chapter 59: The rise of China, India and Indonesia

1 John Keane, *When Trees Fall, Monkeys Scatter*, World Scientific, 2017, p. 8.
2 See Peter Jennings, 'Canberra alone must control our China ties', *The Australian*, 3 November 2018.
3 'Australia's trade in goods and services by top 15 partners', DFAT trade statistics, July 2018.
4 See James Lawrenceson, 'If China sneezes, there's no reason for Australia to get pneumonia', *AFR*, 9 January 2019.
5 James Laurenceson, email to the author, 6 March 2018, explaining that these figures are based on updated statistics in the IMF's *World Economic Outlook* series. Laurenceson is an economist and deputy director of the Australia China Relations Institute at University of Technology Sydney.
6 'Figure 2.4: GDP forecasts to 2030', *Foreign Policy White Paper*, DFAT, 2017. The figures are in purchasing power parity terms.
7 PwC, 'The Long View: How will the global economic order change by 2050?', PricewaterhouseCoopers, February 2017.

8   James Lawrenceson, *Do the Claims Stack Up? Australia Talks China*, Australia China Relations Institute, UTS Sydney, 28 October 2018, p. 7.
9   *Foreign Policy White Paper*, DFAT, 2017, op. cit.
10 Kishore Mahbubani, 'What China threat? How the US and China can avoid war', *Harper's Magazine*, 29 January 2019.
11 David Brooks, 'The chaos after Trump', *NYT*, 7 March 2018.
12 'China lifting 800 million people out of poverty "Great story in human history": World Bank chief', *New Indian Express*, 13 October 2017.
13 Mahbubani, op. cit.
14 Simone van Nieuwenhuizen, 'China: Party of governance and control, not revolution', *The Interpreter*, 23 November 2018.
15 Keane, p. 8.
16 Brian Toohey, 'Xi's technocrat crackdown risks China's growth', *AFR*, 8 August 2016.
17 Keane, p. 3.
18 Stephanie Nebehay, 'UN says it has credible reports that China holds million Uighurs in secret camps', Reuters, 11 August 2018.
19 Vicky Xiuzhong Xu and Bang Xiao, 'China's Social Credit System seeks to assign citizens scores, engineer social behaviour', ABC News, 2 April 2018.
20 Charles Morris, 'We were pirates too: Why America was the China of the 19th century', *Foreign Policy*, 6 December 2012.
21 John Edwards, 'The first rule of a trade war: know thine enemy', *The Interpreter*, Lowy Institute, 17 April 2019.
22 *National Support for Emerging Industries*, National Academies Press, Washington, 2012, p. 1; See Jerome W. Schnee, 'Government programs and the growth of high-technology industries', *Research Policy*, 7(1), January 1978, pp. 3–24; and 'Uncle Sam's favorite corporations', Good Jobs First, 17 March 2015.
23 Department of Defense Testimony, 'Military technology transfer: Threats, impacts, and solutions for the Department of Defense', House Armed Services Committee, 21 June 2018.
24 I was one of several Australian journalists who visited Huawei's Shenzhen campus in 2016 on a trip funded by the Australia China Research Institute's Chairman's Council, comprising seventeen Australian companies and four Chinese-linked ones.
25 Mike Burgess, ASD Director-General, 'Then and now: Coming out from the shadows', speech to ASPI National Security Dinner, 29 October 2018.
26 *The Economist*, 'The right call on Huawei: Technology and security', 27 April 2019.
27 Geoffrey Sachs, 'The war on Huawei', *Project Syndicate*, 11 December 2018.
28 Chris Uhlmann and Angus Grigg, 'Spy chief's campaign to kill Huawei', *SMH*, December 2018.
29 Laurenceson, *Do the Claims Stack Up?*, pp. 62–72.
30 Ibid.
31 Transcript, *Media Watch*, ABC-TV, 15 August 2016.
32 Email to the author, 27 March 2018.
33 Davis Brophy, 'The book Xi Jinping wants you to read for all the wrong reasons', *SMH*, 28 February 2018.
34 Brian Toohey, 'China alarmism is costing us dear', *AFR*, 24 September 2017.
35 Dylan Welch, 'Chinese agents are undermining Australia's sovereignty, Clive Hamilton's controversial new book claims', ABC News, 22 February 2018.
36 Laurenceson, *Do The Claims Stack Up?*, pp. 62–72.
37 Stephanie Borys, 'China link possible in cyberattack on the Australian Parliament computer systems, ABC understands', ABC News, 8 February 2019.

38 Amanda Hodge and Nivell Rayda, 'PNG base upgrade worries Jakarta', *The Australian*, 15 December 2018.
39 J.R. Walsh and G.J. Munster (eds), *Documents on Australian Defence and Foreign Policy, 1968–1975*, self-published, 1980, p. 220.

Chapter 60: Going to war against China
1   Congressional Research Service, 'Instances of use of United States Armed Forces abroad, 1798–2016', 7 October 2016.
2   Mark Thomson, *The Cost of Defence: ASPI Defence Budget Brief 2017–18*, Australian Strategic Policy Institute, 2017, p. 185.
3   Hugh White, *Without America: Australia in the New Asia*, Quarterly Essay 68, Black Inc., 2017, p. 57.
4   Matthew Harper, 'Chinese missiles and the Walmart factor', *Proceedings Magazine*, US Naval Institute, July 2011.
5   Confidential sources.
6   'Nuclear weapons: Who has what at a glance', Arms Control Association, 21 June 2018.
7   See Chapter 56 in this book.
8   Sam Bateman, 'No need to rock the boat in the South China Sea', East Asia Forum, 6 March 2018.
9   See Lynn Kuok, 'Progress in the South China Sea?', *Foreign Affairs*, 21 July 2017.
10 For more details, see Clinton Fernandes, *Island off the Coast of Asia*, Monash University Publishing, 2018, pp. 120–7.
11 Bateman, op. cit.
12 Ibid.
13 Ibid.
14 'Taiwan, Japan coastguards collide near islands', *AFP*, 4 July 2012.
15 'Washington playing "Whack-a-Mole" in South China Sea, says ex-US official', *Wall Street Journal*, 28 May 2015.
16 Patricia Lourdes Viray, 'ASEAN, China see South China Sea code first draft by 2019', *Philippines Star*, 14 November 2018.
17 *Foreign Policy White Paper*, DFAT, 2017.
18 Ibid.
19 Shashi Sharoor, *Inglorious Empire: What the British Did to India*, Hurst, 2017.
20 Ulsa Patnaik, 'Transfers from India to Britain', in S. Chakrabarti and U. Patnaik (eds), *Agrarian and Other Histories*, Columbia University Press, 2018, pp. 278–317.
21 Alexander Davis, 'How the Conservative Anglosphere fell in love with India', *The Interpreter*, 19 December 2018.
22 Hugh White, 'The White Paper's grand strategic fix: Can Australia achieve an Indo-Pacific pivot?', *Australian Foreign Affairs*, 24 November 2017.
23 Kim Beazley, Lockheed Martin Vernon Parker Oration, Canberra, 22 June 2016.
24 Office of the Secretary of Defense, *Annual Report to Congress: Military and Security Developments Involving the People's Republic of China 2018*, Department of Defense, p. 43.
25 Allan Hawke and Rick Smith, *Australian Defence Force Posture Review*, 30 March 2012, p. 13.
26 Turnbull interview on 3AW radio, 11 August 2017.
27 'Malcolm Turnbull, Julie Bishop say China is no threat to Australia', *AFR*, 29 January 2018.
28 Graham Allison, 'The Thucydides Trap: Are the US and China headed for war?', *The Atlantic*, 24 September 2015.

BIBLIOGRAPHY

Allies, film produced by Sylvie Le Clezio, directed by Marian Wilkinson, Sydney (Grand Bay Films International; distributed by Cinema Enterprises, 1983), 95 mins; transcripts of interviews.

Ball, Desmond. *A Suitable Piece of Real Estate: American Installations in Australia,* Hale & Iremonger, Sydney, 1980.

Barton, Rod. *The Weapons Detective: The Inside Story of Australia's Top Weapons Inspector,* Black Inc., Melbourne, 2006.

Blair, Anne. *There to the Bitter End: Ted Serong in Vietnam,* Allen & Unwin, Crows Nest, NSW, 2001.

Blaxland, John. *The Protest Years: The Official History of ASIO, 1963–1975,* Vol. 2, Allen & Unwin, Crows Nest, NSW, 2015.

Blaxland, John and Crawley. Rhys. *The Secret Cold War: The Official History of ASIO, 1975–1989,* Vol. III, Allen & Unwin, Sydney, 2016.

Casey, R.G. Diaries, *Papers of the Casey Family, 1820–1978,* National Library of Australia, MS 6150. The diaries were reclassified after being quoted in Toohey and Pinwill.

Cleary, Paul. *Shakedown: Australia's Grab for Timor Oil,* Allen & Unwin, Crows Nest, NSW, 2007.

Colby, William. *Honorable Men: My Life in the CIA,* Simon & Schuster, New York, 1978.

Cox, Arthur Macey. *The Myths of National Security: The Peril of Secret Government,* Beacon Press, Boston, 1975.

Curran, James. *Unholy Fury: Whitlam and Nixon at War,* Melbourne University Press, Carlton, Vic., 2015.

Davies, Bruce, with McKay, Gary. *Vietnam: The Complete Story of the Australian War,* Allen & Unwin, Sydney, 2013.

Edwards, John. *John Curtin's War, Vol. 2: Triumph and Decline,* Viking, Melbourne, 2018.

Fettling, David. *Encounters with Asian Decolonisation,* Australian Scholarly Publishing, North Melbourne, 2017.

Fowler, Andrew. *Shooting the Messenger: Criminalising Journalism,* Routledge, London, 2018.

Fraser, Malcolm with Roberts, Cain. *Dangerous Allies,* Melbourne University Press, Carlton, Vic., 2014.

Gyngell, Allan. *Fear of Abandonment: Australia in the World Since 1942,* La Trobe University Press in conjunction with Black Inc., Carlton, Vic., 2017.

Hager, Nicky. *Secret Power: New Zealand's Role in the International Spy Network,* Craig Potton Publishing, Nelson, NZ, 1996.

Ham, Paul. *Vietnam: The Australian War,* HarperCollins, Pymble, NSW, 2007.

Hamilton, Clive. *Silent Invasion: China's Influence in Australia,* Hardie Grant, Richmond, Vic., 2018.

Holdich, Roger, Johnson, Vivianne and Andre, Pamela (eds). *The ANZUS Treaty 1951,* Department of Foreign Affairs and Trade, Canberra, 2001.

Horner, David. *The Spy Catchers: The Official History of ASIO, 1949–1963,* Vol. 1, Allen & Unwin, Crows Nest, NSW, 2014.

Horton, Scott. *Fool's Errand: Time to End the War in Afghanistan,* CreateSpace Independent Publishing Platform, 2017.

Howard, John. *Lazarus Rising: A Personal and Political Autobiography,* HarperCollins, Pymble, NSW, 2010.

Keane, John. *When Trees Fall, Monkeys Scatter: Rethinking Democracy in China,* World Scientific, London, 2017.

Kelly, Paul and Bramston, Troy. *The Dismissal: In the Queen's Name,* Penguin, Melbourne, 2016.

Kelly, Paul. *The Unmaking of Gough,* Angus & Robertson, Sydney, 1976.

Lindsey, Robert. *The Falcon and the Snowman: A True Story of Friendship and Espionage,* Simon & Schuster, New York, 1979.

Long, Gavin. *The Final Campaigns: Australia in the War of 1939–1945, Series 1, Army, Vol. VII:,* Australian War Memorial, Canberra, 1963.

Marchetti, Victor and Marks, John D. *The CIA and the Cult of Intelligence,* Knopf, New York, 1974.

Masters, Chris. *No Front Line: Australian Special Forces in Afghanistan,* Allen & Unwin, Crows Nest, NSW, 2017.

McClelland, James. *The Report of the Royal Commission into British Nuclear Tests in Australia,* Australian Government Publishing Service, Canberra, 1985. (Jill Fitch and William Jonas were commissioners.)

McGrath, Kim. *Crossing the Line: Australia's Secret History in the Timor Sea,* Schwartz Publishing, Carlton, Vic., 2017.

McNeill, Ian. *The Team: Australian Army Advisers in Vietnam 1962–1972,* University of Queensland Press in association with Australian War Memorial, St Lucia, Qld, 1984.

Medvedek, Zhores A. *Nuclear Disaster in the Urals,* Norton, New York, 1979.

Milliken, Robert. *No Conceivable Injury,* Penguin, Ringwood, Vic., 1986.

Moran, Christopher. *Classified: Secrecy and the State in Modern Britain,* Cambridge University Press, Cambridge, 2012.

Parkinson, Alan. *Maralinga: Australia's Nuclear Waste Cover-up,* HarperCollins, Sydney, 2016.

Pembroke, Michael. *Korea: Where the American Century Began,* Hardie Grant, Richmond, Vic., 2018.

Perry, William. *My Journey at the Nuclear Brink,* Stanford University Press, Stanford, CA, 2015.

Ross, A.T. *Armed and Ready: The Industrial Development and Defence of Australia, 1900–1945,* Turton & Armstrong, Wahroonga, NSW, 1995.

Snepp, Frank. *Decent Interval: An Insider's Account of Saigon's Indecent End,* Vintage Books, New York, 1978.

Symonds, J.L. *A History of British Atomic Tests in Australia,* Australian Government Publishing Service, Canberra, 1985.

Tange, Arthur. *Defence Policy-Making: A Close-up View, 1950–1980*, ANU Press, 2008.

Toohey, Brian and Pinwill, William. *Oyster: The Story of the Australian Secret Intelligence Service*, William Heinemann Australia, Port Melbourne, 1989.

Toohey, Brian and Wilkinson, Marian. *The Book of Leaks: Exposés in Defence of the Public's Right to Know*, Angus & Robertson, North Ryde, NSW, 1987.

Tynan, Elizabeth. *Atomic Thunder: The Maralinga Story*, NewSouth Publishing, Sydney, 2016.

Walker, Frank. *The Tiger Man of Vietnam,* Hachette Australia, Sydney, 2009

——*Maralinga: The Chilling Exposé of Our Secret Nuclear Shame and Betrayal of Our Troops and Country*, Hachette Australia, Sydney, 2014.

Walker, John R. *British Nuclear Weapons and the Test Ban 1954–1973*, Routledge, London, 2010.

Walsh, J.R. and Munster, G.J. (eds). *Documents on Australian Defence and Foreign Policy, 1968–1975*, self-published, 1980.

Wessels, Andre. *The Anglo-Boer War 1899-1902,* Sun Press, Bloemfontein, 2011.

INDEX